THE FOREIGN POLICY
RESEARCH INSTITUTE SERIES

The Foreign Policy Research Institute
University of Pennsylvania

Number 8

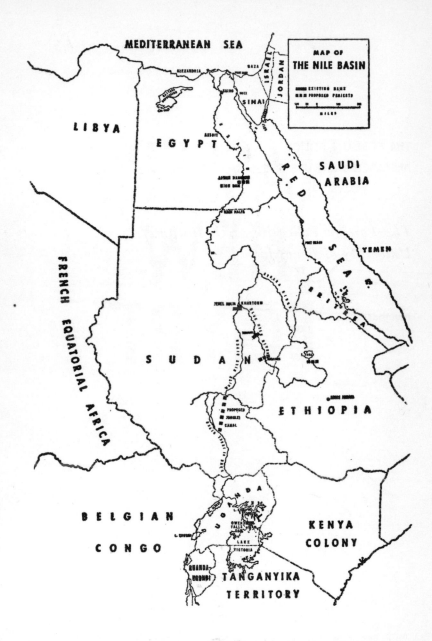

THE FOREIGN POLICY RESEARCH INSTITUTE
UNIVERSITY OF PENNSYLVANIA

NASSER'S NEW EGYPT

A CRITICAL ANALYSIS

By Keith Wheelock

FREDERICK A. PRAEGER, Publishers • NEW YORK, N. Y.

BOOKS THAT MATTER

First published in the United States of America in 1960
by Frederick A. Praeger, Inc., Publishers
64 University Place, New York 3, N. Y.

This is the eighth in a series of studies to be published by
Frederick A. Praeger, Publishers, under the auspices of the
Foreign Policy Research Institute at the University of Pennsyl-
vania, established under a grant of the Richardson Foundation,
Greensboro, North Carolina. This study was subjected to the
extensive and critical discussion of the Associates of the Foreign
Policy Research Institute. However, the views expressed in
NASSER's NEW EGYPT: A CRITICAL ANALYSIS are those of the
author.

Preface
and Acknowledgments

A study of Egypt since the Revolution provides insight into many of the major problems confronting the world today. The phenomenon of military regimes replacing civilian governments throughout the Afro-Asian world is of urgent concern to the West and to the Communists alike. Gamal Abdel Nasser's peculiar brand of neutralism has thrust Egypt into the center of the cold war. The problems of internal development facing this country are similar to those encountered in many of the underdeveloped areas of the world. And Nasser's appeals for Arab unity reflect the growing movement toward greater regional cooperation, a hallmark of the twentieth century.

This book is not intended to be a history of Egypt of the past seven years; rather, it is an analysis of the contemporary scene. While I have endeavored to present the highlights of the period since the military coup of 1952, my primary purpose has been to analyze Nasser's military regime.

The study of an entire country is a difficult task for one person. It is all the more difficult in the case of Egypt, where an authoritarian government and widespread censorship compound the problems of research. Thus, I realized at the outset that this study could be completed only with the cooperation of President Nasser himself. His approval was not easy to obtain. Indeed, several of his advisers informed me that my request was presumptuous—that I needed no such guarantee to conduct my study. I felt, however, that I could not enjoy the freedom of action essential to my work without the President's personal support.

In September, 1957, when my request had not been met, I abandoned the entire project. But my homeward journey was interrupted by a telegram awaiting my plane's arrival in Paris: President Nasser wished to see me the following day. He graciously acceded to my request and placed the facilities of the

Presidency at my disposal. Thus, *Nasser's New Egypt: A Critical Analysis* was made possible by Nasser's willingness to permit such an analysis of his regime. This should not imply, however, that the President concurs with the conclusions in this book; in fact, he has, in the past, indicated strong disapproval of many of my views. Nevertheless, he permitted me to complete this study.

I first visited Egypt in 1953. Subsequently, I returned to Cairo for extended periods in 1954, 1956, 1957, and 1958. Much of my background information has been gleaned from published materials. Dr. Husni Khalifa's *Misr Egyptian News Agency,* Jon Kimche's *Jewish Observer and Middle East Review,* the *Cairo Press Review,* and the perceptive dispatches of *The New York Times* correspondents Robert Doty and Osgood Carruthers and those of David Holden of the London *Times* have proved most valuable. But the book depends primarily upon information obtained through scores of personal associations in Egypt formed over the past six years.

President Nasser's approval of my project came as a direct result of the initiative taken by Mohamed Abdel Kader Hatem and Fakhry Gaber. Kamal Bakr, of the Egyptian Department of Information, charged with arranging many of my official appointments, repeatedly met my difficult demands; this book is a tribute to his refusal to be deterred by governmental red tape. I am indebted, also, to Saad Afra, Director-General of the Department of Information, and his assistant, Issam Khodairy, with whom I enjoyed a pleasant working relationship.

Many people exceeded their official obligations in facilitating my investigations. In the field of economics, Hassan Abbas Zaki, Minister of Economy for the Egyptian Region, Mahmoud Ibrahim and Gamal Elish at the National Planning Commission, Ahmed Sulimon Bakr of the Economic Organization, and Dr. Abdel Moneim el Banna gave unstintingly of their time. My work on social development was facilitated by the assistance of Hussein Shafei, Central Minister of Social Affairs and Labor, and his colleague, Zaki Imam. My understanding of Egypt's labor problems is a direct result of extensive interviews with Ahmed Abdullah Toiema of the National Union, Abdel Mony Said Salama of the Ministry of Social Affairs and Labor, and Abdul Halim el Kadi, Administrative Secretary at the Egyptian

Federation of Labor. Ahmed Rifaat, Assistant Under-Secretary of State at the Ministry of Municipal and Rural Affairs, deserves credit for bringing the problems of Egyptian housing to my attention.

For three years, Sayed Marei, Central Minister of Agriculture, took time from a crowded schedule to answer my detailed questions on agriculture, while his charming and competent associates, Mrs. Rashad Badran and Mahmoud Fawzy, provided me with a comprehensive picture of Egypt's Agrarian Reform program. My special thanks go to Eva Garzouzi, author of *Old Ills and New Remedies in Egypt,* who provided me with expert counsel on Egypt's internal development.

Mohammed Naguib, Gamal Salem, Amin Shaker (formerly Nasser's aide-de-camp), Anwar Sadat, and Moursy Saad el-Din were among those most helpful on matters concerning Egyptian internal politics and foreign affairs. Regretfully, personal considerations require me to leave unnamed many others who made significant contributions to my research.

I am deeply grateful to the Foreign Policy Research Institute of the University of Pennsylvania, under whose auspices I have pursued my work since 1956. I am indebted particularly to the Institute's Director, Robert Strausz-Hupé, and its Deputy Director, William R. Kintner. Walter F. Hahn, Executive Editor of *Orbis,* the quarterly journal published by the Institute, contributed invaluable editorial assistance.

Hans Kohn, Norman D. Palmer, Arthur P. Whitaker, and H. Field Haviland, Jr., Associates of the Institute, as well as Sanford Griffith, Irving Kravis, Charles Issawi, Hal Lehrman, and Richard H. Nolte, among others, kindly submitted critical comments on various draft chapters. While their suggestions improved the manuscript, their assistance in no way relieves me of sole responsibility for the contents of this book.

In conclusion, it is only fitting to thank the members of the "Hard Core" of Cairo for sharing with me their objective impressions of the Egyptian political scene, and my patient wife, who experienced many lonely hours during my work on this book.

—K. W.

Philadelphia, Pa.
December, 1959

To Kamal, Mahmoud, and Omar
Egypt's future is secure with such men

Contents

I. PRELUDE TO TAKEOVER   1

II. COUP AND CONSOLIDATION   12

III. THE ENTRENCHMENT OF THE MILITARY REGIME   37

IV. AGRICULTURE AND AGRARIAN REFORM   74

V. EDUCATION AND SOCIAL DEVELOPMENT   109

VI. ECONOMICS AND INDUSTRIALIZATION   137

VII. THE HIGH DAM   173

VIII. PRELUDE TO "NASSERISM"   206

IX. THE WEST AT BAY   228

X. THE TACTICS OF "POSITIVE NEUTRALITY"   249

XI. NASSER'S NEW EGYPT IN PERSPECTIVE   277

NOTES   287

INDEX   323

I

Prelude to Takeover

Background

Egypt is not a great nation, nor has it been one for many centuries. Lacking adequate resources with which to feed a hungry population, and infested with a parasitic bureaucracy so common to Eastern societies, the country has been hard-pressed merely to exist. Perhaps, at the time of Napoleon's invasion, some pride existed for what once was Egypt; however, the Egypt of the eighteenth century excited the imagination of but few of her people. Once notable traditions long since had given way to a national stagnation nurtured by successive foreign occupations.

Then came Mohamed Ali, first a mercenary under the Turks and later the ambitious ruler of Egypt. Whatever the shortcomings of his internal policies, he awoke the lethargic Egyptians. But when Mohamed Ali's reforms could not keep pace with the requirements of an extensive empire, Egypt lapsed once again into political inertia. Twenty years later, the construction of the Suez Canal and Khedive Ismail's gross mismanagement of his financial affairs again attracted the interest of the chancelleries of Europe. During Ismail's reign, a well-meaning attempt was made to develop the country: new schools sprang up throughout Egypt, and a fetish for industrialization resulted in the undertaking of several highly uneconomic projects; but this brief upsurge produced few lasting results. Soon after the British and French deposed Ismail in favor of his son, Tewfik, a band of discontented Egyptian army officers organized the first concerted and truly Egyptian protest against the government and its foreign advisers. Their efforts, however, were short-lived, for the British occupied Egypt and disbanded the Egyptian army.

With the advent of the twentieth century, a new nationalist movement, born of the frustrations of the preceding century, asserted itself. Using the rallying cry of "Egypt for the Egyptians," several youthful Cairo lawyers molded this growing resentment into an embryonic political movement. After undergoing the humiliation of being made a British protectorate during World War I, Egypt ultimately gained her legal independence in 1922. The mere trappings of monarchy and control over certain domestic matters, however, did not make Egypt into a viable nation. As British influence in the country rapidly receded, local autocrats captured many sectors of the government administration. And with large landowners and other conservative elements firmly entrenched in Parliament, the country scarcely could expect to attain rapid economic and social development.

During the succeeding generation, nominal progress was recorded in many fields: local industry, under the leadership of Bank Misr, expanded significantly; several universities and many new schools were in evidence; and British garrisons were confined to a few major cities. But the real per capita income of the country decreased during the same period. With a ratio of almost four persons to an arable *feddan* and with industry providing less than 4 per cent of the national income, forceful measures were needed if Egypt hoped to keep her deteriorating standard of living in check. Moreover, while the *fellaheen* (farmers) were a passive political element in this depressing picture, the growing petty bourgeoisie—the unemployed university graduates and the middle-class members of the military—all potentially were agitators against the *status quo*.

As in other Arab countries, the government was controlled by a small clique of men who were concerned primarily with protecting their own vested interests. While political parties diligently included reform measures in their campaign platforms, the wealthy landowners refused to permit any but the most trivial of innovations; the ordinary farmer was denied even the most elementary safeguards of land tenancy, and large estates were amassed at the expense of hundreds of thousands of small owners. Moreover, since the Parliament was reluctant to tax the income of the wealthy classes which it represented, scarcely 5 per cent of the national income was available for government expenditures. Corruption was commonplace, and the poor in Cairo and elsewhere waited in vain for their long-promised potable water projects, for stable incomes and steady jobs.

There were, of course, occasional voices raised against the system. Sometimes, also, these voices were heard throughout the country, but they could not budge the "old order." The Wafd, the Saadists, or even the Liberal Constitutionists would support the cause of a reformer momentarily; once they reached office, promises quickly were forgotten. Perhaps one should not judge the politicians too harshly, however, for they were but the creatures of a Cairene society which had long flourished by the systematic exploitation of the countryside.

The large cities, Cairo and Alexandria, were supplied with modern conveniences: public utilities were installed in the early twentieth century and, at least in the fashionable residential districts, the inhabitants enjoyed purified water, a modern sewage system, and other facilities expected in a busy metropolis. This, however, brought few benefits to the country-at-large. But as the old order became less dependent upon the British, new avenues were provided, through which middle-class Egyptians could vent their spleen at the country's corruption and lethargy.

Perhaps the first cohesive group organized to alter Egypt's traditional political structure was the Moslem Brethren under Hassan el Banna, but this band of religious zealots was heavily burdened by a dogmatic Islamic conservatism. Instead, it was the military which provided the greatest hope for breaking the existing structure of government which the country as a whole had found so stifling. In 1936, as an aftermath to the new Anglo-Egyptian treaty which defined and restricted Britain's military position in Egypt, the doors of the military academy were opened to more candidates: applicants from the villages and middle-class youths with high-school diplomas were permitted to compete for positions once reserved for Cairo's social elite.[1] In early 1936, a serious youth, already branded a troublemaker for his participation in several nationalist riots, had been denied entrance to the military academy—and subsequently had enrolled as a student of law.[2] But the new policy to develop a larger Egyptian officer cadre encouraged him to apply again; so in early 1937, Gamal Abdel Nasser, along with scores of other cadets, entered the first "egalitarian" semester of the military college.[3]

A Conspiracy Takes Root

Eighteen months later, a new class of twenty-year-old lieutenants was graduated. A group of these officers, fresh from Abbassia Military Academy, was posted first in Mankabad in Upper Egypt. There the loneliness of evening was nightly filled with long conversations around the campfire. Often the men preferred light-hearted chatter, but Gamal Abdel Nasser regularly injected serious discussions of existing social and political problems.[4] In the isolation of Upper Egypt, these men—Nasser, Zacharia Mohieddine, Anwar Sadat, and others—passionately discussed their dreams for the salvation of Egypt. Nasser expressed the sentiments of many when he urged his compatriots to "fight imperialism, monarchy, and feudalism"; soon, however, the officers were assigned to other units, and the group was broken up. Nasser was posted to the 3rd Infantry Battalion in the Sudan, while Lieutenant Sadat, more fortunate, was stationed near Cairo. In the following years, none of these junior officers was able to take decisive action.

Perhaps Sadat, impulsive and reckless, came closest to translating emotion into action. Driven by an intense hatred of the British, Lieutenant Sadat gathered a small band of followers and plotted the defeat of the British. With the support of General Aziz el Misri, former Chief of Staff in the Egyptian army who had been retired because of his pro-German sympathies, Sadat sought to establish contact with Rommel's forces.[5] Fearing that Egypt, if conquered, might be given to Italy as war booty, Sadat favored a program of cooperation with the Germans which would defeat the English and, at the same time, gain for Egypt her independence.[6]

A scheme in May, 1941, to smuggle General el Misri out to the Germans failed; the first attempt was abandoned when the car carrying the fleeing officers broke down, and on the second attempt the plane carrying the General crashed upon take-off.[7]

The pilot, Hussein Zulficar Sabry, and Abdel Moneim Raouf were interned along with the General. Undaunted, Sadat's group planned other adventures. A plan was drawn up by which Sadat, with no more than thirty followers, would seize British General Headquarters, cut off the British garrison in Cairo, and "eliminate" the old politicians.[8] However, Sadat finally deemed this plan too ambitious.

Sadat was the self-appointed leader of a band which, according to his account, included Abdel Latif Boghdadi, Hassan Ibrahim, Khalid Mohieddine, Abdel Moneim Raouf, and Gamal Abdel Nasser (who was then stationed in the Sudan).[9] When, in February, 1942, Sir Miles Lampson, the British Ambassador in Cairo, forced King Farouk to appoint Mustapha Nahas Prime Minister, Sadat's band again decided to act. Several weeks later, Farouk snubbed the British Ambassador during a reception for Princess Fawzia of Iran. Sir Miles protested, and the conspirators, anticipating British reprisals, prepared to counterattack. Sadat, waiting to give the signal to strike, circled Abdine Palace all night in Zacharia Mohieddine's car;[10] but the British did not move against the palace and the suicidal plan was abandoned. Sadat was involved in so many intrigues—with the Moslem Brethren, German agents, and his fellow officers—that, not unexpectedly, he was soon arrested, after being implicated by several captured German spies.

Later in 1942, Nasser was transferred to Lower Egypt and renewed contacts with his officer friends. Apparently the incident at Abdine Palace, when the British encircled Farouk's palace with tanks and forced Mustapha Nahas' Wafd government upon Farouk, had made a deep impression upon Gamal Abdel Nasser, for he often refers to this date as the start of the Revolution. There was little opportunity for conspiratorial activities during the war years, but by the fall of 1943, Nasser formed within the military a small organization which was united against the British. During this period he also maintained close liaison with the Moslem Brethren, having been introduced to the group several years before by Abdel Moneim Raouf. By the end of the following year, according to Khaled Mohieddine's later recollection, the leading officers in Nasser's group included, in addition to Mohieddine, Kamal el din Hussein, Abdel Hakim Amer, and Abdel Moneim Raouf, while Abdel Latif Boghdadi and Hassan Ibrahim, although not on its executive council, also were important members of the group.[11] It is safe to assume that this was the group which, in 1945, issued circulars attacking imperialism; "The Army Gives Warning" was one of its first efforts.[12] By then, more members had been recruited and a hard core was created: Abdel Hakim Amer, Zacharia Mohieddine, his cousin Khaled, Salah Salem, Sarwat Okasha, Abdel Moneim Raouf, Kamal el din Hussein, Abdel Latif Boghdadi, and Anwar Sadat (then a civilian) were considered part of Nasser's group.[13]

Nasser organized his men into two groups: a military one led by him, and a civilian branch commanded by Anwar Sadat, then in hiding after having escaped from prison. In theory, this organization was most impressive. Different "sections" were established to deal with administration, economic affairs, combat personnel, security, terrorism, and propaganda. In reality, however, these titles held little significance. The economic affairs division, for example, collected dues and was charged with providing funds for the families of imprisoned members, but the officers' salaries seldom permitted such luxuries. The other sections were, by and large, also ineffective.

At least until the Palestine War, the movement's primary concern was the defense of the officers' interests.[14] Except for some miscellaneous pamphlets and occasional meetings at officers' homes, the group did little to distinguish itself as a revolutionary body. Furtive contacts with the Moslem Brethren and, indirectly, the Communists, however, brought the officers under the close surveillance of the police and of Palace spies; several arrests in November, 1947, brought their activities almost to a halt. At that time, claims a member of the executive council, the group numbered over one thousand,[15] but a more conservative estimate by another council member puts the figure at ninety.[16] With the outbreak of the Palestine War, the military section became dormant, while the civilian section (Sadat had again been jailed in 1946 for allegedly participating in an assassination) dissolved completely.

Five days before the Arab armies marched into Palestine, sev-

eral army officers, including Brigadier Mohammed Naguib, submitted a report to Prime Minister Mahmoud Nokrashy; the report
showed conclusively that Egypt was not prepared to fight.[17] But
when palace advisers brought this document to the King, Farouk
ordered it suppressed. Subsequently, the Egyptian army suffered
a humiliating defeat at the hands of a smaller, ill-equipped Israeli
enemy. Following the Palestine campaign, a number of the
younger officers bitterly blamed the "old order" for their failure.
Refusing to recognize their own share in Egypt's humiliation,
they singled out incompetent leaders, political intrigues, and defective weapons as the reasons for defeat. The young officers were
anxious to vindicate themselves and the army.

It was this legend of the "stab in the back" which breathed
new life into Nasser's conspiratorial group. Another reorganization of the executive council occurred in 1949. Nasser, still the
leader, gathered around himself men like Abdel Hakim Amer,
Kamal el din Hussein, Khaled Mohieddine, Hassan Ibrahim, and
Abdel Moneim Raouf; in the following two years, Salah Salem,
Abdel Latif Boghdadi, Anwar Sadat, and Gamal Salem joined
the inner circle.[18] Forming cells of five men, the organization
successfully eluded police detection. Only once was the movement in real danger: this occurred when the Army Chief of Staff,
Ferik Heydar Pasha, caught Lieutenant Hassan Allam writing a
revolutionary tract. Nasser's group, now calling itself the Society
of Free Officers, abandoned Allam to his fate.[19]

Nasser strongly believed that the Free Officers could succeed
only if they established a firm base within the army; and, in
opposition to Anwar Sadat, he generally refused to engage in
terrorist activities. Instead, he sought slowly to build up the
strength of his organization. In late 1950, with the assistance of
Khaled Mohieddine's facile pen, the *Voice of the Free Officers*
was established.[20] Inexpensive pamphlets, published irregularly,
increasingly became commonplace in the officers' messes. In 1951,
Nasser believed that the Free Officers would be prepared for a
takeover by 1955.[21] Meanwhile, Nasser decided to challenge the
government over the Officers Club elections, scheduled for December, 1951. After distributing a circular, "The Army Says
'No!' to Farouk,"[22] Nasser sought to enlist a popular army gen-

eral as the Free Officers' candidate against Farouk's man, General
Hussein Sirry Amer. Nasser's choice fell on a man who had
recently been replaced by General Amer as commander of the
crack Frontier Corps, and the chosen officer readily agreed to
oppose the King's candidate. Thus, Mohammed Naguib became
associated with Nasser and his men.[23]

The elections came as a shock to the government. General
Naguib, generally recognized as the candidate of a secret officers'
group, received 276 of 334 votes for President.[24] The board of
the Club included Hassan Ibrahim and Zacharia Mohieddine,
while Colonel Rashad Mohanna, although not a candidate on
the unofficial Free Officers' slate, was elected Secretary-General
by acclamation. In January, 1952, when Cairo was pillaged by
mobs and disorder reigned in the country, the Free Officers felt
ready to act. Amid rumors that King Farouk intended to flee
Egypt, plans were set for a coup in March. The King, however,
remained in Cairo, and when Rashad Mohanna, who had
pledged the support of his artillery battalion, requested a transfer
to el Arish, the March plan collapsed.[25] Upon the suggestion of
Khaled Mohieddine, the new target date was set for November,
when the government would be back in Cairo and Parliament
would be in session.[26]

Thus, the Free Officers plotted the overthrow of the existing government, but the objectives of the proposed takeover were
not clear. Was the goal a *coup d'état* or a revolution? The most
striking feature of the clandestine pamphlets circulated by Nasser's group was a strong emphasis on imperialism. While "corruption, bribery, favoritism, and abuse of influence" were castigated,
the pamphlets contended that these evils could not be combatted
until Egypt was "completely freed from imperialism." A circular
dated March 22, 1952, included the following slogans: "Down
with imperialism!" "Down with any alliance with imperialism!"
"Down with joint defense and with any collective security pact
under imperialism!"[27] Other stated objectives of the Free Officers
included the abolition of martial law, the lifting of censorship,
the dismemberment of the political police, the release of political
detainees, the proclamation of an amnesty for all political prisoners, and the abrogation of all previous reactionary laws. While
these goals were liberal, they were not revolutionary.

The Free Officers Act

Nasser, in the months following the burning of Cairo, carefully prepared for the military takeover. Aware of the fact that he still lacked adequate military backing, he enlisted two field colonels into the movement: Hussein Shafei of the cavalry and Ahmed Shawki of the infantry.[28] After three changes in government within the first six months of 1952, there was increasing tension in Cairo, and the government's security forces were becoming extremely apprehensive of rumored military conspiracies. Nasser, after the abrupt July dissolution of the Officers Club board by the government, decided to act on August 5.[29] By then the army would be paid and, more important, Shawki's 13th Infantry Regiment was scheduled to return to Cairo.

But events were moving so quickly that this timetable soon had to be abandoned. Hussein Sirry, the Prime Minister, aware of the army's restiveness, sought to include Mohammed Naguib in his Cabinet as Minister of War.[30] Farouk, however, refused to make this appointment, and Sirry Pasha resigned on July 20. Concurrently, according to *Al Misri,* the King had requested that Miralai Safwat, chief of the palace police, draw up a plan to arrest Naguib and assassinate his colleagues; this plan was drafted on the eventful day of July 20.[31] When Ahmed Abdul Fath of *Al Misri* informed Colonel Sarwat Okasha, a Free Officer, of these developments, a hasty council was held at Colonel Nasser's home, and the decision was made to move within forty-eight hours. One of his colleagues quoted Nasser as saying: "If it is to be a battle of liquidation, why not start a revolution?"[32] Over Nasser's strong objection, plans were discussed for the mass assassination of political leaders in the event of the failure of the military coup.[33] Although Mohammed Naguib later claimed that he participated in these decisions, other members of the Free Officers state categorically that General Naguib, even at that late date, was not privy to the executive council's decisions.[34] On the evening of July 20, Nasser and Abdel Hakim Amer attempted to brief the General on the most recent developments, but they were unable to see Naguib alone.[35]

Plans to move on the night of July 21 proved premature, so the coup was postponed until July 22.[36] Then, while the Army

General Staff was meeting in emergency session to discuss means of checking the rising military unrest, the Free Officers acted. Despite several mishaps, the operation was successful beyond the plotters' wildest hopes; within four hours the city was occupied, and only two soldiers, guards at army headquarters, had been killed.[37] All ranking members of the General Staff but one were arrested. By seven the next morning, the weary conspirators had summoned Naguib to Abbassia, and Anwar Sadat had been ordered to broadcast the news to the nation. The proclamation, composed by Major Abdel Hakim Amer under Nasser's close supervision, gave the following explanation of the coup: "Led by fools, traitors, and incompetents, the army was incapable of defending Egypt. That is why we have carried out a purge. The army is now in the hands of men in whose ability, integrity, and patriotism you can have complete confidence."[38]

Was this the manifesto of a revolution? Hardly. Rather, it sounded more like an apologia for the military's past shortcomings. The Free Officers, almost without exception, were men in their thirties. They had experienced the humiliation of being withdrawn from the battlefront by the British during World War II, and they had suffered defeat under an amazingly inept high command during the Palestine campaign. It must be remembered, also, that their coup was partly in self-defense. They knew that the Palace was prepared to crush them.

While these circumstantial factors explained many of their actions, we must probe more deeply to gain a true measure of their motivations. Many of the Free Officers came from the middle class, others from the villages. Being honest, eager young men who had acquired a sense of discipline in the army, they could not but be affected by the dismal spectacle of Egypt's political and social life. Rising prices, unemployment, palace suppression of opposition political parties, and the King's personal life—all these were part of the decay which corroded Egypt. While they had no clear notion of what should be done, they knew that some action had to be taken. Their movement was not based on the masses; yet, inarticulately perhaps, it expressed the revolt of the suppressed middle class. As Nasser himself remarked, "If the army does not move, who else will?"[39] He further admitted that "the full picture of a soldier's duty did not become clear until long after the Revolution."[40]

It was surprising how ill-prepared the Free Officers were for success. After finding that their swift military action was welcomed by much of the country, they hastily improvised an *ad hoc* plan of action. Upon deciding in favor of Ali Maher as the Prime Minister, they had to ask a local journalist to guide Anwar Sadat to the home of the new head of government. With Maher sworn in, the next problem was how to deal with the King. According to some sources, the Free Officers, until July 24, were willing to retain the monarch;[41] initial statements by Naguib and Sadat seemed to support this impression. But even after Farouk accepted the military group's original list of demands, there was strong sentiment in favor of deposing the monarch. On the night of July 25, two groups, one under Naguib and Sadat in Alexandria, the other under Nasser in Cairo, decided the King's fate. Although there was strong feeling that he should be placed on trial for his many crimes against the state, Nasser's moderate view prevailed.[42] The following day, while British troops in Suez made no move to save the King, he abdicated in favor of his six-month-old son. At six in the evening, Farouk left Egypt.

II

Coup and Consolidation

Rout of the "Old Order"

The day after Farouk's departure, General Naguib, publicly recognized as leader of the Free Officers, declared: "Our military movement has nothing to do with politics."[1] Refusing to make a statement on foreign affairs, he asserted that the military accepted responsibility for an investigation of the Palestinian arms scandal and for the defense of Gaza against possible Israeli attack. These objectives were added to a previous Free Officer commitment to a campaign against graft and nepotism. The absence of more detailed plans was understandable, for the Free Officers never had expected to govern. As Colonel Gamal Abdel Nasser has somewhat naïvely written: the army's role was that of a "commando vanguard"; he and his associates sincerely felt that "good politicians" would run the country once the army had eliminated the "bad elements."[2] Later, a member of the Free Officers' executive council, Khaled Mohieddine, commented frankly: "We didn't discuss what we would do after the Revolution."[3] It was on an *ad hoc* basis that the military had to cope with the problems of governing.

The first week's achievements were impressive. Some of the King's closest advisers were arrested, and a number of political prisoners were released; investigations were reopened in the Palestinian arms case and in the murder of Hassan el Banna, founder of the Moslem Brethren. The inefficient practice of moving the government to the sea resort of Alexandria during the summer months was ended, and all officials were ordered to return immediately to Cairo. The titles of "pasha" and "bey," claimed to be representative of Egypt's past social inequality, were abolished. A purge against Farouk's supporters was initiated by the army, and a Regency Council, including Colonel Rashad Mohanna, was established to substitute for the absent infant, King Fuad II. An anticorruption law was enacted, and political parties were ordered to purge themselves.

By the end of the week, however, many of the Free Officers openly had become disillusioned. Some of them had thought at first that the new regime could function with the old politicians; Nasser and Major Khaled Mohieddine even favored the immediate recall of the suspended Parliament.[4] But it soon became evident that the powerful Wafdist Party's as well as the dangerous Moslem Brethren's alliances with the Ali Maher government were only tactical and temporary ones. Upon Mustapha Nahas' hasty return from France, the leader of the Wafdist Party publicly supported the proposed Regency Council on the condition that the Wafd-dominated Parliament be recalled to ratify it.[5] Invoking Naguib's pledge to "uphold the Constitution," Nahas further suggested that nationwide elections be held. Observers agreed that they would result in an overwhelming Wafdist victory.

The Moslem Brethren, pleased that one of their followers, Rashad Mohanna, held such an important position, felt that they could also depend upon support from former sympathizers such as Nasser, Anwar Sadat, Hussein Shafei, and Kamal el din Hussein.[6] Although the Brethren, on two occasions before the overthrow of Farouk, had refused actively to support the Free Officers,[7] the Supreme Guide, Hassan el Hodeiby, informed Nasser in late July that any law which was to be promulgated had first to be approved by the Moslem Brethren.[8] Moreover, on August 3, the Brethren issued a "White Paper" which stated that "the Koran is our only Constitution," thus pressing their concept of a theocracy.[9] The Free Officers, in rejecting a coalition with the Brethren, realized that the army was now opposed by the two most powerful political forces in the country.

What started as a simple *coup d'état* soon became a struggle for political survival. The Free Officers, in an effort to consolidate their power, substantially raised military salaries and added Lt. Colonel Zacharia Mohieddine, Lt. Colonel Hussein Shafei,

Lt. Colonel Abdel Moneim Amin, Lt. Colonel Yussef Saddik Mansour, and, according to many reports, Major General Mohammed Naguib to their executive council. While a political parties reorganization law was being implemented, Naguib and his colleagues believed that the country could be governed by the nonparty civilian government of Ali Maher. But they were soon disillusioned even on this score. Ali Maher was a conservative politician of the old regime. Although he was willing to accept the premiership after the coup, he displayed strong reluctance to implement the sweeping reforms urged by the military. When an agrarian reform bill was first discussed, the Premier was loath to impose such severe financial penalties upon members of his own social class. Moreover, in opposition to Naguib's expressed wishes, he authorized additional indirect regressive taxes on such commodities as tobacco.

By August 8, the die had been cast. Naguib publicly set the campaign in motion with the warning that it might become necessary to proclaim a dictatorship unless Egypt's political parties thoroughly "cleansed" themselves.[10] Referring to the Wafd, he declared: "Most of the evil element extending to the very top still remains untouched. What I think of the Wafd cleanup goes for all the other parties, too."[11] Two days later, General Naguib continued his attack in a leading Cairo newspaper, *Al Misri:* "We have advised. Now we warn. Next we shall act. We have had enough of corruption. Political parties must get rid of bad elements. The next step should be to bring these bad elements to book and let justice take its course. . . . Our parties are founded on personalities, not on principles."[12] The Free Officers, however, were laboring under a self-imposed handicap: they had committed themselves to peaceful means. And the opposition to the army, taking heart from the absence of forceful measures, became increasingly virulent.

The first serious challenge to the new regime came from the Delta. On August 12, riots broke out in the mill town of Kafr el Dawar. An organized band of workers, shouting "Long live the army's Revolution, the people's Revolution!," seized the factory installations, setting fire to several buildings and damaging equipment. When the police force could not cope with the rioters, army troops had to be called from Alexandria to subdue the workers in a pitched battle; nine were reported dead and twenty-two wounded. The Free Officers, panicked by this show of violence, took forceful action. Naguib, until then represented as a mild and moderate leader, declared bluntly: "All sections of the population, and particularly labor, should notice that any disorder or infringement of public security will be considered as an act of treason against the country, the penalty for which is well known to all."[13] A special military court, headed by Abdel Moneim Amin of the Free Officers' executive council, was created to try the arrested textile workers.

Government officials to this day have failed to give a consistent account of the riots. The controlled local press strongly suggested that the same "secret hands" which had organized the January burning of Cairo were behind the Kafr el Dawar rising.[14] General Naguib stated flatly that it was a "Communist-inspired" strike,[15] and Major Ahmed Abdullah Toiema, the military coordinator of labor affairs since 1952, declared in 1958 that the responsible individuals were Communists.[16] On the other hand, leading figures in Egypt's labor movement claim that no definite proof of Communist involvement has yet been established.[17] It is generally accepted, however, that Communist influence in labor unions at the time was strongest in the textile industry. At any rate, the public prosecutor obtained the first death sentence within five days of the strike and, during the following week, another worker was given the death penalty, while a score of others received prison terms. The two condemned to death were offered clemency if they turned state's evidence; but when they refused to name the instigators of the disturbance, the Free Officers upheld the original sentences and the two were hanged early in September.

On the Monday following the strike, the Ministry of Interior announced the formation of a "State Security Department" to fight against Communism and Zionism,[18] and before the Kafr el Dawar trials ended, the Ministry announced the breakup of a major Communist cell and the arrest of twenty-four persons charged with belonging to the outlawed Communist movement. This vigorous campaign against the Left alienated a leading

Communist faction which previously had supported the Free
Officers. The MDLN (Democratic Movement for National
Liberation), which claimed Colonel Yussef Saddik Mansour and
Khaled Mohieddine among its members,[19] soon became openly
antagonistic; it denounced the "military dictatorship which,
after sparing Farouk, the feudal lords, traitors, and embezzlers,
spilled only the workers' blood."

In an impromptu address, Naguib told a group of soldiers
that the army would "crush" anyone caught spreading the false
idea that the army was tainted with Communism. Then, in an
apparent reference to right-wing politicians, he continued: "Elements belonging to the corrupt era are still at large and they are
actively working to frustrate our movement. But we will crush
them. We will shoot them, if necessary."[20] This blunt warning
followed his announcement that parliamentary elections, originally scheduled for October, would be held in February, 1953.
It was felt that, before the elections, the army, after implementing
a retroactive illegal profits act and after initiating a general purge,
would approve only substantially reconstituted parties. The Free
Officers believed, also, that the agrarian reform law, once enacted, would destroy the dominant influence of large landowners
in Egyptian politics. As was to be expected, most political parties
reacted sluggishly to official orders for a purge, awaiting the
outcome of the expected showdown between the Wafd and the
regime.

Naguib and other Free Officers met with various leaders of
the Wafd in an effort to reach a compromise. But, in a speech
at Alexandria on August 23, Mustapha Nahas claimed that
violence had been done to the Constitution and demanded a
return to parliamentary rule. The army, fearing that wealthy
landowners and others affected by recent reform measures might
rally in support of the Wafd, moved tanks to strategic positions
throughout Cairo, only to withdraw them the following day.
Then, on September 5, the Wafd defiantly announced that the
decisions of purge committees should be regarded as accusations,
subject to approval in duly constituted courts of law.

Ali Maher's position, during these turbulent days, was fast
becoming untenable. The Free Officers group, impatient for

reform, accused Maher of deliberately delaying the land reform bill and other measures. Early on September 7, 1952, simultaneous with the arrest of forty-three politicians of the old regime, General Naguib, prodded by the more impatient members of the Free Officers' junta, established himself as Prime Minister of a new civilian Cabinet.

Yet, the struggle was far from over. The Egyptian masses, although disgruntled at the failures of the "old order," still were not captivated by the minor reforms initiated by the new regime for the benefit of the poorer classes. So the Free Officers, realizing their lack of firm popular support, sought an alliance with the Moslem Brethren against the Wafd. Supreme Guide Hodeiby was approached with an offer of two ministries in return for Brethren support.[21] But Hodeiby's candidates, Munir Dallah and Hassan Ashmawi, were unacceptable to the Free Officers. When the new Cabinet accepted a more moderate Brethren member, Sheikh Ahmed Hassan Baquory, he was immediately expelled by the Brotherhood. A coalition with Hodeiby consequently being out of the question, the Free Officers nevertheless decided to challenge the Wafd. Thus Suliman Hafez, a bitter foe of the Wafd, was appointed Deputy Premier and Minister of the Interior.

The mass arrest of old-regime politicians did not appear to be directed solely against the Wafd. Rather, the coming struggle was foreshadowed by the new Cabinet's first meeting. After a session of nine and one-half hours, Minister Fathy Radwan announced, on September 9, that the Agrarian Reform Law had been enacted and a law for the compulsory reorganization of political parties had been approved. The Agrarian Reform Law was, of course, more than a purely political move. Nevertheless, it was clear to many observers that the legislation, aimed at breaking up the feudal hierarchy of the countryside, was designed—at least in the short run—to cripple Wafdist power in the villages. Nor was there any mistaking the fact that the party reorganization act was directed against Mustapha Nahas' leadership, for the Free Officers had made it amply clear that a Nahas-dominated Wafd would be unacceptable.

The septuagenarian Nahas struggled against the October 8

deadline set by the government for "political reorganization."
Meanwhile, a Wafdist faction friendly to the military regime
urged the dismissal of Nahas and his replacement by a former
senator from Tanta, Salem Fahmi Gomaa. While the Wafd was
thus split internally, other parties hastened to reorganize in compliance with the law. Four cabinet ministers founded a new
party, and the Moslem Brethren, after fighting bitterly over the
decision of whether to register as a religious society or political
party, finally enrolled as a political organization.

But the Wafd had not yet come to heel. Indeed, as the
other parties complied meekly with the government's ultimatum,
the Wafd was becoming the rallying ground for civilian opponents of the Free Officers. Wafd leaders realized that their backs
were against the wall—that the party, having already been
humiliated several times since the July coup, could not retreat
further without forfeiting its political future. Nahas, therefore,
launched a counteroffensive with the declaration that "No power,
Allah and the Egyptian people excepted, can oust me." [22] He
followed this up, on September 27, with an attack against
Deputy Premier Hafez, when he referred to "those who exploit
political events to feather their own nest." [23] The government,
realizing that a compromise was impossible, decided to act. After
placing the military under a "state of alert," Naguib and his
fellow officers left on a tour of the Delta, traditionally the
Wafdist stronghold. His trip turned into a triumphal procession.
As one veteran newsman commented: "The Wafd is dead." [24]

Ultimately, the Wafd elected Nahas as Honorary President.
Deputy Premier Hafez, however, refused to recognize this reorganization. A Wafdist attempt to challenge this ruling through
the courts was countered by a Cabinet decree which conferred
supreme powers, not subject to judicial review, upon General
Naguib for six months, retroactive to July 23, 1952.

This decree was not the only indication of the government's
drift toward complete military dictatorship. New roundups of
civilian politicians were conducted, and, on September 25, the
Cabinet retired 450 army officers of all ranks. [25] Five days later,
staff officers were assigned to many of the more important government departments. [26] It came, therefore, as no surprise when

Naguib declared in early October: "We have already declared that our principal aim is to establish a 'true democratic government' in Egypt. *If political parties will become perfectly reorganized by that date* [February, 1953], elections will take place at the fixed time, and without undue delay." (Italics added.)[27] Obviously, the military junta, becoming accustomed to governing, was reluctant to surrender its newly acquired powers to civilian politicians.

With the Wafd subdued, the government turned to the Moslem Brethren, still a major threat because of their widespread religious appeal and its many active supporters even within the army and the police. Two days after pardoning Brethren members imprisoned for political crimes, the government dropped a leading Brethren sympathizer, the popular Colonel Rashad Mohanna, from his position on the Regency Council, charging that Mohanna had opposed the agrarian reform program, had sought to gain undue personal influence, and had refused "to conform with the principles of the military movement."[28] A local newspaper charged that he tried to proclaim himself as Caliph of Islam;[29] and a government source revealed that Mohanna had summoned the Prime Minister to inform him that he did not wish to remain a mere figurehead.[30] It is entirely possible that Colonel Mohanna did seek greater personal recognition, for the Regency Council possessed no real power. More significantly, however, Mohanna had attracted attention by his criticism of the existing "godless" government, and it is likely that he was chastised primarily for his close working relationship with Hassan el Hodeiby. Upon his removal he was placed under house arrest; the Regency Council was thus reduced to a single man, the affable Prince Mohamed Abdul Moneim.

The Military Takes Over

With some of the more formidable organized opposition thus eliminated, the regime felt ready to lay the groundwork for a new political structure. Ali Maher, still on friendly terms with General Naguib, publicly announced, on November 15, what many believed to be the political beliefs of the Free Officers' junta. He declared that "the Constitution must be modern. The present Constitution does not meet the needs of a free and developed democracy because it was based on nineteenth-century principles of democracy. Parliament must actually represent all sections of the nation, political and economic, workers and technicians. It must be a living mirror of the nation. The major outlines for this project must be submitted to a Constituent Assembly or to a National Congress, so that the people may make its choice." [31] While the press carried reports of army efforts to form an "organization of liberation youth" (thought by some to be a new political party), continued publicity was given to the need for a "truly sound Constitution."

Ahmed Abdul Fath, the Wafdist editor of *Al Misri*, was not alone when he declared that "the people are looking forward to the day when they will be able to enjoy the freedom of speech and the freedom of assembly, as well as all other basic rights." [32] But by the time Naguib announced, on December 10, that the Constitution had been abrogated and authority had passed to a "transitional government," a majority of the population was conditioned to accept this *fait accompli*.

Through December and much of January, the drive against existing political parties continued. A government decree, retroactive to 1939, barred all persons convicted of corruption or abuse of power from political activity and public office. Still another court, consisting primarily of army officers, was established to try cases of corruption, and a number of former ministers, including Wafdist Fuad Serag el Din, were indicted. Then, shortly after a fifty-man constitutional committee was set up under Ali Maher's direction, twenty-five officers, the most prominent being Colonel Mohanna, were arrested on charges of conspiring to overthrow the government; Colonel Nasser, then acting Army Chief of Staff, also announced that fifteen civilians had been taken into custody and that the arrest of every known Communist was planned. These arrests preceded Naguib's announcement that there would be a "transitional period" of three years before constitutional government would be resumed. Moreover, the Cabinet decreed a ban on all political parties and authorized the seizure of party funds. And so, on the six-month commemoration of the coup, with the announcement of the formation of a "Liberation Front" to replace the dissolved political parties, military dictatorship was a fact. The authority of government was transferred to a newly created Revolutionary Command Council (RCC), composed entirely of Free Officers' executive council members.

Thus, a small band of officers, who had initiated a modest *coup d'état* with no professed desire to govern, had become, within the brief period of six months, rulers of their country. A historian, looking back upon this turbulent period, will find cause to indict Nasser and his group: their systematic elimination of political opposition and their abandonment of principles which they had held aloft in the battle against the "old order." But in fairness to these young insurgents, one cannot escape the conclusion that their hand, at least in part, was forced by circumstances. Dedicated nationalists, and imbued with a devotion and honesty rare in Egyptian public life, they entered the political arena with the naïve preconception that a simple change at the top could halt the deterioration of Egypt's national life. This attitude was natural in men whose military careers had kept them relatively removed from the miasma of Egyptian politics. Once they came face to face with the corruption and irresponsibility of the "old order," the conclusion became inevitable: the implementation of reforms could not be entrusted to the old politicians with their vested interests and their cynical disdain for the public good. A new system had to be wrought.

Their efforts at reform were praiseworthy. Inheriting a nation close to bankruptcy, the new Cabinet bravely introduced an austerity budget which was not expected to gain favor with many civil servants and local businessmen. Furthermore, the reduction of rents and food prices, the introduction of minimum agricultural wages, the establishment of "anticorruption courts," the enactment of a land reform program, the drafting of new labor laws, the introduction of more progressive taxes, and a host of other measures all reflected the spirit of the military group.

By January, 1953 what had begun as a coup turned into a revolution. No longer was the old political system to be tolerated;

no longer would the traditional social and economic structure remain intact. The Revolutionary Command Council, rapidly consolidating its power, pressed the Revolution which had begun to take form during the preceding months. Perhaps some of the Free Officers still remembered the aims which had been expressed in their pamphlet of March, 1952, entitled *Down With Martial Law*:

1. The abolition of martial law.
2. The lifting of censorship.
3. The shattering of the political police.
4. The release of political detainees.
5. Amnesty for political prisoners.
6. The abrogation of all previous reactionary laws.
7. The restoration of the Constitution.[33]

But what had become of these lofty goals? Martial law, in January, 1953, was still in force. The press already had threatened to strike over local censorship. Sections of the old political police had been disbanded—only to be replaced by army personnel. Many political victims of the old regime had been released from prison—only to be replaced by new detainees, arrested in January "for the security of the State." The Constitution had been abrogated. Political freedom was sacrificed as the RCC undertook the reconstruction of Egypt.

The first phase of the Revolution had been easy, perhaps deceptively so. The Free Officers, by virtue of their physical control of the government, were able to split, isolate, and contain their immediate opposition. Their success, however, was due largely to the apathy and submissiveness of the Egyptian people. Egyptians traditionally have been accustomed to domination. But there is also a deep-rooted passive resistance among Egyptians against any authority beyond that of the family or the local village. This refusal to cooperate with the central government had plagued Cairene rulers for many centuries. Destroying the "old order" by degrading leading political figures, by confiscating party funds, and by redistributing existing wealth was one thing; creating a viable alternative system was quite another. The RCC was determined to initiate a political revolution which, by necessity, also entailed an economic and social transformation of the first magnitude.

The new "Liberation Rally," headed by Colonel Nasser, was expected to provide the new regime with popular support. Nasser, by recruiting Abdel Latif Boghdadi as Comptroller-General, Major Ahmed Tahawy as Deputy Secretary-General, and Major Ahmed Abdullah Toiema as Deputy Secretary-General in charge of Labor Affairs, and by appointing other officers like Major Wahid Ramadan and Captain Adel Tahir to manage the Rally's youth activities and its paramilitary formations, sought to create a Falange-type organization whose loyalty to the government would be unquestioned. As Colonel Nasser expressed it: "Liberation Rally is not a political party and was never intended to be. The creation was prompted by the desire to establish a body that would organize the people's forces and overhaul the social setup. The Liberation Rally is the school where the people will be taught how to elect their representatives properly."[34]

It was apparent that the Liberation Rally would wean few members from the old political organizations. Since the Rally was determined to create a new political base, it decided to cast its appeals to labor and the youth. Ever since after the Kafr el Dawar incident, the military had consciously wooed the working classes. Although legislation was passed which for all practical purposes outlawed strikes, efforts were made to expand trade unionism, and a new conciliation and arbitration law was enacted. Certain key union leaders were allegedly placed on the government payroll. The other target group, the youth, was more difficult to control, for the universities traditionally had been arenas for paid political agents; moreover, the Moslem Brethren had unusually strong support among Cairo's students. Brethren members had explicit orders to infiltrate the Rally and, as Major Toiema later observed, it was the Brethren members who were most anxious to receive paramilitary training.[35]

The government had become an unwieldy mechanism for policy implementation. Final authority rested in the RCC, which scheduled weekly joint sessions with the civilian Cabinet headed by General Naguib. The RCC, however, exercised little executive control since, except for Naguib, none of its members occupied official administrative posts. Moreover, RCC decisions were determined by majority vote, each officer, including Naguib, casting but a single ballot. Understandably, some of the members deemed this system burdensome; and Naguib himself felt bridled by the equal votes of his young, often unknown, colleagues. It is surprising, indeed, that decisive action resulted from such an awkward arrangement; and as operational decisions became more pressing, the group appointed a vice-chairman, Colonel Nasser.

The political climate during the spring of 1953 was calm. Colonel Mohanna and a number of other officers, arrested on the eve of the start of the "transitional period," were tried before a Revolutionary Tribunal headed by Nasser and including eight other RCC members. After a trial in which the defendants were not permitted counsel, all the accused were found guilty, with some sentenced to life imprisonment. Later, still another committee was established, this time composed of Minister Fathy Radwan and RCC representative Sadat, charged with screening defendants for yet another "treachery court"; public accusations were directed against Mustapha Nahas' wife and against Fuad Serag el Din of the Wafd, who already had been arrested on three previous occasions. In June, the Palestinian "arms scandal case" came to a surprising end. Since Naguib and his associates long had claimed that defective arms were mainly responsible for the army's poor performance in Palestine, it was generally expected that scapegoats would be produced from ex-King Farouk's entourage. Instead, eleven of the thirteen defendants, including Prince Abbas Halim, second cousin to Farouk, were acquitted; the other two were let off with fines.

Beginning in early 1953, the rumor was current in Cairo that the RCC, with Ali Maher's hearty approval, had decided to proclaim Egypt a republic, and that Nasser, now recognized by many as the *primum mobile* of the Free Officers, would supplant Naguib as premier. The General was scheduled for elevation to a new position of president. Indeed, this had been the plan, but Naguib strongly protested the proposed change. Naguib's objection confronted the other RCC members with a difficult decision. While the younger officers had remained in the background, Naguib had become the popular figure of the Free Officers movement. His humble manner, the cheap cigarette tobacco in his musty pipe, his simple honesty—these had become the symbol of the Revolution, and he its only personality. The Free Officers, having created the image of Naguib the leader, found it impolitic to deny his wishes.

On June 18, 1953, the Republic was proclaimed, with Mohammed Naguib as its first President. Since Naguib also retained the Premiership, Nasser was sworn in as Deputy Premier and Minister of the Interior; Wing Commander Abdel Latif Boghdadi became Minister of War and Marine; Major Abdel Hakim Amer, close friend of Nasser and once director of Naguib's office, was promoted to Major General for his new job as military Commander-in-Chief; and Major Salah Salem assumed office as Minister of National Guidance and Minister of State for Sudanese Affairs. These changes were significant, for they drastically reduced what civilian participation there had been in the government. Nearly all of the key posts were now held by officers. The only critical ministry not headed or staffed by officers was that of Finance, for the Free Officers still felt incapable of coping with the intricacies of economics.

While Naguib remained titular leader of the RCC and of the government, it became increasingly clear that Nasser wielded the actual power. More and more, Nasser, or his colleague, Major Salem, issued policy statements; and on occasion, major decisions were taken without Naguib even having been consulted. An incident in August, 1953, illustrated Naguib's faltering authority. President Naguib had decided to leave on a pilgrimage to Mecca in the company of Colonel Ahmed Shawki, Commandant of the Cairo garrison and an outspoken opponent of Nasser. Apparently deeming this a potentially dangerous combination, Nasser ordered three of his trusted RCC associates, Salah Salem, Hussein Shafei, and Gamal Salem, to accompany the President on his trip. Yet, despite these restrictions, Naguib still seemed to enjoy his symbolic role, although obviously overwhelmed by huge quantities of factual material which he did not fully comprehend. A visitor to Naguib's modest home (overrun by nine cats, for whom he had been unable to find "good homes"), was struck by the President's simple honesty. His growing political isolation was reflected in such comments as, "I really don't remember," or "They haven't told me."[36]

Although Nasser had now become the most important single leader within the RCC, he was still forced to rely upon a hard core of Free Officers. With the assistance of Zacharia Mohieddine, promoted to Minister of the Interior on October 4, the vise against individual politicians and dissident officers was tightened. On October 11, 1953, Major Salah Salem announced the discovery of a major "conspiracy" involving "certain . . . professional politicians [who] are in constant touch with the British Embassy."[37] Four days later, an extraordinary "Revolutionary Tribunal," responsible only to the RCC, was established, with Abdel Latif Boghdadi as President of a triumvirate including Anwar Sadat and Hassan Ibrahim. Among the thirty-four defendants were some of the most prominent politicians of the old regime: Mustapha Nahas; Serag el Din; Hafiz Afifi, former Chief of the Royal Cabinet; Ibrahim Abdel Hadi, the former Premier who had personally censured Nasser in June, 1949; Ibrahim Farag; and Prince Abbas Halim. They were arraigned on charges ranging from treason to "rumor-mongering" and "working against the interests of the country."

The trials made a mockery of judicial procedure. While the defendants were permitted counsel, defense lawyers often were barred from visiting their clients. When one defense lawyer protested against the high-handed methods of the tribunal, Chairman Boghdadi replied bluntly: "You forget that this is a revolutionary court."[38] Some of the lawyers found these conditions so intolerable that they withdrew from the trials. Hadi received the death sentence "for high treason and corruption" (later commuted to life); Farag, former Assistant Secretary-General of the Wafd, was given life imprisonment, and other prominent politicians faced at least fifteen years in prison. A *New York Times* correspondent commented: "Many observers here believe that the alleged conspiracy with foreigners is a shrewd blind to justify the removal of still influential leaders of the abolished political parties."[39] These political prisoners were more fortunate than four other men, accused of spying for a foreign power.

The colorful "King Sabri" was hanged within forty-eight hours of conviction; three others were executed five days later. Shortly after the trials, the RCC announced still another "reform," one which was not unexpected after the abolition of the monarchy: the confiscation of all land and other wealth belonging to the former royal family of Mohamed Ali.

It was at this time also that Major Salem, by then official spokesman for the regime, implied that the three-year "transitional period" leading to the restoration of constitutional government might be extended indefinitely. In answer to a question concerning the future government, he replied sharply: "And why should you worry what will happen after the three-year period is over?"[40] Politicians, however, were not the only victims of systematic repression. Local Communist splinter groups, increasingly critical of the "dictatorial regime," which they termed a "tool of American imperialists," were the targets of concerted police action. Several major cells had been uncovered, and over a hundred alleged members of the outlawed Communist Party were tried before military courts. Furthermore, the Cairo Court of Cassation ruled that Communist prisoners were not entitled to amnesty under the General Amnesty Law, for they had been jailed for committing a "social" rather than political crime[41]—i.e., the attempted overthrow of the existing social system of Egypt.

Still unresolved, however, was the struggle with the Moslem Brethren. By October, 1953, it was clear that the only two political organizations of consequence left in Egypt were Nasser's Liberation Rally and the Brethren. Of the two, the Brethren, having effectively infiltrated the Rally, were by far the stronger. Nasser, reluctant to risk a direct clash between two mass organizations, resorted to more subtle tactics. He exacerbated the friction which still rent the Brethren after Hodeiby's selection as Supreme Guide over the former Executive Vice-President, Salah Ashmawi, and Hassan el Banna's brother; he also encouraged an attempt to depose Hodeiby's faction. Immediately after Hodeiby had summarily expelled four members of the Executive Committee in November, 1953, a dissident group led by Salah Ashmawi, a close friend of Naguib, seized the Brethren's headquarters.[42] The insurgents, under police protection, passed a resolution which dissolved the Supreme Guidance Committee and established a temporary ruling body of four members, including Ashmawi. On the following morning, however, thousands of Hodeiby supporters reoccupied the premises.

The personal intervention of Naguib and Nasser went for naught, as the Executive Committee immediately expelled Ashmawi and his followers.[43] Nasser's attempted coup thus backfired badly; not only had the military regime openly abandoned its professed neutrality over intra-Brethren politics, but the bungled intervention also served to strengthen Hodeiby's position. The Supreme Guide remained defiant. When asked about possible Brethren participation against the British in the newly organized National Guard, he replied deliberately: "It is the duty of all men and women, young and old, to struggle to get the enemy out of their country. We have desired to participate with the National Guard with all our power so that we shall be prepared *in the struggle demanded by religion.*" (Italics added.)[44]

Nasser, on several occasions, had requested that the RCC dissolve the Brethren; each time a majority of the officers opposed him. Then, on January 12, 1954, a serious disturbance occurred at Cairo University. While Brethren students were conducting memorial services for "martyrs of the Suez Canal campaign," a sound truck from the Liberation Rally chanced by. Within minutes, a riot had broken out and dozens of students were injured, four seriously. This was the excuse Nasser needed. After an emergency meeting of the RCC, the Brethren were proscribed and Hodeiby and other Brethren leaders arrested. The official communiqué stated: "The Moslem Brethren organization is considered a political party and is, therefore, subject to the Revolutionary Command Council's decision for the dissolution of political parties."[45] Thus, the Brethren were forced underground.

The Nasser-Naguib Controversy

With the last civilian challenge to the RCC ostensibly eliminated, attention turned to the widening split within the regime. No longer was there any lip service paid to the myth of unity; as

early as September, 1953, the resignation of Colonel Ahmed
Shawki as chairman of a military court was generally interpreted
as a protest against Nasser's ambitions for the premiership. Moreover, Naguib became outspokenly critical of his colleagues. Naguib is reported to have told one foreign diplomat: "These
young men are imprudent . . . they no longer listen to me. They
are piling up stupid mistakes and heading for disaster."[46] To
another diplomat he complained that Fuad Serag el Din's sentence was a "blunder and an injustice."[47] The tension within
the RCC erupted in several crises, and each time Naguib threatened to resign unless he had his way.[48] Feeling that he had
become leader of the country in fact as well as in formality,
Naguib insisted upon greater authority. As he later reflected:
"I was responsible for every action taken by the government. . . .
I was no longer willing to assume responsibility for actions regarding which I was either not consulted or of which I did not and
could not approve."[49]

The conflict between Naguib and Nasser broke into the open
on February 25, 1954. Three days previously, the RCC had sent
Gamal Salem and Kamal el din Hussein to visit Naguib and
seek a compromise.[50] Upon leaving Naguib, they informed him
of an RCC meeting scheduled for February 24. Instead of attend-
ing, President Naguib submitted his letter of resignation. Startled,
the assembled officers voted to accept it, with only Nasser voicing
some reservations.[51] The following day, Nasser was proclaimed
Chairman of the RCC and Prime Minister, while the presidency
was declared vacant. Naguib was placed under house arrest,
and a state of emergency was proclaimed throughout Egypt.

The move evoked immediate opposition: the Sudanese, who
had idolized Naguib, himself part Sudanese, rushed a three-man
delegation to Cairo; the fifteen-thousand-strong Frontier Corps,
composed primarily of crack Sudanese soldiers, threatened to
mutiny;[52] and pro-Naguib officers seized the offensive. A climax
came on the evening of February 26, when a group of cavalry
officers under Major Khaled Mohieddine's leadership met in
Abbassia. Mohieddine refused to recognize Salah Salem as the
RCC's spokesman;[53] he and his fellow officers demanded to speak
with Nasser. While General Amer deployed his troops to guard

against a possible insurrection, Colonel Nasser faced this mob
of angry men alone and unarmed. He tried to reason with the
officers for over two hours, then gave up in despair: Naguib
and Mohieddine were to be appointed President and Prime
Minister respectively.[54] Mohieddine then went to Naguib's house
and convinced the General that he could return to office only
if he accepted Khaled as Prime Minister.[55] Shortly after Naguib
had reluctantly accepted this condition, some pro-Nasser officers
kidnapped Naguib, abducting him into the desert. Apparently
they were prepared to kill him, if necessary. Nasser, however,
ordered Naguib's immediate release.[56] By noon of February 27,
the RCC had reappointed Naguib as President. To Khaled
Mohieddine's surprise, however, Nasser remained Prime Minister.

Early on February 28, Naguib's day of "victory," there were
signs of an approaching showdown. When Cairo University students demonstrated against Nasser, security forces fired upon
them near the Kasr el Nil Bridge; thirteen were wounded, three
of them fatally. The incident was officially described as "inspired
by the Brethren."[57] Cairo was a restive city that morning, as
huge throngs turned out to cheer Naguib's triumphal return to
Abdine Palace. When Naguib addressed his welcomers in Abdine
Square, it became apparent that many in the crowd were Moslem
Brethren, and some of the Kasr el Nil Bridge survivors, waving
handkerchiefs dipped in blood, were rapidly becoming unman-
ageable.[58] Naguib, in an apparent effort to forestall possible
disorders, invited Brethren leader Abdel Kader Aouda to join
him on the balcony; this, in turn, gave ammunition to those
who claimed that Naguib's reinstatement was instigated by the
Brethren. Moreover, Naguib cast for the support of the "old
order" when he announced (without the RCC's permission)
that parliamentary elections soon would be held.[59] Suddenly, his
appearance on that balcony made him the symbol for all the
forces which opposed the regime. The Moslem Brethren and the
Wafd, for different reasons, openly supported him, while even
the Communists, who previously had referred to his rule as "a
military cloak serving the ends of imperialism,"[60] saw in Naguib
a foil against Nasser. But by appealing directly to the people,

Naguib had committed himself to another showdown with his former comrades.

As an aftermath to Naguib's reappointment, the return to civilian parliamentary rule became a distinct possibility. Indeed, Naguib, in his letter of acceptance to the RCC, referred to the "Parliamentary Republic of Egypt,"[61] a term which had not been used previously. There already was a movement afoot to dissolve the RCC, and many observers believed that Nasser had suffered a major defeat; nevertheless, a majority of the RCC, including the Salem brothers, Boghdadi, Ibrahim, and Sadat, stood firmly by him, while two other important members, Colonel Zacharia Mohieddine, Minister of the Interior, and Amer, military Commander-in-Chief and Nasser's close personal friend, did not openly identify themselves with either camp.

Well-informed foreign correspondents were convinced that Nasser could have crushed the cavalry's threat with the help of the army; these same persons believed that Nasser shunned such a course of action lest he provoke a civil war.[62] Perhaps, also, Nasser's capitulation to the cavalry was a spur-of-the-moment decision, prompted in part by his chagrin at the cavalry officers' flat rejection of the RCC's principles, principles in which he sincerely believed. Whatever Nasser's motives, however, the fight was far from over. While Naguib imagined that the RCC could not govern without him (this was how he explained his reinstatement), Nasser realized that Naguib could not rule alone. Without the army's support, he would be forced to rely on the Brethren or, perhaps, a revived Wafdist movement.

After Naguib and Major Salem had left for the opening of the Sudanese Parliament, a spokesman for the RCC claimed that the agitation which led to Naguib's reinstatement had been instigated by "eight Communist officers."[63] Linking the Communists to a united front which included the Moslem Brethren and the Socialist Party, it was further announced that these officers would be court-martialed. This was in direct violation of an agreement between Naguib and Nasser that there would be no retaliation against participants in the February events. And while Naguib was greeted in Khartoum by bloody disorders (generally attributed to the Sudanese political group which opposed union with Egypt), the Egyptian government announced the arrest of 118 persons who had plotted "to provoke disorders in connection with the return of Naguib to Cairo";[64] Brethren, Socialists, Wafdists, and Communists were included in the roundup. Meanwhile, Nasser strengthened his hold over the army, transferring two cavalry colonels, promoting about fifteen colonels to brigadiers, and dismissing other officers.

Even while these actions were being taken, the RCC obligingly deferred to Naguib's announced wishes. On March 5, the junta supported the decision to conduct elections in June for a constituent assembly which would precede a new parliament, planned for July 23. The RCC promised that martial law would be abolished one month before elections, and press censorship was lifted, effective March 6. It appeared that Naguib, with the strong backing of Ali Maher and Abdel Razzak Sanhoury, former President of the State Council, had won a decisive personal victory. Although politicians were puzzled by the roundup of thirty-eight Communists immediately following this announcement, they seemed reassured by Naguib's March 8 resumption of the Premiership and of the Chairmanship of the RCC. It was evident, however, that a majority of the RCC members did not relish the idea of parliamentary rule, for, as one of them remarked: "A quick return to parliamentary life would mean a return to the scene of the dissolved political parties and the corruption they [the RCC] fought."[65]

Nasser remained in the background as Naguib claimed authority "by the will of the people."[66] When the unbridled press presented demands for complete and immediate freedom, it was Naguib to whom this plea was directed. Egypt was rapidly approaching chaos. The politicians, taking advantage of the RCC's apparent fear of opposing Naguib, openly lobbied for a parliamentary government; the universities, opened after having been closed for two weeks, again were shut following anti-Nasser demonstrations; the sentiments of civilian groups were expressed by the Egyptian Bar Association when it passed a resolution urging the junta "to go back to the barracks."[67] On March 20, the day on which Cairo hosted a state visit by King Saud, five bombs exploded in various sections of Cairo. Naguib no longer appeared to be in control of the situation.

This was the moment for which Nasser had prepared. On March 25, the RCC announced its latest decisions, which were tantamount to the abdication of its authority:

1. Political parties may reorganize immediately.
2. The RCC will be dissolved on July 24, 1954.
3. The RCC will not form a new political party.
4. There will be no deprivation of political rights.
5. The Constituent Assembly will be elected freely and directly, with no appointees.
6. The immediate task of the Constituent Assembly will be to elect the president of Egypt.[68]

In the light of Nasser's comment four days previous ("I am a revolutionary, not a politician"[69]) and of the editorial comments of *Al Gomhouria* (the paper edited by Colonel Anwar Sadat of the RCC),[70] this move was interpreted by many as a tactical maneuver against Naguib and the political parties. Immediately, scores of Brethren members, including Hassan Hodeiby and Abdel Kader Aouda, were released from jail; eight civilian ministers reportedly submitted their resignations as a preliminary to the formation of an all-civilian cabinet;[71] the Bar Association called for the cancellation of all military court verdicts;[72] and serious efforts were underway to reactivate the old political parties.

While Naguib helplessly surveyed the general disorder, a well-coordinated protest was initiated against the return of civilian rule. About one hundred and fifty members of the Liberation Rally staged a demonstration against the return of political parties; then a clandestine pamphlet, signed by "free revolutionary officers" and supporting the continuation of RCC rule, was circulated; Major Amin Shaker, aide-de-camp to Nasser, accused Naguib of becoming a tool of "dishonest politicians of the old regime."[73] He asserted: "At this stage the RCC has to take a decision to leave it to the Egyptian people to decide between the General and his associated elements, on the one side, and the Council on the other side. . . . We are confident that the traditional wisdom of the Egyptian people will decide their own future and avoid the trap that is being made for them in the name of lofty principles."[74] The trap was being closed.

The army, under Amer, staged a sit-down strike against Naguib. Then the Federation of Cairo Transport Workers, of which Naguib was an honorary member, made the next move. Nasser, through Major Toiema of the Liberation Rally, had gained the support of Sawi Ahmed Sawi, the transport union's President. Cairo was paralyzed by a bus, tram, and taxi strike. The police announced its refusal to supervise the June elections, and the navy sailed from Alexandria, pledging allegiance to the RCC. Meanwhile, demonstrators organized by the Liberation Rally gathered at strategic areas throughout Cairo, giving the impression of strong popular support for Nasser.

On March 28, the strike spread to many parts of Egypt. Naguib began the day in conference with Moslem Brethren leaders, then went to the Council of Ministers for a scheduled RCC meeting. Forcing their way through a pro-Nasser street crowd with drawn revolvers, Naguib and his aides waited a full hour for Nasser and his associates to arrive. Nasser and Salah Salem, after their arrival, continually went to the balcony, ostensibly to calm the "spontaneous" demonstrations. It was clear that Naguib had lost. The following morning, Naguib, Nasser, and other members accompanied King Saud to Almaza Airport. Then, according to one report, Naguib attempted to escape aboard the King's aircraft, but was stopped by Anwar Sadat.[75] Naguib collapsed and was carried to a nearby hangar. Under "doctor's orders," he was confined to his home.

That same afternoon Major Salem, speaking for the RCC, announced that the revolutionary junta, "bowing to popular demand,"[76] had reversed its decisions of March 5 and 25. Instead, political parties would again be outlawed (except for a special dispensation granted the Moslem Brethren), and the RCC would continue to rule until the end of the transitional period—January, 1956. Before that date, a national advisory assembly would be formed.

Representatives of the Moslem Brethren, the Communists, and the Socialists, boldly identifying themselves by name and party, sought to lead the students at Egypt's three secular universities against the military regime, but troops quickly dispersed demonstrations, and the universities again were closed down.[77] Then, Major Khaled Mohieddine left for a prolonged stay in Europe at the government's expense, while the RCC prepared for a large-scale purge. Perhaps the only major civilian group to be spared was labor, for support from several key unions had been vital in the overthrow of Naguib. Indeed, Egyptian labor reached, for a brief moment, a position of unprecedented influence, and it proposed the formation of a labor organization (remarkably similar to the organization suggested by Hodeiby of the Moslem Brethren in 1952) to work side by side with the RCC. Cairo trade-union leaders met on April 7, to consider ways of creating a national confederation: this they sought as reward for their previous support of Nasser and the RCC. Major Toiema, however, did not approve this move.

The press, again subjected to strict censorship, was singled out for special retaliatory treatment, while civilian politicians and the universities were warned that they would pay heavily for their opposition to the RCC during the March crisis. On April 15, the "cleansing of Egypt's political life" began. Members of the Wafd, the Liberal Constitutionalists, and the Saadists who held ministerial rank after July 1942—thirty-eight in number—were barred from politics for ten years; they were excluded, also, from membership in executive councils of unions and other organizations. The Press Syndicate's ruling council was dissolved; fourteen publications and twenty-three journalists were publicly accused of having taken bribes from previous governments.

On April 18, for the second time in two months, Nasser became Prime Minister, while Naguib retained the post of President. With the appointment of Wing Commander Hassan Ibrahim as Minister of State for Presidential Affairs and of Lieutenant Colonel Hussein Shafei as Minister of War, only two members of the RCC were excluded from the Cabinet: General Amer, Commander-in-Chief of the military, and Colonel Sadat, editor of the semiofficial newspaper *Al Gomhouria*.

Nasser had now become the undisputed leader of Egypt. No longer was he obliged to depend on RCC majorities, although the façade of majority vote still was maintained. After skillful manipulation, he had achieved effective control over the government. Yet, as he realized only too well, a majority of the country did not support him. But Nasser, whatever his faults, had several attributes which were unusual in Egypt: at least in 1954, he was a dedicated Egyptian nationalist, willing to endure personal enmity in his quest to develop the country. As he envisaged it, the creation of a new Egypt "would be accomplished at the expense of popularity." [78] And his blueprint for development certainly was not designed to placate the Egyptian dislike of authority, for he declared that "Egypt needs social and economic strengthening by authoritation methods and political purge . . . before [a] democratic constitution." [79]

III

The Entrenchment of the Military Regime

Nasser Consolidates His Position

Gamal Abdel Nasser was now dictator of Egypt. In his struggle to power he had managed to alienate almost every group which traditionally had been considered a power in Egyptian politics. The local parties and their leaders had been humiliated. The rich ex-pashas eyed this youthful upstart with disdain. Professors and students alike had been victimized by his authoritarian tactics, and the middle-class merchants and civil-service bureaucrats felt the squeeze of the government's austerity budgets.

The secular character of the RCC estranged Moslem Brethren adherents, and the regime's open appeals to the West for foreign capital and military assistance, combined with continued internal suppression, disheartened Egyptian leftists. Tenuous control of the labor movement through the Liberation Rally provided Nasser with a minimum of public support, but his power ultimately came from a single source—the military.

Nasser, however, did not seem overly embarrassed by the title of military dictator. For almost thirty years Egypt had lived behind a façade of democracy in which less than 20 per cent of the voters were literate and a majority of the votes were "delivered" by a few wealthy men. This system had not been overthrown; instead, it simply had collapsed under its own dead weight. No longer did Nasser feel called upon even to pay lip service to this "democracy." His power-political position incurred the wrath of many influential men in business and agriculture, not to mention the ranking civil servants whose careers had been linked closely to specific political parties; but Nasser was willing to accept this as a price of authoritarian government. He did not envisage an easy task, for what he aimed at was a political and social revolution. It was his firm belief that such a revolution could be triggered and carried through only by a nonpolitical government capable of enforcing decisions made "in the interests of the country." At the time, he summarized his philosophy as follows: "We are like a father who gives his son medicine, however painful it is to him, for he knows that he thus saves the life of his child."[1]

Nasser was uniquely qualified for the "father" role. His cleverness and patience had long distinguished him from the other RCC members; indeed, as a tactical thinker he had few peers, a fact he proved by easily outmaneuvering such men as Ali Maher, Mustapha Nahas, and Mohammed Naguib. Moreover, he had a quick grasp of problems and a prodigious capacity for work. Yet, he lacked one important trait of the dictator: the ability to exhort large masses of people. Before a crowd he appeared ill at ease—at times even timid. In his early career as Egypt's leader he seldom departed from a dry, factual presentation merely to gain mob approval. This man, who was at his persuasive best in small meetings, would become awkward and abrupt before large gatherings. And, in dealing with a loquacious Egyptian people, this was a serious handicap. In a country where personalities had dominated politics for so long, Gamal Abdel Nasser, despite his administrative ability and political acumen, was at a distinct disadvantage.

Nasser decided that it was not necessary for him to seek national popularity, at least over the short run. As a general rule, he refused to endorse programs which were primarily political palliatives. Instead, he increasingly sought to "cleanse" the instruments of power with which to impose his own social and economic programs. The army, his immediate source of power, was continually purged of opposition elements. Not even the Free Officers' executive council (which became the RCC) was spared: three members—Abdel Moneim Amin, Yussef Saddik Mansour, and Khaled Mohieddine—had been dropped by April, 1954. Perhaps it was more than a coincidence that these officers were well known for their leftist proclivities. Nasser later emphasized his antileftist stand when he permitted Colonel Sadat

to report in *Al Gomhouria* that Khaled Mohieddine had admitted
to the Free Officers that he was a Communist.[2] Further evidence
of this policy came with the arrest of sixteen army officers accused
of plotting May Day disorders with Communists. According to
Major Salah Salem, these officers, many of whom had originally
been arrested in February, 1954, as Communist supporters of
Naguib's reinstatement, confessed to a plot to overthrow the
regime and establish a Communist rule. In the wake of these
arrests, twenty-four civilians and ex-Captain Mustafa Kamal
Sidky, once considered an important member of the Free Officers, were seized on the same general charges. A second court
of the Revolutionary Tribunal was established to try the sixteen
officers, fifteen of whom were in the cavalry. Their leader,
Captain Ahmed Ali Hassan al Masry, a close associate of RCC
member Hussein Shafei, was most seriously compromised during
the trial; it was claimed that he sought to reinstate Naguib in
case of a successful coup.[3] He and twelve others subsequently
were convicted and given prison sentences ranging to fifteen
years. Colonel Ahmed Shawki, who less than a year before had
accompanied Naguib on his pilgrimage to Mecca, was also
brought before the tribunal. After Abdel Latif Boghdadi pronounced a ten-year sentence against Shawki for "preparing an
insurrection," the Revolutionary Tribunal, established the preceding September, was dissolved.

Other purges followed. The press paid a heavy penalty for
its attacks upon Nasser and the military government; the leading Wafd paper, *Al Misri*, was confiscated, and orders were
issued for the arrest of the Fath brothers and certain other
"antiregime" newspapermen. A campaign was conducted against
those papers and reporters who previously had accepted funds
from now defunct political parties or from former governments.
The "cleanup" campaign became complete with the dissolution
of the standing council of the Press Syndicate; plans hurriedly
were prepared to substitute a pro-Nasser body.

While Nasser thus dealt decisively with the regime's political
opposition, his efforts to establish a proregime political movement were less successful. The once highly vaunted Liberation
Rally had proved ineffectual. Further discredited by its role in

the March disturbances, the Rally was no longer actively supported even by government officials. On one occasion, government officials had described it as a "front," but after the connotations of this were explained, the term "rally" was adopted. Perhaps the only unanimity over the movement's purpose was a negative one: all of the Rally's supporters agreed that it was not a political party. As a mass organization the Rally was a failure; its claimed two-million membership never was realized. Nasser, Boghdadi, Tahawy, Toiema, and others used this Falange-type organization successfully for specific purposes—to control labor, to organize a cadre of proregime youth, and to "create" demonstrations. But the government found it impossible to impose this political organization upon the masses of Egyptian people. Moreover, much to the chagrin of its organizers, some of the Rally's enthusiastic participants were the very people whom it had meant to combat: the Moslem Brethren and the Communists.

By July, another highly touted goal of the regime—the establishment of a national consultative assembly—was no longer discussed publicly. Occasional reports had been published as to its tentative composition, and a ministerial committee claimed that two hundred of three hundred potential candidates had been approved, but these plans were not implemented. Nasser, commenting on the fact that all members were to be appointed rather than elected, explained that he "desired to eliminate all traces of the past by avoiding election contests which create unnecessary ill feeling, so that a new era of sincere cooperation for the public welfare might be started."[4] In a private interview, the Premier further stated that "the army, after ten years' preparation for politics, could not return to normal activities in less than ten years. My friends would still be my friends, in or out of uniform."[5]

Nasser found it exceedingly difficult to create the foundation of a broadly based political machine, for he was determined to demand sacrifices from his people rather than offer them the "bread and circuses" so often promised by previous regimes. In a characteristic speech he exhorted his fellow citizens "to be hardy and to sacrifice some of the pleasures of this evanescent life"[6]—

certainly not an appealing thought to a nation with an annual per capita income of one hundred dollars. In a break with the past, the rural areas, traditionally a dormant factor in Egyptian politics, were given special attention, to the detriment of the politically vibrant masses of Cairo; this was underscored by the appointment of the popular and competent Abdel Latif Boghdadi as Minister of Municipal and Rural Affairs.

The beautiful new avenues and countless luxury apartment buildings built in Cairo could not solve the problems of a city composed primarily of slums. In a metropolis of over two million persons, well over one hundred thousand males were classified as unemployed; and a majority of the families existed on less than twenty dollars monthly. Even more important, the petty bourgeosie—the minor civil servants, teachers, transport workers, and the multitude of unemployed or underpaid graduates of the universities—was discontented. Now, with the formal political structure of Egypt dismembered, these people took on a greater significance, for it was through them that civilian opposition to Nasser could best be channeled.

Indeed, it was these elements who wildly cheered Naguib on July 22, 1954, in his first public speech after he relinquished the Premiership to Nasser. When, on this day, during the commemoration of the second anniversary of the Revolution, Naguib shouted, "Whoever thinks that the Revolution is the deed of any one person is much mistaken,"[7] his words were drowned out by deafening roars of approval. His brief speech was extended to thirty minutes by the numerous interruptions. Then Premier Nasser faced the same crowd. He read from a prepared text; two hours and twenty minutes were devoted to internal improvements and another ten minutes were spent outlining Egypt's foreign relations. Anyone surveying the scene from the speaker's platform was impressed by the crowd's response; a group of men, huddled close to the platform, periodically shouted laudatory slogans. However, a walk through Midan Gomhouria revealed a different picture. While members of the Liberation Rally, perhaps twenty deep, formed a ring about the foreign dignitaries and dutifully followed the signals of professional cheerleaders, the mood of the rest of the "two hundred thousand enthusiastic listeners" was different. The center and rear of the square resembled a county fair on a festive occasion. Magicians performed their sleight-of-hand tricks on the sidewalks, beans and confectionaries were hawked to the passing strollers, and the loudspeakers blared over an obviously listless audience. The only signs of interest from the large majority of the crowd would come when Nasser, apparently annoyed by the Liberation Rally's claque, would impatiently raise his voice above their chants— then some of the unorganized spectators would hoot derisively at their Prime Minister.

The most significant lesson of the evening was that Naguib still retained tremendous popularity among the masses. Naguib, under constant surveillance since April by an RCC-appointed Minister of State for Presidential Affairs, still remained to many the symbol of the Revolution; to others he appeared as the only focal point around which opposition to Nasser could be gathered. Only two militant groups still remained uncrushed: the Communists and the Moslem Brethren. The Communists, rent by internal dissension, were continually being harassed by the government. Hardly a month went by without another cell being uncovered, or a major trial being staged. According to the chief of the Criminal Investigation Department at the Ministry of the Interior, 252 Communists had been arraigned in the first five months of 1954,[8] and the pace of arrests showed little sign of slackening during the remainder of the year. Moreover, the Communists provided an easy target for the government, representing as they did, at least indirectly, foreign subversion and an antireligious movement dedicated to the violent overthrow of the existing regime.

Nasser lashed out vigorously against them: "Take Communists, for example. We know this type of person aims only at anarchies, for they can only live in anarchy. They are printing leaflets filled with lies and deception. From where do [they get the funds] . . . they spend on these leaflets? . . . It was the Communists who set fire to Cairo while patriots in the Canal Zone were fighting imperialists. Communists aim at anarchy in order to satisfy their masters who are spending on them. Their appearances are rosy, but, under the surface, they are filled with grudges. Their objective is to rule the country by a Communist regime led by their chiefs."[9]

The Communists realized that alone they were ineffectual. So, using the contacts which they had made in prison with Brethren members following the government's anti-Brethren campaign in January, 1954, the leaders of several Communist factions sought a tactical alliance with the Brethren. One clandestine Communist pamphlet, issued on June 29, 1954, exhorted that "two forces led the opposition to the Revolution, the Communist Party, and the Moslem Brotherhood. A strengthening of the alliance between them is the first step in building the National Front and uniting all nationalists of all parties in a single struggle to bring down Gamal Abdel Nasser's regime."[10] There is little evidence, however, that the Brethren responded to these overtures. Instead, Supreme Guide Hodeiby decided on a "go-it-alone" showdown with the government over the Suez Canal Agreement issue.

On July 27, 1954, Nasser initialled an agreement with British Minister of State Anthony Nutting which provided for the gradual withdrawal of British troops from Egyptian soil; certain provisions were included which permitted British civilian technicians to remain in the Canal Zone and reserved for British troops the right to return if Turkey or a member of the Arab League were attacked. The following morning, soon after Naguib's arrival at Abdine Palace, a crowd began to gather outside his office. As its chants grew louder, Hassan Ibrahim, the Minister of State for Presidential Affairs, nervously closed the windows: the crowd was cheering Naguib. Later in the day, the official Moslem Brethren position was announced: the new agreement bound Egypt to unfavorable conditions at a time when the 1936 Anglo-Egyptian Agreement had almost expired. July 28, originally meant to be a festive holiday to celebrate the departure of the British, was fast becoming a day of violence. Abruptly, Zacharia Mohieddine banned all public demonstrations, and order was restored in Cairo, at least temporarily.

But Hodeiby was not content to drop the issue. Claiming that the agreement with Britain contained "every kind of harm to the interests of Egypt and Arabism," he challenged Nasser to publish the Brethren's objections.[11] Nasser replied sharply before a meeting of Liberation Rally faithfuls: "In April, 1953, when we found that Hodeiby and Mr. Evans, the Oriental Counselor at the British Embassy, had talks, I met the Supreme Guide at the residence of Munir el Dallah. I say at this time that they had not only accepted this agreement, but a worse one. This opposition is only for deception. . . . They [the Brethren] oppose this regime and all its achievements and they say that Islam is their objective. No, their objective is power. Religion to them is but a means to power."[12]

Much like the Wafd nearly two years earlier, the Brethren were now fighting for their very existence. No longer was the government prepared to compromise, as it did in January, 1953, and again in March, 1954. Nasser, aware of the Brethren's bent for assassination, introduced what he jokingly referred to as his own system of "collective security"; if he were killed, the other RCC members were instructed to "wipe out the three hundred leading Brethren in a matter of hours."[13] Nasser took steps to strengthen the regime. His close friend Major General Abdel Hakim Amer was appointed Minister of War, and Kamal el din Hussein, newly appointed Minister of Education, purged forty Egyptian university professors;[14] for the first time, all active members of the RCC were accorded ministerial rank. Within ten days, 109 high-ranking police officers, including 31 brigadiers and generals, were placed on pension.[15]

Clashes between Brethren members and the government became commonplace. On August 27, after a sheikh at a Cairo mosque denounced the Suez Canal Agreement, the police intervened; in the ensuing fight, about fifty persons were injured and another twenty arrested. Several days later, the police announced that thirty Brethren were injured in a riot which was touched off when a student leader urged Moslems to oppose the Nasser government "with force." On Friday, September 10, a Brethren sheikh attacked the Nasser administration in a sermon in a Delta mosque; following a battle with the National Guard, seventeen Brethren were arrested. Four days later, it was announced that the government had undertaken the job of preparing all sermons to be delivered in Egyptian mosques.[16] Meanwhile,

Brethren leaders in Syria bitterly criticized the Nasser regime and accused the Premier of conducting secret negotiations with Israel. Then, on September 24, in the face of strong government opposition, the Brethren Constituent Assembly reaffirmed its faith in Hodeiby's leadership. A later attempt was made by a Brethren faction desirous of accommodation with the RCC to place Hodeiby "on leave," but this attempted coup failed.

Since July, 1954, Brethren pamphlets had been distributed praising Naguib as the "savior and true leader of the country."[17] On October 19, the day of the signing of the Suez Canal Agreement, Naguib sent a letter to Nasser. In it, he stated his opposition to the signing of any agreement with the British, on the grounds that the atomic and hydrogen bombs had changed the nature of war and there was no longer any need for conceding to British troops the right to return under certain circumstances. He placed full responsibility for the agreement on Nasser and declared that it was "against the aspirations of the people."[18] Two days later, this letter was distributed by the Brethren under the title "Mohammed Naguib Is Not Responsible."[19]

On the night of October 26, a Cairo plumber named Mahmoud Abdul Latif fired eight shots at the Premier while he was addressing a large audience in Alexandria's spacious Midan Gomhouria. Nasser dropped to the floor; then, arising unscathed, he screamed almost hysterically to the crowd: "If Gamal Abdel Nasser dies now, he will be content, because everyone of you will be another Gamal Abdel Nasser."[20] All this was registered on a nationwide radio hookup. When the would-be assassin was identified as a member of the Brethren's "Secret Order," the plot seemed tailor-made for Nasser's objectives. For here was a perfect excuse for a bloody purge of the Brethren—with Nasser emerging as a hero to boot.

Mass arrests commenced on the night of the 26th; the following day, local authorities did not restrain mobs from burning the Moslem Brethren headquarters. Bit by bit, sensational facts were released to the public. Latif, the police claimed, was carrying a picture of Naguib in his pocket. The original plan had been to assassinate the Prime Minister during evacuation agreement celebrations in Cairo on October 21.[21] Latif and Hindawi Duweir (a young Cairo lawyer arrested with Latif) confessed that they had received instructions from the Brethren's underground terrorist organization;[22] retired Colonel Abdel Moneim Raouf and Youssef Taalet were named among the commanders of this group. Hodeiby was arrested in Alexandria and accused of plotting the overthrow of Nasser's administration by scores of assassinations: 160 officers allegedly had been marked for extermination, with Naguib the notable exception.[23] Meanwhile, over a thousand Brethren, mainly of the "Secret Order" and the Executive Committee, were arrested, and a special "people's tribunal," headed by Deputy Premier Gamal Salem and including RCC members Hussein Shafei and Anwar Sadat, was established to try them.

Many observers doubted that Hodeiby knew of, much less had ordered, the assassination plot. Capitalizing on these doubts, a ranking Brethren leader, Abdel Kader Aouda (the man who had joined Naguib at Abdine Palace on the morning of his triumphal February return to office) sent a petition to Nasser. Aouda promised to disband the "Secret Order" and surrender all arms and ammunition within fifteen days, to reform the general organization and limit it to purely religious and educational activities—at least during the transitional phase and until constitutional rule returned to Egypt—and to stop the antirevolutionary campaign within two weeks after an agreement.[24] In return, he demanded the release of all arrested Brethren, pardon for all those who surrendered their weapons within the fifteen-day period, permission for all Brethren to consult openly upon an agreement with the government, and a promise of no arrests during this fifteen-day period.

Nasser, however, was in no mood for compromise. The trials commenced on November 9, with Latif and Hindawi Duweir, leader of a Brethren branch in a Cairo suburb, as the first defendants. In pleading guilty, they soon implicated a number of the Brethren hierarchy. Duweir created a sensation when he testified that Ibrahim Tayab had informed him that Naguib agreed to make a radio broadcast to "calm the population"[25] if the assassination of Nasser succeeded. Captain Mahmoud Riad, aide-de-camp to President Naguib, was identified as the liaison man for the "Secret Order."[26] (Captain Riad managed to escape trial by fleeing to Saudi Arabia.) This evidence provided Nasser with sufficient excuse to depose Naguib. On November 14, Major General Amer and Hassan Ibrahim escorted Naguib from his Abdine Palace office and placed him under house arrest in Marg, thirty miles from Cairo. Shortly thereafter, the post of president was declared vacant, and Nasser assumed the functions, although not the title, of that office.

The trials resembled a circus side show. Hearings were carried over the Egyptian broadcasting facilities, and more caches of arms or fugitive Brethren leaders were produced for public inspection. It was interesting to note, as the trials progressed and several more "people's tribunals" were hastily established, that the "Secret Order," as opposed to the Moslem Brotherhood *in toto,* bore the brunt of the government's attack. The idea of returning to a society governed by the fundamental principles of Islam still attracted many adherents in Egypt and elsewhere. While the highest Islamic religious body condemned the work of the "Secret Order," it pointedly neglected to condemn the Brethren as a whole.[27] Of the first seven defendants sentenced to death, six convicted members of the "Secret Order" were executed; the sentence of the seventh, Supreme Guide Hodeiby, was commuted to life imprisonment. According to Nasser's later statement, 867 Brethren ultimately were convicted by the "people's courts."[28]

Prelude to Political Reconstruction

With the demise of the Moslem Brethren, the RCC under Premier Nasser entered a critical period. The obvious scapegoats had been eliminated; henceforth, the regime would find it more difficult to disavow responsibility for Egypt's shortcomings. After more than two years of authority, the revolutionary cadre still had not created the foundations of a new political order to replace the old. And as the months passed, Nasser and his colleagues appeared increasingly fearful of turning the authority of government back to the "people." The military gradually was being "civilianized"; the *foule* sandwiches eaten at the office desk, the bread and cheese wrapped in newspapers, the .45

automatic pistol lying on the desk as a symbol of authority—these were giving way to well-tailored suits, an occasional American or British car, and membership at the Gezira Sporting Club. A new society was taking shape, but it was a far cry from Nasser's original conception of a new order. The young captains, majors, and colonels were creating their own elite, and they were loath to surrender their newly gained privileges. In a way, it might be said that the revolutionaries of 1952 were the political conservatives of 1955; indeed, a cynic might suggest that they were the new Wafd.

This should not be taken to mean, however, that, reminiscent of traditional Egyptian politics, the officers, by and large, were indulging in bribery and corruption. A strong sense of dedication and honesty still prevailed, and their standards of personal integrity remained admirably high. But who would complain if an officers' cooperative, utilizing a government loan, should import automobiles at wholesale prices? And who would begrudge them apartments which they would find difficult to maintain on a captain's meager salary? Such fringe benefits had been taken for granted by generations of Egyptians. These small things, however, served to underscore the fact that the regime's original *esprit de corps* was waning. As the novelty of governing wore thin, many of the officers lost much of their idealism, and some observers began to see evidence of a trend toward power for power's sake.

It was against this background that Nasser embarked upon his next phase of political revolution. First he had to dispose of some troublesome internal problems. In the past, he had encouraged harmony among non-Islamic groups; with monotonous regularity, the Grand Rabbi and leaders of the Coptic Church had been produced at major official functions. With apparent regret, Nasser authorized two trials against Jews, one involving espionage for Israel and the other "Zionist cooperation with local Communists." Foreign criticism notwithstanding, both cases appeared bona fide and the distinction between Jew and Egyptian seldom was made publicly.[29] Although Nasser received unfavorable publicity from abroad when two persons convicted of spying were executed, it should be noted that the same penalty previously had been inflicted upon Moslems convicted of espionage.

Later in 1955, however, another governmental act gave Egypt's non-Moslem community valid cause for concern. On September 21, the Council of Ministers announced that Sharia (Moslem religious) courts and non-Moslem religious community courts would be abolished on January 1, 1956, and their functions assumed by national courts. Several of the qualifying provisions of this announcement gave obvious advantages to Moslems: Sharia judges were to be incorporated within the national judicial system and all lawyers practicing before the Sharia courts transferred to the national rolls.[30] Most likely, the government's action was designed in part to restrict the traditional influence of the conservative sheikhs of Al Azhar University, but it also abolished the private courts of the non-Moslem religious communities. The Catholics spearheaded the fight against this decree, but, after a number of bishops and priests were detained for several days, the courts were abolished on schedule.

Another government measure was aimed at curbing the influence of the numerous foreign schools throughout Egypt. These schools, with an enrollment of well over one hundred thousand, generally were run by mission groups and maintained an academic standard far superior to the government schools. When a law was enacted requiring all primary and secondary schools to teach each Egyptian student the religion of his parents, this was widely interpreted as a deliberate blow against non-Moslem (considered by many to mean non-Egyptian) schools. By mid-1956, there were definite advantages in being a Moslem Egyptian. Although there were no laws to this effect—the legislation specifically protected general freedom of religion—members of the Coptic and Jewish faiths cited instances of apparent discrimination. Their fears were not allayed by the new Constitution, which declared that "Islam is the religion of the State." By inference, the non-Moslems increasingly were considered second-class citizens—this despite the fact that the tradition of including a Copt in the cabinet was retained (in the nonessential Ministry of Supply), and the government vigorously denied charges of bias.

This growing religious friction, however, continued to be overshadowed by political problems—particularly the abiding problem of Communism. Although membership in the Egyptian

Communist splinter groups, according to Nasser's own estimate, numbered no more than five thousand in 1955,[31] he recognized Communism as a major internal danger. He bluntly observed: "When Communism became a form of government, it was turned into an absolutely different thing from what its advocates hoped for. There are many luring and dazzling theories which, when practically tested, the painful truth about them is laid bare in all its sordid ugliness. . . . They have lost faith in religion which, in their opinion, is a myth. . . . They have lost faith in liberty because it springs from the individual's faith in his worth where the individual in the Communist system has no worth or will. . . . Our final conclusion is that we have a pattern of life which we shall never repudiate in exchange for the Communist doctrine."[32]

Arrests of Communists continued through 1955 and the first half of 1956. In April, 1955, while Nasser left for the Bandung Conference, Zacharia Mohieddine conducted yet another major roundup of Communists. But as Egypt began to espouse a policy of "positive neutrality," local Communists curbed their attacks against the "fascist Nasser." By 1956, most of the factions openly supported his government, and the government seemed to reply by easing its pressure against Communist organizations. In February, 1956, sixty-five alleged Communists were arrested in Cairo, with Professor Ismail Abdullah Sabri, accused of being the Secretary-General of the Egyptian Communist Party, the principal defendant. But five months later, immediately following a visit to Cairo by Soviet Foreign Minister Dmitri Shepilov, Sabri was acquitted. The same month, Khaled Mohieddine, who had been exiled to Europe and publicly denounced by RCC member Sadat as a Communist, was accepted into the Egyptian Press Syndicate and became chief editor of a new afternoon daily, *Al Missa*, reputedly financed with Egyptian government funds.

Many foreign observers saw in the government's volte face vis-à-vis Communism a domestic application of Nasser's newly proclaimed "positive neutrality" in Egypt's foreign dealings. Yet, the government gave different reasons. As Anwar Sadat of the RCC explained: "There were really very few true Communists in Egypt; a large majority of those claiming membership in the various local Communist organizations were actually left-wing nationalists. After the military takeover, they failed to realize that this was their revolution, but after a few years of opposition, many of the Egyptian Communists realized their mistake."[33] This, however, did not explain why, in March, 1956, a Communist pamphlet called for the second phase of the Communist takeover —the National Front.[34]

Indeed, the government's changed attitude toward the Communist danger symptomized a profound reorientation of Nasser's policy—a reorientation toward the East. The Egyptian propaganda machine, refined under the combined efforts of the Free Officers and some German expatriates including Johann von Leers, continued to exhort against "imperialists, reactionaries, tools of imperialism, and traitors to the Arab cause." Yet, these epithets now were directed not so much against the battered old "enemies" at home—the Wafd, the Brethren, and the followers of Naguib—as against the "imperialistic" Western powers.

The reasons for this shift were domestic as well as foreign-political. While Nasser was groping for his nebulous "new society," he wished to divert the people's attention from the paucity of internal progress. Moreover, after a strong Israeli retaliatory raid in Gaza on February 28, 1955, the army became restive. In what generally was regarded as a political coup, the Egyptian Premier obtained armaments from the Soviets, thus pacifying the army, upon whose support he depended, as well as gaining the applause of his fellow citizens for outsmarting the West. Partly for tactical and partly for pseudoideological reasons, he saw fit to continue this policy, which, while alienating the West, gained him the popular support at home which previously had eluded him.

But while Nasser mounted these attacks against the West, he was still uncertain as to how to implement his "political revolution" at home. Gamal Abdel Nasser was confronted with a dilemma. While he could declare bluntly, "We are going to have no Parliament in Egypt until we liquidate the influence of the feudal landlords and capitalists,"[35] there was no assurance that other segments of the society would provide a viable foundation for government. Nasser was obviously troubled by this political vacuum, for he desired to give continuity to the movement which he had initiated. Perhaps apprehensive that the structure which he had created, dependent as it was upon support from the military, would crumble if he, the linchpin, were removed, Nasser on occasion expressed this fear in public: "A person goes, another comes. The nation should always have those who can lead and those who may be trained to lead. Parliamentary life gives the opportunity to show up abilities which the country needs."[36] In Cairo, a topical question was: "But what if something happened to Nasser?" And the general answer was "chaos," for there was no obvious successor to Nasser. In his own sphere, General Abdel Hakim Amer had considerable influence, but his authority ultimately came from the Premier, as did the power of Ali Sabry, generally regarded as Nasser's right-hand man. Zacharia Mohieddine, the trusted Minister of the Interior, proved efficient at his job, but few Egyptians seriously believed that he was qualified to run the country. Perhaps Abdel Latif Boghdadi was of Nasser's caliber, but the chances were slim that he could ever gain the support of a majority of the Free Officers. It seemed reasonable to predict that Nasser's sudden death would precipitate coups and countercoups in which the Egyptian nation would be the loser.

Nasser was painfully aware of this prospect and wished to build a political structure which would lend permanence to his work of the preceding years. But in this quest he was blocked by a serious personal shortcoming: Gamal Abdel Nasser did not like to share authority, either with his closest associates or with some advisory or consultative civilian assembly. He was loath to surrender power to people less qualified—and this, in his opinion, included almost everyone. Moreover, when a man did outstanding work and gained public recognition for his efforts—the popular Abdel Latif Boghdadi is a case in point—he risked demotion, for Nasser was jealous of his power. As he once asserted boastfully: "I know everything that goes on in the Nile Valley";[37] and he was unwilling to relinquish the power of his position. Furthermore, Egypt was patently unprepared for a responsible federal government with free interplay between executive and legislature, for, in the brief span of the Revolution, a national sense of public responsibility had not yet taken root.

While the Premier could proclaim that "the Revolution aims at creating a socialist society without class distinction,"[38] he could not ignore the lack of public responsibility. One could almost visualize Nasser's mental reservations as he alluded to the coming parliament. On one occasion he declared that it was "unlikely" that Egypt would return to a "partisan democracy" within the "predictable future," although he recognized the need for a "sort of parliament" to serve as a "meeting ground" for new civilian leadership.[39] Later he referred to a "national assembly" which would be established "next January" (1956); it would exercise a "majority rule based on laboring, peasant, and professional working classes."[40] And as if trying to subdue his own misgivings, he continued: "I have confidence in this army and I know that Gamal Abdel Nasser will be with you today, but he does not know whether he will be with you tomorrow. But I am confident that this army will protect these [the Revolution's] principles and adhere to them."[41]

Another indication of Nasser's indecision was his relaxation of press censorship, ostensibly to allow free discussion of the future form of government. But even this move was tempered by Anwar Sadat's stern rejoinder to the nation: "I would like to remind you of the shape of the system of government after the transitional period, as clearly outlined by [Premier] Gamal—a nationalist rule, a social community, no political parties, freedom of employment, individual freedom, and collective freedom."[42]

The promise to hold parliamentary elections in January, 1956, was not kept, but on January 16, at the end of the three-year "transitional period" originally proclaimed by Naguib, a new constitution was announced and a National Assembly was scheduled to convene in November. This constitution, however, did not provide a ready solution to Nasser's—indeed, the country's—problem. The right to freedom of expression and of the press, the right of orderly assembly, and the inviolability of private residences all were respected, but only within "limits defined by law." These rights, so restricted, had existed previously. While the National Assembly was granted considerable powers, including that of overriding a presidential veto by a two-thirds majority, a "national union," whose method of formation was to be determined by the president, was granted sole authority to present candidates for membership in the National Assembly. In fact, this permitted the president to handpick candidates for the National Assembly.

The National Union, as a successor to the listless Liberation Rally, was a nebulous organization. According to Fathy Radwan, then Minister of National Guidance and the government's official spokesman on this subject: "The National Union is not a party; nor is it a one-party system. As specified in the constitution, and as its name indicates, it is an all-embracing union of the Egyptian people. In other words, it is the kind of system which all prudent nations adopted at important stages in their history."[43] Nasser gave a somewhat different explanation: "The National Union is a national front which includes all the members of the nation except the reactionaries and the opportunists and the agents of imperialism, because it is they who controlled us in the past and proved to be traitors."[44] Whatever the nuances of its character, it seemed obvious that the National Union was to have a twofold purpose: to screen prospective candidates for the National Assembly and to organize a political front favorable to the existing regime.

Nasser did not take kindly to mounting Western criticisms of his "dictatorship"—criticisms which were directed at the constitution and at his unopposed candidacy for the office of president. He believed that Egypt needed an authoritarian government, and he answered foreign attacks against his rigid censorship and restrictions on civil liberties by pointing to the chaos which had occurred in March, 1954, when many curbs were temporarily lifted. In a major policy speech before the Cooperative Congress, he invoked history to justify his actions: "There was political freedom in the United Kingdom, but such freedom could not be directed against the monarchy—a system which was keeping pace with the nature of Britain and her people. In the United States, there was also political freedom, but such freedom was banned where it was thought to be an instrument for Communist principles. In the Soviet Union, political freedom could not be used to resist the political setup there. Political freedom was thus adapted to conform with the interests of society, and there was no such thing as political freedom for everybody."[45]

On June 23, five days after the last British troops had left the Canal Zone, Gamal Abdel Nasser was elected President; he gained 99.9 per cent of the vote, with only 5,267 of nearly 5.5 million votes registered against him. The constitution fared slightly worse: "only" 99.8 per cent of the electorate voted approval. The Revolutionary Command Council was then dissolved and its members, with the exception of Major General Amer, became civilians. No longer did the authority of government rest formally in the hands of the RCC. With the closing of this political phase, further personnel changes took place. Major Salah Salem, once Minister of National Guidance and Minister of State for Sudanese Affairs, had been retired the previous September; he was made the editor of a new daily newspaper. His brother, Gamal Salem, was dismissed as Deputy Premier and relegated to political oblivion. Anwar Sadat, while no longer a minister, still managed the government's newspaper, *Al Gomhouria,* and headed the Islamic Congress. Hassan Ibrahim, however, was less fortunate: he became an ordinary member of the National Production Council.

At last the government had assumed at least the semblance of constitutional rule, and there was every expectation that National Assembly elections would be held in October. Now that the RCC was disbanded and only six of the original fourteen members remained active in the government, was it possible to evaluate this group's effectiveness over the preceding years? Perhaps it would suffice to measure their achievements against the goals previously set by Nasser.

1. *Eradication of imperialism.* The influence of the British and French in Egypt had diminished considerably and the foreign communities no longer dominated the country's social and economic life. But much of the campaign against imperialism was a fight against a paper tiger: the regime would create its "imperialist adversaries," then proceed to destroy them. If, as the regime later claimed, foreign economic holdings in Egypt were a manifestation of "economic imperialism," then the new leaders

of Egypt certainly had not been hostile to this force during the
first four years following the Revolution. The regime promulgated
legislation to encourage foreign investment. Moreover, the government gladly accepted forty million dollars of American
assistance. It is true that a few Western nations no longer received
a majority of the seasonal cotton exports, but many observers
wondered whether Egypt, by shifting substantial exports to the
Communist bloc, had indeed escaped "imperialism." It was clear
that the campaign against "imperialism" (generally conducted
verbally against Western interests in the Afro-Arab world) served
a psychological as well as political need: it turned the attention
of Egyptians from their abiding problems to real and imaginary
"enemies" at home and abroad, and gave them a new feeling of
national pride.

2. *Abolishment of feudalism.* The redistribution of over
400,000 *feddans* and the reduction in agricultural rents were
steps in this campaign. Mention should be made of new legislation which required employers to provide greater benefits for their
workers. A more progressive taxation program also could be
claimed as an achievement.

3. *Eradication of monopolization.* Although the largest landholdings had been broken down, the industrial monopolies remained almost untouched. Indeed, the government on occasion
encouraged the establishment of new monopolies. Ahmed
Abboud, the most notorious Egyptian monopolist, was a welcome
visitor to the Ministry of Finance and even at Nasser's office. It
was clear that the government, at least in the initial years after
the Revolution, did not want to alienate these "monopolists,"
whose experience and power were needed during the "growing
period" of the new Egypt.

4. *Establishment of social justice.* There was a more egalitarian approach to the distribution of social services, and cases
of flagrant corruption were seriously curbed, but it is questionable
if "social justice was imposed." A new privileged class emerged
and only a fortunate few benefited from massive government
schemes.

5. *The building of a strong national army.* Under the RCC,
military expenditures almost doubled, and scores of German

military advisers under General Otto Farmbacher were employed to train the new army. The result was a military force which performed impressively on parade. But battle-preparedness was another matter, and the Egyptian army earned few laurels in its first real test, the Sinai campaign in the fall of 1956.

6. *Establishment of sound democratic rule.* Since Nasser himself presented lucid reasons in favor of continued authoritarian government, no astute Egyptian looked forward to "democratic rule," except within the narrowly defined limits of a national assembly.

Ranged alongside these announced objectives, the RCC's political achievements hardly were impressive. President Nasser's following statement attests more appropriately to the political achievements of the RCC: "These [past] four years equal forty years of demolition—demolition of the old society which was based on exploitation, partisanship, despotism, oppression, egoism, individualism, and opportunism."[46]

Suez and After

The withdrawal by Secretary of State John Foster Dulles of America's offer to assist in the construction of the High Dam at Aswan provided President Nasser with a convenient excuse for deferring the political reconstruction of Egypt. When, in retaliation, he announced the nationalization of the Suez Canal Company, Egypt entered into a major crisis, and many past promises were forgotten in the excitement of the moment. For Nasser, it was a moment of glory; never before had the Egyptian people so solidly supported him. When the President drove to Alexandria's Midan Gomhouria to make his "nationalization" speech, a small mongrel dog, running bewilderedly beside his large limousine, received more applause from the crowd than did he. Two and one half hours later, however, Nasser was the nation's hero. The boldness of his plan and his open defiance of the West stirred the imagination of his people. The crowds responded with hysterical abandon: "The British and French say that they will send troops? One hundred million pounds is blocked by the Bank of England? *Maalish.* The Canal is ours and we will keep it."

Internal security was tightened during the summer of 1956. Egyptians were advised to avoid "certain" foreigners, members of the foreign community became accustomed to the whirl of a tape recorder as they telephoned, and the CID (Criminal Investigation Department) man in his small black car and the *galabiyaed* lollers with their well-polished shoes became common sights on the streets of Cairo. Five journalists working for British newspapers were expelled from Egypt, and an allegedly British-controlled espionage ring was exposed, complete with passwords, code names, and contacts in the British Embassy. Yet, despite this deepening tension, individual foreigners were not molested. Even during the general strike called on August 16, 1956, to protest the first Suez Conference meeting in London, while over two million Egyptians roamed the streets of Cairo, not a single incident against foreigners was reported.

The new unity of Egypt was demonstrated during the British and French attack of October-November, 1956. If Prime Minister Eden and Premier Guy Mollet believed that Egyptian resistance would collapse and the Nasser government would tumble after the first aerial bombardment, they were mistaken. While bombs landed near Cairo, the city's life continued as usual. And while the Egyptian army fled Sinai, professors at the universities implored their students to take to the trenches—and they themselves followed. Port Said became the symbol of the new spirit. After much of the army had withdrawn from the city, the citizens of Port Said—young boys, university students, and old men —armed with rifles and equipment abandoned by the army, fought the British and French invaders. Port Said finally was occupied, but only after bitter street fighting. It was a credit to the new spirit of Egypt that few of Port Said's citizens collaborated with the Anglo-French invaders.

Significantly, the worst showing during the campaign was made by the army. Once off the parade grounds, the officers lost much of their bravado, and stories of officers abandoning their men under fire made the rounds in Cairo—stories which uncomfortably reminded Egyptians of the dismal performance of the army during the Palestine campaign of 1948-49. Nasser tried to screen Egypt's military defeat by diverting the nation's attention to the "heroes of Port Said"; but while he claimed that the soldiers and civilians had fought "side by side," the residents of Port Said knew better. What followed was an attempt at metropolitan bribery, as Nasser sought to "buy off" an entire city. It has been estimated that over 9 million pounds (almost 27 million dollars) had been allocated to the city during the following year, as Port Said was enshrined as a national monument. An indication of the President's chagrin at his army's performance was that he did not dare visit this "glorious battlefield" until thirteen months after the battle.

While the defense of Port Said and the abortive Anglo-French attack bolstered Nasser's prestige, the Israeli victory in Sinai was a bitter pill for the regime: the Egyptian army—Nasser's army, the nucleus of his "new society"—had been disgraced. Scores of officers were dismissed and rumor had it that others were executed. The damage, however, was done. In a pitiful effort to save face, the Cairo propaganda machine ground out endless stories of Egypt's "victories": according to these reports the French battleship "Jean Bart" had been sunk (it was decommissioned in Marseilles the following spring), and eighty-seven British and French planes had been destroyed. Accounts of bombing attacks against Israeli bases were fabricated. Reams of news space were devoted to explanations of Egypt's "strategic withdrawal" from Sinai; one local Cairo weekly even printed a 120-page supplement on Egypt's "victory" in Sinai.[47] The same newspapers, however, found it difficult to explain the return of five thousand Egyptian soldiers from Israeli imprisonment.

As the truth about Sinai and Port Said filtered back to Cairo, the privileged position of the military appeared to be in jeopardy. Yet as Nasser realized full well, there was no alternative to the existing military government—and the country, still strongly pro-Nasser, could not have him without the military. There was one minor crisis: some disgruntled officers, including a close colleague of Anwar Sadat, sought to organize an army coup. This, however, was quickly subdued and prison sentences were passed *in camera*. This was one trial which Nasser wished to shield from the public.

The "Suez affair" gave Nasser the excuse to act against the

remaining symbols of "foreign imperialism" in Egypt: the foreign-controlled banks and commercial and industrial firms. After the Anglo-French attack, those two countries were branded "enemy nations," and their citizens, in accordance with Military Proclamation No. 5 of 1956, became "enemy subjects," losing all their legal rights.[48] The Minister of the Interior's denials notwithstanding, a number of Jewish citizens also were subjected to forced confinement and to the sequestration of their businesses and possessions. The mood of the day was reflected in the Alexandria Bar Association's decision to prevent British, French, and Jewish lawyers from practicing their profession in Egypt.[49] Late in November, the Minister of Finance, Dr. Kaissuny, "issued instructions to the banks to afford every facility to all Egyptian citizens wishing to acquire the shares of enemy companies under sequestration so that they may be speedily Egyptianized."[50] That British and French citizens be requested to leave the country was understandable, and the temporary sequestration of their assets also accorded with general wartime practice. But the rapidity with which British and French companies were redistributed among Egyptians suggested that Nasser's government sought to capitalize upon the existing circumstances by preventing the eventual return of the former owners. Moreover, the government liquidated a substantial portion of the sequestered assets at far below their actual value.

There was even less justification for the government's campaign against the Jews. Egypt long had been a haven for stateless persons—some of them victims of World War II and others resident in Egypt for generations. In November, 1956, those Jews who did not qualify for Egyptian passports bore the brunt of the government's drive against "foreigners." Many of them were requested or advised to leave the country within forty-eight hours or less; none of them was permitted to carry with them more than a small portion of their possessions. Before leaving Egypt, they were obliged to renounce all claims to possessions left behind.

It is impossible to state accurately how many of the Jews left under compulsion and how many fled in the fear of future reprisals. Zacharia Mohieddine, denying that the government was persecuting Jews, explained the government's action as follows:

"They [Egyptian Jews] are Egyptians like you and me. All we did was to put some of their establishments under sequestration to make sure that there would be no capital that would leave the country."[51] The government's drive against "foreigners" reached grotesque proportions when an under-secretary at the Ministry of Education announced in all seriousness that the Ministry was "reviewing all English and French books . . . now in use in schools and universities throughout Egypt with a view toward removing from them any trace connected with Britain and France and their history. British- and French-run schools from now on will be 100 per cent Egyptian in every respect."[52]

The campaign against Western interests was intensified when, on January 15, 1957, an "Egyptianization" decree required all banks and insurance companies to come under exclusive Egyptian management within five years. The British and French banks and insurance companies seized by the government were immediately "Egyptianized." Thus an indirect aftermath to the British-French-Israeli attack was the elimination of much of the West's remaining influence in Egypt. In the wake of this upheaval, there was a paucity of qualified Egyptian civilians to fill the available business posts, and a number of ex-officers were able to pre-empt many of these lucrative positions. Through a new government establishment, the Economic Development Organization, Nasser was able to gain control of a sizable segment of the country's industrial and financial sector. This organization, by supervising a majority of the nation's banking institutions, also permitted the government to consolidate its control over the local Egyptian business community.

Egypt's largest foreign communities, the Italians and the Greeks, had a long tradition of loyal service in Egypt. Many of these families had lived in Egypt for two or three generations and were active and influential members of the local business community. They, too, were placed in jeopardy by the "Egyptianization" laws and by the rising xenophobia. According to one report, three thousand Italians had left Egypt between November, 1956 and April, 1957.[53] Nor was the campaign restricted to "foreigners" and Jews; non-Moslem Egyptians increasingly felt the sting of discrimination. Father Robert Chidiac, writing in the

Egyptian Catholic weekly *Le Rayon d'Egypte,* reported a "great fear" among the Christians of Egypt because of a series of new laws on Egyptian nationality and "Egyptianization" and because many firms were telling Christian applicants that "we have instructions to hire only Moslems."[54]

These measures did not stint Nasser's popularity with the Egyptian masses. As the West's economic and political campaign against Egypt intensified, the Egyptian people rallied in support of their President. Hardly a month passed without Egyptians being exhorted against another "imperialist conspiracy" and the actions of "stooges of imperialism" (King Hussein of Jordan was a favorite target). The serious shortages in local markets, created by the war and the subsequent economic warfare, were blamed on the West. Nasser had stated correctly in August, 1956, that the Western economic freeze could scarcely hit any but the small middle class in Egypt, because more than three-quarters of Egypt's pitifully miserable people were already on the borderline of starvation.[55]

The National Assembly Discredited

By May, 1957, Nasser deemed the time favorable to select candidates for the embryonic National Assembly. But instead of calling upon the full facilities of the National Union to perform this task, he resorted to a subterfuge by appointing a temporary executive committee of the National Union consisting of Abdel Latif Boghdadi, Minister of Municipal and Rural Affairs, Major General Abdel Hakim Amer, Minister of War, and Zacharia Mohieddine, Minister of the Interior—men who were directly responsible to the President. They were assisted in their duties by a new law which excluded from candidacy any person liable to "administrative custody" under the June 22, 1956, ruling of the Revolutionary Command Council. This ruling included:

1. Those whose property was confiscated by the RCC.
2. Those who were deprived of their political or civil rights.
3. Those who were convicted and sentenced by the Revolutionary Tribunal, the People's Court, or the Antigraft Court.

4. Those who were convicted and sentenced by military or civil courts for crimes against the security of the state.

5. Those who were arrested or confined to restricted residence on orders given by martial law authorities in the period from July 23, 1952, to the date of coming into force of the new constitution.[56]

This effectively excluded from the elections a great many of Egypt's old politicians and the entire leadership of the outlawed Moslem Brethren.

Of 2,508 registered candidates, the executive committee, with Nasser's approval, accepted only 1,320;[57] the disqualified candidates had no right of appeal. A government-inspired article in the daily newspaper *Al Shaab* sought to explain these selections. It was claimed that selection by the National Union committee did not constitute a recommendation, but merely indicated that there were no objections to the candidate. Among those eliminated were "imperialist agents, reactionaries, or opportunists"; "amateurs who applied for nomination only to make publicity for themselves"; "those who used their financial resources to buy votes"; and "those who were not considered fit . . . because of the nature of their present work or because of certain political considerations, even though they are known to be good citizens."[58] By election day—July 3—73 candidates had withdrawn and another 76 were running unopposed, so that 1,171 candidates were competing in the election.[59] Only about one-third of the candidates were elected on the first ballot, while in five districts no candidates had been found qualified by the National Union. Runoff elections were conducted on July 14.

While, generally speaking, pro-Western elements were eliminated by the selection committee, so also were such rabid pro-Communists as Kamal Bindary, the notorious "Red Pasha," and labor's political role was abruptly curtailed. Nasser, who previously had taken great pains to encourage a "directed syndicalist movement," had refused the request of Anwar Salama, President of Egypt's new Federation of Labor, for a large slate of candidates. In the end, only six of labor's seventeen candidates were successful[60]—perhaps a sign that Nasser feared labor as a potential political rival. Sawi Ahmed Sawi, President of the Cairo Transport Workers Union and the person directly responsible for the pro-Nasser strike in March, 1954, was eliminated on the first ballot. Another vicitim of the election was Colonel Samir Helmy, the man most closely associated with the ambitious High Dam scheme. According to well-informed officials, Helmy blamed Zacharia Mohieddine personally for his defeat. Ahmed Fuad, a leading leftist economist known to be close to Nasser's inner circle, was defeated by a Rawia Attia, one of the two successful female candidates.

At the polling booths, the formalities of secret elections generally were observed. Some of the defeated candidates, however, produced convincing evidence that the totals in their districts had been fabricated. Before the National Assembly convened to elect its officers, a local newspaper, *Al Ahram,* prematurely published the results; this somewhat unusual procedure triggered a minor "revolt" at the first meeting, when a few deputies refused to make the selections unanimous.[61] But Nasser, seemingly unperturbed, opened the National Assembly in grand fashion. After traveling through Cairo in an open car, providing an easy target for any of his enemies, he was enthusiastically received in the renovated Parliament building, whose royal crest had been replaced by a fifty-foot-tall replica of the symbol of the Revolution—Saladin's eagle.

Four days later, on July 26, Nasser spoke in Alexandria; it was the first anniversary of the nationalization of the Suez Canal Company. But this time he had no surprises for the audience. As he recited Egypt's "successes" in foreign affairs during the previous year, the audience obviously was bored. At the conclusion of his speech, there was not a sound from the crowd of over a hundred thousand; no chants, no applause—nothing. Nasser turned from the speaker's platform and departed quietly. It seemed that the luster of Egypt's hero had dimmed.

It came as no surprise, therefore, when Egyptians were treated to another full-scale conspiracy trial. The defendants included seven army officers and five civilians, among them the popular Dr. Mohamed Salah el Din, former Wafdist Minister of Foreign Affairs, and Abdel Fattah Hassan, once Wafdist Minister of Social Affairs. The trial, which was brought before a special High Military Court, was opened on August 12 with full radio and press coverage. The prosecutor's opening charge to the court was a curious one. "With regard to the accused," he said, "they all approved the foreign policy pursued by the present regime but objected to what they proudly termed procrastination in restoring representative life. It was necessary to let the country, so to speak, have a period of convalescence. In its efforts to put matters right, the Revolution had spent five years, which is an infinitely short period in the life of a nation. The alleged delay in restoring parliamentary life had not been the reason which had induced the accused to hatch this conspiracy, because the revolution government had fulfilled its promise. [sic] A general election had been held and the National Assembly had come into existence."[62] He concluded by pointing out that "it was the duty of the accused toward their fatherland to support the government during the tripartite aggression against Egypt and not to attempt to cause a gap in the lines of the nation."[63] He then demanded severe punishment for the defendants.

The only witness for the prosecution, Ahmed Kadry, who had been convicted previously of participating in a leftist military conspiracy against the government in 1954, did little to assist the prosecution's case. When asked how he knew that America was involved in this conspiracy, he blandly replied: "It is a question of being aware of public opinion and current political affairs."[64] He added that it was a well-known fact that all silencers for pistols were "only produced by foreign nations, and so I concluded that the contacts of the plot were imperialists."[65] Laughter resounded through the crowded courtroom. It later developed that Kadry had been allowed to hear all of the defendants' recorded confessions. But, unfortunately for him, he often contradicted himself. At one time he even claimed that the accused were in league with both the Communists and the Americans.[66]

When the defendants took the stand and one by one repudiated their previous confessions which, they claimed, had been extorted from them, the regime's "show trial" suddenly became a trial of the regime itself. And when daily radio coverage was abruptly discontinued, Cairenes competed for court passes to witness "the most amusing spectacle in all of Egypt." On one occasion, a counsel for the defense berated the court for violating Article 265 of the Military Law;[67] then another lawyer objected to the competence of the court, pointing out that the accused should have been committed for trial before the Court of Criminal Assizes. The military governor-general, he contended, had no power to exercise absolute authority, but must act within the specific limits of the Constitution. Why, then, he asked, should these men be committed for trial before a military court, while Britons accused of espionage were brought before an ordinary civilian tribunal?[68] Advocate Mohamed Hashem centered his attack on the prosecution's flimsy case: "With regard to Ahmed Kadry, the only witness for the prosecution, he certainly is an extraordinary man. His statements were disconnected and trivial, but they had to be, for they were framed in order that they might be expanded to the desired proportions."[69] The defense refused even to discuss the accusation that Mohammed Naguib was connected with the "conspiracy."

The trial proved disastrous for the government. There was no definite proof of a conspiracy; the prosecution witness had been thoroughly discredited; promised evidence could not be produced; and the authority of the court had been challenged. The government had to choose between two distasteful alternatives: it could order the acquittal of the defendants, thus making the court and the regime appear foolish, or, in the face of overwhelming evidence to the contrary, it could press for conviction. In a private interview early in September, Ali Sabry, then Minister of State for Presidential Affairs, revealed the government's decision: "Maybe the trial was handled too harshly and quickly, but we never would have put them on trial had there not been a conspiracy. In other cases we can afford to be more cautious, but with conspiracies one cannot wait. We wanted to catch the case before it became too large."[70] The following month, eleven of the thirteen defendants were sentenced to prison, four of them for life.

Meanwhile, the government did not fare well in the deliberations of the National Assembly. After the ministers reported on progress within their ministries since the Revolution, the deputies displayed surprising boldness in their interpolations. When Dr.

Aziz Sidky, Minister of Industry, reported on the production of a milk-processing plant near Alexandria, a deputy promptly challenged him, producing figures which suggested strongly that the Minister had falsified his report. And the Minister of the Interior, Zacharia Mohieddine, had some trying moments when he was challenged by Abdul Fadel el Gizawi on the subject of political detainees.[71] According to one report, three questions had been asked of the Minister: What is the number of political prisoners and what are their political affiliations? Are any citizens under house arrest, and if so, on what charges? Are there detainees under restriction for other than political reasons? In reply, the Minister stated that the only political prisoners were those sentenced by tribunals or courts, that nine political detainees were under house arrest, and that a number of people were detained for criminal reasons. El Gizawi's rejoinder was a request to end house arrests. Over the uproar that followed, Mohieddine retorted sharply: "We do not regard them as being political, because all citizens are equal before the law and Government. . . . I think that when we speak of freedom, we speak of freedom for sincere citizens, not of freedom for conspirators and reactionary citizens."[72] Gizawi shouted in return: "And I demand the release of those whose loyalty to the Revolution and whose faith in its aims has been proved by events."[73] The exchange ended, but Mohammed Naguib was not forgotten.

The future of the National Assembly was determined by two debates. The first concerned the regime's agricultural showplace, the highly publicized Liberation Province. It had been widely recognized for several years that this experiment had become unreasonably expensive, and rumors of the Province's wasteful and corrupt administration made the rounds. Deputy Ali Shishni finally raised the matter in the National Assembly, accusing the Province of spending an incredibly large sum on public relations.[74] The commotion which followed this charge was so great that the Speaker, Abdel Latif Boghdadi, finally suspended the meeting. Members of the Assembly demanded that Magdy Hassanein, Managing Director of the Province, and three other deputies be expelled, but these officials subsequently were exonerated by a specially appointed committee of ministers. The disgruntled members drew little solace from the fact that Nasser dismissed Magdy Hassanein from the administration of Liberation Province a few days later. The following week, Kamal el din Hussein, Minister of Education and former RCC member, resigned from the National Assembly in disgust. According to one reporter, the Minister was angered by Nasser's failure to endorse the Assembly's attack against political corruption. It was only after Nasser's personal intervention that Hussein withdrew his resignation.[75]

Only a month later, after another dispute with the National Assembly, Kamal el din Hussein again submitted his resignation. The issue was the admission of additional "external" students to Egypt's already crowded universities. A majority of the Assembly refused to accept the Minister of Education's recommendations and, instead, voted to admit a large number of secondary-school graduates. According to the Constitution, the Assembly was empowered to "forward desires or proposals to the Government regarding matters of public concern."[76] Hussein, claiming that he could not implement such a policy, resigned. The situation was not helped by the fact that the "people's representatives" had seen fit to debate this issue *in camera*. The most far-reaching implication of the crisis was that the National Assembly had assumed, at least temporarily, the authority to override a minister's policy. It was largely because of this that Anwar Sadat, Abdel Latif Boghdadi, and Gamal Abdel Nasser came to the support of Hussein.[77] Eventually it was decided that the resolution had merely been the expression of a wish, not the promulgation of a law, and Kamal el din Hussein was restored as Minister.

The prestige of the Assembly dropped even farther in early January. On January 7, the Speaker, Abdel Latif Boghdadi, was absent and, before an afternoon session was convened, the two Deputy Speakers departed. Ahmed el Harmil, the oldest deputy, presided in their absence. Fearing the absence of Boghdadi's firm hand, a government official passed el Harmil a note ordering adjournment.[78] With not even a semblance of parliamentary procedure, the Assembly was adjourned. The hasty announcement met with sarcastic laughter. Perhaps the deputies realized what most of Egypt already knew. As Mohamed Hassanein Heikal, Nasser's political confidant, put it: "The role of the National Assembly is that of the second phase of a transitional period toward real democracy. It won't play the primary role in policy formation, but it will participate. It is not an ultimate end."[79] Apparently, the deputies had been guilty of interpreting the Constitution too literally.

Nasser in Search of an Ideology

While the comedy of the National Assembly was being enacted, President Nasser worked diligently to develop a functional political philosophy. At the Cooperative Congress, on December 5, 1957, he elucidated in detail his concept of Egypt's desired new society. Emphasizing that the political and social revolution had to progress side by side, he observed that a happy and prosperous society depended upon the elimination of the exploitation of the majority by a few. In his view, the country was "moving to a new phase, a transitional phase," in which the objective was the establishment of a "socialist, democratic, and cooperative society, free from political, social, and economic exploitation."[80] While he was determined to eliminate "opportunistic individualism," he did not believe that the alternative was "state capitalism."[81] Instead, he anticipated the state in the role of "trustee" over the people, with protection of the "small capitalists and small savers" as a principal objective. He also distinguished between eliminating individual opportunism and doing away with individualism itself. It was his view that the profit motive could often be subdued by individual citizens who were willing to invest "social capital" in such projects as low-cost housing.[82]

The ultimate goal was a cooperative society. "Instead of the merchant exploiting the customer when the latter goes to buy anything from him, there should be cooperation—the merchant gains, and the customer is not duped. It is taken for granted, of course, that a cooperative concern, or a cooperative society, should make a reasonable profit and that the customer is served without being exploited."[83] This was to be the blueprint for the new Egypt, but no one in Egypt knew how to implement it. Neither private capitalism nor state capitalism was deemed suitable. Cooperatives were suggested as a solution, but Egypt's previous experiences with cooperatives had not been encouraging. Moreover, since the results of this reconstruction were not expected to appear "within a year, or two, or five,"[84] it was tacitly implied that nondemocratic controls would have to be maintained over the nation.

The hasty union with Syria in February, 1958, provided Nasser with an excuse to adjourn the National Assembly, on the promise that a new parliament would be constituted from the memberships of the existing Egyptian and Syrian assemblies after a brief "transitional period." This was in February. Then, almost as an afterthought, a decree was published in August which declared that the salaries of Assembly members would be suspended as of September 1.[85] The National Assembly passed into limbo, and President Nasser was in no apparent hurry to create another troublesome substitute.

As the National Assembly drifted from the scene, attention was directed toward the National Union. This organization had experienced a slow beginning. Although its decree of formation was issued on May 28, 1957, and its articles of organization were drafted by November, the Union suffered from several false starts. Membership rolls were opened on November 25, and local committee elections were first scheduled for January 3, 1958, but, inexplicably, in the summer of 1958, Anwar Sadat, Secretary-General of the National Union, stated that only National Assembly members had been admitted to date.[86] And even then, 8 of the 350 deputies had been excluded from participation in the Union.[87] Anwar Sadat, Mohamed Abdel Kader Hatem, former Director-General of the Department of Information and then Political Counselor at the Presidency, and Ahmed Tahawy and Ahmed Abdullah Toiema, former Deputy Secretary-Generals of the Liberation Rally, worked diligently to make the Union a success. One government official attributed the public's obvious apathy toward the National Union to a lack of "ideology." In his opinion, Sadat and his colleagues failed to provide a cadre and a doctrine which would appeal to the

Egyptian people. He derisively mocked Hatem's statement that "the Union's ideology could be found in Nasser's statements." Toiema presented a different view. As he explained it, the National Union, unlike the Liberation Rally, was giving priority to quality in members over quantity.[88] According to many observers, it obtained neither.

The impression grew that the Union was to become a club for the government's more trusted supporters. It became apparent, also, that the National Union was to be used as a weapon against those whom the government deemed undesirable. A case in point was its management of labor affairs. Anwar Salama, once installed by Toiema as president of Egypt's labor federation, had fallen into disgrace with his former sponsors. It was a relatively easy task to depose Salama from the federation's presidency, but Toiema further wanted to consolidate his control over local trade-union councils. In a ruling aimed, according to some, primarily against Salama, Toiema decided that any member of a syndicate council (these were large boards often with as many as twenty-one local representatives) must be an active member of the National Union.[89] The reaction of a labor leader from Port Said seemed typical: "What is the National Union? I am not a member nor will I join. And that goes for the rest of my members, too."[90] Partly because of labor's reaction, no effort has yet been made to enforce the condition for syndicate membership. Its promulgation, however, did much to damage the National Union's campaign to establish itself as a popular mass organization.

Even the leaders of the National Union were not agreed as to its operating principles. Anwar Sadat seemed firmly convinced that the organization's cadre should continue to be the representatives of the National Assembly.[91] Mohamed Abou Nour, director of the Union's organizational structure throughout Egypt, strongly dissented. According to him, many of the National Assembly members were not "good people."[92] "It was not necessary to depend upon all National Assembly members, but 'they' [apparently Sadat and Hatem] said we must."[93] He saw great danger in imposing leadership from the top and presented his own scheme for avoiding this problem. If ten men were selected in every village, he foresaw an opportunity to undercut "undesirable" National Assembly deputies within two years.[94] He had fought vigorously, and with some apparent success, to include "opposition members" (often the defeated opponents of successful Assembly members) on the local councils, some of which began their existence in September, 1958.

Anwar Sadat and Gamal Abdel Nasser have ambitious plans for the National Union, but to date the Union's progress has been unimpressive. Moreover, there is considerable friction among its top leadership. Some claim that it was a matter of the highest policy which kept Tahawy and Toiema of Liberation Rally days isolated in the old Rally offices, while Sadat and his handpicked staff worked in the former headquarters of the Revolutionary Command Council, over a mile away. Whatever the reasons, the National Union has encountered many of the difficulties experienced by its predecessor, the Liberation Rally.

The net result is that, at this writing, the "transitional period" of 1953 has yet to end. Nasser, brilliant tactician that he is, fears the development of a political force which ultimately might challenge his authority. The same attitude apparently has guided his policy toward local Communists. During much of 1956 and 1957, many men accused of left-wing or Communist tendencies were permitted to assume positions of importance. Several of the most prominent leaders in the labor movement generally were regarded as Communists. Dr. Ismail Abdullah Sabri, once indicted as Secretary-General of the Egyptian Communist Party, occupied a vital post as research director of the government's powerful Economic Organization. Dr. Yussef Idris, a brilliant writer who had been imprisoned in 1954 as a Communist, later became a close confidant of Anwar Sadat and worked as director of the National Union's foreign affairs section. Ahmed al Masry, convicted as the ringleader of a Communist plot against the government in 1954, was installed in the Ministry of Social Affairs, working in close contact with the Minister, his old friend Hussein Shafei. The return to influence of Khaled Mohieddine also fitted the general pattern.*

---

* In 1959, Khaled Mohieddine was relieved of his post as editor of *Al Missa* during Nasser's anti-Communist campaign.

Then, in December, 1958, Nasser startled a Port Said audience with a vicious attack against Communist infiltration in the U.A.R. Within a week it was reported that over two hundred Egyptian Communists had been arrested, and that two major printing houses, financed by the Soviet and Chinese Embassies to publish and distribute Communist propaganda, had been closed.[95] It remains to be seen, however, whether Nasser's break with Communism is final.

Nasser has shown himself extremely reluctant to delegate authority—an attitude which has been reflected in his treatment of provincial and district governments. The last local government elections were held in 1950. The next were scheduled for 1955, only to be postponed.[96] The Ministry of the Interior ruled later that every governor of a province must be a police officer, thus terminating the previous practice of appointing prominent civilians to these posts.[97] During this period, a battle developed between the Ministry of the Interior and the Presidency over the issue of decentralization. It appeared that the advocates of decentralized government had gained a victory when local elections were scheduled for June 24, 1957; these elections subsequently were postponed for a year because of the "Interior Ministry's preoccupation with preparations for the National Assembly elections."[98] This postponement has since been extended for an indefinite period, and there are strong indications that control over the *moudiriahs* (provinces) will be transferred to the Presidency.

Whatever Nasser's shortcomings and abuses of power, the Egyptian President generally has been a tireless and sincere patriot. His task has not been easy and the alternatives often distasteful. President Nasser has grasped tightly the reins of power, and his regime is an authoritarian one. But Gamal Abdel Nasser has not developed an insatiable lust for power; more accurately, it would appear that President Nasser has lost faith in the Egyptian people.

IV

Agriculture and Agrarian Reform

Problems of Egyptian Agriculture

The Nile has long occupied a sacred position in Egyptian my-
thology—and with good reason. In many respects it is accurate
to say that Egypt is the Nile. This mighty river, spewing forth
its fertile flood waters, brought the Pharaohs wealth and power.
Later it made Egypt the granary of the Roman empire. But by
the end of the nineteenth century, the irregular flow of the river
Nile no longer was able to provide sustenance for the rapidly
swelling population of the Nile Valley. Formerly, farmers would
await the flood, trap water in man-made basins, and contentedly
farm their yearly crop. These ancient methods, however, proved
inadequate to provide for the increase in population during the
nineteenth century.

Under the skilled direction of the British, great strides were
made toward establishing a nationwide system of perennial
irrigation under which two and even three crops could be
cultivated. Between 1897 and 1947, the total crop area was
expanded from 6,764,401 *feddans** to 9,166,589 *feddans*, an
increase of 35 per cent.[1] However, 80 per cent of this increase
was attained in the first thirty years, during the major transition
from basin to perennial irrigation. Only nominal progress was
recorded in the succeeding generation. But during this half century, Egypt's population more than doubled.

After World War II, Egyptian agriculture entered into a
period of crisis. During the war, fertilizer imports had been
sharply curtailed, with the subsequent result that yields per
feddan declined substantially. These losses were not easily recov-

---

* 1 *feddan* = 1.038 acres.

ered and, during the 1948-52 period, average yields of major crops attained only 91 per cent of 1935-39 productivity.[2] With local industry still making only a nominal contribution to the national income and with a low rate of development in agriculture, per capita income had declined and there was a deterioration in the country's general standard of living.

Agriculture is the backbone of the Egyptian economy. In 1952, over 65 per cent of the Egyptian people derived their living directly from agriculture, and 70 per cent of the country's industrial labor force worked in factories which depended upon raw agricultural products.[3] In the same year, 93 per cent of the country's exports were agricultural, while over a third of Egypt's imports was food or other agricultural products.[4] At the time of the military coup, a country with a population of over 21 million eked out a subsistence from 5,974,784 arable *feddans* —substantially below the one-half *feddan* per person required for a modest existence.[5] Egypt's agricultural problems were aggravated by an astonishing inequality in land distribution: much of the arable land was owned by relatively few absentee landlords. One authority noted in 1953: "Should the present trend continue, Egypt will be facing a situation in the year 2000 where she must feed ten people per *feddan* of cultivated area . . . notwithstanding the planned expansion of area. This appears to be quite impossible."[6]

These, then, were the problems inherited by the new regime: agricultural output was dependent upon a capricious Nile; the feudal economic structure of the agricultural society obstructed extensive land reclamation and increased productivity; and 400,000 more Egyptians annually had to be fed from less than 6 million *feddans*.

No easy solutions were available for Egypt's agricultural difficulties; in fact, many an expert dismissed the problem as completely hopeless. When Wing Commander Gamal Salem of the Free Officers, in cooperation with several civilians of the "old order," drafted the agrarian reform program, none of the goals was especially novel. Raising productivity was an obvious aim, one which the Ministry of Agriculture had held aloft for several decades. Expanding the land under cultivation was another proposal which had been raised continually by the Ministry of Public Works and in Parliament. And the third objective, establishing more efficient management of existing agricultural resources, had been supported, in principle, by Egypt's leading agronomists. The major difference between the old and the new regime lay not in conception but in execution. For years, even decades, men like Mirrit Boutros Ghali and Mohamed Khattab had suggested viable alternatives to the prevailing agricultural structure, but their imaginative proposals fell upon the deaf ears of parliamentarians and ministers. The British agrarian authority Doreen Warriner noted: "In thirty years of parliamentary government not one measure was passed for the benefit of the *fellaheen*."[7]

Then the Free Officers seized power. The new leaders did not depend upon Parliament or upon the "old order" for their political support; instead, they were determined to eject the entrenched conservative elements which had controlled Egypt's political and economic scene for so long. Thus, the new regime could embark upon an agricultural development program with national rather than vested interests as their prime concern.

The first step toward agricultural reform and, significantly, the issue upon which the civilian Prime Minister, Ali Maher, was forced to resign, was redistribution of the land. Previously, bills had been presented to Parliament on this subject. A 1945 bill sought to prohibit further acquisition of land over 100 *feddans*, and in 1950 a bill was introduced which would have placed a 50-*feddan* limit on individual landholdings. Both proposals were overwhelmingly defeated.[8] Then, early in 1952, it was announced that a fourteen-man committee under Abdel-Wahab Ezzat was to be established for the purpose of distributing reclaimed land of the State Domain in lots of five *feddans* or less.[9] This committee never was given the opportunity to fulfill its announced function, nor did the past record of the State Domain Department suggest that the committee would have met with great success: from 1935 through 1950, 182,523 *feddans* of state land had been sold, with 90.7 per cent going to large landowners and only 1.7 per cent being allotted to small farmers.[10] When, in early August, 1952, a draft agrarian reform bill was circulated, many of the leading landowners sought a compromise with the government. Some suggested progressive tax-ation as a remedy (agricultural holdings had largely been exempted from direct taxes by successive parliaments). Others, including Prime Minister Ali Maher, favored a limit of 500 *feddans* per person.[11] The Free Officers' executive council, while finding these proposals unacceptable, permitted landowners to retain 200 *feddans*, a moderate figure in the light of socialist demands for more radical restrictions. The military was careful not to alienate the middle class from which most of its members had been drawn.

Implementation of Agrarian Reform

Although no organization had yet been established for its implementation, the Agrarian Reform Law was decreed on September 9, 1952. A ministerial Higher Committee was created to supervise the land redistribution, and this committee's newly appointed Executive Director, Sayed Marei, was charged with the execution of Law No. 178. Marei set out to assemble a skeleton staff, then acquaint them with the regulations which they would be required to enforce. Some of his initial encounters with governmental bureaucracy attested to the frustrating inertia of Egypt's civil service, as department after department refused to cooperate with his as yet undefined organization. Having no official lien on state budgetary funds, he sought an advance from the Ministry of Finance. When this proved unsuccessful, he applied at the Agricultural Credit and Cooperative Bank for a loan, but this government-sponsored bank refused his request because he lacked collateral.

Marei's efforts to gather a nucleus of trained personnel met with more success, as a few men were obtained on loan from the Ministries of Social Affairs and of Agriculture. But this makeshift group was hardly prepared for the difficult task of enforcing the first land requisition orders which were issued to 112 landowners on October 26, 1952. Twenty-two rather bewildered men, each with the princely sum of 50 Egyptian pounds to meet "unexpected expenses,"[12] were deployed to the provinces to implement these orders. At first, the result was chaos. Wealthy landowners, understandably upset by the requisition orders, set out to make life as miserable as possible for these government representatives.[13] When tractors ran out of fuel, tenant farmers were told to find "the government man." Local credit was suspended, and landlord-tenant relationships were disrupted. If the landlords hoped in this way to sabotage the entire agrarian reform scheme, they succeeded—at least for the moment.

Mr. Marei, an extremely capable administrator, came to an obvious conclusion: matters could not be dealt with within the existing framework of government bureaucracy. The problem came to a head when, during 1952, the responsible governmental departments failed to meet his personnel and monetary requirements. Wing Commander Gamal Salem, who claimed authorship of the Agrarian Reform Law, brought the matter before the Free Officers' executive council. The issue was simple: the "old order" was sabotaging the regime's most highly publicized reform, and, unless drastic measures were taken, the entire program would collapse. Marei soon obtained what he needed. The Agricultural Credit and Cooperative Bank, once so reticent with his application, granted him a 1-million-pound advance, guaranteed by the government. Even more significant was the permission to recruit personnel without the limitations of civil service regulations: this meant that greater pay inducements could be offered and incompetent employees could be more easily dismissed. By the end of 1953, the Higher Committee, then officially called "The Higher Committee for Agrarian Reform" (HCAR), had become widely known for its competent staff, and the government proudly gave foreign visitors guided tours of its "showplace" at the Committee's headquarters in Abdine Palace.

Even with the support of this staff, Mr. Marei found the task of land requisitioning and distribution an extremely difficult one. According to Law 178/1952, all landowners were permitted to retain 200 arable *feddans* for their personal use and up to 100 additional *feddans* for their children. The land held in excess of this limit was to be requisitioned within a five-year period, unless the large landholders sold their surplus in 2 to 5-*feddan* lots to small farmers who owned less than 10 *feddans*. Moreover, all of the requisitioned land was supposed to be distributed by the government within five years, which meant that extensive credit and marketing facilities had to be established for the new owners. The problem was all the more complex because antiquated methods of land registration made it impossible to ascertain, with assurance, precisely how much land was subject to expropriation.

Government figures on land ownership were hopelessly outdated. Title to considerable land still had not been transferred from long-dead owners, and government statistics on total landholdings could not be assessed against total ownership, since many people possessed more than a single tract. Indeed, Mr. Marei himself once referred to 2,136 owners of 1,176,801 *feddans,* then later in the same publication mentioned 1,786 owners of the same land area.[14] In an early pamphlet, Marei claimed that 655,640 *feddans* would be requisitioned over the following five years,[15] and the same figure was mentioned in HCAR material as late as November, 1954.[16] But by March, 1955, estimates of the land area subject to the law had been reduced by 100,000 *feddans.*[17] Five hundred and sixty-five thousand *feddans* has served as the official government figure since that time.

The estimate of land available for distribution underwent another substantial revision when large landholders hastened to take advantage of Article 4 of Law 178/1952. Under this article, land subject to requisition, but not yet requisitioned, could be sold to small farmers (not related to the seller) within the limits of 5 *feddans* each. Landowners naturally preferred dealing with individual farmers to accepting non-negotiable government bonds, and these local transactions soon reached major proportions. By June, 1953, according to the National Bank of Egypt, about 50,000 *feddans* had been sold under Article 4.[18] Several HCAR publications in 1954 set the total at 85,000 *feddans,*[19] and another usually reliable source estimated the figure at 92,000 *feddans.*[20] It was evident that Article 4 could jeopardize the entire land-distribution program. Therefore, on July 15, 1954, an official decree was issued forbidding the approval of any sales under Article 4 which had not been registered in court by November 1, 1953.[21] It would appear, then, that this retroactive regulation would have frozen land sales at substantially less than

100,000 *feddans*. In 1955, however, an official source placed the figure at 145,000 *feddans*,[22] a total which was subsequently confirmed by Sayed Marei. Although the available figures appear incompatible, it would seem reasonable to assume that more than 200,000 *feddans* had been sold under Article 4 before the government forcibly intervened.

With 565,000 *feddans* subject to the Agrarian Reform Law, and after 145,000 *feddans* had been privately sold, about 420,000 *feddans* were available for requisition. Discrepancies in the official figures on land requisitioning blur an accurate assessment. Probably more than 150,000 *feddans* were taken over by the HCAR by November, 1953;[23] by November of the following year it was claimed that the HCAR had control over 254,532 *feddans*.[24] Of this total, 180,000 *feddans* were confiscated from the Mohamed Ali family, so that less than 75,000 *feddans* had been acquired from ordinary citizens. The requisition goal of 420,000 *feddans* reportedly was reached by 1957.[25] Thus, this phase of the program has been completed.

Yet, new problems arose in the distribution of requisitioned land. The large landowners, in selecting the land to be given up to the government, naturally chose their less fertile areas. Moreover, with a maximum of 420,000 *feddans* available for distribution, an optimum of only 120,000 families would be able to become new landowners. Certain areas, expropriated from large, fertile Delta estates, were ready for almost immediate distribution. These first 18,402 *feddans* were handed over to the *fellaheen* amid much fanfare on the first anniversary of the military coup. It was not until April, 1954, however, that the next distribution was scheduled; then another five thousand *feddans* were parceled out. By October, 1954, 101,299 *feddans* had been distributed to 28,353 families, with over 50 per cent of this total being given to the farmers during the celebrations of the Agrarian Reform's second anniversary in September.[26] According to HCAR figures, another 145,941 *feddans* were turned over in 1955, bringing the total to 247,240 *feddans* distributed among 66,220 families.[27] The pace slowed appreciably, however, for by June, 1957, according to Agrarian Reform authorities, only 282,000 *feddans* had been released.[28]

Since 1955, Agrarian Reform officials have been conspicuously reticent about giving details of the distribution program. The HCAR press department announced the further distribution of 20,578 *feddans* on July 23, 1957,[29] the fifth anniversary of the military coup, and, according to local press reports, another 15-20,000 *feddans* were handed out the following July.[30] These figures, if accurate, would bear out Mr. Marei's press statement in July, 1958, that 320,000 *feddans* had been distributed to 78,000 families.[31] Later in the year, Mr. Marei stated that another 50,000 *feddans* would be turned over to small farmers by November, 1958. This would mean that 370,000 *feddans* were to have been distributed by the end of 1958.

The preceding figures, taken at face value, suggest that the government's land distribution program is nearing completion. There is, however, reason to question the validity of these statistics. For example, a substantial portion of the requisitioned land was found unfit for immediate distribution. As Mr. Marei put it: "In certain cases, a few plots were rented to farmers, but title will remain with the High Committee."[32] Moreover, the HCAR was reluctant to distribute fruit orchards in uneconomic 3- to 5-*feddan* plots. Some requisitioned land also was set aside for public utilities. Finally, there are profound discrepancies in the government's figures. The following memorandum, prepared by an Agrarian Reform official in January, 1959, bears this out:

1. The area of land requisitioned from
   private individuals   240,000 *feddans*
2. The area of land confiscated from the
   Mohamed Ali family   180,000 *feddans*
3. The area of land privately sold by
   the ex-owners over the maximum
   limit, according to Article 4 of the
   law   145,000 *feddans*

            Total   565,000 *feddans*

4. The area of land retained by the
   Agrarian Reform Organization not
   to be distributed at present, either
   because not fertile or because subject to judicial appeals, or retained
   indefinitely for future public utilities   130,247 *feddans*

Lacking further information which might clarify the figures mentioned in section four of the above memorandum, it would appear that a discrepancy exists between the 130,247 *feddans* therein recorded and the estimated figure of 370,000 *feddans* distributed through 1958. Realizing the problems which have beset the HCAR, the 130,247-*feddans* figure is not surprising; but if it is correct, then deception certainly has been practiced in the claims of the land distribution program.

As Doreen Warriner noted in reference to the requisitioning and distribution under the HCAR, what once were large holdings and small farms now are small holdings and large farming units.[33] Large Egyptian landowners increasingly had found it more profitable to rent out their land, rather than farm it themselves. As a result, it was estimated by 1950 that over 60 per cent of Egypt's arable acreage was tilled under a system of cash rental or crop tenancy. Large estates enjoyed the advantages of large-scale farming, but only through implementation of a strict rotation system on small plots. Under the monolithic structure of a feudal society the small farmers were heavily dependent upon their local landlord, for it was he who could provide them with short-term credit, fertilizers, and other agricultural necessities. The HCAR recognized the pressing need to create a substitute for these ex-landowners. The new landowners could not obtain private credit at reasonable terms, for, by the terms of the Five-Feddan Act of 1913, it was impossible for them to use their land as collateral. Moreover, their former landlords were unwilling actively to support the Agrarian Reform program. In dire necessity, the new landowners might call on local usurers to borrow funds at a prohibitive rate, but it was considered the government's responsibility to provide these farmers' requirements at a reasonable cost.

The Agricultural Credit and Cooperative Bank alone was incapable of meeting these demands; it lacked the trained personnel and would require massive government subsidies. Similarly, the agricultural cooperatives which previously had been organized under the Ministry of Social Affairs were unable to help, for they generally were mere purchasing societies, formed to obtain discounts on fertilizer, insecticides, or other agricultural commodities. Sayed Marei saw only one solution to the problem: supervised credit through Agrarian Reform cooperatives. It was with this purpose in mind that he persuaded Mahmoud Fawzi, formerly of the Ministry of Social Affairs, to create a massive cooperative system for the HCAR.

These new cooperatives have become a vital part of the Agrarian Reform program. All recipients of land distributed through the HCAR were obliged to become members. And, according to the local cooperative statutes, every member had to sign a contract agreeing to deliver his crops to the cooperative for marketing and to purchase his agricultural requirements through his local cooperative.[34] The HCAR funnelled Agricultural Credit and Cooperative Bank funds through the Agrarian Reform cooperatives to the new owners. "With these loans," explained Marei, "went complete supervision of the various agricultural activities undertaken, since it was feared that some farmers might misuse the loans which they had drawn."[35] All of this was to be achieved through local cooperatives which the members did not control, for they could not refuse to accept the HCAR's nominee for the dominant position of supervisor.

It would have been too sanguine, perhaps, to assume that the Egyptian *fellaheen* were then capable of managing their own cooperatives. But the very fact that restrictions were imposed from Cairo caused considerable difficulties, and embittered ex-pashas recounted with relish some of the incidents which befell inexperienced supervisors. Moreover, the Egyptian farmer is a stubborn individual, and it is not easy to tell him what to do. Perhaps this is why the new cooperative system was not, at first, forced upon HCAR land recipients. While, according to the law, members of cooperatives were obliged to market their goods through the local organizations, in practice coercion proved to be an ineffective method. Instead, incentives were offered. Agrarian Reform officials made every effort to render their marketing services profitable to the cooperative farmer. During the first agricultural year, only 9,000 cantars* of cotton (the produce from 2,000 *feddans*) were marketed through Agrarian Reform

---

* 1 cantar = 99.05 lbs.

facilities.[36] But these farmers, because the HCAR eliminated the middlemen by bulk sorting and then holding auctions in Cairo, realized over two pounds a cantar more than those who relied on traditional marketing methods. The following year, about 86,000 cantars of cotton were marketed through cooperatives, and by 1957, the figure had risen to more than 300,000.

There were other incentives for marketing crops through cooperatives. For example, a farmer could not obtain cooperative loans unless he sold his cotton through his local cooperative. As Marei expressed it: "Supervised credit is strongly linked with cooperative marketing of cash crops to guarantee the repayment of the loan as it falls due."[37] In fact, deductions were made for government taxes, cooperative services, and outstanding loans before the individual farmer received his cash. This system, while it was hardly "cooperative" in a strictly voluntary sense, was effective and essential. Hostility toward these cooperatives gradually has waned and by January, 1959, there were 276 such units in land reform areas.[38]

Highest officials of Agrarian Reform still desire to control large-scale production in these areas. In an effort to increase efficiency, experiments in crop rotation were conducted. Now a majority of the cooperative areas are obliged to practice triennial crop rotation. Juxtaposed to this are the plans in some areas to remove the appointed supervisors and let the local members manage the cooperatives themselves. This already has occurred in two cooperatives. When this practice becomes widespread, the success of the Agrarian Reform cooperative system is likely to be ensured.

The Egyptian government has made much of the incentive resulting from individual ownership following the redistribution of land under Law 178/1952.[39] In fact, however, none of the land distributed is yet owned by those who farm it. According to Article 16 of the Agrarian Reform Law: "Neither the owner of the land nor his heirs may dispose of the land before effecting full payment of the price. Prior to such payment, the land shall not be subject to expropriation in settlement of a debt unless due to the Government, to the Agricultural Credit and Cooperative Bank, or to a cooperative society."[40] This means that the farmer is little more than a tenant until full payment is made, although local cooperative societies have tended to interpret this provision liberally when an individual farmer has had difficulty in making prompt payment on his loans. In 1955, for example, a brief moratorium was declared on certain loans after disease had damaged severely the cotton crop in several provinces. More important was Law 554/1955 which permitted the HCAR to confiscate property "if the new owner fails to make proper use of his land."[41] This law could conceivably be invoked against a farmer who refuses to abide by cooperative crop rotation regulations or decides to market his crops independently. The very existence of such a decree suggests that all members do not adhere willingly to their cooperatives' directives.

The HCAR deserves praise for establishing a functional system by which it was able to maintain and even increase agricultural production during a transitional period in which land was requisitioned, then distributed. It is still too early, however, to pass judgment on this system as a viable cooperative structure, for it has not had sufficient time to operate. Doreen Warriner believes that "the cooperatives are managed by state officials in what is, in effect, a system of collective farming."[42] Sayed Marei finds the term "collective" distasteful. In his view, there is a "great difference between collective and cooperative farming; the key is individual ownership, not collective ownership."[43] But by this very definition he classifies the agrarian reform movement with neither. This distinction, however, is only of academic importance over the short run, and it should not detract from the achievements of Mr. Marei and Mr. Fawzi. They were faced with tremendous and immediate problems at the outset of the agrarian reform program and they met the challenge forthrightly and effectively. Whether the structure which they erected can be maintained without modifications over a long period of time remains, however, to be seen.

Economics of Agrarian Reform

An economic evaluation of the land redistribution program is difficult, especially since available statistical data are unreliable. The HCAR has been reticent to explain the financing of agrarian reform to the general public; and the government has proved none too eager to discuss the reserve funds which supposedly are being amassed for the eventual repayment of the former large landowners. When the Agrarian Reform Law was announced, provisions were made to compensate the owners of requisitioned land. In a way, these landowners paid for their low tax assessments of preceding years, for compensation was calculated from the government land tax which had been determined in the forties. Assuming that land should rent at a figure seven times this tax, the total value of a *feddan* was fixed at the sum of ten-years' rental. In general, calculations computed on this basis provided compensation equal to one-third to one-half of the land's current market value.[44] This sum was to be repaid over thirty years, with 3 per cent annual interest being paid during the interval.

The Agrarian Reform Bonds were not highly regarded in Cairo's financial circles. They were non-negotiable and could be used only to pay certain land taxes, for the purchase of fallow land, and in settlement of death duties. Moreover, even when the bonds first were issued, knowledgeable Egyptians predicted that they never would be redeemed. Indeed, a low opinion of the bonds was one of the reasons why so many Egyptians sought to dispose of their requisitionable land under Article 4 of Law 178/1952 in a depressed land market. At first it was estimated that upwards of 150 million pounds in bonds would be issued as compensation. Then, official publications of the HCAR continued to insist that at least 120 million pounds of bonds would be issued in payment for requisitioned land and equipment. Since 1954, well-informed Egyptians have pared this figure down further. The Director of the Economics Department at the HCAR expects 75 million pounds in bonds, of which 4 million would be compensation for requisitioned buildings and equipment.[45] This estimate appears reasonable, although even this may eventually prove too high. It is interesting to note that, although all land had been requisitioned by early 1957, only 22.3 million pounds of Agrarian Reform Bonds had been registered with the government by December 31, 1957. According to Sayed Marei, this delay was caused by the difficulty in verifying land ownership: he assured the writer that over 30 million pounds in bonds would be issued by December, 1958.[46] He also stated that interest accumulated on these bonds (calculated from the day of requisition) would be paid immediately upon issuance of such bonds.

The recipients under the land distribution program, on the other hand, benefited from the large landowners' financial losses. Agrarian Reform cooperative members were expected to purchase their land in thirty annual installments. The purchase price was arrived at by using the assessed purchase value as a base, then adding 3 per cent yearly as interest on the bonds and another 15 per cent over thirty years to cover the Agrarian Reform's handling expenses. The annual cost was substantially below the rental value of the land. Thus it came as a great surprise to many people when, on September 29, 1958, it was announced that the bonds would be extended to forty years, the yearly interest rate was reduced to 1.5 per cent, and Agrarian Reform charges were cut to 10 per cent. Because the loss of income to the former large landowners was of little concern to the government, some observers surmised that this step was taken in order to further placate the *fellaheen* in the Agrarian Reform areas. Another common view, however, was that the move was simply another effort to redistribute agricultural income at the expense of the wealthier classes. Because the reduction cost the government millions of pounds in expected revenue, there must have been a compelling reason for it. Mr. Marei (by then Central Minister of Agriculture for the United Arab Republic) described it as an attempt to improve conditions for the farmer.[47] A member of his staff expressed it more succinctly: "Families are expanding and what satisfied the *fellaheen* five years ago is no longer sufficient." It may be that this move was, in part, designed to allay some criticisms which were being leveled against Agrarian Reform cooperatives.

At the outset of the land reform program, the Ministry of Finance claimed that all rent accruing to the HCAR should be considered state revenue. Then, after the HCAR had been established as an organization independent of direct government control, Sayed Marei obtained a government ruling exempting from payment of the land tax all land which had been requisitioned, but not yet distributed. Therefore, in order to assess accurately the economics of agrarian reform, it is necessary to appraise the finances of the HCAR and the government separately.

Originally, the HCAR was obliged to obtain a loan of one million pounds from the Agricultural Credit and Cooperative Bank in order to finance its first year's expenses. The requisitioning of land, however, soon enabled it to repay this debt. As soon as land was requisitioned, the HCAR assumed the responsibility for making payments on Agrarian Reform Bonds, including the 3 per cent interest. But until this land was distributed, the Higher Committee was permitted to charge rent, generally calculated at seven times the land tax. On a *feddan* of land taxed at 2.5 pounds, the rent charged would amount to 17.5 pounds, while the total amount due the Ministry of Finance was only 11.1 pounds, thus resulting in a handsome net revenue for the HCAR. By October 31, 1955, the Higher Committee netted at least 2,754,800 pounds in this manner,[48] and the subsequent slow-down of distribution probably will have more than doubled this "profit" by 1959. This "profit," in turn, resulted in further savings.

During its first two years, the HCAR borrowed money from the Agricultural Credit and Cooperative Bank and lent it through local cooperatives at almost the same rate that it paid the Bank; the Higher Committee lost money on these banking transactions. Then the HCAR decided to use its own reserves along with installment payments on bonds to finance its own credit system, keeping the 3 per cent interest return on loans for its own purposes. Every June, it would deposit the bond installments with the Ministry of Finance, after having used those funds for up to ten months without interest. Of course, there also was income from various service charges. A separate fund established for Agrarian Reform cooperatives never failed to show a net gain, partially as a result of the commissions received from cotton and fertilizer sales.

Although, according to the provisions of Law 178/1952, the

transitional period of land distribution should have been completed within five years, the government granted the HCAR permission to retain certain land beyond 1957. Much of this land, however, is substandard, and the rent often has been reduced below the permissible maximum rate. It would appear, therefore, that the HCAR's future income from these areas will be marginal. Moreover, with the introduction of the forty-year, 1.5 per cent bonds, there will be far less funds available for a self-financed credit system. According to Sayed Marei "the government must pay 1 to 1.5 million pounds for Agrarian Reform projects during the year 1958-59."[49] He also voiced his concern lest the Agricultural Credit and Cooperative Bank would again have to provide credit facilities for Agrarian Reform areas, thus burdening the government with an additional expense.

The government found itself in an unusual financial situation. Its major direct benefit from the land redistribution program came from a supplementary tax imposed as of January, 1953, on all unrequisitioned land scheduled for ultimate expropriation. At a rate of five times the original tax, it has been estimated that four million pounds accrued from this levy. Ostensibly, the Agrarian Reform Fund at the National Bank of Egypt, reported to be ten million pounds by the end of 1958,[50] could provide the Ministry of Finance (later the Ministry of the Treasury) with some ready cash. Even this source of liquid capital, however, is questionable, for the funds there generally were used to redeem Agrarian Reform Bonds which had been paid to the government for death duties or certain land taxes. It may be claimed that the government, as owner of 180,000 *feddans* confiscated from the Mohamed Ali family, was the heaviest direct loser from the land distribution program; it had claim to Agrarian Reform Bonds nominally valued at 31 million pounds, which originally provided interest of almost 1 million pounds yearly. With the extension of the bond period, smaller annual payments would be available with which to redeem the government's bond holdings, while income on the bonds was reduced by nearly half a million pounds yearly.

The redistribution of land under the Agrarian Reform program also has resulted in a redistribution of income on a considerable scale. Some of the wealthiest men in Egypt lost much of their annual income, while perhaps a hundred thousand fortunate families may receive up to twice their former income, at least temporarily. Moreover, substantial increases in productivity have been reported for Agrarian Reform areas, and these, too, should boost the country's economic development. It seems too early to determine whether the higher incomes in Agrarian Reform areas are primarily a result of a redistribution of the wealth which occurred through lower land charges. Perhaps Agrarian Reform cooperatives have reduced production costs, but this is difficult to assess in the absence of reliable figures on the costs of cooperatives and of family labor. Available information suggests that the cooperative system has proved substantially more efficient than individual small farmers, but all HCAR expenses must be taken into account.

One other point needs to be made concerning the "economic worth" of Agrarian Reform areas. Unquestionably, production has risen in many of these areas; at times yields have increased more than 30 per cent during the past six years. On the other hand, imported chickens, hybrid seeds, and increased amounts of fertilizer have been distributed through these HCAR cooperatives long before they have been made available to other farmers. It is fair to assume that these cooperative areas have received special treatment; this fact, while it does not necessarily detract from their agricultural achievements, should place claims of higher productivity in proper perspective. In short, the Agrarian Reform program has contributed to Egypt's economic development, but the magnitude of this contribution remains to be determined.

"Land distribution, which has caught public attention most, is probably the less significant of the two major provisions [of the Agrarian Reform Law] . . . the other major provision being that which fixes annual rent at seven times the original land tax."[51] While 420,000 *feddans* were included in the land distribution program, about two-thirds of Egypt's arable area, or 4 million *feddans,* were affected by the rent reduction and land tenure regulations. The new rent prescribed by law was, like the Agrarian Reform Bonds, calculated on the basis of the low land tax assessments of the forties. Thus, a landlord might be required to rent a *feddan* for 14 pounds in 1953, while he had received over 30 pounds for the same tract in the preceding year. This was another effort to reduce the wealth and influence of the large landowners and to increase the income of the small farmer. In cases of crop tenancy, the owners were permitted to claim no more than one half of the crop after "all expenses are deducted."[52] According to Ministry of Agriculture estimates, these provisions added 40 million pounds annually to the income of the tenant class.[53] The same figure has been used continually by Agrarian Reform officials, but has never been fully substantiated.

During 1953 and 1954, with the cotton market depressed and land values falling as a result of the Agrarian Reform Law, rents had declined by as much as 40 per cent.[54] By 1955, however, agricultural rents rose, and the pressures of supply and demand often led to violations of the rent laws. Although detailed information on these contraventions is lacking, they appeared to be sufficiently widespread to worry the government. In July, 1956, the local press announced that a law was being drafted under which severe penalties would be inflicted upon anyone disregarding the official rental rates: "It has been decided to stop the manipulation in the value of land rentals, thus wiping out the black market from the Egyptian villages."[55] A year later, Sayed Marei, then Minister of State for Agrarian Reform, admitted before the National Assembly that some tenants were paying rents which exceeded the limits prescribed by law.[56] The campaign against offenders was climaxed by a 1958 amendment to the Agrarian Reform Law, approved by Nasser, which authorized imprisonment of all lessors who deliberately obtained rents above those stipulated by law.[57] Although it is doubtful that rent laws have been fully enforced, without question these regulations have brought an aggregate of many millions of pounds annually to the small cultivators. Their added income, in turn, has permitted farmers to purchase more fertilizers for their land, but their major increase in expenditure has been on personal consumption. And one wonders how much of this added income has been absorbed by the rise in the cost of living over the past several years.

An attempt also was made by the government to establish a minimum wage for agricultural workers: 18 piasters daily for men (about 50 cents) and 10 piasters for women and children. This was considerably above the existing rate, and to date the government has found it impossible to enforce such a pay scale. Indeed, it would appear that the hired agricultural worker not only has failed to benefit from this decree, but also has lost in absolute terms from the Agrarian Reform Law. Large land-owners, farming their reduced acreages, have tended toward more economical management of their holdings, thus reducing their dependence on migrant labor. Moreover, farmers under the Agrarian Reform cooperative system have less need for out-side labor, since access is provided to tractors and other labor-saving devices. According to the Statistical Administration of the Presidency, wages of male agricultural laborers rose less than 10 per cent between 1953 and 1956. Even if these figures are assumed to be correct, this is far short of the 50 per cent increase envisaged by the drafters of the agricultural wage law. There is reason to believe, moreover, that even this reported increase is an exaggeration.

Assuming that its purpose has been to redistribute a portion of Egypt's agricultural wealth and to redistribute land without loss in production, the Agrarian Reform program has been a tremendous success. Perhaps fault might be found in the original law. Some critics believed that the 200-*feddan* figure was too generous; others were critical of Article 4 (on private sale of requisitionable land) and of the increased measure of govern-ment control inherent in the proposed cooperative structure. Nevertheless, Law 178/1952 was executed exceedingly well. This achievement can be attributed to several major factors. First, the HCAR was freed from government routine and, in many respects, operated as a private business, complete with its own financing schemes and separate budgets. Secondly, and of equal importance, Sayed Marei was able to assemble a highly competent administrative team to manage the Agrarian Reform program. He was not obstructed by civil service regulations in acquiring the necessary personnel, and he also was able to offer more attractive salaries than those generally granted to government officials.

There is yet another factor in the administrative structure which should not be overlooked—namely its operation by competent civilian professionals. Granted, in the beginning Wing Commander Gamal Salem was very much interested in the land distribution scheme, yet nevertheless, the entire program was achieved without a single military official actively engaged in administrative affairs. Instead, competent members of the "old order" like Sayed Marei, formerly a member of Parliament, and Abdel-Wahab Ezzat, a ranking official during the monarchy, managed a civilian secretariat which, generally, had been drawn from other ministries. Perhaps it is significant that the most successful of the "revolutionary proposals" originally instituted by the Free Officers was executed by nonmilitary men. Also, it seems fair to conclude that its success would have been in jeopardy had the HCAR been an integral segment of the governmental structure.

The dispossessed landowners certainly have not been pleased with the land distribution program, for they have lost a significant portion of their capital and yearly income. Likewise, the introduction of rent ceilings has also cost wealthy landlords tens of millions of pounds annually. Conversely, the way of life of many *fellaheen* has been profoundly changed. The small farmer now enjoys a larger cash income; even more important, he has been given a sense of security. Those who cultivate redistributed land have a tangible possession, one which cannot be lost except under extraordinary circumstances. Those farmers who still rent are given the security of three-year leases, a luxury seldom enjoyed before Law 178/1952. Whether it is owned or rented, the *fellaheen* feel more attached to the land which they now cultivate. And, considerable evidence refutes the claim that the *fellaheen* are no better off than before the Revolution.[58]

One should not, however, overestimate the "revolutionary change" which accompanied the land redistribution program. Unlike many agricultural countries, Egypt traditionally had been farmed in small units. Sayed Marei stated in 1954: "There has been very little change in agricultural methods since the land reform."[59] It was only after the land was distributed that the more significant changes, such as compulsory crop marketing through cooperatives and obligatory crop rotation, were instituted on a large scale. There is still much to be done in Agrarian Reform cooperatives. The lack of adequate social services, for example, inhibits the development of a viable cooperative system under which the Agrarian Reform supervisor can be replaced by a functional board of *fellaheen* co-op members. The most severe criticism with which Agrarian Reform officials must cope is that the peasants simply have changed masters under a system of collective farming.[60]

Now that many of the HCAR's original objectives have been achieved, there are indications that its activities will be expanded. Already, a General Agrarian Reform Cooperative Society has been formed to supplant the HCAR, and the HCAR has been renamed the Agrarian Reform General Organization. There are also plans to distribute upwards of 135,000 *feddans* of State Domain land and 110,000 *feddans* belonging to the Wakfs (government religious trust).[61] Although certain technical problems still must be resolved, the distribution is expected to be in accordance with the Agrarian Reform Law of 1952. Now that the Agrarian Reform administration is entering into a new phase of operations, its members should be content that its first phase, that of executing Law 178/1952, has been fulfilled most admirably.

Land Reclamation

The Agrarian Reform Law did not concern itself directly with another major agricultural problem, that of land reclamation. This was a program which the military government marked for its own—one which it decided to "kick off" with the spectacular development of an entirely new province. This area, managed by Major Magdy Hassanein, one of the Free Officers, was to be named Liberation Province—symbolic, it was claimed, of the Revolution's achievements. The moderation practiced under the Agrarian Reform was singularly absent in this project, as

Major Hassanein endeavored to conquer the desert with an army of machinery and a complex of irrigation canals.

His self-set goals were most ambitious: an original 600,000 *feddans* of desert land were incorporated into the Province (with another 620,000 *feddans* to be added later) and this feat was to be accomplished without foreign assistance as "a test for the competence, ability, and honesty of Egyptians."[62] It was further decided that Liberation Province settlers would form the nucleus of Egypt's new rural society; a program was quickly formulated by which families from Delta villages would be placed in modern, utilitarian homes (no animals were to be allowed in their living quarters), a uniform dress was designed for the Province (overalls for the men to replace their "outmoded" native dress), and nurseries would be provided for children from the age of two, so that their mothers would be available for "productive tasks."

The Province was "created" on April 5, 1953, and construction began in earnest. Heavy earth-moving equipment worked, on occasion, around the clock, and huge quantities of machinery were purchased to assist in carving an oasis out of the desert. Some agronomists protested that sufficient water was not available to reclaim such large tracts of desert, but their warnings went unheeded. A few wells had already been drilled to a water table under the Province, and the officers in charge of the project felt confident that adequate water supplies would be found. Work proceeded at a rapid rate as roads were constructed, several housing settlements were established (the first was named "Om Saber," after a woman martyr of the Suez Canal struggle against the British), and the first *feddans* of sandy soil were ploughed according to schedule. The idea of Liberation Province was a compelling one: the project, if it succeeded, would point the way to a solution to Egypt's critical shortage of cultivated land. And as the plans took shape, hundreds of foreigners were brought to admire this revolutionary scheme of which so much was expected.

As the program gained momentum, plans became more far-flung. Why should such a Province rely only on agriculture, it was asked? If it were to be truly representative of a new Egypt, it also should have an industrial nucleus. Thus, plans for many new industries mushroomed even before the first permanent residents had been settled. By 1954, some criticism was in evidence, especially from members of Cairo University's Faculty of Agriculture, but this was summarily dismissed as antiregime. Indeed, it became increasingly unwise to question the economic worth of Liberation Province. Experimental plots ("whose costs should not be considered, because they were experimental") produced luscious fruits and vegetables. And visitors to the Province could attest to the high quality of its produce. But when would the program start large-scale and economic production?

Finally, in 1955, the first settlers came from Menoufia Province. They were undoubtedly a superior group of Egyptians. The admission requirements were stringent. The males were expected to have completed military service, and they could have no more than one wife and three children. Moreover, they had to be young and capable of passing a psychological examination. Upon acceptance, they were moved into a new house and worked for an adequate daily wage. After three years, if they proved satisfactory, the families would be permitted to purchase their houses over an extended period and would be given shares, equivalent to 5 *feddans,* in the Province. Although Major Hassanein insisted that one "must keep the word collective out of our vocabulary,"[63] no individual ownership of land was envisaged. By 1956, about twenty-five hundred settlers' homes had been constructed,[64] but, at most, only 389 families had been accepted by the Province. In the meantime, over a thousand agricultural workers from nearby provinces tended the fields.

The program for an industrial center was off to an equally poor start. The Province was isolated from Cairo and Alexandria. Any industrial project entailed the importation of the raw material and workmen and the transport of the finished product to an urban market. Two factories were established for the government to make shoes and clothing for the needy, but more expansive plans, such as the creation of a cement factory which was to utilize waste materials from an iron plant over one hundred kilometers away and the building of an automobile assembly plant, did not materialize. Some plants, however, were constructed to utilize the Province's produce and to supply the

Province's necessities. An ice factory, a mechanical repairing unit, and a tile factory were of some use, but the fruit and vegetable canneries failed to receive sufficient agricultural goods to justify their operation.

The bubble of Liberation Province burst dramatically before the National Assembly. Scandal or, more charitably, rumors of mismanagement had long been associated with the Province's activities. It was not, however, until the issue was raised within the National Assembly that President Nasser felt compelled to take decisive action. Within two weeks, Major Hassanein and some of his aides were dismissed and, ironically, Sayed Marei, as newly appointed Minister of Agriculture, became responsible for the Province's operations. His colleague from Agrarian Reform, Abdel-Wahab Ezzat, was given the task of unraveling the Province's tangled affairs. This change in management made one fact clear: the "social experiment" had ended. Earlier, when plans for collective farming originally had been discussed, Mr. Marei had delegated his Director of Cooperatives, Mahmoud Fawzi, to fight collectivization.[65] Now, with Marei in active control, the "settler scheme" lived on borrowed time. At the peak, only 389 settler families had been assembled in the Province; by mid-1958, the number had dropped to 372.[66] According to Marei, these families had the choice of either receiving land within a year or of being transferred to Agrarian Reform areas.[67] Meanwhile, they served as foremen over the temporary agricultural workers who still farmed the Province's fields.

The economics of Liberation Province have been shrouded in secrecy—and for good reason. It seems evident that the industrialization program was a failure: a fruit-packing plant and two government clothing factories are still operating, but the radio plant was sold to the army and removed. It is still questionable whether the existing fruit and vegetable canneries can be operated economically. At any rate, no further attempts to establish major industries at the Province are expected.

An evaluation of the Liberation Province's agricultural experiment is most difficult because of the usual clash of government statistics. One fact is certain: the original objective, to have 201,500 *feddans* under cultivation by 1958, has not been achieved.[68] According to a Liberation Province official, 17,000 *feddans* had been reclaimed by April, 1958, of which 13,000 were under cultivation.[69] This would seem reasonable in the light of Abdel-Wahab Ezzat's remark that by June, 1958, a total of 19,000 *feddans* would be reclaimed.[70] According to Sayed Marei, however, by October, 1958, 30,000 *feddans* had been reclaimed in the southern part of the Province and 10,000 in the north, with another 10,000 *feddans* in the northern part in various stages of reclamation. Even allowing for a generous use of the term "reclamation," this seems difficult to reconcile with information obtained from one of his most competent assistants who is actively concerned with Province affairs. The latter claimed that, at present, there are only 12,000 *feddans* of "cultivated" land, with little Nile water available for further expansion. Of this, possibly between 5,000 and 6,000 *feddans* can be planted with citrus trees, but the remaining area is troubled by seepage from the Nile, so less profitable crops must be grown on this land. He stated definitely that there were no immediate plans to initiate new land reclamation programs.[71]

Official figures suggest that the entire project has cost at least thirteen million pounds.[72] Although President Nasser, in a major speech, accused foreign broadcasts of gross exaggeration when they put the cost at eighty millions, he has not yet produced detailed evidence to justify the estimate of thirteen million pounds. It has been suggested, for example, that the army assisted in some of the Province's programs. How should such aid be evaluated? Should rebates on customs duties also be considered a Province expense? And when a premium had to be paid for purchases in foreign currencies, was this included in the Province's budget? In all, there is ample evidence to bear out the statement by one of Nasser's most intimate associates: "Liberation Province is not economic, and I don't know if it ever will be economic."[73]

The government claims that Liberation Province was a great experiment and should be judged as such. Yet, even by empirical standards the project has proved a failure. The social experiment ended ignominiously, and the great industrialization plans did not materialize. Certainly, the program yielded some valuable lessons, but they were purchased at enormous cost. Perhaps, if and when the High Dam is constructed, water will be available to irrigate the Province's wastelands. But until then, the scheme seems destined to lie dormant.

There has been one other major land reclamation program under the regime: a joint Egyptian-American project undertaken in 1953. Under the terms of the agreement, the Egyptian-American Rural Improvement Service (EARIS) was to receive 5,450,000 pounds from the Egyptian government and 3,469,000 pounds from the United States, contributed proportionally over a period of years, with which to reclaim and distribute 37,000 *feddans*. Early in 1954, the program was initiated at the Abis area in the Province of Beheira. From all appearances, work progressed rapidly. By February, 1955, land was available for the first eighty-nine families, and housing facilities and primary irrigation canals had been established throughout much of the area. It has been reported, however, that the land then distributed already had been almost completely reclaimed by the State Domains Department.[74] If this is correct, EARIS' accomplishment is not so impressive. Moreover, the project was marred by an unfortunate error in policy. Originally, land was handed over in 6-*feddan* lots, but this allotment exceeded the specifications of the Agrarian Reform Law. EARIS was obliged, therefore, to take a *feddan* back from each family. Complications naturally arose.

Another problem was posed by the low yield of the area. The reclaimed land produced substantially less per *feddan* than other farms in Beheira Province. EARIS, in an effort to make the project financially attractive to potential settlers, proposed nominal purchase costs. Land donated by the Egyptian government and valued by some at over 50 pounds per *feddan* was assessed at 30 pounds a *feddan* by EARIS officials. Furthermore, reclamation costs were calculated on the assumption that all 24,000 *feddans* would be distributed. But even these inducements attracted no new settlers to Abis. This failure was the result partly of politics and partly of the incompetence of the Ministry of National Guidance, which was entrusted with the task of selecting qualified settlers. The fact remains that, even before the complication resulting from the Suez crisis, Abis had a great shortage of settlers.

Those farmers who had moved to Abis were given many advantages. Funds were made available to them, with EARIS as the cosigner. A local cooperative, using EARIS money, offered interest-free loans to meet agricultural expenses. Moreover, regulated payments for the occupied land have yet to commence. According to the director of EARIS, by 1958 no money had been collected directly from the settlers. A certain amount, "voluntarily contributed by the individual farmer," has been deposited with the local cooperative pending final settlement of land costs.[75] This suggests that the program has not met original expectations.

In late 1958, there were 820 houses prepared for settlers, yet only 89 of these were occupied. Apparently, 3,125 *feddans*, capable of producing 60 per cent of a full crop, were ready for distribution as early as October, 1955. In November, 1957, the United States released another 600,000 dollars for EARIS, and local officials are optimistic that further land distributions can be facilitated. In another area, Qoota, 6,000 *feddans* were scheduled for cultivation; yet, hilly country reduced this total to 4,500 *feddans*. Of this area, about 3,500 *feddans* are under some degree of cropping, but the task is made extremely difficult by the existing 3 per cent slope in the land. A village which was to be constructed by 1956 has yet to materialize. No major work has been done at the third area of the project, Kom Oshin, where EARIS expected to place 7,000 *feddans* under cultivation. To date, over four million pounds have been committed to these projects with disappointing results. Perhaps, with closer cooperation promised between American officials and the Egyptian government, reclamation can proceed at a faster pace and land distribution, now placed under the Agrarian Reform administration, will prove more successful.*

Since 1952, other efforts have been made to create more arable land in Egypt. Invariably, however, the expectations of some officials have clashed with Egypt's traditional enemy: the

---

* It has been reported in 1959 that nearly 1,000 families have been resettled in the Abis area.

critical shortage of water. Whatever the legends of ancient Egypt may claim, there is to date no convincing evidence that the deserts, through the use of underground water sources, can provide more than marginal relief to Egypt's arable land problem.

With the establishment of the Permanent Organization for Land Reclamation, an effort was made to consolidate individual projects for land reclamation. Great publicity has attended these various proposals. The National Production Council, for example, listed in detail the areas in which 234,500 *feddans* were to be reclaimed.[76] Another official publication in 1955 listed under achievements of the Revolution the fact that "350,000 *feddans* have been reclaimed for agriculture and the Liberation Province has been founded."[77] While the National Production Council's plans could conceivably be realized over a number of years, the latter statement is unquestionably in error. The 350,000 figure may refer to the expansion in total crop area since 1952; such expansion, however, merely requires the marginal cropping of land already under cultivation—a far different matter than land reclamation. Other references have been made to the reclamation of 300,000 *feddans* by 1956, but such claims either were made for propaganda purposes or were the result of erroneous terminology.[78]

Even in 1958, responsible officials have differed extensively in their estimates of what had been achieved. Sayed Marei claimed that 130-140,000 *feddans* had been reclaimed since the Revolution, but 80 per cent of this land previously had been cropped.[79] Apparently, he included those areas in which irrigation and drainage facilities had been improved since 1952. An official bulletin placed the figure for reclaimed and cultivated land at 100,000 *feddans*.[80] Perhaps the most accurate information comes from Mansour el Sayed, Director-General of the Permanent Organization for Land Reclamation. Excluding Liberation Province and the EARIS project, his figures showed that 20,000 *feddans* had been reclaimed since 1952. About 12,000 of this total area utilized water directly from the Nile, while the rest was reclaimed with drainage water or in oases. Seven thousand *feddans* currently are under cultivation, while the remaining 13,000 *feddans* are to be cultivated within two years. Sayed's plans call for the reclamation of another 20,000 *feddans* within the next two years and of 150,000 *feddans* within five years; 50 per cent of these projects will rely exclusively upon Nile water.[81] Sayed ventures the cautious hope that the oases will provide water for substantial future reclamation.

If Egypt's land reclamation projects over the past seven years are any indication, then the reclaimed land will not substantially reduce the country's critical shortage of arable land. What land has been reclaimed has proved far more expensive than originally estimated. Moreover, reclaimed land, at least for the first few years, produces low yields. Since the Revolution, far less than 75,000 *feddans* have been reclaimed. Of this total, about 20,000 *feddans* are under economic cultivation. This rate falls far short of keeping pace with the needs of Egypt's rapidly expanding population.

Scientific Farming

Assuming that expansion of arable land is severely restricted, Egypt is called upon, in the words of Abdel Razzak Sidky, a former Minister of Agriculture, to build "skyscrapers in agriculture."[82] With land area limited, great emphasis must be placed on increasing productivity. This problem is not new to Egyptian agronomists. For decades, the research departments in Dokki have worked diligently to develop better strains of seeds and livestock, while the qualities of Egyptian long-staple cotton have become world famous. And today, Egypt's closely cropped *feddans* produce some crop yields which are among the world's highest.[83] It is possible, however, to further increase these yields through the extensive introduction of scientific farming methods. Hybrid seeds, for example, might increase substantially the productivity of wheat and maize at only a nominal cost. Already, a large-scale program has been conducted toward this end. Similarly, the proper use of fertilizer can produce higher yields per *feddan*, but the cost is greater. Surprisingly enough, larger crops also could be obtained if Egyptian farmers could be persuaded to use less water on their crops. When given the opportunity, not only do they literally drown their fields, but the resulting drainage problems have contributed to lower yields over more than 1 million *feddans*.

Another obstacle with which agronomists have had to cope is pest control. Ministry of Agriculture officials estimate that as much as 40 million pounds worth of crops annually are destroyed by insects and other vermin. Substantial progress has been in evidence during the past few years as a result of widespread application of scientific farming methods. If these same methods can be applied throughout the entire country, some agricultural experts expect an increase in productivity approaching 30 per cent over the next five years.[84] This figure should be considered close to optimum, however, for there is a point after which increased yields are of marginal economic value.

While great increases in productivity have been achieved experimentally, the major problem is to channel these benefits to the *fellaheen*. Likewise, although a uniform government-controlled system of crop rotation may prove beneficial to the country as a whole, it may be extremely difficult to persuade individual farmers to adopt such a method. It is also recognized that many new farming techniques require financing which is not readily available to most Egyptian farmers. In the past, resort was made to the Ministry's agricultural extension stations and individual agricultural cooperatives, which generally were operated for the benefit of a few large land cultivators. Now, however, a concerted attempt is being made to consolidate the nation's factors of agricultural production. And for Sayed Marei there is only one way to do this: through agricultural cooperatives.

Agricultural Cooperatives

In 1955, when Sayed Marei was Managing Director of the HCAR and Chairman of the Agricultural Credit and Cooperative Bank, Agrarian Reform authorities, after a long fight, were permitted to introduce their cooperative methods in five or six cooperatives under the Ministry of Social Affairs. In the past, the Ministry's cooperative departments had not exercised close supervision over their cooperatives, and Mr. Marei was anxious to demonstrate his idea of "supervised credit." While this experi-

ment proved a success and as the Social Affairs Ministry sought
to employ some of the HCAR's techniques, Marei's plans for
cooperative societies suffered a severe setback in late 1956. It
was his idea to organize cooperatives nationwide on the same
principle as employed in his own cooperatives, but the Ministry
of Social Affairs, jealous to maintain control over the country's
cooperatives, refused to relinquish its hold.[85] Apparently, Marei's
voice carried less weight than did Hussein Shafei's (formerly a
member of the RCC and then Minister of Social Affairs). All
cooperatives, except those within Agrarian Reform, remained
directly under Shafei.

It was evident, however, that Zaki Imam, Director-General
of the Ministry of Social Affairs' Agricultural Cooperatives Department, and others on his staff had been impressed by Mahmoud Fawzi's experiments, for they were quick to adopt many
of the HCAR's methods. Marei believed that the existing cooperative system had to be changed. In its place, cooperatives
should be established through which the Agricultural Credit
and Cooperative Bank could work. In his opinion, the Agricultural Credit and Cooperative Bank "should support well-
established co-ops composed of the majority of landowners in
one village to serve its members. These co-ops should represent
the Bank as the only credit agency in the village."[86] He suggested further that such cooperatives could provide "collective
guarantees" for loans.[87] Although the practical advantages of
this policy, from the government's standpoint, could not be
denied, the implementation of such a comprehensive program
appeared to present many serious difficulties. Unlike in Agrarian
Reform areas, the bait of cheap land could not be offered farmers subject to these cooperatives. Moreover, Agrarian Reform
cooperatives had proved successful because of extenuating circumstances. To expect this same formula to succeed throughout
the country in a few years appeared to be a highly optimistic
goal.

Agrarian Reform officials had not abandoned hope that they
might obtain some authority over this experiment. In February,
1958, all holders of less than 5 *feddans* were permitted to join
Agrarian Reform cooperatives in their areas.[88] Later, Mahmoud

Fawzi suggested that holders of 15 *feddans*, or even more, be permitted to join existing Agrarian Reform cooperatives. Meanwhile, Hussein Shafei and Zaki Imam had organized several General Cooperative Congresses and were hard at work to establish new agricultural cooperatives throughout the country, province by province. Three of these were formed in 1957, another forty in 1958. If existing plans are realized, the Agricultural Credit and Cooperative Bank will be obliged to operate only through these cooperatives by 1961.[89]

In theory, this should be an ideal economic arrangement: low interest credit can be provided to small farmers, fertilizers and seeds can be made available at nominal cost, all loans will benefit from collective guarantees, and crops marketed through these cooperatives will benefit from bulk handling. The experience of Agrarian Reform cooperatives, however, was unique; and even then, after six years, cooperatives have been unable to function in accordance with their statutes. Some observers feel that the farmers are not yet ready to accept such strong regulations as the government plans to impose. And it is generally felt that the ability and dogged determination of Zaki Imam are not sufficient to surmount an extreme shortage of proper personnel.

The strongest advocates of the Agrarian Reform cooperatives are shocked by the manner in which Hussein Shafei expects to blanket the country with cooperatives. If, in the face of so many obstacles, these can succeed, then the country's agricultural development will be well under way. But if, instead, this policy evokes strong resentment from the farmers, Egypt's agricultural program will suffer a severe setback. Hussein Shafei, like Major Hassanein of Liberation Province, has decided that the situation calls for decisive action. Success, however, is not a foregone conclusion.

Assuming that the government wishes to impose strong controls over agricultural production, it can resort to vehicles other than the Social Affairs cooperatives. The most exciting Egyptian agricultural experiment in years was conducted by Mahmoud Fawzi in the Delta village of Nawag, not under Agrarian Reform jurisdiction.[90] Instead of imposing a cooperative upon the farmers, great efforts were made to win the support of the *omda* (mayor) and local elders for a village-wide crop-rotation scheme. Once their backing was obtained, the remaining villagers supported the program, but not without strong initial opposition. It was more than coincidental that necessary funds and farm materials were to be supplied through a new cooperative. With crop fragmentation seriously reduced and the economies of large-scale cultivation achieved, the villagers experienced substantial economic gains by the end of the first season.

For a number of years, the government has fixed maximum limits on cotton areas under cultivation, while a minimum has been placed on the amount of wheat acreage a farmer is required to plant. Government crop requisitioning at fixed prices also has become common practice. In addition, the Ministry of Public Works, especially during the summer season, maintains tight control over available water supplies, limiting certain crops when the Nile is low. With these various other means available, perhaps the government would be wise to employ a more conservative cooperative program, at least over the next several years.

Balance Sheet of Egyptian Agriculture

Many extravagant claims have been made concerning Egypt's increased agricultural production since 1952. Although the complete picture is obscured, partially by the interchangeability of certain major crops, several general observations can be hazarded. Between 1952 and 1954, the total cropped area under winter, summer, and *nili* cultivation increased from 9,298,735 *feddans* to 9,885,229 *feddans*, an increase of over 6 per cent. Since then, however, further increase has been negligible.[91] Total production of agricultural crops is greater than during the 1948-52 period, as was to be expected. Rough calculations based on total cultivated area and official indices of agricultural production suggest that total agricultural production in 1956 reflected a 6 per cent increase in productivity over 1952 figures.[92] During the same period, the population increased by 10 per cent. Other figures, however, indicate that yields of major crops rose substantially more than a modest 6 per cent. Wheat and rice showed the most remarkable advances; wheat productivity over the four-year period 1953-56 showed a 19 per cent higher productivity than over the 1949-52 period, while rice yields showed comparable gains.[93] One can conclude that the decline in agricultural productivity experienced during and after World War II has been checked and a modest upsurge in productivity should be expected. It should be remembered, however, that a majority of Egypt's crops currently cannot match the agricultural productivity recorded during the years 1935-39.

Cotton accurately reflects the dilemma of Egyptian agriculture. In 1957, raw cotton alone accounted for 72 per cent of Egypt's total exports. When the foreign cotton trade is booming, Egypt's economy appears buoyant and the farmers do well with their major cash crop. But the cotton market, like any raw-commodity market, experiences large price fluctuations, and these in turn are reflected by Egyptian agriculture. Between 1949 and 1955, gross income from cotton was calculated to represent over 40 per cent of all income from field crops. Although agronomists recognize the dangers of such great dependence upon one crop, no alternative can yet be provided. Moreover, it has now become a matter of government policy to speculate on future cotton demand, as cotton and wheat acreages are regulated. Wheat is an essential food crop (and often a major import item), but a successful cotton season proves more lucrative. In this vicious circle, the government has found it necessary, since 1952, to establish minimum support prices for cotton in an effort to stabilize the internal market, and in so doing the Egyptian Cotton Commission has accumulated cotton surpluses. All of this, while perhaps unavoidable under the circumstances, can prove onerously expensive for a poor country like Egypt.

The future prospects for Egyptian agriculture are not encouraging. Excluding the construction of the High Dam at Aswan and the proposed "New Valley" project, which, according to President Nasser, may see over 3 million *feddans* irrigated with underground water (which is not yet assured), approximately 150,000 *feddans* of new land can be expected to be brought under cultivation during the next ten years. And even if this optimistic goal can be attained, a population increase of 25 per

cent will far outstrip this 4 per cent rise in arable land. Moreover, even if the Ministry of Agriculture's ambitious ten-year
plan, which is expected to cost over 60 million pounds, is implemented successfully, its primary achievement will be to maintain
Egypt's existing minimal standard of living. Currently, about
46 per cent of Egypt's total cultivated area is devoted to cereals
for human consumption; another 23 per cent is planted with
nitrogen-producing animal fodder.[94] While the latter figure may
be reduced in future years, there is every indication that, as
more income becomes available to individual Egyptians, per
capita food consumption will increase.[95] Tentative figures suggest that the rise in wheat consumption between 1952 and 1957
is substantially more than should be expected strictly on the
basis of population rate of growth.

Definite agricultural progress has been made since 1952. But
more positive results were certainly expected from the efforts at
land reclamation, and valid criticism can be directed at the
Ministry of Agriculture for not making the benefits of its experiments available to a larger number of small farmers; on the
other hand, the Agrarian Reform Law initiated a significant
new era, and the use of cooperatives may enable the government
to manipulate more efficiently the factors of agricultural production. When Sayed Marei was asked, in his position as Central
Minister of Agriculture for the United Arab Republic, if he
would describe Egypt's agricultural development since the Revolution as "very good, satisfactory, or unsatisfactory," he replied,
"satisfactory."[96] This can be considered an honest assessment.

V

Education and Social Development

Egypt's Social Lethargy

Egypt's poverty is reflected in her highly underdeveloped human resources. Traditionally, so long as agricultural production was maintained and taxes collected, the government found little occasion to interfere with "those neuter objects" which tilled the soil.[1] Local government often was left to village councils, education to religious bodies, and few steps were taken to improve the squalid conditions throughout rural Egypt. Epidemics and low life expectancy were accepted as a matter of course. In the major cities, especially after the advent of Mohamed Ali, the government made an effort to establish a minimal system of education, to inculcate social consciousness, and to encourage industriousness. Viceroy Mohamed Ali felt these to be a prerequisite foundation for his sizable military establishment. Later, under Khedive Ismail, notable progress was made toward creating a base upon which Egypt's future educational and social development could be projected. The British military occupation abruptly cancelled these plans. During the first half of the twentieth century, several commendable programs for the modernization of Egypt's educational system and the creation of basic public services for the entire population were adumbrated. Most of those projects, however, were stillborn.

Egypt of the mid-twentieth century was plagued by those social problems characteristic of a feudal, agricultural society. To many, the symbol of success was to live in Cairo or Alexandria, for these two cities were the commercial and social centers of the country. Urban residents, no matter how lowly their occupations, tended to look down upon those who lived in rural areas. Large landowners often passed their time in these cities or in Europe, traveling to their country villas only occasionally to oversee their managers. Many less prosperous city dwellers chose idleness to employment in Upper Egypt. And since Cairo, with its cinemas, coffee houses, and many other diversions, was considered to be a veritable Mecca by Egyptians, it was only natural that students from the villages, once exposed to Cairo life, seldom returned to the homes of their families; in fact, many *fellaheen* endured hardships in order that their sons may escape the dreary confinement of the village.

Rural Egypt had changed little in the course of four centuries. The mud and reed huts, the omnipresent filth and poverty, and the dreary routine of the village held little appeal for those who had tasted another life. Escape was possible because class barriers were not unbreakable. Certainly the uneven distribution of wealth produced great social cleavages, and a few large landowning families banded together in an exclusive social elite. But to the landless, education still offered the credentials for social advancement.

The urban-rural dichotomy was reflected in governmental development of the country. According to some estimates, over 75 per cent of the government's development funds prior to the Revolution had been spent in cities which housed less than 30 per cent of the nation's total population. This, of course, made the division all the more acute. The policy was myopic not only because of Egypt's heavy dependence upon her agricultural production, but also because, with an annual population increase of 400,000, there simply were not enough jobs available in the cities. During World War II, British and American military installations required the services of many Egyptian laborers and wages skyrocketed. This in turn swelled the migration to the cities, and the postwar period found Cairo burdened with a serious unemployment problem. To this number were added those who annually graduated from secondary schools and the universities. True, job opportunities were no greater in the villages. But Egyptian families traditionally provided for their members and, in terms of national welfare, many people deemed underemployment on the farms preferable to unemployment in the cities.

In the wake of the unchecked migration to the major cities came serious social problems. Village life imbued its inhabitants with strong moral and social values: the mosque, the village council, and the family were the unquestioned sources of authority. With the transition to city life, however, many of the social restrictions disintegrated. Although respect for the family still survived, the village council was replaced by a more nebulous municipal government, and religious devotion became more a matter of individual choice rather than of social obligation. With the shift from village to city life, many of the traditional social values fell by the wayside, and the materialism of the city replaced the spiritualism of the rural community.

It was not surprising that most Egyptians lacked a sense of public responsibility and a pride in their work. The villagers historically had been oppressed. Cheating the tax collectors and matching wits with landlords were necessary stratagems in the battle for survival. Indeed, resistance to authority became a national characteristic. The Egypt of 1952 was a nation of people who abhorred responsibility. The country's problems were apparent to all, and possible solutions had been advanced by many of Egypt's most competent men. Domestic politics, however, had blocked meaningful reforms.

What was written by Mirrit Boutros Ghali in 1938 still was valid in 1952: "Only a political party confident of its strength, firmly believing in its convictions, prepared to execute its programs and to assume for them full responsibility, can prepare a reasonable, practical program and present it to the nation."[2] Ghali did not picture the military in the role of reformers; but when Egypt's political system collapsed in 1952, it was the military which assumed control. To the Free Officers, many of whom hailed from the villages, the problem seemed simple: blueprints for reform already existed; they "merely" had to be implemented. Under the slogan "Unity, Discipline, Work!" the Revolution, proclaimed to be "by the people and for the people," committed itself to a vigorous program of educational and social development.

Education on the Rise

Symbolic of this new spirit was the promise of 400 new schools yearly, or more than a school a day. Even as early as 1914, a plan had been drawn up calling for the construction of 200 schools annually over a twenty-five-year period;[3] and primary education through the age of twelve was made free and compulsory by law in 1923.[4] Few schools, however, actually were constructed, especially in rural areas, and the *fellaheen* often believed that their children could spend their time more profitably in the fields. Education was the key to social development in the opinion of the military junta, and for the first time a serious effort was made to provide primary schooling throughout Egypt. True, the slogan "a school a day" also had propaganda value. Whatever the motivations, however, the new school program was impressive. According to the published schedule, 4,000 new primary schools were to be constructed between 1955 and 1964.[5] By 1964, primary education was to be made available for all Egyptian children between the ages of six and twelve.

The primary-school building program was entrusted to a newly established organization, the School Buildings Foundation, which was financed by government-guaranteed loans. The Foundation was responsible for the design and the construction of the schools, while the Ministry of Education was expected to provide qualified teachers. The program got off to a slow start in 1953, and less than half of the budgeted funds were expended during the first year. By July, 1958, it was reported that about 848 primary schools had been constructed at a cost of 13,865,000 pounds, a figure which would suggest a per-classroom cost of 1,260 pounds.[6] Although these results fell well below the original target, the efforts to extend primary education throughout the country far exceeded similar attempts before the Revolution. Unfortunately, this program was restricted by a shortage of funds. For all practical purposes, this segment of the School Buildings Foundation's activities had been financed entirely by loans from the Civil Servants Insurance and Pension Fund. These loans originally had been for twenty years at 4.5 per cent, but the interest rate later increased to 5.5 per cent. And as the government became hard pressed to finance its many other projects, especially in the industrial field, it became apparent that the program for new primary schools was given a low priority.

Already the program had burdened the government with a substantial increase in expenditures. According to the 1954-55 budget for the Ministry of Education, 12,530,000 pounds had been allocated for primary education. In the 1957-58 budget, the figure approached 20 million pounds[7] (more than half of the entire Ministry's budget), and there were indications that it would increase further once existing schools were properly staffed. Thus it was not surprising that the School Buildings Foundation's plans for 1958-59 called for only forty-three new primary schools.[8] The Foundation's Assistant Director explained that the original plan had been to construct about one thousand primary schools, then concentrate on the establishment of more technical and secondary schools.[9] This seemed very much like an ex post facto rationalization.

A major function of primary schooling in Egypt is to provide the rudiments of an education to the large number of students who never will advance to secondary schools. At the same time, it is the expressed policy of the government, especially in agricultural communities, to prepare the students for living effectively within their immediate environment. The schools attached to the Combined Service Units provide an excellent example of this principle; they combine elementary instruction in reading and arithmetic with practical training in rural industry and agriculture. Many classes actually are conducted in workshops or on fields adjacent to classrooms. This type of education has many merits, not the least being that it might curb the current exodus from the villages to the cities. It would be unrealistic, however, to place great hope in Egypt's system of primary education. The quality of teaching is low, for the starting salary is 10 pounds monthly (1 dollar a day), and no university graduates apply for these positions.[10] Instead, students with intermediate-school degrees often are recruited, and the results are not encouraging. Since 1952, major efforts have been undertaken to revise the teacher-training program. There are indications that some of the least competent teachers have been replaced, but the very nature of the job excludes from candidature those individuals who are intellectually best suited for the task. And these persons will not be attracted until salaries are raised substantially and the villages can provide some of the social comforts currently found only in the larger cities.

According to official government statistics, there were 1,611,000 students in primary schools during 1951-52;[11] after a massive construction campaign and after the Ministry of Education's budget for primary education was more than doubled, this figure had risen to 2,104,000 by 1957-58.[12] It would seem unrealistic to expect Egypt's primary-school building program to maintain this pace. The needs, also, are disproportionate: while urban schools, on rare occasion, have as few as twenty students per class, the average student-teacher ratio in rural areas is already about 40 to 1. Egypt, therefore, will be hard pressed to maintain, let alone increase, the current percentage of school-age children who actually attend school, and the hope for universal primary education is little closer to realization than it was before the Revolution. According to the 1947 census, approximately 15 per cent of the population was of primary-school age.[13] Assuming that the same proportion holds in 1958, 3,750,000 children were eligible for primary school, of which only 56 per cent could be accommodated. The military regime attacked the problem of primary education with admirable enthusiasm, but in time it became obvious that the challenge outstripped the resources which the government could mobilize. Thus, plans for social development have had to undergo modification, since universal education had been an apparent foundation stone for the "new society."

Higher education also has been beset by serious difficulties. Even before the Revolution, it was recognized that the standards at the universities were discouragingly low. Classes were overcrowded, and professors were unable to supervise individual study and research. Students were encouraged to memorize rather than interpret material. A member of the Faculty of Science was able to graduate without becoming qualified to conduct a laboratory experiment, while a liberal arts major could obtain a diploma after committing perhaps a dozen books to memory. What was true of the secondary-school system applied equally to the universities: educational standards were rapidly deteriorating, and business and government circles expressed widespread dissatisfaction with the new graduates.[14] Many suggestions for improvement had been made in the past: one obvious proposal was to raise the requirements for admission to universities. With a university degree increasingly becoming a prerequisite for employment with the government or in private business, however, the government was under considerable pressure to expand enrollment. College doors were opened to almost all secondary-school graduates who mustered a score of "60" or above in their examinations for admission. A majority of these substandard students enrolled in liberal arts courses, which seemed to offer the easiest route to a degree. Upon graduation, however, these persons found job opportunities extremely limited, and many of them felt that the government somehow was obligated to care for them. What the country needed instead was increased enrollment in technical institutes, but pre-Revolution politicians were unwilling to impose such a policy upon the country.

These were the outstanding problems which faced the would-be reformers of the new regime. The increased emphasis on industrialization required many more trained technicians than were currently available. In attempting to redress this shortage, the new regime faced a subtle barrier. The Revolution had been declared in the name of "the people," and it was generally understood that "the people" would have greater opportunities under the new regime. As an extension of this thesis, higher education came to be considered a right rather than a privilege— a principle which was hardly conducive to a more selective approach to higher education.

In 1951-52, the three major universities (excluding Al Azhar) had a total enrollment of 30,641 students;[15] six years later, this had increased to 71,994.[16] More important, during the same period the percentage of students in the faculties of arts, law, and commerce rose from 53 to 69. Although Kamal el din Hussein, Minister of Education, once boasted of university education in Egypt that "its per capita proportion was considered to be the highest in the whole world,"[17] few informed Egyptians were proud of the state of their country's higher education. Indeed, following the Revolution many of the more qualified professors had been removed from the universities, some to take positions with the government, others because their political opinions were unacceptable to the RCC. Since the universities traditionally had been political trouble spots, the new regime took precautions: it decided that faculty deans were to be replaced every two years,[18] and military secretaries were assigned to the universities. These measures hardly served to boost the morale of the faculties.

In December, 1957, Kamal el din Hussein reached a long-overdue decision to restrict further enrollments in the universities. A major crisis ensued in the National Assembly. When the Assembly members voted to admit all successful secondary-school graduates into the universities, Hussein submitted his resignation to President Nasser. For political reasons which transcended the immediate issue, Nasser persuaded Hussein to continue as Minister, and the National Assembly's view was overridden. The problem, however, has yet to be solved. According to local press reports, over fifteen thousand new students have been admitted for the 1958-59 academic year.[19] Until the government adopts a policy of encouraging the training of qualified students who can make a gainful contribution to the country's development, Egypt will continue to pay a heavy price for condoning mass-education policies at the highest academic levels.

Progress in other fields of education has been more satisfactory. The vigorous program of teacher training deserves special commendation. It has produced noticeable results despite the generally low quality of available personnel. Great strides have been taken, also, toward establishing a functional network of technical schools, although to date the caliber of instructors is disappointing and graduates, therefore, often have not been welcomed by private industry. Efforts have been continued, also, to extend the scope of the Popular Culture Institute, originally established in 1946: this experiment in adult education has recorded a modest success, but the Institute will never have more than a marginal effect upon the country's educational program.

One of the most deleterious developments in Egyptian education since the Revolution has been the closing of many foreign schools. In part, this policy was an aftermath of the Suez crisis of 1956; there also is evidence that the government is following a deliberate policy to eliminate "foreign elements" from local schools. For those who could afford it (including some ministers in Egypt's present cabinet), these foreign schools traditionally have provided the best primary- and secondary-school education available in Egypt. Their "Egyptianization" is not likely to enhance educational standards.

Since the Revolution, there have been serious attempts to increase the enrollment in Egypt's educational institutions. During the first five years following the military takeover, about 22 million pounds was spent on new school buildings; in contrast, about 4 million pounds was expended from 1947 to 1952.[20] During the same period, total enrollment rose from 1,901,000 to 2,696,000,[21] with about half the increase being recorded in primary education. Today, the government bears 80 to 90 per cent of the total cost of Egypt's education.[22] State schools are free and many student expenses at the university level are underwritten. The government thus exercises considerable control over general educational policy: most students could not afford higher education without subsidies from the Ministry of Education. Unfortunately, the post-Revolution government in Egypt has failed to initiate an educational policy which will fulfill the country's basic needs while also being economically feasible. And it seems fair to conclude that such a policy will not be adopted until President Nasser is willing to brave political unpopularity by initiating an educational program geared to the nation's best interests.

Rural Development Eclipsed

Education is but one segment of a larger program of social development, which, in turn, is an integral part of the regime's over-all program. Nasser himself has acknowledged that "the political and social revolutions have to progress together."[23] In an effort to make good on its social promises, the government, on October 17, 1953, created the Permanent Council for Public Welfare Services (PCPWS). Early in 1954, soon after Nasser had consolidated his position of control, the capable Abdel Latif Boghdadi was shifted from the Ministry of War to the Ministry of Municipal and Rural Affairs to emphasize the regime's desire to develop rural Egypt. The Council was authorized to "study general policy and lay down broad lines for education, health, reconstruction, and social affairs" with representatives from the Ministries of National Guidance, Social Affairs, Municipal and Rural Affairs, Health, Education, and the Wakfs serving as Council members.[24] In deference to the national austerity budgets, it was decided to finance the various projects through funds accruing from confiscated Mohamed Ali properties.

Attention was focused on the Council's most ambitious project —the establishment of 864 Combined Service Units throughout the country. Each of these units, designed to serve communities of fifteen thousand, was to be equipped with health, social, agricultural, and cottage-industry facilities, and twelve primary-school classrooms. According to Council publicity, these facilities were estimated to have cost 55,850,000 pounds under the monarchy, but the PCPWS claimed that, with "new methods," they could be constructed for 22 million.[25] According to their calculations, a unit in Lower Egypt would cost about 22,880 pounds, while in Upper Egypt expenses would total about 31,700. The program was launched amid great fanfare. In July, 1955, Gamal Abdel Nasser inaugurated the first unit, although thirty-two units had been scheduled for completion by March.[26] Two hundred were to have been turned over by December, 1955, but by mid-1956, less than one hundred had been finished, let alone staffed.[27] The original plan to construct 600 units within three years was abandoned, and the entire program underwent drastic modification. By early 1956, according to a leading Council member, lack of funds and "politics" reduced to fifty the number of new centers to be undertaken during the year.[28] His comments implied that social development had lost its former priority on the RCC's agenda.

One of the main problems which beset this worthwhile venture was the serious lack of competent personnel. According to Salah Ismail, assistant to the Council's chairman, it was difficult to obtain people to administer Combined Service Units, especially in Upper Egypt. A Council tender in the spring of 1956 for one hundred persons had brought only seventy responses;[29] and the qualifications of many of the applicants were low. Moreover, it seemed that the more urbanized Delta area had received preferred treatment over Upper Egypt. Using much the same system employed by the Ministry of Social Affairs in establishing pre-Revolution Rural Social Centers, preference was given to some communities which could donate a few *feddans* of land. In addition, it was far easier to recruit personnel for posts within convenient commuting distance of Cairo. This writer noted, in August, 1956, that not a single Combined Service Unit was functioning between Kena and Aswan in Upper Egypt, a distance of over 400 kilometers.[30] And except for a few "display units" near Cairo, it was questionable as to how fully staffed the other centers were.

By August, 1957, it was claimed that 200 centers had been completed, of which 170 were in operation[31] (another source put the figure at 134 in October, 1957).[32] In May, 1958, 210 units were reported to be in full operation.[33] It may be assumed, therefore, that the original objective of 250 functioning units should be reached by the end of 1959. According to Hussein Shafei, Minister of Social Affairs, there are no plans to construct further new units in the immediate future.[34] The next stage, once funds are available, will be the expansion of existing pre-Revolution social and health centers so that they can provide the multiplex services offered by a Combined Service Unit.

Fundamentally, the Combined Service Unit is a good idea. Using cheap medical facilities to attract nearby villagers, the government sought to provide certain basic facilities in Egypt's rural areas. The problem of personnel was not peculiar to this program, for it always has been difficult to obtain qualified persons to serve in rural provinces. Perhaps more valid criticism could be leveled at the manner in which these units were imposed on various communities. Mohamed Shalaby, widely recognized as one of Egypt's few authorities on the establishment of social centers, expressed this criticism as follows: "Before the Revolution, the government and the individual social worker sought to give confidence, then funds, to local communities, but now they build a unit, then try to obtain the people's confidence."[35] His observation that "the *fellaheen* as a rule cannot be hurried into adopting new ways of doing things"[36] seems to be correct. Although it is extremely difficult to evaluate the effectiveness of existing units, strong criticism of their operation appeared in the semiofficial newspaper *Al Gomhouria* in August, 1958. Hussein Shafei replied apologetically that they "still were in the experimental stage."[37]

The cost of the 250 Combined Service Units has been obscured by a welter of conflicting figures. The Under-Secretary of State for Combined Service Units claimed that costs totaled 10 million pounds. When the writer pointed out that President Nasser already had announced before the National Assembly that expenditures had reached 13 million pounds by 1957, a member of the Under-Secretary's office agreed to "rework the calculations." The new estimate came to less than 12 million pounds. According to statistics from the Ministry of Municipal and Rural Affairs (the organization which contracted for the construction of the units), the cost had exceeded 13 million pounds, and this total did not include equipment.[38] And it never has been explained adequately why an official publication on Combined Service Units, printed in April, 1957, stated that 16 million pounds *had been* expended on the construction of 250 units.[39] Even assuming the figure of 13 million pounds to be correct (and there are indications that this estimate is conservative), this would mean a per unit cost almost double that estimated in 1954. In addition, a minimum of 8,200 pounds yearly (excluding education costs) is required for the administration of each center.[40] Measured in terms of original expectations, this has proved to be an expensive experiment.

Originally it was expected that the confiscated Mohamed Ali

properties would provide revenues in excess of 60 million pounds, a sizable sum with which to execute the Council's projects. Until the properties were converted into liquid funds, the Council received advances from the government, using the confiscated land and other holdings as security. When the Ministry of Finance undertook the liquidation of these properties, however, the PCPWS received only a fraction of their worth. Many former royal palaces were taken over by government agencies, and no apparent payment was made for confiscated land holdings which, according to Agrarian Reform figures, had a value of approximately 30 million pounds. Ultimately, about 15 million pounds was turned over to the Council, but funds in excess of this figure already had been committed on various projects.[41] With anticipated Mohamed Ali funds thus greatly reduced, the ambitious plans of the PCPWS were scaled down to the capacities of the responsible ministries: primarily the Ministries of Social Affairs, Municipal and Rural Affairs, Education, and Public Health. The Combined Service Units became the responsibility of an under-secretary of state who reported directly to the Minister of Social Affairs. In January, 1957, the Permanent Council for Public Welfare Services officially was dissolved.

The major development program for rural areas was the implementation of the potable water scheme—which had been planned and initiated before the Revolution. According to official figures, the program to provide Egypt's rural areas with pure water had cost 7,758,589 pounds by June, 1952, and another 13,830,335 pounds was spent through July, 1957.[42] Dr. Abu Nosseir, Minister of Municipal and Rural Affairs, claimed that 28 million pounds had been expended by June, 1958, and that 4.5 million would be allocated during 1958-59.[43] By 1962, potable water should be available to all rural communities at a total cost of about 36 million pounds.[44] Thus, it would appear that an important rural development scheme is nearing completion.

The Egyptian government does not seem to have any plans for another massive village development program. Rather, the regime's enthusiasm for extensive rural development seems to have waned as the enormity of the task has become apparent. Increasing emphasis is currently being placed on developing the less populous, but economically more productive, urban areas. Abdel Latif Boghdadi, whose appointment as Minister of Municipal and Rural Affairs had symbolized the regime's concern with rural development, was removed from his post in July, 1957. During the following six months, no one was named to replace him; it generally was acknowledged that his ultimate successor, Dr. Abu Nosseir, was not vitally concerned with problems of rural development. Indeed, Nosseir considered the potable water scheme his Ministry's major achievement during the past five years; during the coming five years he plans to place primary emphasis on urban housing projects.[45]

Housing Gains the Spotlight

The new emphasis upon housing highlights a problem which has become increasingly acute since World War II. With the creation of new industrial centers and the swelling of already overcrowded cities, there has been an extreme shortage of adequate, low-cost living accommodations. While buildings, especially after Agrarian Law 178/1952, have been a preferred investment for private citizens, none of this capital has gone into the construction of housing within reach of the laboring classes. Instead, numerous luxury apartments, priced far above the average Egyptian's income in order to yield an annual return of 8 to 10 per cent, have been built. Moreover, rent ceilings on old buildings discouraged landlords from making even minor repairs.

In 1949, the government had initiated a scheme to provide inexpensive housing for workers near Cairo, but this move benefited scarcely a thousand families.[46] The new regime pledged itself to a far more ambitious program. Although the government itself did not wish to participate directly in constructing low-cost housing units, it did grant generous subsidies for this purpose to various official and semiofficial organizations. Major municipalities, such as Cairo, Alexandria and, after the Anglo-French attack, Port Said, benefited most from this policy. Urgent political reasons prompted a concerted effort in Port Said, where accommodations for 4,549 families were provided between early 1957 and late 1958;[47] Cairo and Alexandria managed to erect over 5,200 municipal apartments for rent, not to mention other more specialized projects.[48]

In keeping with the government's wishes, most of the "popular housing" was to be channeled through the Popular Housing and Development Company, established in 1953. The Company, dependent primarily upon governmental or semigovernmental sources for its financing, undertook the construction of a variety of projects: homes for railroad workers, fashionable apartments for police officials, "popular houses" near Cairo, accommodations for Al Azhar students, and new quarters for petroleum workers at Suez were among its original commissions. As in so many other Egyptian projects, work did not proceed according to expectations. Preliminary cost estimates proved inaccurate, and by December, 1957, the government prohibited the initiation of further self-financed building projects by the Company. It is entirely possible that original cost projections were highly unrealistic. Whatever the reason, the government felt that it could no longer underwrite new construction at the previous level of expenditure.

From 1954 to the second half of 1958, the Company had spent 6,250,000 pounds of its own funds, while another 1,750,000 had been received from other companies for services rendered.[49] Of the 6,250,000 pounds, 3.9 million had been obtained in direct loans from governmental institutions, with interest varying from 2 to 5 per cent; another 800,000 came from government investments or outright subsidies. It was obvious that the company could not continue without strong financial support from the government. In early October, three more loans totalling 1.5 million pounds were granted the Popular Housing and Development Company; these funds, from the National Bank of Egypt, the Postal Savings Fund, and the Civil Servants Insurance and Pension Fund, apparently were to ensure completion of projects already initiated. Other new construction, however, was authorized only on a contract basis with industrial companies or government departments.

In another effort to stimulate more housing construction, the government encouraged the development of housing cooperatives. By December, 1953, fifteen societies, including one army

officers' and one police officers' cooperative, had been registered
with the Ministry of Social Affairs. Members were required to
make a down payment of 40 per cent, and the government
guaranteed the rest; a total of 1.5 million pounds at 3 per cent
was made available for a twenty-year period. In addition, more
than 1 million pounds was obtained from the Civil Servants
Insurance and Pension Fund in an effort to meet the demands
of housing cooperatives, but by 1956, the entire sum had been
spent, primarily in the Cairo area, and only seventeen of the
ninety-seven existing cooperatives had been serviced.[50] Instead
of financing low-cost dwellings, the Ministry of Social Affairs
generally had sponsored luxury cooperative housing; at one cooperative along the Pyramids Road, a loan of 3,000 pounds was
provided for each apartment, while the owner, on the average,
paid another 2,000.[51]

This experiment seemed to disillusion some government officials, and no further funds have been allocated for the cooperative housing program. In an effort to rectify this situation, a
law passed in April, 1956, placed a 1,000-pound limit on the
total cost of each cooperative house or apartment; moreover,
to be eligible for a government loan, the owner could not have
a monthly income exceeding 50 pounds. A plan has been drafted
whereby 10 million pounds would be devoted to cooperative-
housing schemes over the next five years.[52] By late 1958, no
action had been taken on this proposal, and it is doubtful that
the government is in a position to commit such a large sum,
because "popular housing" would appear to have first lien on
any government funds available for housing projects. At President Nasser's insistence, even the Ministry of Wakfs (religious
endowments) is currently committing over 1 million pounds to
low-cost housing. The Wakfs have limited funds, however, and
it is unlikely that they will continue to participate in such non-
remunerative investments unless ordered to do so by Nasser.

It is extremely difficult to obtain an accurate estimate of
expenditures for these low-cost housing projects. Perhaps the
best approximation can be arrived at by a per unit analysis.
The houses at Embaba, Helwan, and Helmiet-Zeitoun were the
first projects entrusted to the Popular Housing and Development

Company. Low bids from private contractors and a plentiful supply of materials resulted in a nominal per unit price of about 567 pounds; it has been stated by a responsible authority that the same house would cost over 800 pounds if constructed in 1958.[53] In Abu Zaabal, at the employees' and workers' settlement being constructed for the Egyptian State Railways, current figures suggest that the per family cost will be over 1,000 pounds, while civil servants' flats in the provinces are expected to cost at least 800 pounds each. Somewhat luxurious accommodations in Suez will require about 1,300 pounds per family,[54] while the more austere dwellings of Port Said average about 500 pounds per unit.[55] It should also be remembered that, in addition to the above prices, the government provides such assistance as cash subsidies, land at nominal cost, and, at times, free installation of public utilities. Except in the case of the construction for Al Azhar (where students lived in dormitories), it may be assumed that "popular housing" in post-Revolution Egypt seldom has cost less than 500 pounds per family. Although the Cairo municipality claims that its slum-clearance program is being achieved at a substantially lower cost, the accompanying figures are open to serious doubt.

Since the "popular housing" schemes are restricted to those families earning less than 25 pounds monthly, the problems of self-financing are apparent. Originally, it was planned to sell dwellings to the occupants, and this was done in the case of 4,300 houses constructed near Cairo. Since then, except for 108 luxury apartments built for police officers, the government has decided to rent rather than sell.[56] Perhaps this was prompted by the fact that few workers could make the required down payment of one-third of the purchase price. Currently, two- to four-room units are being rented for between two and three pounds monthly. Assuming a 2-pound rental on a 500-pound capital investment, this would bring an annual return of 4.8 per cent before collection and upkeep expenses are deducted. Since private apartments in Cairo are expected to bring a minimum annual return of 8 per cent, it is plain to see why private investors have not participated in low-cost housing.

From 1952 to July, 1958, the Egyptian government, through

the Popular Housing and Development Company, the various municipalities, the Ministry of Wakfs, and housing cooperatives, has constructed between 21,116 and 24,136 family units, with another 3,805 to 8,847 units not yet finished.[57] Since a concerted effort was launched to construct "popular houses," approximately six thousand family dwellings have been built yearly at a cost of about 4 million pounds. While this is a notable achievement when compared to governmental efforts before the Revolution, Egypt's housing needs are still far from satisfied. In Cairo, where an estimated 63 per cent of the country's private construction is centered, no more than 4,500 new private apartments have been built in any one year since the Revolution, and these have cost an average of over 3,000 pounds each.[58] A few companies have constructed private communities for their skilled workers, but little attention has been given to the plight of the semiskilled worker and day laborer. Rent reductions and licensing restrictions have now been decreed to curb further construction of luxury-apartment buildings, but it is doubtful that these measures, even if effectively enforced, will alleviate the housing problem.

According to Ahmed Rifaat, the Assistant Under-Secretary of State responsible for housing, 40,000 housing units yearly are needed merely to keep pace with the growth in urban population that now totals 8 million; he estimates that another 32,000 units will be required annually to replace existing antiquated accommodations.[59] Without considering the needs in the villages, this means that 72,000 units are required yearly. At the nominal cost of 500 pounds per family unit, this would entail an expenditure of 36 million pounds, almost double the amount the government has spent over the past *six* years. A detailed study undertaken by the Ministry of Municipal and Rural Affairs seems to verify the magnitude of the need.[60] It would appear that over 75 per cent of the costs would have to be met directly by the government— an expenditure which, in the light of the government's total commitments, is out of the question. Perhaps, as some officials believe, the cost per family unit can be reduced to 400 pounds (a move which, undoubtedly, would have the strong support of Nasser, who, after his trip to the Soviet Union in 1958, vigorously attacked the "lavishness" of new workers' dwellings).[61]

Egypt's totally inadequate housing facilities, especially in the major cities, are and will continue to be a problem of the first order. The workers' primary desire, after food, is for decent housing. And because they form the productive force in Egypt's new industrial complex, a sincere effort must be made to satisfy their demand. Since the government's limited resources available for housing projects must be directed toward satisfying the industrial workers and the civil servants, it seems doubtful that the regime can also engage in large-scale slum clearance.

Government Domination Over Labor

An overriding consideration in establishing a priority for housing projects is the relationship between labor and the government. After the Kafr el Dawar riot, the new regime made a serious effort to woo labor. In December, 1952, the scope of individual contracts was extended, and legal status was accorded to collective bargaining and conciliation and arbitration. Even though the right to strike was prohibited, the new laws were a substantial improvement over old legislation. Moreover, the formation of new trade unions was encouraged, and, for the first time, agricultural workers were permitted to organize. In September, 1953, the Higher Consultative Council for Labor was reconstituted to permit greater labor representation, and by 1955, an "All Egypt Trade Unions Congress" had been established, predecessor to the Egyptian Federation of Labor founded in January, 1957.

Some observers interpreted these moves as a *quid pro quo:* the government wished to cultivate labor as a proregime cadre, in return for which labor would be granted greater authority in determining its own affairs. Yet, Ahmed Abdullah Toiema, the government's "commissar" of labor affairs, made it clear that the government's reins on labor would not be released: "Labor unions are not allowed to strike, because now we must rebuild our country. You must have [take] precautions to finish building without any struggle."[62] The key is his reference to "struggle." Toiema realized that organized labor was potentially the strongest cohesive civilian force which could challenge the government's authority—that labor, indeed, could assume the political significance held by student groups before the Revolution. By offering labor certain tangible benefits, such as higher wages and better working conditions, the government hoped to gain the workers' support. But labor leaders had to watch their step lest they became too powerful; if they asserted themselves forcefully they were likely to be dismissed. An example was Anwar Salama, perhaps Egypt's most qualified labor leader. He was the government's choice for President of the Egyptian Federation of Labor. Subsequently, he began agitating for more workers' rights and even suggested that labor might be obliged to strike for the right to strike.[63] Salama, more than any other man, was in a position to bring unity to the Egyptian labor movement. The government felt, not without good reason, that a functioning trade-union organization, whatever its social benefits, would not be compatible with the regime's immediate economic objectives. And so Toiema, with Nasser's approval, stripped Salama of his posts.

To date, organized labor has been kept subservient. Because the government fears a strong trade-union movement, Toiema has been careful to select innocuous men as labor leaders. The government's wariness of labor was demonstrated by an incident involving a factory at Sornaga. When the owners announced that the factory would close, a group of workers, possibly on Anwar Salama's suggestion, offered to invest their indemnities (terminal pay) in order to keep the plant running. While the government was afraid to let the workers become owners, it could not reject the offer out-of-hand. Ultimately, workers and others acquired 285,000 pounds in shares, while the Industrial Bank purchased the remaining shares in the amount of 115,000 pounds. Nevertheless, the government was able to place five representatives of the Bank on the factory's board, while labor was allowed only four members.[64] Toiema was outspoken in his disapproval of even this representation; he did not want labor to hold direct shares in industry ("he had heard about this happening in the United

States").[65] In his opinion, workers should never have more than 5 per cent direct ownership in a firm.[66] When the issue arose again, this time in Shoubra, the government refused to let the workers participate; instead, funds were provided for the existing owners.[67]

The government is well aware of the fact that, as industrialization plans materialize, organized labor will gain a greater power potential. And because the government is convinced that an independent labor movement would prove detrimental to the country, little is being done to identify the workers as a distinct social class. Whether labor can be suppressed over the coming years is open to doubt, but there is no mistaking the government's policy.

Social Security Enacted

The most significant achievement for labor in the social field has been the enactment of the Insurance and Savings Fund Law 419/1955. In 1950, a social security scheme was established which drew funds only from the government; its major beneficiaries were old people and workers' dependents. When the government failed to provide the 6 million pounds required annually, the program collapsed.[68] Under Law 419/1955, workers were required to contribute 5 per cent of their wages and their employers added another 7 per cent, in return for which the Insurance and Savings Institution assumed responsibility for workers' indemnities, pensions, and certain sick leaves. Although the benefits, like the workers' contributions, were necessarily low, the program was the government's first practical endeavor to provide some form of financial security for Egypt's industrial and commercial workers. In the past, most large private companies had sponsored insurance or retirement plans, but these generally had been highly restricted. Although the government and labor were strongly represented on the Insurance and Savings Institution's board, the Institution was able to develop a sound financial policy because of the brilliance and determination of its Director, Dr. Mohamed Wasfy. At first, the law applied only to those industrial establishments in Cairo and Alexandria which employed more than fifty workers;[69] by 1957, the law included any plant or factory in the Republic which engaged fifty workers; and it was expected that by 1959, or 1960 at the latest, all workers subject to the 1952 individual-contracts law would be registered with the Insurance and Savings Institution.

During its first two years, the organization functioned smoothly. Administrative costs were kept below 2 per cent, and a sound portfolio was assembled. Since then, however, several incidents have suggested that future operations may be less successful. At the outset, the Insurance and Savings Institution was, to all intents and purposes, a one-man organization: Dr. Wasfy managed it superbly with a small group of qualified assistants. In 1958, several ex-officers in the administration sought greater managerial power, and Hussein Shafei, himself a former officer, condoned their grab for power. Subsequently, Dr. Wasfy's most competent assistant was forced to resign. If, in a continuation of this trend, Dr. Wasfy is ousted from his post, the future of the Insurance and Savings Institution will be seriously endangered.

With the government in great need of liquid capital for its various industrial enterprises, the Insurance and Savings Institution is a likely prospect for funds; over 3 million pounds had been collected by 1957, and over 10 million pounds annually is expected after 1960.[70] Anwar Salama once claimed that this entire sum would be available for industry,[71] and Hussein Shafei felt that these funds should be "invested in the interests of the working classes."[72] If license is taken with actuarial tables, then the entire social security system could easily become a shambles. To date, Dr. Wasfy has been able to invest the Institution's money safely and profitably; when larger amounts are available, it may be more difficult to obtain a safe, reasonable return on capital. But if this leads to speculation in government securities which have currently been underwritten by semiofficial organizations, and necessarily so, then the entire program may be placed in jeopardy.

The government has its own social security system, the Civil Servants Insurance and Pension Fund, which has been in operation since February, 1953. Currently, about 200,000 civil servants are members of the program. They contribute 10 per cent of their basic salary, which is then matched by the government. It is expected that government laborers and servants also will be included in this fund by 1960. The scheme's major advantage is that it affords government employees a minimum of security. At the same time, it places a great responsibility on the Fund's administrators (headed by the Ministry of the Treasury), for it often is the most readily available source of large sums of liquid capital for government enterprises.

By the end of 1958, its assets totaled about 42 million pounds,[73] and its annual receipts exceeded expenditures by over 9 million. More than 13 million pounds has been invested in industry, including 3.6 million in the government-sponsored KIMA fertilizer plant (which will not commence operations until 1960 at the earliest); a 1.5-million loan at 5.5 per cent interest was granted for the railroad housing settlement at Abu Zaabal; another loan at 5.5 per cent was extended to the military officers' cooperative for the purchase of private automobiles; and about 12 million pounds was provided for the School Buildings Foundation at 4, then 5.5 per cent.[74] In October, 1958, the Popular Housing and Development Company received a 500,000-pound loan, with the interest rate raised to 6 per cent. Earlier, the housing cooperatives had received 2.8 million pounds at 5.5 per cent. It is encouraging to see that the director can command commercial interest rates, even from government concerns; this is a privilege not always accorded the National Bank of Egypt. But with so much of its funds involved in nonproductive projects, the fact remains that the Fund's solvency depends upon the government. If, for example, the School (now the General) Buildings Foundation were unable to repay its principal and the government refused to intercede, the Civil Servants Insurance and Pension Fund would be in serious trouble.

Both this Fund and the Insurance and Savings Institution are extremely important contributions to Egypt's social welfare. It remains to be seen, however, whether they will be treated primarily as social instruments or as financing agencies for governmental projects. Significantly, in the final budgetary accounts for the government's 1955-56 fiscal year, the excess of revenue from the Civil Servants Fund was used to counterbalance deficits in the budgets of other semiautonomous organizations.[75]

Nasser's "New Society" Unrealized

During the past seven years, the Egyptian government has sought to establish a more equalitarian society, but many of these endeavors have been tempered by political and economic considerations. In public health, for example, medical needs call for a nationwide health campaign, for an Egyptian's life expectancy is about thirty years, and a majority of the country's citizens are plagued by bilharzia, trachoma, and other major diseases. But any substantial efforts to improve health facilities will, in turn, accentuate the population problem, for increased per capita productivity and extended life expectancy would, in a static economy, reduce job opportunities.

An effort has been made to introduce birth-control methods,[76] but only slight progress has been made. Although the Mufti of Egypt has pronounced that Islam has no theological objection to birth control,[77] it has proved most difficult to popularize this program in the villages. Another deterrent to a massive national health campaign is that many of the most effective medicines must be purchased with hard currencies. Under the existing economic situation, Egypt finds these items less essential than goods for economic development. In an effort to overcome this problem, plans are now being initiated to produce certain basic medicines locally. Between 1952 and 1956, the number of registered doctors increased from 4,470 to 6,420, while the number of beds in hospitals under the Ministry of Public Health increased at most by less than 10 per cent.[78] All of this suggests that the government is committed to providing a minimum of medical care for its citizens (most notably through the Combined Service Units), but that the program does not merit major emphasis. This is borne out by Ministry of Municipal and Rural Affairs figures. They show, for example, that, between 1952-57, the government spent more on constructing new roads in Cairo and Alexandria than it devoted to the building of new hospitals throughout the entire country.[79]

Religion has been a controversial subject in Egypt ever since the eighteen-seventies, when Mohamed Abdou and his followers advocated the modernization of Islam. An increasing number of Egyptians felt that Islam, as reflected in the teachings of Al Azhar, proved incompatible with Egypt's aspirations in the modern world. As one vocal critic of the "priesthood" expressed it, a nationalist government was more capable than a religious government in liberating the country because it could unite the entire nation on a nonsectarian basis.[80] During the first half of the twentieth century, Al Azhar lost much of its pre-eminence in Egyptian education, and there was an obvious trend toward national secularization, at least in the leading cities. The Moslem Brethren, under Hassan el Banna's vigorous leadership, sought to restore a theocratic government based on the Koran, but their efforts failed.

Islam remains an important factor in Egyptian life. Especially in the villages, the mosque is the center of the community. But the present government refuses to submit to religious dogma; instead, Islam must remain subservient to the nation-state. Religion can be a potent political force, as was demonstrated by the Moslem Brethren's challenge to the regime, and President Nasser is understandably wary of its latent power. Although the 1956 Constitution recognizes that "Islam is the religion of the State,"[81] Nasser has abolished religious courts, and Al Azhar, the academic center for the Moslem world, is financed and controlled by the Egyptian government. The government's position has been summarized by Ahmed Toiema's statement that "it is most dangerous for any country to have a religious government."[82] For political and social reasons, the government has attempted to place loyalty to the state over devotion to Islam in the Egyptian's hierarchy of values. This, in turn, has led to the development of a new secularism which challenges many of Egypt's traditional values.

It is the government's announced purpose to establish new values which are concomitant with the goals of the "new Egypt." One of the instruments of this campaign is the cooperative system which, according to a leading cooperative authority, is "primarily a social movement."[83] If one of the purposes of the cooperative system is to instill in its members a spirit of comradeship, however, the task is an ambitious one. The Minister of Social Affairs himself attaches a predominantly economic meaning to the co-operatives. "Co-ops," he stated, "are an economic means to enable a community to make best use of its resources."[84] He appears unawed by the "social mission" of cooperatives. In the opinion of Mohamed Korani el Badawi, head of the Cooperative Department at the National Union, Egypt's cooperative spirit is "bad," and he does not envisage a rapid transformation to a more satisfactory cooperative philosophy.[85]

Nasser described his vision of the "new society" at the General Cooperative Congress in June, 1956: "At present, our society is capitalistic . . . it is still based on exploitation. . . . In the exploitative state, if you want to raise your income from 50 to 100 pounds, you don't resort to work, but you resort to trickery. But in a cooperative society, if you want to raise your income, you resort to work and not to trickery. You raise the quality of your work and get more pay. This is the society I want for my country."[86] If this somewhat crude simile indeed describes Egypt's "new society," then it is difficult to imagine this social order springing full-blown from the cooperative movement. The experience of Egypt's cooperatives thus far suggests that, while they may result in substantial economic benefits for the country, they do not necessarily engender a greater social awareness among their members.

Yet, the "new society" envisaged by President Nasser has broader implications. He wishes to minimize, if not eliminate, the existing class differences and develop a functional citizenship dedicated to the creation of a strong Egyptian nation. Even in the early days of the Revolution, the Liberation Rally was commissioned "to teach the people how to make a democratic standard of living."[87] This attempt to level the class structure also was implicit in the efforts to create a new agricultural society at Liberation Province. But Nasser's ideal is marred by two harsh realities: the economic plans of the state require strong central control over the population, and the officers who participated in the Revolution have formed their own privileged class. The government is highly sensitive on the latter score, for the formation of a new elite would undermine the entire structure of the embryonic "new society." When Nasser and Hussein Shafei were questioned on this "new class," both quickly denied that such a group existed, at least in the sense that Djilas had described its counterpart in Communist society.[88]

Hussein Shafei, Minister of Social Affairs, took considerable pains to explain his viewpoint: "It is difficult to say that there is a new class of officers who took any advantages, but you may put it that way. After the abolition of the old regime, there were new positions, posts, responsibilities; when the Revolution started, it had no party. In the initial stage, until you find those in whom you can put your faith, the most difficult problem which faces a leader of a *coup d'état* is how to make a limit between the army and the leadership of the country. The army should be an instrument to serve the country and defend it, and I think that no country which has passed such a situation could have put the army so quickly in its place. . . . Of course a lot of—some of— the key positions in which you want a real success were taken by some of the army officers and, of course, those who have been making use of the different positions of the old time can always feel that they have lost something."[89] He is correct in stating that the military has distinguished itself in the manner in which it assumed the responsibilities of government; and some of the leading RCC members, including the President, Hussein Shafei, Kamal el din Hussein, and Abdel Latif Boghdadi, have continued to display high personal integrity and devotion to their country. But it is impossible to blink the fact that the military, even after becoming civilians, expect and often receive special treatment.

Social development cannot be imposed upon a country; instead, it comes as a by-product of political and economic growth. Definite progress has been made since the Revolution in providing for the social welfare of the Egyptian people, but the capabilities of the Ministry of Education and of the Ministry of Social Affairs are limited. Although current plans for the next five years place heavy emphasis on developing cooperatives and dealing with labor's problems, Hussein Shafei acknowledges that,

"Egypt must restrain social spending until the economy improves."[90] There is no quick or easy solution for Egypt's social problems for, as Gamal Abdel Nasser recognizes, "Building factories is easy, building hospitals and schools is possible, but building a nation of men is a hard and difficult task."[91]

VI

Economics and Industrialization

Economic Crisis

Egypt's economy never has been heavily dependent on industry. During the reign of Mohamed Ali, vigorous efforts were made to create industries in support of a substantial military establishment, but a sharp retrenchment in Egypt's armed forces and a British-imposed reduction of the high protective tariffs abruptly ended the country's industrialization plans. Later, under Khedive Ismail, another and much less ambitious attempt was made to establish extensive local industries, but this experiment, too, proved prohibitively expensive. In both cases, the difficulties encountered were similar to those found in other agricultural economies: a large majority of the population, living at a bare subsistence level, provided a negligible market for industrial products; it was difficult to assemble a reliable force of skilled laborers; and an irregular power supply, together with primitive conditions, often resulted in unsatisfactory finished products requiring excessive tariff protection which the government was not in a position to provide. In addition, Egypt was handicapped by her lack of raw materials. Except for cotton and a few minerals, Egypt had little upon which to construct an industrial complex.

In the twenties, with the establishment of the first truly Egyptian bank, further plans for industrial development were initiated. Bank Misr used its resources to establish the "Misr Group," an impressive array of new industrial enterprises; but inadequate technical surveys, combined with the many difficulties of operating industries in Egypt, led to a disproportionate number of failures.[1] Indeed, after a run on Bank Misr in 1940, only government intervention saved the "Misr Group" from dismemberment. Yet, the activities of the bank, despite its failures, were significant, for, with the exception of foreign-controlled concerns, there was little other Egyptian industry.

Tightly controlled family concerns and the absence of investment houses deterred industrial development. Moreover, even when enterprising individuals submitted sound technical surveys for industrial projects, banks were extremely reluctant to grant the necessary funds. The government, recognizing that potential enterprises were deterred by lack of financing, provided Bank Misr with nominal industrial credits. Money alone, however, was not the answer. In 1932, for example, of 193 applications at that bank for industrial loans, 185 were rejected for lack of adequate collateral.[2] And in the prewar period, a number of new Egyptian companies, after obtaining the financing requested, failed when original market research or construction estimates proved in error.[3]

With World War II came a boom in Egyptian industry, for British and American troops were a ready market for almost everything local industries could produce. At the same time, many wealthy Egyptians, in the face of restricted cotton exports and a sharp decline in general agricultural profits, sought to invest in industry. This investment flow was accompanied by the expansion of joint-stock companies, which assured better protection to individual investors. During the war years, "new capital issues running into millions of pounds were oversubscribed within a short time of opening the subscription lists."[4]

In the postwar period, however, protective tariffs and "progressive monopolization" were insufficient to insure continued high profits.[5] Several major industries, notably those associated with Bank Misr and others under the control of Ahmed Abboud, flourished during this period. Their effectiveness was due to superior management and, often, to substantial assistance from the government—Abboud's sugar company, for example, enjoyed a complete monopoly over sugar production. However, after the war, scores of less efficient factories closed down, and agricultural investments rose once more. By 1952, industry (including foreign concerns) contributed only 8 per cent of a national income estimated at over 800 million pounds.*

The Egyptian government, although it maintained high tariffs in an effort to protect the country's inefficient industrial firms, did little in the way of actively stimulating industry during these postwar years.[6] True, an industrial bank was created, with 51 per cent of its assets government-owned, but the credit policy of this bank proved only slightly less conservative than that of other Cairo banks. A government-owned oil refinery was expanded at Suez, but this was due, in part, to laws which discriminated against foreign investments. In 1947, a companies law required that 51 per cent of all new joint-stock companies be owned by Egyptians; this, naturally, discouraged potential foreign investors. The following year, a mining law made operations prohibitive for several foreign oil firms which already were prospecting in Egypt's deserts. Some companies withdrew completely, while others, including Socony-Vacuum, sharply reduced their capital outlays.[7] By and large, the government proved woefully ineffective in spurring industrial growth. Although plans for a hydro-electric plant at Aswan were drafted in 1947 and tenders subsequently requested, the results were negligible. A five-year development program was announced in 1947, but less than half the budgeted funds were ever spent.

It seemed apparent that, at least over the short run, local industry could give but a slight fillip to the nation's economy. Egypt continued to rely heavily upon agriculture; raw cotton alone regularly accounted for at least 80 per cent of the country's total exports. In many respects, Egypt's economy was at the mercy of international cotton markets. If world demand was high, then these premium prices would be reflected by an expanded money supply, more cash in the villages, and a greater capacity for imports; conversely, a slack demand and low prices generally had a marked deflationary impact. The Korean War boom of 1950-51 in raw materials absorbed that year's cotton crop; prices were exceptionally high and exports spiralled. Much

---

* While the official exchange rate is £E1 = $2.872, the Egyptian pound regularly is discounted 30 to 40 per cent on the open market.

of the profits, however, went toward the purchase of luxury items, as the government's refusal to impose restrictions resulted in record imports and substantial trade deficits. Moreover, private manipulation of the Alexandria Futures Market kept the price of long-staple cotton artificially inflated, so that Egyptian cotton was being priced out of much of the world market.[8]

While the local cotton market was being cornered, world cotton consumption fell off sharply; from early 1952, heavy inventory accumulations resulted in a further decline in demand.[9] Egypt, which experienced large balance of payments deficits even while she received record cotton revenues, suddenly was faced with an economic crisis of the first magnitude. At the end of the first seven months of the 1951-52 cotton season, only one-third of the total supply of cotton had been sold—and the price was falling fast. The government offered to purchase all end-of-season cotton at generous support prices, but this did not alleviate the national problem. An important source of revenue was lost when the Cabinet abolished the government tax on the year's cotton exports. The government, already hard pressed to meet current expenses, also was forced to take delivery of July-August cotton contracts in May* to prevent a major collapse in the country's cotton trade.[10]

The failure of the cotton market had disastrous effects on Egypt's economy. Previous cotton profits had been expended on excessive imports or, only too often, on inflating land values and in the construction of expensive villas and apartment houses. Little preparation had been made during the boom for the eventual readjustment of cotton prices. Suddenly, the government found its sources of revenue drying up. Emergency measures were adopted: all ministries were ordered to curtail general expenditures by 35 per cent. But with wages, salaries, and cost-of-living increments taking up nearly half of the national budget, the ministries found it impossible to comply with this order. Between April and June, 1952, the government spent twice as much as it took in. The 1951-52 budget deficit† brought the General Re-

---

* Egypt's cotton season runs from September 1 through August 31.

† The Egyptian government's financial year runs from July 1 through June 30.

serve Fund from 78.5 million pounds (of which 41.7 million
was committed to the International Bank for Reconstruction and
Development, the International Monetary Fund, and domestic
government obligations) in July, 1951[11] down to 38.4 million
pounds in June, 1952.[12] From January to July, 1952, imports
exceeded exports by 50.6 million pounds.[13]

Economic Stabilization by the Military

The country's precarious economic condition loomed large in
the July military takeover: some businessmen accepted the military coup because of their disgust at the inadequacy of previous
civilian governments. The major economic objectives of the new
regime were obvious and urgent: the economy must be stabilized;
confidence must be restored in the cotton market; and the deficits
in the budget and in the balance of payments had to be eliminated. These pressing issues took precedence over any ambitious
plans for future development. Already, during the first six
months of 1952, Egypt's foreign exchange holdings (including
gold) had fallen by 26.6 million pounds (from 330.4 to 303.8
million),[14] and the country had to cope with a record cotton
crop in addition to a sizable carry over from the previous season.
Moreover, with reduced revenues expected for the fiscal year
1952-53, budgetary expenditures also had to be curbed. Within
four months, a number of emergency measures were enacted. The
revised 1952-53 budget anticipated expenditures of 206 million
pounds, 10 per cent under those for the previous year; in October, import licenses were imposed on all goods not covered by
specific trade agreements. On November 23, 1952, the government closed the Alexandria Futures Market, offering to buy
available cotton at nominal support prices.

These were bold steps, taken as they were in a climate of
political unrest. At first, the results were not encouraging. The
government authorized a 50-million-pound Treasury Bill issue
for the purchase of cotton, as the world price dipped substantially
below the support level. When revenues fell below expectations,
further restrictions were imposed, among them a freeze on government wage increases. All these measures were taken to repair

the damage done by previous governments. Gamal Abdel Nasser properly observed: "We have inherited a heavy legacy: a ruined treasury, an unbalanced budget, and a corrupt government."[15]

The task of checking Egypt's economic deterioration was imperative; and the government, through resolute action, aided by the deflation which accompanied the break in cotton prices, rapidly approached this goal. More difficult, however, was a program of long-range economic development for, in the opinion of Dr. Abdel Galeel el Emary, then Minister of Finance, it would take ten years to raise Egypt's standard of living.[16] Several cautious attempts were made to lay the groundwork for development. In October, 1952, the Permanent Council for the Development of National Production was created; by January, 1953, its members included a number of civilian experts and some qualified army technicians. The National Production Council (NPC) was charged with drafting a three-year national development program within a year, with emphasis on land reclamation and irrigation projects.

Subsequently, a new mining law sought to make oil prospecting more attractive for foreign concerns by giving equal rights to Egyptian and foreign companies and decreeing liberal conditions for the repatriation of foreign capital invested in Egypt. Other laws exempted important new industries from taxes on commercial and industrial profits for seven years, and undistributed company profits earmarked for reinvestment received a 50 per cent tax exemption. In addition, the government, to encourage investment in local industry, agreed to accept securities in payment of up to half of estate taxes.[17] These measures, while they failed to produce immediate results, were an indication of the government's determination to stimulate industrial development.

Although the 1952-53 budget final accounts showed a 10-million-pound deficit, this was no mean accomplishment under the circumstances. For 1953-54, the government still was unwilling to impose new taxes, as the ordinary budget was balanced at a low 197.5 million pounds. Observers noted with satisfaction that, under a military regime, the Ministry of War estimates remained the same. Granted, some Ministry of Education expenses were shifted to the autonomous budget of the School

Buildings Foundation, and certain projects of the Ministry of Public Works were transferred from the ordinary budget; nevertheless, the government's achievement was notable. Now that the economy had passed its most critical period, the government also saw fit to initiate an extraordinary development budget, to be financed by loans and special resources. For 1953-54, 25.4 million pounds was allocated, but this included almost 10 million already committed from the General Reserve Fund for the Aswan hydro-electric plant and the North Cairo electric station.[18] According to the broad outlines of the National Production Council plan, much of the future development budgets would be used to improve agriculture and communications.

A deflationary trend continued throughout 1953 and into 1954. Revenues from government sales of cotton stocks permitted the repayment of some Treasury Bills, yet a slight balance of payments deficit remained; the potentially inflationary development budget expenditures materialized most slowly. Moreover, while the quantity of cotton exports was 25 per cent above that recorded in the 1951-52 season, depressed prices meant that some of the crop still was being purchased at the government's support price. The government, in order to dispose of its surplus, forced farmers to reduce their cotton acreage in favor of wheat. Thus it was able, in 1954, almost to eliminate expenditures for wheat imports whose average, in previous years, had exceeded 20 million pounds. By the end of the 1953-54 fiscal year, Nasser had good reason to feel pleased when he announced: "We have succeeded in balancing our budget in 1953. . . . In 1954, we have been able to draw up a constructive and progressive budget in which services and production are well balanced."[19]

A surplus in the ordinary budget permitted an addition to the General Reserve Fund, and foreign exchange holdings, which had decreased by about 27 million pounds in 1952-53, fell only 2.6 million in 1953-54. Moreover, the Egyptian national debt had not increased, cotton carry over had been reduced to manageable proportions, and a deflationary fiscal policy had proved successful. Now Nasser felt ready to go beyond the modest development program already undertaken. In his opinion, the two major projects of the previous year had been Agrarian Reform and the planning of the mammoth High Dam.[20] Land reform alone, however, could not be expected to produce dramatic improvements in Egypt's economy, and the High Dam, at best, was a distant goal.

In early 1954, a contract for an iron and steel factory was signed with a West German firm; a large-scale expansion program was underway at the government petroleum refinery; and plans for a fertilizer plant at Aswan were being formulated. The 1954-55 budgets made it obvious that economic development had become a vital political issue—that, indeed, it was becoming symbolic of the military regime. The ordinary budget was still a modest 227 million pounds, with 14.3- of the 30.4-million increase being charged to the Ministry of War. But many development programs which previously would have been included in the ordinary budget were now placed under the National Production Council's development budget (41.2 million pounds, as compared with 25.4 million for the previous year) or under the new Public Welfare Services budget of 14,582,000 pounds. In two years, total appropriations for "new works" and development had increased from 34,143,000 pounds to 81.7 million, most of which was to be financed by public loans and by funds confiscated from the Mohamed Ali family.

The government took determined steps to minimize the inflationary impact of this ambitious program. The regime's cautiousness was reflected in the actions of the National Production Council. Its members discerned the pitfalls of hasty economic development and displayed admirable restraint in their development schemes. The Council had no illusions regarding the country's ability to finance a massive development program. According to an NPC study, Egypt's gross rate of capital formation in 1953 was only 8 per cent of the national income. Of the 68.9-million gross total, public and private building accounted for 40.6 millions.[21] Accepting these figures as indicative of Egypt's general magnitude of gross capital formation, the National Bank of Egypt calculated net capital formation at 46 million pounds.[22] Since this rate was considered to be insufficient to maintain the country's existing minimal standard of living, the Council sought first to halt Egypt's economic deterioration before undertaking more ambitious plans for industrial expansion. Soon after the agreement with the British for the evacuation of the Suez Canal Zone was signed, the United States agreed to contribute 40 million dollars in goods towards the various NPC projects. Thus the Council's program reached major proportions.

Rising Government Expenditures

By the end of 1954, the government felt ready to resort to the public market for funds. In December, National Production Loans were floated for 25 million pounds; although the National Bank was forced to absorb 15 per cent of the issue, the results were considered satisfactory.[23] While it became necessary, in the fall of 1954, to lower the required reserve ratio for commercial banks from 15 to 12.5 per cent to permit financing of the cotton crop and subscription of the new bonds, no crisis was indicated. Even when the deflationary trend ended by late 1954, the government did not expand its Treasury Bill holdings. Indeed, throughout this period, a diligent effort was made to further reduce outstanding Treasury Bills.

Yet, progress was not smooth. Despite the warning to local businessmen implicit in the sequestration of Ahmed Abboud's twelve-million-pound sugar company, the members of Egypt's commercial community were not anxious to cooperate with the government, and the slow pace of agricultural and industrial development discouraged the military junta. Perhaps this was the reason why many of the economic principles adhered to through 1954 were compromised by late 1955. Nasser's confidant, Mohamed Hassanein Heikal, explained it another way: internal development took a back seat to "external needs" after the signing of the Baghdad Pact and after the Israeli attack on Gaza on February 28, 1955.[24] In all probability, both motives figured strongly. There was no doubt that the junta was impatient with the slow progress which civilian economists claimed was necessary for Egypt's sound economic development. At the same time, Egypt's new international aspirations demanded an increased military establishment which could be met only through heavy reliance on deficit financing.

Another decline in the Western textile market in the middle

of the 1954-55 season served further to compound the Egyptian government's financial difficulties. Cotton exports were one-third less than the preceding year, with prices substantially under the Egyptian Cotton Commission's support prices. This drop in trade not only reduced the government's revenue, but also necessitated the encouragement of sales to soft currency areas; the government, toward this end, guaranteed a 10-million-pound credit for Communist bloc countries at the National Bank.[25] The slow movement of cotton also tightened the local money market, making it difficult for the Ministry of Finance to cover its growing obligations. Thus, in May, 1955, Dr. Abdel Moneim Kaissuny, the Minister of Finance, was authorized to unify all Treasury Bills within a ceiling of 150 million pounds (they were then at 56 million), with another 50 million permitted upon approval from the Council of Ministers. In the wake of devaluation rumors, this new move was interpreted as a "most inflationary process,"[26] and local stock market prices rose considerably.

The preliminary 1955-56 budgets served further to suggest an impending inflationary trend. Of course, a moderate inflationary rise often is desirable, especially in a rapidly expanding, underdeveloped economy, but the government's bold fiscal policies worried many of Egypt's most competent economists. While the ordinary budget again showed only a modest increase, the development budgets, which were dependent upon "special resources," totalled 77 million pounds—and this amount did not include the various autonomous budgets for school buildings and similar undertakings which also required government funds. According to Dr. Kaissuny "the government finds it [production loans] better than resorting to increased taxation, since it considers [that] any increased taxation above present levels might hinder investment and economic expansion."[27] This principle was commendable, but it left unanswered the question as to how the more than 80 million pounds required during the 1955-56 fiscal year was to be raised. Apparently, the government decided to rely heavily upon Treasury Bills.

Prices were still depressed at the start of the 1955-56 cotton season. The decision was made, therefore, to reopen the Alexandria Futures Market, and export duties were cut by over half.

But the government quickly realized that it could not afford this loss in revenue, and an additional ad valorem tax of 7 per cent was imposed on almost all imports. With development programs demanding large amounts of hard currencies, the government was anxious to utilize its blocked sterling balances. After considerable negotiation, it was agreed that 20 million pounds sterling would be released annually by the British (double the previous amount) in return for increased Egyptian purchases from the sterling area.

By the end of 1955 (following the government's agreement to purchase over 200 million dollars worth[28] of weapons from the Soviets), marked changes were evident in Egypt's economy. Foreign exchange holdings, which actually had increased during 1954, had now fallen by 34.3 million pounds; debits in foreign clearing accounts had increased by 12 million; government deposits in banks declined by about 6 million; and Treasury Bills assumed a greater importance in the expanding money supply.

As the government incurred heavier expenses and economic projects demanded more funds, deficit financing became an integral part of government policy. Another loan of 25 million pounds was successfully floated on the public market (with banks and companies the main purchasers), but this failed to cover current expenses. During the first seven months of 1956, Egypt's national debt rose by almost a third—from 218.6 to 280.3 million pounds. Although budgetary revenue was substantially higher than originally estimated, so, too, were expenditures: the Ministry of War, according to the 1955-56 final accounts, spent 85.4 million pounds—or 30.4 million above its initial budget of 55 million. Moreover, despite a good cotton season, foreign-exchange holdings fell another 27 million pounds through July, 1956.

Nor was any fiscal retrenchment apparent in the 1956-57 budget. The ordinary budget was increased significantly (from 238.3 to 280.5 million pounds), with the Ministry of War showing an actual budgetary increase of 22 million pounds (some observers believed that further expenses were concealed elsewhere). Certain projects formerly carried in the budget of the then defunct Permanent Council for Public Welfare Services were included under their respective ministries. Significantly, the ordinary and development budgets of 1956-57 totalled 326.3 million pounds, as compared with 315.3 million for the preceding year, while the amount allocated to development and "new works" declined by 25.3 million. A new national defense tax and an amended stamp tax produced additional revenue, but it seemed most unlikely that the ordinary budget actually would balance. Moreover, with the 1955-56 budgetary deficit, the General Reserve Fund had been further reduced to 12.2 million pounds.[29]

It was at this juncture that the Suez Canal Company was nationalized. The resulting international crisis upset Egypt's internal economic plans: all foreign-exchange assets in England and France were frozen, and, after the United States blocked Egyptian government holdings in America, Egypt's development program slowed down appreciably. As Western economic pressure tightened, Egypt struggled to consolidate her economic position. Contrary to the hopes of the blockading powers, Egypt's situation was not critical. The country had few imperative requirements from abroad, the most important being petroleum, fertilizers and wheat. After some difficulty, soft-currency supplies were provided by such countries as the Soviet Union and Rumania, and foreign exchange was advanced by several "friendly countries": Communist China provided 5 million dollars worth of Swiss francs, Saudi Arabia made 25 million dollars available, and other nations gave similar emergency assistance. In addition, two 15-million-dollar loans were obtained from the International Monetary Fund.

At least over the short run, Egypt suffered no critical shortage of hard currency for essential items. By September, however, Egypt found it necessary to examine all foreign tenders for the expressed purpose of "expanding trade relations with friendly countries."[30] In a way, Egypt benefited from this situation. The regime long had wanted to impose drastic restrictions on luxury imports, and the currency shortage provided an excellent opportunity to enforce a shift to locally produced goods.

The Suez crisis imposed a more serious strain on the local economy. The added expense of mobilization forced the government quickly to increase the Treasury Bill issue; by the end of the year, the Bills, almost entirely taken by the National Bank, totalled 146 million pounds—a rise of 40 million in five months—and note circulation was increased even more rapidly. The expanded money supply reflected, in part, the season's excellent cotton prices; to a greater extent, however, it reflected the government's serious monetary problem. Especially after the Anglo-French-Israeli military attack, private loans and advances increased appreciably. Much of this increase, however, was a result of the government's inflationary policy, for the National Bank was obliged to make substantially higher advances to the private sector. Even greater damage would have been done to the economy had the government not acted with dispatch. At the time of the military attack, the stock market, whose prices had fallen heavily since July, was ordered to impose minimum prices. Steps were taken, also, to protect the cotton trade. Strict local price controls, a moratorium on debts, and a makeshift system of rationing helped to cushion the impact of the crisis.

By early 1957, several facts had become clear. First, the existing inflationary condition could be simply a transitory phenomenon, for it was still possible for the government to revert to deflationary policies. More difficult to reverse, however, was the shift in the pattern of trade. Already the Communist bloc was receiving over 30 per cent of Egypt's exports. Offers by these nations to supply imports for soft currencies, coupled with Egypt's obligation to make repayment for armaments already received, greatly enhanced the Soviet bloc's politico-economic position in Egypt.

Planning for Development

The government used the military attack on Suez as an excuse to tighten its grip on the entire economy. Foreign banks and insurance companies long had held a dominant position in Egypt's economy; and many of the leading Cairo industrial and commercial firms were managed by foreigners. On January 15, 1957, a series of "Egyptianization" laws were decreed. All British and French banks, which had been "at war" with Egypt,[31] were "Egyptianized" immediately, and plans were hastily drafted for the purchase of these institutions. Other foreign banks which, according to the Chairman of Bank Misr, "aimed at dominating the country's economy and plotted to impair its trade interests," [32] were given up to five years to become Egyptian joint-stock companies under Egyptian management. The same ultimatum was given to insurance companies.

These moves, while they were symptomatic of Egypt's new and strident nationalism, also were prompted by economic realities. Obviously, it would be far more difficult for the Egyptian government to exact the "cooperation" of foreign-controlled concerns. As an official at the Ministry of Economy and Commerce expressed it, " 'Egyptianization' of banks—of savings—is very essential for over-all planning." [33] The 1957-58 official budget report stated that "Egyptianization" permitted the investment of the people's savings for the benefit of the national interest. [34]

But the sudden seizure of British and French holdings posed new problems: the government soon realized that the transfer of foreign concerns to Egyptian ownership and management was more easily decreed than done. The government already was becoming a large-scale owner of capital, and the official machinery was ill-prepared to cope with these new responsibilities. Abdel Latif Boghdadi some time previously had suggested the establishment of an economic development organization, [35] and this idea was now adopted, albeit in modified form. With the creation of the Economic Development Organization, the government formally divested itself of its stock holdings. Beginning in January, 1957, the Economic Organization, financed with government funds and guarantees, was responsible for the implementation of various commercial and industrial schemes. The Organization, by virtue of its control over many of Cairo's leading banks and insurance companies, gained a dominant position over Egypt's business community. To give the government further control over the country's banking system, a new banking and credit law strengthened the Ministry of Finance's power over the National Bank of Egypt and gave the National Bank more authority as a central bank.

These measures for economic centralization, however, were

enacted in the continued absence of an economic plan for the country. The Permanent Council for Public Welfare Services, with its ambitious ten-year program, had been denied a budget in 1956; and the National Production Council still was operating primarily on an *ad hoc* basis. By late 1956, it was decided that the NPC was overburdened by its responsibility to draft and execute projects. The regime felt, also, that the Economic Organization was equipped to cope with recurring financial problems. Thus, in January, 1957, the National Production Council was dissolved and its unallocated funds were deposited with the Economic Organization, which was headed by a former RCC member, Hassan Ibrahim. Drawing upon the staff of the two dissolved councils, a new committee was created: the National Planning Commission, charged with drafting a comprehensive plan for Egypt's economic and social development. This plan, in turn, was to be submitted to a Higher Planning Board presided over by President Nasser.[36]

Yet, these organizational changes notwithstanding, the economy continued to be run on a basis of constant improvisation. While a National Planning Commission staff was gathered in the isolation of Abdine Palace, there were still not even the bare outlines of a national economic program. Although Boghdadi, as Minister of Planning, declared in early 1957, that a plan was being drawn up to invest 1.8 billion pounds over the next ten years (thus raising national income by 65 per cent),[37] it was apparent that no detailed plan existed. Indeed, his high estimate of future investments prompted many observers to question the credibility of the proposed plan.

In the race among government bodies to produce a plan, the newly created Ministry of Industry took an early lead. Since one of the primary aims of the Revolution was to create a "new, industrial Egypt," this Ministry, under the energetic direction of a Harvard Ph.D., Aziz Sidky,[38] had a psychological advantage. Furthermore, a number of industrial surveys already had been conducted, including a quarter-million-dollar study by the Arthur D. Little Company of Boston. The findings of these surveys, however, were too conservative for Dr. Sidky, who pictured his Ministry as the linchpin of Egypt's economic development. Instead, Sidky proposed to embark on an expansive program of industrialization which would far surpass relative growth in the agricultural sector. A responsible economist with the National Planning Commission estimated that "in the immediate future—say the next eight to ten years—a higher standard of living for Egypt seems somewhat utopian."[39] Sidky, however, sought a dramatic breakthrough.

The Ministry of Industry's plan was ambitious: "We are attempting to narrow the gap between our standard of living and that of economically advanced countries at a time when the latter is not static but is continuously increasing."[40] The expressed objective was to double per capita income during the next twenty years;[41] the five-year aim was to increase the industrial sector of national income by 84 million pounds to 184 million.[42] All these calculations assumed, as a matter of course, that other sectors of the economy would experience an annual 2 per cent increase, at constant costs, over the same period. Assuming that the capital coefficient should be about 3:1, the Ministry calculated that 255 million pounds in new investments would be required over the next five years.[43] Manufacturing industries alone were expected to need 181.2 million pounds, while mining, petroleum, and training programs were to absorb the remaining funds.[44]

By the same sort of calculations which have brought grief to Indian planners, it was estimated that, by the end of the five-year plan's third stage, there would be an annual "net saving" of 54.5 million pounds in foreign currency. Leaning on an imprecise interpretation of the "multiplier" theory and a rigid adherence to a formula of national income increment, these planners (among them a ranking ministry official who had been considered incompetent in his position at the National Bank of Egypt's Research Department) made an optimistic projection of jobs which would be provided by their scheme. Assuming that 120,000 workers would obtain direct employment, they estimated, on the basis of a 3:1 ratio of secondary and tertiary occupations, that another 360,000 workers would be employed; for the sake of simplicity, they referred to "500,000 newly employed" through industry within five years.[45]

In a country as hard-pressed to finance its current expenditures as Egypt, it was surprising that the problems of financing were treated in so cavalier a manner. According to the plan "there is no lack of capital for investment."[46] The problem of foreign currency was dismissed by the comment that, by the sixth year, savings in imports would amount to 63,787,500 pounds, while potential exports would increase by 21,410,000.[47] It was further observed that the increase in national income, by the sixth year, would equal the annual sum required for investment.[48] When confronted, during an interview, with the possible fallacies of such reasoning, Dr. Sidky replied candidly: "Financing is not my field, I don't understand it. Go see Dr. Kaissuny."*

This cursory treatment of financing caused considerable concern among Egypt's economists, who did not agree with the Ministry of Industry's optimistic projections. The former Director-General of Foreign Exchange Control, Hassan Abbas Zaki, openly questioned the plan before the National Assembly. In his opinion, the plan's foreign-currency requirements might be more than the country could afford, and he suggested that part of Egypt's gold reserve (held untouched on Nasser's personal order) might be sold to meet the new foreign-exchange demands.[49] Zaki also referred to the scarcity of local savings.

Another noted Egyptian economist, Dr. Nikolai Koestner, backed by twenty years of experience in Eastern European countries and sixteen years as Director of the National Bank's Research Department, was more outspoken. In the National Bank's quarterly *Economic Bulletin* (which must be approved by the Bank's subgovernor) he wrote: "[The plan requires] an expenditure of about 44 million pounds on the average per year, or approximately an amount which may come very close to the total savings of the nation of which heavy sums are needed for communications, agricultural development, including reclamation work and—of course—building. In this sense, the plan is unreal and can only be implemented if the general plan . . . shows the sources of financing. . . . It is a common

---

* Kaissuny was then Minister of Economy and Commerce.

failure of many a planner that he makes the plan of development and leaves to somebody else to make the plan of financing and this somebody leaves to a third party the task of finding the money."[50] Koestner also took issue with the plan's heavy reliance on the "multiplier" theory: "We regret to say that we do not share the optimism of the plan about the automatic multiplier effect. . . . The multiplier, if it exists, is a phenomenon of the free market economy and may be very disappointing in other conditions."[51] This opinion was shared by the Director of Research in the Ministry of Economy and Commerce.[52]

Another shortcoming of the plan was its failure adequately to investigate potential markets for the expected deluge of industrial goods. Dr. Sidky himself had written in his doctoral dissertation: "The pace of industrialization in any country is dependent on the market. It is clear that at this stage [in Egypt] there is very little possibility of production for export, except in a few types of industry, and the purchasing power of the local market is not great."[53] The Arthur D. Little studies emphasized the importance of cost and market analyses *before plants were built*,[54] and the National Production Council observed that "the study of local demand is of paramount importance for the success of development schemes."[55] Dr. Sidky's ministry, however, chose not to heed this advice. While most factories were working a single shift (and even then some were operating at substantially below full productive capacity),[56] the Ministry of Industry seemed confident that the necessary new markets would materialize.

In view of Egypt's low per capita income and the plan's assumption of minimal progress in all but the industrial sector, it would seem evident that much of the new purchasing power would have to come as a direct result of the plan. Accepting the questionable thesis that the plan would "create" about 500,000 new jobs, a substantial increase in the ability to purchase industrial products is unlikely. Even if all these workers came from outside the existing industrial sector (which is not the case), the marketing problem would not be solved. Most of the workers would receive about 35 dollars monthly; after deduction of minimum requirements—including food, housing, transportation, and social security—perhaps 5 or 10 dollars would remain. And if the industrial sector's expansion is proportionally greater than that of agriculture, some of the workers' wages would go toward the purchase of costlier food. The adoption of labor-saving devices by these new industries (found so profitable in the textile industry)[57] would make the marketing problem even more acute.

Few Egyptians had the courage publicly to criticize this plan, which quickly became intimately associated with the regime's political aspirations. But, outside the Ministry of Industry, no Egyptian economist with whom this writer discussed the plan in detail thought that it could succeed if implemented as originally published. Dr. Sidky had contemptuously dismissed the Little study: "It was not a plan [it was never meant to be], but just a series of projects."[58] This description also fitted his own industrial "five-year plan." The "plan" was little more than a catalogue of projects; the means of financing or marketing were not adequately explored. But because Egypt desperately needed a plan for industrialization, and since no other was available, the Ministry of Industry's program was accepted by default. The great danger, however, was that it would, indeed, be accepted as a workable scheme. And in 1957, Gamal Abdel Nasser seemed to believe in its success.[59]

During 1957, Egypt was beset by a foreign-exchange shortage. With sterling balances frozen indefinitely and trade with the Communist bloc often conducted on a barter basis, nearly all hard currency received from the recently reopened Suez Canal was used to defray the cost of western imports. Egypt was anxious to launch her mammoth industrialization program, but it was difficult to see how the foreign exchange could be made available. In the light of the existing international political situation, it seemed most unlikely that western countries would provide the necessary credits. Nasser, therefore, decided to seek Soviet help for the industrial five-year plan. Previously, Egypt had rejected East Germany's offer to participate in local development schemes, "because Eastern bloc offers, deliberately computed at much cheaper prices, involve the risk of the dissemination of prejudicial ideologies."[60] Similarly, Dr. Sidky had recognized in his statement of the five-year plan that "dependence on foreign loans and aids are both limited in extent and risky."[61] These reservations, however, were overridden. General Abdel Hakim Amer, Minister of War, conducted the original negotiations in Moscow. According to Egyptians, the Russians wished to limit their credit offer to 500 million rubles (125 million dollars at the artificial exchange rate of four to one), but Nasser demanded 700 million rubles.[62] It was further claimed that the Russians wished to extend these credits over five years, while Amer insisted on a four-year period.[63] The final agreement, on January 29, 1958, accorded with Egypt's wishes.

The terms of the agreement made it apparent that the Soviets wished to impose a heavy burden upon Egypt's economy. The Russians realized the shortcomings of Dr. Sidky's plan, and it was to their political advantage that Egypt become overextended economically. Thus, they sought to provide Egypt with credits far in excess of the country's absorptive capacity. If the Russians were actually concerned with Egypt's development, they would have acceded to Egypt's request that the credits be extended to include purchases from Eastern Europe; instead, the U.S.S.R. refused, explaining that, although it would try to "cooperate," it did not like the idea of "taking business away from Eastern European countries."[64] This meant, in fact, that Egypt had to finance her purchases from other Communist countries independently. Moreover, some extraordinary conditions were attached to the agreement by a country which, ostensibly, wished to help Egypt and limit the amount of the total credits. For example, the credit extended by the Soviet Union did not cover the expenses of Soviet technicians in Egypt, technical assistance, Egyptians being trained in the Soviet Union, or the costs of ocean freight, insurance, most spare parts, and raw materials; payment for these had to be made to a "collector account" at the National Bank of Egypt.[65] And payment for these items was not governed by the credit terms of twelve years for repayment, with a 2.5 per cent annual interest. While Egypt appeared grateful to receive Soviet credits, some Egyptians recognized the strong political overtones in Russia's economic gambit.

Financing Internal Development

Internal financing of Egypt's development schemes also presented a problem of the first magnitude. Taking capital formation as a point of departure (calculated at market prices, which included customs duties, unlike earlier figures for 1953 and 1954), one authority estimates gross capital formation at 105.8 million pounds for 1954, 128.5 million for 1955, and 128.6 million for 1956.[66] These figures seem compatible with information available at the National Bank and the Ministry of the Treasury. After deducting the balance of payments deficit, this would suggest that local savings contributed 97.6 million pounds to capital formation in 1956. But when the National Production Loans and other claims on past savings are considered, it is evident that current savings provided far less than this sum. Moreover, if an analysis by Dr. Kaissuny is correct, even with investments far in excess of present savings, it would be difficult to raise the country's standard of living.

Kaissuny told a group in 1957 that the population increase "necessitates the diversion of nearly 80 million pounds annually into new investments just to keep the same level in our standard of living. This is in addition to another 50 million pounds or so required to meet the growing consumption and maintain the existing productive capacity. This means that the minimum annual level of new investments must not be less than 130 million pounds in addition to any desired investments in projects which would lead to an increase in our standard of living."[67] Gamal Abdel Nasser has publicly declared that Egypt's annual savings are 130 million pounds[68] (a level which most probably could support the country's present plans). However, one of his leading economic advisers who wishes to remain anonymous places the figure at no more than 90 million pounds; even this figure is considered too high by some government economists. With the government already contributing well over half of total capital formation,[69] it seems obvious that increased capital expenditures may be financed only through sustained deficit financing or further taxation.

After the Revolution, the government was faced with a savings dilemma, for Agrarian Reform and taxation relief, which favored the poor, also tended to reduce savings. So that small savings could be accumulated, government and workers' insurance and pension funds were established, the Postal Savings Bank was made more attractive to potential depositors, and bank interest rates on savings were increased. These measures, however, have not stimulated the accumulation of savings needed to meet the government's monetary requirements. At maximum, net capital formation for 1958, calculated at the optimum, should total between 90 and 100 million pounds. Assuming a capital coefficient of 3:1, and after adjusting for the rise in population, the net per capita increase in national income for 1958 would be no more than 1 dollar. And, at this writing, there are numerous indications that this optimum has not been attained.

Already the public market has been burdened by bond issues; the government-managed Postal Savings Fund alone subscribed to over 25 per cent of a November, 1958, National Loan, the first such public subscription in over two and one-half years. Treasury Bills are considered excessive, and the government is reluctant to impose new direct and indirect taxes. The extensive deficit financing undertaken before much of the country's industrialization program has been initiated means that the government is likely to continue to face serious financing problems. In addition, the High Dam project, if it materializes, will place another heavy demand on internal financing facilities—at least for the first six years of the Dam's construction, at which time the first returns may be realized.

With all of the fanfare attendant to Egypt's drive toward industrialization, it is surprising how little actually has been invested in new industries since the Revolution. Capital issues of joint-stock companies during 1951 totalled more than capital issues for 1952 and 1953 combined. According to one source, paid-up capital in "purely private, new industrial concerns" between January, 1954, and October, 1956, amounted to 5,085,000 pounds,[70] while paid-up capital for "public industrial concerns" totalled 26 million pounds, including 11.4 million for the iron and steel company and 8 million for the fertilizer plant at Aswan.[71] Fifty-five per cent of the total sum came from governmental organizations, including the Industrial Bank; another 5.4 million pounds came from banks and companies; and the rest was supplied by "private capital."

Another source, apparently utilizing different data, placed initial capital for new companies in 1955 at 4,475,000 pounds and at 24,460,000 in 1956.[72] The 1956 figure could be misleading, however, for the paid-up capital of two companies, a new sugar and distillery company and a fertilizer plant, accounted for 20 million pounds (and the sugar company cannot really be considered "new," for it had been dissolved by the government, then reconstituted under a different name with no change in the physical plant). It was estimated that actual net recourse to the capital market in 1956 was 19.3 million pounds.[73] The year 1957 saw 3.7 million pounds in new capital issues,[74] while real investment in industrial concerns totalled 12.7 million, including a capital increase of 7.6 million for the iron and steel company, and an increase of 3 million for existing cotton-spinning firms.[75] While the low level of industrial expansion was noteworthy, equally significant was the fact that private financing of new companies had fallen to about 13 per cent, with the government and semiofficial organizations filling much of the gap.[76]

By 1958, President Nasser realized that Egypt's economic progress was not what he had anticipated. After the union with Syria, he turned his attention to internal development—his first real opportunity since 1956. In 1957, Egypt's economic planning was dominated by Sidky's five-year plan for industry: this program, with its many shortcomings, had become a foundation stone of Egypt's proposed development. The manner of Soviet credits and the establishment of a "General Authority for the Execution of the Five-Year Plan" made revision of this program difficult. While Dr. Sidky's projects had not won the approval of Egyptian economists, his critics were unable to offer a viable alternative. Meanwhile, Egypt's efforts toward economic development continued in the absence of any centralized control.

The Ministry of Industry refused to cooperate with the

National Planning Commission, for Dr. Sidky feared, and justifiably so, that it wished to invade "his domain"; the Higher Planning Board was dismissed by a ranking official at the Ministry of Industry as a "failure";[77] the Economic Organization was building a financial empire of its own; and the Ministry of the Treasury and the National Bank were hamstrung by the lack of fiscal coordination. No one beneath the President seemed to have the authority to control the actions of these various bodies. Indeed, this organizational chaos brought to mind a comment Nasser had once made about pre-Revolution governments: "Various ministries in certain cases . . . went so far as to hinder and spoil the other's work."[78] Orders ultimately were given to Hussein Shafei, a former member of the RCC and the new Minister of Planning, to produce a national five-year plan to start in 1960, and the National Planning Commission finally settled down to constructive work. Other ministries were also requested to submit five-year plans, and the Ministry of Agriculture outdid itself by coming up with a ten-year program. But the major question was still unresolved: what was the status of Dr. Sidky's plan?

According to Hussein Shafei, "Sidky's five-year plan is only a program; if it fits into the National Planning Commission's frame, fine."[79] Meanwhile, however, this "program" was being implemented. And while Zacharia Mohieddine continued to head the Ministerial Economic Committee, and Ali Sabry, the President's chief political adviser, chaired the Committee for Imports and Exports, Sidky's program became further entrenched. Nasser apparently had an inkling that the program was not proceeding according to original plan. At the dedication of the iron and steel factory, he declared that, in the future, "we may have to reorganize our planning in a drastic manner."[80] But still he saw no alternative. He believed that the "Egyptian economy must be conducted on directed lines, so that capital can be mobilized for the service of the national economy,"[81] and he endorsed the existing industrial program pending a viable alternative. Some of the official announcements concerning the plan made observers feel that they were spectators at a comedy. Dr. Aziz Sidky announced at one time that the first five-year plan would be completed within three years, and a second plan would start in 1960.[82] Later Nasser proclaimed that "with the help of God, the five-year plan will be completed in 1960."[83] One wonders in retrospect how seriously these statements were being taken, removed as they were completely from economic reality. It would seem that political considerations had eclipsed the economic imperatives of Egyptian industrialization.

A chronic deficiency in Egypt's governmental planning is that original cost estimates consistently fall far short of ultimate expenditures. If conditions run true to form, the Ministry of Industry's plan is likely to result in even greater economic chaos. The iron and steel company is a case in point. Originally, the concern was expected to cost 17 million pounds, and even then an American industrial consultant firm commented: "It is *claimed* by the National Production Council that this plant will yield steel at costs competitive with the imported product." (Italics added.)[84] According to early estimates, the net gain in external trade resulting from the factory's production would reach 6,250,000 pounds annually. Local papers claimed that the plant would be completed by October, 1956,[85] but this time-table never was taken seriously. At first, the company's public relations department claimed that 220,000 tons of rolled steel would be produced from 265,000 tons of pig iron (the figure for finished steel later was reduced to 200,000 tons). It is likely, also, that original cost estimates of coke requirements were 50 per cent below actual needs.[86] As work on the plant progressed, estimates were made of the foreign-currency savings to be achieved, but little mention was made of internal costs. Another opening date was passed without comment, as construction work continued and expenditures mounted. Nineteen million pounds had already been raised in capital, but even this amount did not cover costs.

In early 1958, production began; electric furnaces, originally purchased in 1952, made steel from scrap metal, while the main furnaces remained unlit. Finally, in July, 1958, Gamal Abdel Nasser officially opened the factory with great fanfare. By that time, the plant already had cost over 25 million pounds, with further expenditures of over 3 million expected.[87] While there is a ready market available for iron and steel products if imports are curtailed, the company's net economic saving to the country is subject to doubt. The government has guaranteed 4 per cent minimum dividend to holders of the company's stock, but this is simply a transfer of an economic burden; and it has been suggested that the government might have to provide further subsidies in order to keep the price of steel products down.[88] One can conclude that the iron and steel company has proved to be a somewhat expensive undertaking.

Another example of chaotic economic planning and execution is the Aswan hydro-electric plant and its adjoining fertilizer factory. The electric plant was supposed to cost 27.5 million pounds and to transmit 1,350 million kilowatt hours of its 1,880 million kilowatt hours to the fertilizer plant.[89] As early as 1954, the Minister of Public Works estimated that the hydro-electric project would cost at least 30 million pounds,[90] but the official government estimate contained in the Ministry of Industry's five-year plan remained at 27.5 million.[91] A Ministry of Public Works publication, corrected to July, 1958, raised the figure to 29.5 million pounds.[92] Mohamed Hassanein Heikal put the sum at 40 million pounds[93]—a figure which approximates the estimates made by engineers working in Aswan. Moreover, it has been discovered that the fertilizer plant will require 90 per cent of the scheme's power output.[94] This, in turn, means a substantially higher capital overhead for the fertilizer plant once it is constructed. While this plant originally was to start production in 1959,[95] the official target date has now been pushed back to 1960.[96] Capital requirements were estimated at 22 million pounds, but this figure subsequently has been raised. Since 1954, estimated capital overhead necessary for the production of fertilizer at Aswan has risen from approximately 41,250,000 to a minimum of 61 million pounds, with no corollary increase in production plans. While this, in part, simply reflects the world-wide rise in capital goods prices, it nevertheless underscores a major problem of Egypt's industrial planning.

Late in 1958, Gamal Abdel Nasser commissioned Abdel Latif Boghdadi, who had been under virtual house restriction, to take charge of coordinating Egypt's economic development. One of Boghdadi's first moves was to enlist the services of five Russian experts for his Ministry's planning staff.[97] But while progress was made in the development of a national economic plan, Boghdadi found it difficult to deal with the petrified forest of Egypt's administration. He found, for example, that the Ministry of Industry had made sustained efforts to consolidate its position of influence. Originally, the Minister had sought to make the importation and exportation of any raw materials contingent upon the Ministry's approval, but the Advisory Council for Industry tempered this to read that "the views of the Ministry of Industry are to be sought."[98] Dr. Sidky had sought from the National Assembly the control of all industrial production, including the right to fix prices and profit margins, but he was refused complete jurisdiction over price controls.[99] Subsequently, industrial chambers and the Federation of Egyptian Industries were reconstituted, all under the Ministry's control.

Concurrently, the Economic Organization established its own economic domain. It had already gained effective control over most of Egypt's banks and insurance companies and held in its portfolio shares nominally valued at 34,217,000 pounds in companies with a nominal paid-up capital of 71,425,000 pounds.[100] Moreover, the Organization had the legal right to appoint top management and review major decisions for any company in which it owned 25 per cent of the stock. Since the Economic Organization, under Hassan Ibrahim, had become a major benefactor, with government money, of private and semiofficial firms, it, too, wielded considerable influence. The problem confronting Boghdadi was how to centralize the authority which was then being exercised locally, and often indiscriminately. Moreover, it seemed important in government planning to enlist the views of officials and of local businessmen. In this task, Boghdadi had the firm support of the Ministry of the Treasury and of the National Bank, who were continually besieged from all quarters by unreasonable demands for financial assistance. Many members of the National Planning Commission also favored this centralization, for it would unify Egypt's diverse economic development programs. By early 1959, however, Vice-President Boghdadi had not been able to establish such centralization.

The Foreign-Exchange Situation

The foreign-exchange picture, by 1959, had become clearer. Financial settlements had been negotiated with the old Suez Canal Company, and with the British and the French. The United States had released Egypt's frozen dollars immediately after the Suez Canal Company accord had been verified. When the Canal Company had been nationalized on July 26, 1956, President Nasser promised to pay compensation at the previous day's market prices on the Paris Bourse (estimated at 71,344,326 pounds),[101] after all Company assets were turned over to the Egyptian government. A conservative estimate of these assets at the time would be well over 95 million pounds, of which perhaps 26 million were in Egypt.[102] After the nationalization, substantial Canal dues still were paid to the old Company. In April, 1957, after the Canal had been cleared following the 1956 military attack, tolls were collected directly by the Egyptian Suez Canal Authority and compensation negotiations were deadlocked, since Jacques-Georges Picot, Managing Director of the Company, demanded compensation for those Canal revenues which would have accrued until 1968.

Finally, on April 29, 1958, with the assistance of the IBRD's good offices, an equitable settlement was reached. The Egyptian government relinquished claim to all Suez Canal Company assets outside the country and agreed to pay another 28.3 million pounds sterling and French francs over a six-year period; the tolls collected between July 26 and October 29, 1956, were considered the first payment. Solely on the basis of the old Company's claims and bargaining position, there would seem little reason for Egypt to make such a charitable settlement, for she already controlled and operated the Canal. But other factors prompted this settlement, among them the American promise to release 23,174,295 dollars[103] in frozen Egyptian government funds (which was implemented the following day) and the prospect of an early settlement of the sterling sum frozen by the British.

The Suez Canal proved a windfall for the Egyptian government, for it provided a profitable source of hard currency. From April through December, 1957, the Canal produced 24,350,000 pounds in negotiable currency, and another 40 million was expected during 1958. Originally, the Egyptian government had promised to set aside 25 per cent of gross revenues in a special fund for future Canal development, but these plans were upset by the pressure of foreign-exchange requirements. Instead, all receipts over and above those required for current Canal operations were deposited with the National Bank and were subsequently spent. It was claimed that the Suez Canal Authority had first lien on these deposits. This claim, however, was without substance. Even with the Canal revenues, Egypt's foreign-exchange holdings dropped 20 million pounds in the last six months of 1957. The same pattern was evident throughout 1958.

Over a million pounds already have been spent in payment for new dredges (ordered by the old Company) and other miscellaneous equipment; in an effort to obtain greater revenue from the Canal, a two-year, eighteen-million-dollar dredging contract has been tendered to three American firms.[104] While there is no reason to believe that Canal maintenance will not continue at a competent level, it is difficult to see how the Canal Authority, under existing financial practices, can expect to finance the proposed 120-million-pound "Nasser" expansion scheme from its own budget.[105] Currently, the Egyptian government is receiving up to 30 million pounds yearly from the Canal to meet expenses. There is little reason to believe that these requirements will diminish.

The financial settlement with the French also was gratifying to the Egyptians (it was claimed that the French agreed to pay 20 million pounds in compensation for "war damages").[106] Yet, Egypt still was extremely anxious to have her sterling balances unfrozen. Not until March, 1959, did Britain and Egypt agree to a settlement. Originally, the issue was complicated by Egyptian "war claims," which were countered by British demands for compensation for the war materiel seized from British arms depots in the Suez Canal Zone. Ultimately, these counterclaims were dropped, and the negotiations focused on the question of compensation for "Egyptianized" properties. The final settlement for a gross sum of 27.5 million pounds was considered an underpayment by some foreign observers, and the Egyptians obviously were pleased to have their sterling accounts unfrozen for such a reasonable sum.

Egypt, however, still was not in an enviable foreign-exchange position. Excluding 60.6 million in gold holdings and deducting various hard-currency obligations, Egypt's uncommitted foreign-exchange holdings on August 28, 1958—with sterling assets calculated at market value and including Free World clearing-account deficits, as well as future compensation and repayment commitments—totalled no more than 28 million pounds. This meant that future hard-currency needs had to be met primarily from Suez Canal revenues and the proceeds from Egyptian exports.

Other sources were available for development purposes—including West German credits for 44 million pounds,[107] a tentative East German credit for 7.5 million,[108] and a reported Japanese credit for 30 million dollars.[109] But Egypt already had committed herself heavily to foreign lenders. And prospects for substantial hard currency from cotton exports were not bright. Much of the crop already was pledged to the Communist bloc, and there was a strong possibility that the world market would soon face a surplus problem in long-staple cotton.[110]

Egypt's foreign trade was greatly complicated by her dealings with the Communist bloc. A comparison of trade and Central Exchange Control figures indicates that Egypt was paying about 15 million pounds annually for armaments already received; and economic circumstances forced Egypt to engage in commercial deals with the Soviet bloc at rates above existing world prices.[111] When Communist countries violated their trade agreements by selling Egyptian cotton at a discount to Western European countries for hard currency, Egypt was powerless to stop them.

In 1958, nearly 65 per cent of Egyptian cotton exports

went to the Communist world, including the People's Republic of China. The proportion may increase once Egypt starts to repay her Soviet credits. Egypt is in an increasingly difficult position, for her traditional Western cotton markets already are finding alternative sources of supply, and the Sudan is willing and able to offer long-staple cotton at low prices. Thus, excluding Suez Canal revenues, Egypt's prospects for large quantities of hard currency are not bright.

The Egyptian Economy After Seven Years

The internal fiscal situation also fails to present an encouraging picture for a country dedicated to rapid economic development. In late 1957, compulsory reserve ratios of commercial banks were again temporarily reduced—from 12.5 per cent to 7.5 per cent—to enable these banks to meet the market's requirements during the cotton-financing season. And there was a touch of irony in the National Bank's annual report for 1957, when the Bank's Governor commented that it was "gratifying to note that the deficit financing practiced in past years—especially as a result of the Suez events—has been abandoned during the present fiscal year,"[112] for at the end of 1957, Egypt's money supply had never been higher, although foreign currencies included under claims on the money supply had declined by 45.4 million pounds during the year. Perhaps he was referring to the fact that the increase of Treasury Bills had been braked, at least temporarily. But this development was not representative of the government's fiscal policy. At the end of the following year, Egypt's money supply, although nearly 10 per cent above the December, 1957, figure, was in a better relative position. Private deposits had shown a substantial increase, while note circulation had declined nominally.

In the past several years, the government has placed heavy dependence upon the National Bank's facilities. The decision to include government-guaranteed securities and discounted commercial papers as banknote cover has further restricted the Bank's role as a functional central bank. In 1956, Dr. Kaissuny wrote: "It was considered that borrowing from the Central

Bank through the expansion of note issues would expose the country to the dangers of inflation which should be avoided by all means."[113] But Treasury Bills and government-guaranteed loans (such as those granted the Economic Organization) both have an inflationary effect, and these measures have been common practice in past years.

Egypt's financial position is not yet critical. But in the coming years, the government will be tempted further to stretch the nation's credit system and rely continuously on deficit financing to meet its current expenses. Deficit financing, in moderation, may stimulate an economy such as Egypt's, but the inherent inflationary dangers of such a policy are considerable. It is to the credit of National Bank and Ministry of the Treasury officials that they are aware of these dangers and constantly seek to restrain less conservative members of the government family. Hassan Abbas Zaki, in particular, displayed courage during his tenure as Minister of the Treasury.* In his opinion, it was essential to float public loans rather than simply create new money through the Central Bank. He further deemed it unsound to issue Treasury Bills at such a low interest rate that the National Bank held almost all of them; in his view, it would actually prove less expensive if the interest rate of Treasury Bills were increased to 3 per cent so that they would become attractive to the public.

In October, 1958, the Cabinet authorized the issuance of another 50 million pounds in Treasury Bills, in part to finance the remainder of the 1957-58 cotton crop. As long as the government continues its heavy expenditures on the military and other nonproductive items, it would seem unrealistic to expect these Bills to be redeemed. There are indications, however, that under Boghdadi's leadership, a more stringent control might be exercised over the various claims currently being made upon the government for financial assistance.

It is difficult to assess Egypt's economic development over the past seven years. Certainly there has been substantial progress in the industrial sector: the index of industrial production reflects

---

* In October, 1958, Zaki became Minister of Economy and Commerce for the Egyptian region.

a rise of more than 20 per cent from 1952 through 1956. But much of this increase may be attributed to the normal growth in a country with a small industrial base, a growth which could have taken place regardless of the regime in power. Impressive increases in the consumption of electricity also were recorded, but much of this rise is explained by a change in the official method of registering power consumption. The production of nitrate fertilizers more than doubled, the result of the expansion of a single plant—Ahmed Abboud's factory at Suez. By 1959, manufacturing output, primarily by pre-Revolution physical plants, was attaining record highs, and mineral production, with the exception of manganese, was above the 1952 level. This expansion in production, however, already has had marked economic repercussions, for markets are not readily available to absorb a great quantity of new goods.

At the end of 1957, the "leading companies in the [cotton] industry expressed their fears . . . about the future marketing possibilities for their exportable surpluses, especially after the creation of the European Common Market."[114] They called for "careful and cautious market studies before any large-scale expansion of the industry is attempted."[115] No such "studies" apparently preceded the Egyptian-Soviet agreement for the construction of three large spinning factories by 1960. Executives in the cement industry indicated that, after the start of production by the National Cement Company (founded by Magdy Hassanein, the creator of Liberation Province), "marketing . . . became a real problem."[116] The problem was equally serious in the artificial-silk industry.

Perhaps the government has recorded the greatest progress in the communications field and the petroleum industry. At the time of the Revolution, over 50 per cent of all railroad equipment required renewing within ten years; since then, the government has imported many millions of pounds of new rolling stock. Extensive efforts have also been made to replace outdated tracks, to centralize repair operations at Abu Zaabal, and to install a modern communications system on the single-track network of Upper Egypt. In a commendable endeavor to make the Egyptian State Railways a self-sufficient operation, freight and passenger rates have been increased and ESR has been established as a semiautonomous organization with an independent budget. The government's only firm financial commitment to the railroad is to provide 40 million pounds over ten years for equipment replacement; it was calculated that railway profits amounting to this sum had gone into the national treasury during the prosperous war years.

An ambitious road-construction program also has been undertaken. The first three-year plan for roads was almost completed after five years,[117] and it is estimated that over 12 million pounds already has been expended on new roads (excluding construction in Cairo and Alexandria). Such a capital investment should provide the nation's economy with sizable indirect returns. A further 4 million pounds has been spent for the improvement of inland river navigation.

The government has also achieved notable results in the petroleum industry. Especially since the 1956 military campaign, the government has assumed direct control over much of the country's petroleum operations—from prospecting to refining and marketing. The credit for this success belongs to three men: Mahmoud Yunis (also Managing Director of the Suez Canal Authority), Mohamed Ahmed Selim, formerly a leading member of the National Production Council, and Salah Nassim, the competent Director of the General Petroleum Authority. Egypt's petroleum industry is centralized under this Authority, and the administration, with a 1958-59 independent budget of roughly 60 million pounds, is exempt from civil service regulations and government-imposed wage scales.

Before 1957, increases in refinery capacity and the construction of a new oil pipeline from Suez were implemented under the auspices of the National Production Council; since then, the Authority has initiated further programs which should soon be in a position to cope with Egypt's growing petroleum requirements. Currently, production from Egypt's petroleum fields is insufficient to meet local needs; and several old fields have passed their peak production. As a result of a new and vigorous prospecting program, new oil fields have been located which more than compensate for this decline in production. The goal of self-sufficiency, however, has yet to be reached. While Dr. Aziz Sidky believes that this could be achieved in 1959,[118] Salah Nassim suggests that no firm estimate can really be made; he ventures the guess that self-sufficiency may be achieved by 1961.[119]

There are no suitable statistical indexes by which Egypt's economic progress can be measured accurately. In a political speech in 1956, President Nasser tried to emphasize Egypt's rapid economic development with the claim that national income had risen from 748 million pounds in 1952 to 868 million in 1954. Such figures, however, can be misleading.[120] Indeed, original estimates by the Ministry of Finance placed national income for 1950 and 1951 above that for 1954, while the figure for 1953 originally was calculated at 856.7 million pounds.[121] More recent estimates by the National Planning Commission attest to the crudeness of Egyptian national-income figures. Government wholesale price indexes and cost of living indexes also prove unsatisfactory, for they use an outmoded base: moreover, only Cairo prices are considered, and official rather than actual (black) market prices are recorded. A private commercial firm's index is more accurate, but spot checks would suggest that the cost of living has risen more than 17 per cent during the six years after the Revolution. It is this writer's impression that the country's per capita income, at 1952 prices, has risen little, if at all, and that government price controls on all basic agricultural commodities will become increasingly necessary. While industrial wages have shown an absolute increase over 1952 levels, the hundreds of thousands of government officials have been hard hit by the creeping rise in prices.

Egypt's main source of economic strength is her broad agricultural base. The government, in its attempt rapidly to expand the industrial sector, courts the danger that the country's economic equilibrium may be upset. To date, substantial progress has been realized in several fields; but the government also has experienced a number of setbacks in its plans for development. Currently, Egypt's future economic programming is undergoing a complete reassessment. If economic considerations are given priority over political ones, then Egypt's economic future should be secure. However, as late as October, 1958, a civilian occupying one of the top-ranking economic posts in the Egyptian government was highly pessimistic: "We are civilians in a revolutionary atmosphere. Very often, they [the ex-officers] don't look to see if a project is economic or not—they want to please the public."

Given Egypt's paucity of resources, her economic future is not encouraging. Already, more than 150 million pounds has been spent on development-budget projects since the Revolution; but these programs were financed partly by American grants and partly with funds from confiscated Mohamed Ali holdings. Such a windfall is not likely to recur. With heavy social expenditures and a scarcity of capital, competent personnel, and local purchasing power, Egypt will be fortunate, at least over the short run, to maintain her existing low standard of living. A slight increase in per capita income would be a considerable achievement. The problem of serious agricultural underemployment and limited arable land forces Egypt to be ambitious in her economic planning—and industrialization appears to be her best hope. But this should not be used to justify gambles of the highest magnitude— "simply because there is no other alternative."

VII

The High Dam

Nile Development Before the Revolution

The greatest deterrent to agricultural expansion in the Nile Valley is the critical shortage of water. For many centuries the government, using basin-irrigation techniques, was able to trap sufficient flood waters so that the *fellaheen* could cultivate their single crops annually. But in the nineteenth century, the rapid increase in population made further utilization of the Nile waters necessary. During the rule of Mohamed Ali, the first of several major barrages was constructed, and extensive irrigation canals permitted part of Egypt's arable land to be placed under perennial cultivation. Later, under British supervision, the system of perennial irrigation was extended further, but little new land was reclaimed, because the minimum water requirements could not be guaranteed.

While barrages and a dam at Aswan permitted some additional cultivation during spring and summer months, the fundamental problem of Nile irrigation remained unsolved. There are great seasonal and annual fluctuations in the Nile's discharge. On occasion, the total annual discharge has been three times the river's volume during an abnormally low year, while the daily discharge during the spring months averages about one-fifteenth of the discharge at the flood peak. Although the annual mean flow of the Nile would yield enough irrigation water to support substantial agricultural expansion, the irregularity of the Nile's discharge and the absence of adequate storage facilities have, to date, made this a theoretical calculation. Instead, during years of a low Nile, land under cultivation must be severely restricted while, in years of high flood, great quantities of silt-laden water flow into the Mediterranean.

Egypt has long considered the question of Nile water of vital political and economic importance. Since her people are predominately agricultural, and rainfall, except along a narrow coastline strip, is negligible, Egypt's economic existence is inextricably linked with the Nile. Egyptian history records a number of plans by Egypt's ancient enemies to divert the flow of the Upper Nile; and a German proposal to drain water from Lake Victoria merited an investigation by the Egyptian government as late as 1926.[1] The prospects of rechanneling the Nile River away from Egypt are slight, however, for such an undertaking would encounter monumental physical obstacles. A more immediate problem is that other riparian states, especially the Sudan, might draw off water during the period when the Nile is low, thus leaving Egypt with insufficient water for her cropped areas. These fears were exacerbated by the British in 1924, when Lord Allenby, after the assassination of Sir Lee Stack, Governor-General of the Anglo-Egyptian Sudan, issued an ultimatum to Saad Zaghlul stating that "the Sudan Government will increase the area to be irrigated at Gezira from 300,000 *feddans* to an unlimited figure, as need may arise."[2] Therefore, it came as a surprise to some Egyptians when the British, in 1929, negotiated the Nile Waters Agreement, under which Egypt received by far the largest water allocation and further development works along the Nile became subject to Egyptian approval.

By the end of World War II, Egypt's water shortage remained acute. A negligible amount of land had been reclaimed in the twentieth century through utilization of Nile water, and, in 1938, the Ministry of Public Works decided to suspend conversion of further basin areas to perennial irrigation pending an alternative means of flood protection.[3] Over the previous three generations, considerable new works had been constructed across the Nile but, with the exclusion of the Sennar Dam, completed in 1925 to service the Sudan's Gezira Scheme, all of these dams and barrages were designed almost exclusively for Egypt's benefit. Moreover, the greater part of the sums expended were used in the development of a perennial-irrigation system, rather than in the expansion of annual storage capacity. During the preceding fifty years, construction of two major reservoirs, at Aswan and Jebel Aulia, had permitted Egypt to irrigate another 1.5 million *feddans* during the spring and summer; but Egypt's extensive perennial irrigation was to a large measure made possible by restrictions which prohibited the Sudan from drawing any water from the natural flow of the Nile from January to July of each year.

Under the expert guidance of Dr. H. E. Hurst, officials in Egypt's Ministry of Public Works had, for decades, been collecting data on the Nile River. They were aided by previous suggestions as to how the waters of the Nile could be better utilized: Sir William Garstin, once Under-Secretary of State at the Ministry of Public Works, had formally proposed in 1904 that the swamps in the Southern Sudan be traversed by a canal. With this suggestion in mind, Dr. Hurst and his colleagues sought to establish a system of over-year storage, whereby surplus water from years of a high Nile could be used to compensate for a series of subnormal years. Their proposals became known as "Century Storage" for, in calculating the probability of water sources available to provide an equalized, annual water supply, one hundred years was found to be a satisfactory statistical period. Much of their work depended on the distinction between "timely" and "untimely" water. Timely water was that which came down during the period when the natural flow of the river proved insufficient to meet all existing irrigation requirements, while untimely water generally was associated with the Nile in flood.[4]

Hydrologically, the Nile could be separated into two distinct entities, the Blue and the White Nile. The Blue Nile experiences wide variations in its daily flow, for almost 95 per cent of its water comes from the runoff in the Ethiopian highlands. Seasonal rains swell the Nile by late May; then, after a maximum daily volume of about 550 million cubic meters in September, early spring sees the Blue Nile reduced to a trickle. At times, as little as 20 million cubic meters daily flow past Sennar.[5]

Between 1899 and 1953, the total annual mean discharge of the Nile at Aswan* was 83.7 milliards,[6] of which the Blue Nile provided over 50 per cent (48 milliards). The White Nile, although it supplies less water annually, provides most of the timely water and enjoys a more constant rate of flow; during most of the year, the White Nile discharges about 50 million cubic meters daily, while during the last four months of the year this figure approaches 100 million cubic meters.[7] The only feeder into the Nile River north of Khartoum is the Atbara River, which has characteristics similar to those of the Blue Nile; during portions of the timely months, the Atbara often is dry.

The plan for Century Storage was to store White Nile water in the equatorial lakes of Lake Victoria and Lake Albert during the untimely season, then to release some of this supply after the Blue Nile flood. On the assumption that Egypt would place 7.1 million *feddans* (including 650,000 *feddans* under rice cultivation) under perennial irrigation, and, assuming that the Sudan would cultivate 1.1 million *feddans* annually, of which 550,000 *feddans* would require timely water,[8] it was estimated that these areas could be irrigated without crop reduction on the average of nine out of every ten years.[9] Although provisions could be made to equalize the flow of even the lowest Nile, the marginal cost of such protection seemed prohibitively high. Instead, Dr. Hurst was content merely to cushion the impact of abnormally low years, such as, for example, 1913-14.

The Blue Nile, although it represented the largest single source of water, was not considered a satisfactory major storage basin. Excluding a proposal for a dam on silt-free Lake Tana and tentative plans for a dam at Roseires, the only other new reservoir proposed for Blue Nile water was at the Fourth Cataract on the main Nile. During average years, these two dams were expected to provide 5.1 milliards of timely water (from February through July) at Aswan.[10] The other major function

* Because of evaporation and other transmission losses, Aswan has been accepted as the most convenient station for measurement of Nile River discharges. It generally is correct to assume that seven milliards at Aswan represents eight milliards at Sennar. Far greater losses are experienced with water coming from the upper reaches of the White Nile.

of the Blue Nile in the Century Storage scheme was to permit storage of White Nile water during the untimely period. The lowest evaporation rate for water stored along the Blue or main Nile was calculated at over 7 per cent annually. Assuming an over-year reservoir with a capacity in excess of one hundred milliards, this would amount to a sizable loss in available water. On the other hand, it was observed that Lake Victoria and Lake Albert, at the source of the White Nile, enjoyed rainfall which generally offset annual evaporation. Thus it seemed wise to store water in the equatorial lakes during the untimely season, then release it as required when the Blue Nile supply proved insufficient.

The swamp area between Mongalla and Malakal in the Southern Sudan posed a problem, for the Bahr el Jebel River through the Sudd swamp experienced extraordinary losses whenever it carried more than 40 million cubic meters daily to Malakal.[11] According to estimates on the equatorial lakes project, a maximum discharge of 100 million cubic meters would be expected at Mongalla. The most reasonable solution to the problem seemed to be the Jonglei canal scheme, which would permit the excess over 40 million cubic meters daily to be carried by a new canal.[12] The equatorial lakes scheme suffered from several handicaps. First, even if the Blue Nile's untimely water proved excessive, a minimum volume of eight milliards was required to flow through the White Nile during this period to prevent weed growth and to permit year-round navigation. This meant, in a normal year, that approximately sixteen milliards would be available during the six timely months.

In times of a low Nile, assuming that the water was available in the over-year storage reservoirs, more water could be released. This, however, was subject to the capacity of the river bed north of Malakal. Since a daily discharge at Malakal over 100 million cubic meters would cause excessive ponding and spilling, it seemed reasonable to consider 18 milliards at Malakal as the optimum timely limit according to the proposed Century Storage program.[13] Another problem lay with establishing a satisfactory reservoir in the equatorial lakes. Total storage capacity required for Lake Albert and Lake Victoria originally was

estimated at about 195 milliards, including flood protection[14]—
a volume equivalent to more than two years of the Nile's total
mean flow at Aswan. When Uganda proved unwilling to permit
a large reservoir at Lake Albert, Dr. Hurst suggested that a
100-milliard reservoir in Lake Victoria could prove satisfactory.[15]

It had been estimated that, upon completion of dams at
Lake Tana, at the equatorial lakes, and across the Nile north
of Atbara, and after the excavation of a Sudd canal, timely
water, measured at Aswan, would be increased from 23.5 to
approximately 34 milliards.[16] In addition, substantial flood-pro-
tection benefits would accrue. Even after deducting the water
supply set aside as the July reserve, this quantity would be more
than adequate to irrigate Egypt's 7.1 million *feddans* and the
amount designated for the Sudan. Moreover, during periods of
a low Nile, a constant supply could be expected from Lake
Tana and the White Nile. Indeed, it would be reasonable to
expect another one or two milliards from these sources during
the timely period, when the natural river proved inadequate.

The Century Storage plan was the only comprehensive official program for Nile Valley water development compiled during the first half of the twentieth century. The plan's authors
believed that the Century Storage reservoirs could become a
reality in as little as twenty years,[17] and it was anticipated that
this would coincide with the completion of the Sudd Canal.
Dr. Hurst preferred not to suggest the cost of these various
projects. According to an Egyptian government publication, the
cost was estimated at 73 million pounds,[18] but so many variables
were included in these calculations that it would be difficult to
determine their accuracy.

Dr. Hurst felt that Egypt, after this program was implemented, might well be able to place more than 7.5 million
feddans under perennial irrigation, and his estimates for Century
Storage benefits were on the conservative side. He took issue,
however, with an Egyptian government report which claimed
that the Nile ultimately could support 10 million Egyptian
feddans under cultivation,[19] for, he pointed out, the Sudan
appeared capable of cultivating more than the 2 million *feddans*
assumed as a maximum in the original Century Storage calcu-

lations.[20] As the initial phase of the Century Storage program, Egypt participated with Britain in the construction of the Owen Falls Dam, below Lake Victoria, and a dam at the Fourth Cataract was anticipated when the military takeover intervened in 1952.

Initial Planning of the High Dam

As the Egyptian Revolution gained momentum, its military leaders enthusiastically anticipated massive schemes for agricultural development. Mohammed Naguib, then President and Prime Minister, stated: "If we get capital, we will redeem 4 million *feddans* of land from the Nile Valley and 5 million *feddans* in the desert."[21] While even his strongest supporters did not concur with these figures, other members of the new regime seemed confident that about 10 million *feddans* could be placed under cultivation.[22] These goals could not be realized by the Century Storage scheme alone; moreover, it seemed doubtful that the military had the patience to wait twenty-five years for the major benefits of the scheme. Instead, a more spectacular program was undertaken.

For over a generation, the possibility of a large reservoir on the Nile north of the Atbara river had been considered.[23] In the forties, Adrien Daninos, an Egyptian agronomist, and Dr. Luigi Gallioli of Milan had done considerable work on drafting an outline of this proposed storage basin.[24] In late 1952, Dr. Hurst and his associates were commissioned to prepare hydrological studies apropos a possible mammoth dam across the Nile River.[25] Several Egyptian technical missions surveyed possible sites for the dam in October, 1952, and the German firm of Hochtief was commissioned to prepare a preliminary plan by March, 1953.[26] The original plan proved unsatisfactory, for it assumed a rock base close to the river bed, while subsequent and more extensive geological investigations demonstrated that the granite bed was covered by about 210 meters of sand and silt.[27]

The Egyptians wisely recognized their shortcomings in attempting to plan a project of the scope proposed for the

High Dam (Sadd el-Aali). Thus, a committee of Egyptian engineers, headed by Colonel Samir Helmy and including Dr. Mohamed Ahmed Selim and Dr. Hassan Zaky, was attached to the National Production Council and was granted authority over the High Dam scheme. It quickly established a board of international consultants. It was this board, meeting in April, 1953, which provided the guidelines for the entire project after the hasty Hochtief study had been rejected. With the assistance of an aerial survey contracted by the American Technical Cooperation Administration and borings undertaken by a German firm, it was decided by late 1954 that the most suitable site for the High Dam was 6 kilometers south of the present Aswan Dam.[28]

The board of consultants met again in November, 1954, and the members generally were in agreement; three Americans and a Frenchman favored the Hochtief proposal for a horizontal sealing connected with a central core, while a German, Dr. Preuss, supported the difficult "freezing method."[29] It was agreed that an upstream cofferdam over 40 meters high and 500 meters in length would be required before actual construction on the main dam could commence, and the consultants seemed confident that work on the cofferdam and diversion tunnels could begin without undue delay.[30] An estimated 110 million pounds for the construction of the entire High Dam project, excluding the power plant and high-tension switching station, was considered reasonable by the international consultants.[31]

The High Dam, as proposed in 1954, was to be a huge edifice; the Egyptians claimed that the volume of materials required would be seventeen times that of the Great Pyramid.[32] The dam was to reach 110 meters above the river bed and extend about 5,000 meters in length. Seven diversion tunnels in the east bank were to carry the river's normal flow. Another four tunnels, constructed through the west bank, were to lead to an extensive hydro-electric station. The main dam would consist of rock-fill, with the foundation in the river channel consisting of dune sand compacted by vibration, but extensive grouting operations also were considered necessary. Without doubt, the most impressive feature of the High Dam was the size of its proposed reservoir. According to tentative estimates, up to 130 milliards could be stored, with the reservoir extending 150 kilometers inside the Sudanese border;[33] the capacity of the existing Aswan Dam was little more than 5 milliards.

According to Egyptian estimates, 30 milliards should be set aside for sediment accumulation, another 30 would be required as flood protection (especially after Egypt's remaining basin lands were converted to perennial irrigation), and 70 milliards would be available for purposes of over-year irrigation. With the additional water anticipated, the Sadd el-Aali Department of the National Production Council, in February, 1955, expected the High Dam to permit the cultivation of an additional 1.5 million *feddans*, a guaranteed water supply in low runoff years, and an ensured 700,000 *feddans* of rice annually.[34] In March, 1955, Dr. Mohamed Ahmed Selim announced that 2 million *feddans* would be reclaimed, all basin lands would be converted to perennial cultivation (estimated at about 700,000 *feddans*), and a yearly 700,000 *feddans* of rice would be guaranteed.[35] Still later that same year, the National Production Council Yearbook claimed that, after Sadd el-Aali, land under cultivation would expand by 2 million *feddans*, including the conversion of 700,000 *feddans* of basin lands.[36] The discrepancies in these estimates indicated the difficulty in assessing potential Sadd el-Aali benefits.

Perhaps the calculations for hydro-electric production were more accurate, for fewer variables were involved. It was assumed that the constant water flow from the High Dam would raise annual production of the Aswan hydro-electric plant to three billion kilowatt hours—an increase of more than 50 per cent over its original capacity. Moreover, after ten years, the High Dam power plant was expected to produce 4.3 billion kilowatt hours annually, whereas the total measured power consumption in Egypt for 1954 was 1.3 billion kilowatt hours.[37] It was assumed that much of the High Dam production could be delivered to the Cairo area at about one-half the current cost of a kilowatt hour from thermal stations. Using these tentative figures, and apparently assuming that alternative crops can be found which have the equivalent cash value of cotton, it was claimed that, after the first ten years of the High Dam scheme, national income was expected to increase by about 30 per cent (255 million pounds), that annual imports could be reduced by some 60 million pounds, and that agricultural exports could be increased by 50 per cent.[38] After another fifteen years, during which power facilities were to be expanded and more land reclaimed, the total annual increase in national income resulting from the High Dam was estimated at approximately 355 million pounds.[39]

According to 1955 estimates, the first ten-year stage of the High Dam project was to cost 209.5 million pounds, of which 102 million was required in foreign exchange.[40] This amount included construction of the dam, all diversion and power tunnels, estimated indemnities, eight turbines and generators, a transmission line to Cairo, conversion of 700,000 *feddans* from basin irrigation, and reclamation of 400,000 *feddans*. These cost figures, however, seemed conservative. An average of 30 pounds a *feddan* was allocated for land reclamation; in some areas it might take ten times that figure to fully prepare barren land for cultivation. Moreover, although the benefits from 300,000 *feddans* in Liberation Province were calculated, no provision was made even for land-reclamation costs in this area.[41] It is evident, also, that extensive expenditures would be required to utilize adequately the new supply of electric power. Expenditure of another 56 million pounds on further land development and new power potential was projected for a period of fifteen years following the completion of the High Dam, and this would require even greater indirect investment from the private or government sector. On the basis of calculations published in 1955, it would appear that Egyptians tended to overestimate the benefits of the Sadd el-Aali while minimizing the amount of indirect expenditures which would be incurred by the project.

Problems of Nile Water Distribution

A major problem which complicated Egyptian calculations of agricultural benefits to be derived from the High Dam was that of Nile water distribution. From 1870 through 1953, the

Nile river had an annual mean flow of 92.9 milliards measured at Aswan; perhaps, however, the flood estimates were exaggerated during the early years, for between 1899 and 1953, the mean was only 83.7 milliards.[42] Since much of this flow came during the untimely period, Egypt was anxious to ensure a sufficient water supply for her spring and summer crops.

In 1929, the Nile Waters Agreement was negotiated between Egypt and Great Britain, who also acted as agent for the Anglo-Egyptian Sudan. Under its terms, the Sudan was expected to fill Sennar Dam (with a capacity under one milliard) during the untimely period; then, from January 1 to July 15 of each year (Sennar dates), almost the entire natural flow of the river was to be reserved for Egypt.[43] Moreover, "save with the previous agreement of the Egyptian government, no irrigation or power works or measures are to be constructed or taken on the river Nile and its branches, or on the lakes from which it flows, so far as all these are in the Sudan or in countries under British administration, which would, in any such manner as to entail any prejudice to the interests of Egypt, either reduce the quantity of water arriving in Egypt, or modify the date of its arrival, or lower its level."[44] It would appear that this agreement provided Egypt with a carte blanche as regards supervision over Nile waters. Granted, at that time Egypt was by far the largest user of Nile waters; in 1920, it was estimated that Egypt used about 40 milliards annually, the Sudan no more than 1.5 milliards, and other riparian states a negligible amount.[45] But it should be remembered that Egypt enjoyed a well-developed agricultural system, whereas the Sudan's first major project, the Gezira Scheme, was just in its inception.

The Anglo-Egyptian Sudan's movement toward independence coincided with Egypt's plans to construct the High Dam; and when talks were initiated on distribution of future Nile waters, Egyptian negotiators faced a nationalist Sudanese delegation. Talks were held in 1954, but it was not until the following year that the issue became critical. The Azhari government, then in power, had depended heavily upon Egyptian assistance during the Sudanese elections, and the Egyptians believed that Prime Minister Ismail el Azhari, in return, was committed to friendly relations, or even a union, with Egypt. But by spring of 1955, Egyptian-Sudanese amity had cooled, and Egypt found it exceedingly difficult to reach an agreement on the Nile waters.

Colonel Samir Helmy, speaking for Egypt, claimed that all amounts used by each country in the past should be considered "vested rights."* Moreover, he insisted that "since 1886, the whole natural flow of the river Nile during the low season became fully under [Egyptian] control, a natural and historical right to Egypt alone, in addition to her vested rights on the flood water."[46] While the Sudan did not dispute Egypt's right to the volumes of water which she actually used for irrigation,[47] strong exception was taken to Colonel Helmy's statement that "it is indisputable that the present irrigation requirements for both Egypt and the Sudan, estimated at 55 milliards per annum, 51 milliards for Egypt and 4 milliards for the Sudan, are undoubtedly acknowledged as vested rights which should be respected."[48] The Sudanese placed Egypt's current consumption at 48 milliards for irrigation and their own at 4; it is interesting to note that Dr. Hurst, in a 1955 study for the Sadd el-Aali Department, assumed that Egypt's current requirements for irrigation *and* navigation were 49 milliards.[49]

Another impasse was encountered in discussions over the distribution of water impounded by the High Dam. Again Colonel Helmy sought to introduce figures found unacceptable by the Sudanese. According to his calculations, the High Dam would provide, at Aswan, 80 milliards yearly, of which 10 would be lost through evaporation. After deducting the 55 milliards which he previously had assumed as "vested right," this left 15 milliards to be divided. The Sudanese objected on several grounds; they argued that a minimum figure of 84 milliards annually at Aswan should be accepted, for this was the mean flow from 1900 to 1947. Furthermore, by calculating 52 milliards as total "vested right" and refusing to assume any of the High Dam evaporation loss, the delegation of the Sudan arrived at an annual "surplus" of 32 milliards.[50]

---

* Both delegations came to accept "vested rights" to mean the unquestioned right to the Nile water used for areas currently under cultivation, but no agreement could be reached on definite figures.

While both sides employed ingenious arguments, neither proposal provided the basis for a settlement. Egypt was determined to protect her existing right to Nile waters, while also ensuring her right to more than a negligible share of the water provided by the High Dam. The Sudanese were equally determined to redress a wrong which they believed had been committed in 1929. While they acknowledged the principle of "vested right," the Sudanese then proposed the proportional distribution of the gross water from the Nile. Using different formulae, including population ratios, Sudanese delegates laid claim to between 23 and 35 milliards annually.[51]

Originally, the Egyptians suggested that the "surplus" 15 milliards be distributed with total populations being used as the criterion for division.[52] When this was rejected, Gamal Abdel Nasser offered, on May 20, 1955, to distribute this "surplus" on a "fifty-fifty basis";[53] since the Sudan's share would be calculated at Sennar, this would mean that at Aswan Egypt would obtain eight milliards, while the Sudan would receive seven. This apparently would provide the Sudan with a maximum of 11 milliards yearly from the Nile, while Egypt would be assured about 61 milliards after construction of the High Dam. The Sudanese did not deem this an equitable solution.

A good case could be made for either the Egyptian or Sudanese position. Egypt had become accustomed to drawing heavily upon the Nile waters and was loath to jeopardize her "vested right," especially her "right" to the flow during the timely period. And it seemed inconceivable to the Egyptians that they should construct the High Dam and then receive only negligible water benefits from it. On the other hand, it could not be denied that the 1929 Nile Waters Agreement had failed to provide adequately for the Sudan's subsequent agricultural development. The Sudanese were determined to establish their right to a share of Nile waters sufficient to provide for the Sudan's further agricultural expansion. Remembering that Egypt, since 1920, had established by use her "vested right" to another eight milliards annually, the Sudanese delegates were quick to reject a "tentative share" proposal. The basic difficulty arose from the fact that the Nile seemed unable to provide water sufficient to irrigate all the lands which Egypt and the Sudan ultimately would like to bring under cultivation. Given this dilemma, it was understandable why a quick agreement was not forthcoming.

Negotiations were disrupted when the chief of the Sudanese negotiating team in Cairo, Khadr Hammad, the Minister of Irrigation, was surprised by Egyptian police while arranging the publication of a pamphlet unfavorable to the Egyptian government.[54] The resultant publicity increased the friction between the negotiating teams. Then Colonel Helmy, at a press conference, read the following communiqué: "During the past two days, discussions were held between the Egyptian and Sudanese sides on the Nile waters; but the Egyptian side could not conduct the discussions with the Sudanese side on engineering or technical grounds. The Sudanese side, most unfortunately, refused to discuss the technical means by which full use of the waters of the Nile could be made in both Egypt and the Sudan—insisting rather upon dividing an unknown quantity. As technical men, we regret that political circumstances should affect technical points on which no one in the world could differ."[55]

Not unexpectedly, the negotiations collapsed completely Egypt was still drawing her needs from the Nile, and the Sudan was not permitted to interrupt the flow of the Nile during the timely period. But the Sudanese began to give more urgent consideration to a proposal that a dam be constructed on the Blue Nile at Roseires. As Azhari observed: "The Nile flows through the Sudan first, and we can no longer be content to receive our share last."[56]

Financing the High Dam

Financing the High Dam was a formidable problem. According to original Egyptian estimates, the project, including initial power installations, would require at least 180 million pounds, of which 60 million would be in foreign currency.[57] Since Egypt had little prospect of providing the necessary foreign exchange herself, vigorous efforts were made to interest Western business concerns. A West German banking mission arrived in Cairo in

December, 1953, to discuss arrangements for financing,[58] and in June, 1954, a mission of French bankers visited the country.[59] Mohammed Naguib even claimed that the International Bank for Reconstruction and Development (IBRD) had been approached early in 1953, but that at that time the plans for the High Dam had not been considered sufficiently advanced.[60] Toward the end of 1954, it appeared that a British–French–West German consortium was interested in participating in the Sadd el-Aali project. However, because extensive international competitive bidding on individual High Dam contracts was ruled out by the very nature of the consortium, it was impossible for the World Bank to consider the consortium's plan.

Instead, the emphasis shifted to direct participation by Western governments and the World Bank. During 1954, especially after the initialling of the British agreement to withdraw from the Suez Canal Zone, the United States considered the possibility of contributing to the financing of the High Dam project. The World Bank, in its own right, also agreed to investigate the possibilities of an investment in the Sadd el-Aali scheme. As more definite technical plans for the High Dam were formulated, Egyptian officials felt that the matter of foreign financing was being prolonged unnecessarily.

It was more than coincidental therefore, when, in October, 1955, "reliable reports" from Cairo indicated a strong Soviet interest in financing the High Dam. According to Wing Commander Hassan Ibrahim, Minister of Production, a Soviet offer had been made directly to Gamal Abdel Nasser;[61] this was not denied by the Soviet Ambassador in Cairo, Daniil Solod, who stated that "economically, we are in a position to give aid to any country which is willing to accept it."[62] The following week, Egypt's Ambassador in Washington, Dr. Ahmed Hussein, personally informed John Foster Dulles that Egypt would prefer to have the United States and the IBRD rather than the Soviet Union finance construction of the High Dam.[63] He added that the Russians had submitted a firm offer to contribute at least 200 million dollars of the cost, repayable in cotton and rice over a period of thirty years at 2 per cent interest. In November, it was reported that Solod told Egypt's Deputy Premier, Gamal

Salem, that the Soviet Union proposed to build and finance the High Dam with repayment in cotton extended over a twenty-five-year period.[64]

Despite some official skepticism of the validity of these reports, the United States, perhaps to counter the Soviets' successful intrusion into Egypt with massive arms shipments, decided to give urgent consideration to Egypt's request for financial assistance. When Dr. Kaissuny, Colonel Samir Helmy, and Dr. Mohamed Ahmed Selim came to the United States in late November, 1955, the High Dam project still was tentative, for the crucial water issue with the Sudan had not been settled. This economic consideration notwithstanding, the United States and the United Kingdom urgently reviewed their possible participation in financing Sadd el-Aali.

Fearing that Egypt might feel obliged to accept Soviet financing (a December *New York Times* dispatch placed the Soviet offer at 600 million dollars, repayable over fifty years at 2 per cent),[65] the Americans and British hastily sought to conclude their part in the High Dam construction. A major problem confronted the United States for, in accordance with existing legislation, it was impossible for the Department of State to make a long-term financial commitment; and since the Sadd el-Aali project would require sustained financing over a number of years, this presented serious complications. In an effort to placate Congress, it was claimed that economic assistance for Egypt then under consideration would be for a self-contained first stage—a cofferdam which, even by itself, would be a permanent contribution to Egypt's economy. From an economic viewpoint, however, the IBRD did not believe that the High Dam project could properly be considered anything but a single entity, for most of the capital expenditure would bring substantial returns only upon completion of the entire first stage. The administration also considered asking Congress for special legislation which would permit grants or long-term loans to Egypt totalling 200 million dollars over ten years, to be released at the rate of 20 million dollars yearly.[66]

On December 17, 1955, the United States and Great Britain announced that they had offered to Dr. Kaissuny an initial grant of 70 million dollars, of which about 56 million was coming from America and 14 million from England.[67] This first installment was to be used in the construction of the cofferdams and seven diversion tunnels. In accompanying *aide-memoires* it was indicated that, although no long-range contractual commitment could be made, the two governments would be sympathetic to further requests for financial support. These offers were made contingent upon an Egyptian-IBRD "understanding" on matters related to the rights of the Sudan to indemnities and access to Nile waters and upon Egypt's future ability to provide the necessary internal financing. When Solod remarked that the U.S.S.R. still intended to participate in the High Dam "unless there is something in Egypt's agreement with the West which specifically excludes us," a U.S. official retorted that exclusion of the Soviets was implicit in the Western offer.[68]

A comprehensive technical survey of the High Dam project was undertaken by the World Bank. In October, 1955, in a memorandum to the Bank's directors, President Eugene Black suggested that Egypt "should be able to mobilize the necessary funds at home and abroad, but only if she adopts sound methods of financing the project and rigorously adheres to sound fiscal and economic policies."[69] He further observed that the total of Egypt's present and contemplated economic commitments "is substantially in excess of the resources which will probably be available during the critical period that the Dam is being constructed."[70] The IBRD had established a reputation as a conservative banking institution, and its attitude toward Egypt's application bore this out.

On December 16, 1955, the day that the American and British *aide-memoires* were completed, President Black drafted another memorandum in which he stated that the Bank could not reach a firm conclusion on the economic soundness of the entire High Dam project until allocation of additional Nile waters was determined. Egyptian planning assumed that over ten additional milliards would be available for irrigation in Egypt, and the Bank based its calculations of benefits on that assumption; agreement with the Sudan on a lower figure would call for a complete reassessment of the project.[71]

These reservations were included in an IBRD draft memorandum submitted to Gamal Abdel Nasser. Objecting to the clauses which suggested that the IBRD might assume a supervisory position over the Egyptian economy and which required competitive bidding (restricted to member-nations of the Bank), Nasser took the initiative of inviting Black to Cairo. It seemed doubtful that Mr. Black could substantially revise his previous memorandum without compromising the Bank's economic principles: clearly the IBRD's assessment of Egypt's economy was not optimistic. In an economic report of August, 1955, the Bank stated that, even if the full potential of the High Dam were realized, in the light of an anticipated population increase "there is little or no prospect that Egypt will have done much more than maintain the present standard of living . . . by 1975." [72] And a firm regulation of Egypt's finances would seem in order if the Bank was correct in its observation that the Egyptian government was "seeking to move ahead on all fronts at once and at a speed out of proportion to its organizational and managerial capacity and to the financial resources prospectively available." [73]

After more than a week of intensive negotiations, a joint communiqué stated that "substantial agreement" had been reached.[74] Although President Black was noncommittal, Dr. Kaissuny stated that the IBRD loan had been accepted "in principle." [75] It was evident to informed observers, however, that the Bank's position remained substantially unchanged. In deference to Nasser's nationalist sensitivities, great care was taken to avoid creating the impression that the IBRD was "dictating conditions." Instead, emphasis was placed on the fact that a "close relationship must be attained" on a number of matters. This emerges clearly in the following representative clause of the February memorandum:

> The [Egyptian] Government's own contribution to the project will be provided in such a way as to avoid inflation and impairment of Egypt's credit worthiness. To this end, the Government and the Bank will reach an understanding on, and will periodically review, an investment program which will recognize the priority of the High Dam project and the need

for adjusting total public expenditures to the financial resources which can be mobilized.[76]

As Nasser later disclosed, the proposed Bank loan had never progressed beyond the stage of draft memoranda. In February, Nasser had asked Black that "we write the agreement now and sign it, and we postpone it to come into effect after the signing of the waters agreement."[77] Black, however, replied that the Bank's policy prohibited such an arrangement. Moreover, he reiterated that the economic feasibility of the High Dam project was contingent upon the terms of an Egypto-Sudanese water agreement. Nasser also took issue with Black's insistence that conditions for IBRD loans would have to be negotiated "from time to time"; that "the Bank must be fully assured that the foreign currencies which come from the British and American grants are not stopped"; and that "the agreement of the Bank for assistance is, without doubt, subject to reconsideration in the event of exceptional circumstances."[78] Although the IBRD did declare the High Dam project technically sound, available evidence indicates conclusively that at no time did the Bank commit itself to any agreement which could properly be construed as a firm offer to contribute to the financing of the Sadd el-Aali. Moreover, published materials suggest that under no circumstances would the Bank have provided funds for Egypt in the absence of adequate assurances for its investment; not only was the High Dam an enormous undertaking for Egypt, but, at an estimated 1,350,000,000 dollars, it would also be the largest enterprise in which the World Bank had participated.[79]

The Egyptian government's position vis-à-vis the Anglo-American offer was substantially different, for the political overtones of these proposed grants were evident to all parties concerned. Fearful that the Soviets could gain a stronger foothold in Egypt, some Western observers also believed that Egypt, once she became preoccupied with the High Dam project, would forfeit aggressive actions against Israel in favor of internal development. It must have come as a disappointment, therefore, when Nasser hesitated in accepting the Western offer. Notes were delivered to the American and British ambassadors in Cairo

which claimed that the terms accompanying the December offer
"adversely reflected upon Egyptian dignity";[80] a number of
countersuggestions were then submitted.[81] These, in turn, did
not meet with State Department approval. In March, a Department spokesman brusquely summarized the U.S. view: "We
have made an offer and the offer stands."[82]

There were other indications that Anglo-American enthusiasm for the High Dam project was on the wane. Senator Walter
F. George, Chairman of the Senate Foreign Relations Committee, took strong exception to the administration's indirect request
for authority to grant a long-term commitment on the Aswan
High Dam.[83] Moreover, Dulles publicly indicated his annoyance
at Egypt's diplomatic recognition of Communist China. The
changing climate of opinion was also reflected in an American
announcement that funds earmarked for the High Dam no
longer were being held, and that a new Congressional appropria-
tion most probably would be required.[84] During this period,
Gamal Abdel Nasser hinted that Egypt had not rejected the
Soviet offer. He professed that "the Soviet offer was very general
and, really, we have not studied it."[85]

When, in June, Soviet Foreign Minister Dimitri Shepilov
visited Cairo, the Egyptian government deliberately sought to
foster the impression that Russia had offered to underwrite the
entire High Dam program. Nasser commissioned Mohamed
Hassanein Heikal to inform Western newsmen that Shepilov
wished to lend Egypt 400 million pounds (almost 1.2 billion
dollars) repayable over sixty years at 2 per cent interest, or,
perhaps, interest-free.[86] Incredible as such terms might appear,
most of the Western press seemed to accept them as facts.

American opposition to the High Dam project grew on a
number of grounds. There was general annoyance at Nasser's
game of "economic neutralism," which pitted Western offers
against those of the East; Congress never was keen on supporting
Sadd el-Aali; the pro-Zionist lobby vigorously opposed such a
move, and a Southern group feared that the scheme would increase Egyptian cotton production. The Senate Appropriations
Committee went so far as to order the Administration to spend
no Mutual Security funds on the High Dam.[87]

By mid-July, the American press was openly discussing the possibility that the United States no longer would participate in the High Dam scheme. Perhaps it was for this reason that President Nasser instructed Ambassador Ahmed Hussein to publicize widely his impending return to Washington. According to Cairo newspapers, Hussein was instructed to enter into negotiations with the Department of State over the Anglo-American offer;[88] in London, however, Hussein reputedly said that he was "instructed to inform the United States Government that Egypt was accepting Western aid to finance the Aswan High Dam."[89] According to President Nasser, Ahmed Hussein returned to Washington merely to meet Dulles and "request sending replies" to the Egyptian note of February, 1956.[90] In Hussein's view, there were "still some differences between Egypt and Britain and the United States," but they were not "basic points."[91] It may well be, as Egypt subsequently claimed, that Hussein was authorized to reach a firm agreement with the West. If this was true, however, he never had that opportunity. Upon arriving in Washington, he was summoned to meet the American Secretary of State and was handed the following note:

At the request of the Government of Egypt, the United States joined in December, 1955, with the United Kingdom and with the World Bank in an offer to assist Egypt in the construction of the High Dam on the Nile at Aswan. This project is one of great magnitude. It would require an estimated twelve to sixteen years to complete, at a total cost estimated at some 1.3 billion dollars, of which over 900 million represent local currency requirements. It involves not merely the rights and interests of Egypt, but of other states whose waters are contributory, including the Sudan, Ethiopia, and Uganda. The December offer contemplated an extension by the United States and the United Kingdom of grant aid to help finance certain early phases of the work, the effects of which would be confined solely to Egypt, and with the understanding that accomplishment of the project as a whole would require a satisfactory resolution of the question of Nile water rights. Another important consideration bearing upon the feasibility of the undertaking and thus the practicability of American aid was Egyptian willingness and ability to concentrate its economic resources upon the vast reconstruction program.

Developments within the succeeding seven months have not been favorable to the success of the project, and the United States Government has concluded that it is not feasible in present circumstances to participate in the project. Agreement by the riparian states has not been achieved, and the ability of Egypt to devote adequate resources to assure the project's success has become more uncertain than at the time the offer was made.

This decision in no way reflects or involves any alteration in the friendly relations of the Government and people of the United States and the Government and people of Egypt. The United States remains deeply interested in the welfare of the Egyptian people and in the development of the Nile. It is prepared to consider at an appropriate time, and at the request of the riparian states, what steps might be taken toward a more effective utilization of the water resources of the Nile for the benefit of the peoples of the region. Furthermore, the United States remains ready to assist Egypt in its efforts to improve the economic condition of its people and is prepared, through its appropriate agencies, to discuss these matters within the context of funds appropriated by Congress.[92]

The British withdrew their offer on the following day.

The High Dam and International Politics

In many respects, the reference to Egypt's dubious ability to finance the Sadd el-Aali project appeared to be the most valid point included in Dulles' note. The Anglo-American conditional offer of December, 1955, was made with the tacit assumption that Egypt would find it difficult to provide the necessary internal financing. It became known subsequently, however, that Egyptian commitments for Soviet armaments exceeded 250 million dollars, far more than had been assumed originally.[93] Moreover, local fiscal policy boded ill for the future austerity program which had been deemed a prerequisite for financing the High Dam; in the seven months following the Anglo-American offer, Egypt's national debt rose by almost a third, and the economy was definitely embarking on an inflationary bent. Few observers believed, however, that Dulles' action had been prompted primarily by economic considerations.

The United States' willingness to participate in financing Sadd el-Aali had generally been interpreted as a move to give political backing to Egypt. Nasser's brand of "positive neutrality," however, was proving increasingly distasteful to Western interests, as he assisted the Algerian rebels, attacked the West's position in the Arab world "in the name of Arab nationalism," and flirted with the Communist bloc. Egypt's recognition of Communist China was considered by Dulles as proof of the anti-Western direction of Nasser's policies. Moreover, the prospect of financial assistance for Nasser had drawn strong protests from America's staunch allies, especially Turkey, Pakistan, Iran, and Ethiopia.

By mid-1956, influential voices in the United States rose against American policy vis-à-vis "neutrals." Tito, with his on-again–off-again philanderings with the Soviet camp, had obtained nearly a billion dollars from the United States; similarly, Nehru, despite his moral censure of the West, had drawn heavily on American aid grants. But the neutralism of neither Tito nor Nehru could be considered aggressively anti-Western; the same did not apply to Nasser's "positive neutrality." Moreover, American policymakers were growing restive under what seemed to have become a generally accepted game of uncommitted nations: the threat to turn to the Communists if the U.S. refused to meet their manifold, and often unreasonable, demands. As a member of the British Parliament observed: "This policy of outbidding Russia puts a premium on the local governments in the various so-called underdeveloped areas to invent special departments for thinking up fantastic schemes."[94]

If Dulles had so desired, the American offer to Egypt could have been pigeon-holed in accordance with acceptable diplomatic procedure; after Congress refused to provide funds for the High Dam project, the entire issue could have been quietly dropped. Instead, Dulles chose a deliberate rebuff which carried its "own built-in moral for neutrals."[95] The Secretary of State firmly believed that the Soviet Union was not in a position to make good her alleged economic offers to Egypt.[96] Moreover, he wished to scotch any attempt at economic blackmail.[97] He later posed the question: "Do nations which play both sides get better treatment than nations which are stalwart and work with us?"[98] His withdrawal of America's High Dam offer was a dramatic attempt to undercut President Nasser's prestige in the Afro-Asian world; it was also a warning directed to other would-be neutrals. As a bold diplomatic riposte designed to check a deteriorating political situation, it had much in its favor.

Gamal Abdel Nasser was informed of Dulles' action as the neutralists' "summit conference" was ending at Brioni, and, accompanied by Nehru, he prepared to return to Cairo. The setback was all the greater because it was rapidly becoming apparent that the Soviet Union was not immediately going to grant him massive assistance for the High Dam.

On July 14, Shepilov, at a cocktail party in Moscow, indicated publicly for the first time that Russia was not committed to underwriting the Aswan High Dam.[99] Then, on July 21, two days after Hussein's meeting with Dulles, Shepilov stated: "I had the impression after my visit [to Egypt] that there are now more vitally important problems for the Egyptian economy, particularly problems of industrialization, although I do not minimize the importance of the Aswan [High] Dam."[100] This tended to confirm earlier rumors that Egypt had sought to mislead the West into believing that general Soviet offers of industrial credits actually had been extended to include the High Dam. In a deliberately ambiguous statement, the Soviet Ambassador in Cairo said: "Russia will live up to its word in connection with the High Dam project. It will not back down if Egypt requests such assistance. This has been made clear in the declarations of the Soviet Foreign Minister. I believe that nobody in Egypt doubts the sincerity of our intentions. In our opinion, every responsible government should fulfill the promises it makes and should not back down on them. For our part we shall continue to be bound by our promise to Egypt. If and when Egypt asks us to finance the High Dam project, it becomes our duty to grant such a request in fulfillment of our promise."[101] On the same day, Reuters reported that a Soviet press attaché in Cairo had denied that Kisselev had pledged Soviet financing for the High Dam project if Egypt asked for such aid.[102] Subsequently, President Nasser declared that he had not discussed a High Dam loan offer with Shepilov in June, 1956,[103] and Mohamed Hassanein Heikal, who had originally "leaked" to the West Shepilov's reputed terms, claimed that no High Dam offer had ever been discussed in detail with the Soviets.[104]

As was to be expected, the Egyptian press heaped vitriol on the "treacherous" Anglo-American act. One government-sponsored newspaper even declared in mock gratitude: "Praise be to God for having saved our High Dam scheme from the curse of American dollars!"[105] But suddenly, in an abrupt reversal of the local propaganda machine, the press shifted its attacks to the World Bank. According to Bank officials, the withdrawal of the Anglo-American offer meant that the Bank's proposal "automatically expired."[106] Although Senator Fulbright, after reviewing classified State Department documents, later claimed that the United States decision to withdraw the High Dam offer was made against the advice of Eugene Black,[107] this had no bearing on the Bank's position; from the beginning, IBRD assistance had been contingent upon British and American grants. But the Egyptian government chose to ignore this fact. In seeking a political scapegoat, President Nasser went so far as to compare Eugene Black with Ferdinand de Lesseps (the Frenchman responsible for the construction of the Suez Canal) in his speech announcing the nationalization of the Universal Maritime Suez Canal Company.

Yet, there is no question that the World Bank's position on the High Dam project had been scrupulously proper. The Bank determined the minimum guarantees necessary to protect its proposed investment, then refused to abandon its conservative banking principles. Perhaps, if President Nasser sincerely believed that the High Dam was imperative for his country's future well-being, Egypt would have acceded to the Bank's requests. Many observers, however, including prominent Egyptians, voiced the feeling that Nasser, while presenting the High Dam as the focus of his image of a "new Egypt," was unwilling to make the necessary sacrifices. Certainly this impression was strengthened by Egypt's increased internal commitments and her growing involvements in the Arab world. Assuming this to be the case, Dulles' decision was a wise one, for if Egypt would be unable to support the internal costs of the High Dam, the entire project would redound to the West's detriment. There is no question that the United States had compelling economic and political reasons for withdrawal of its original High Dam offer. As President Eisenhower observed: "The conditions that had prevailed at the time the offer was made no longer prevailed."[108]

The High Dam Scheme in Limbo

Upon nationalizing the Suez Canal Company, President Nasser announced that revenues from the Canal would finance the High Dam. This boast, however, evaporated in the crisis triggered by the nationalization. Canal revenues first were denied the Egyptian government, then were required to meet current expenses. Preliminary work continued at the High Dam site, and Colonel Samir Helmy regularly claimed that "if an agreement is reached with the Sudan today, work will start tomorrow."[109] It was obvious, nevertheless, that less emphasis was accorded the Sadd el-Aali project. In 1957, Helmy, after demurely protesting that "financing is not our business, we are engineers," estimated that the construction of the necessary cofferdams and diversion tunnels, with concomitant expenditure to convert basin lands to perennial irrigation, would take five years (previously the government had claimed four) and cost 80 million pounds.[110] Ali Sabry's announcement that work on the Aswan High Dam would begin in 1958 was generally received with skepticism.

Prospects for external financing of the High Dam seemed remote through 1957 and much of 1958. Although Shepilov announced that the Soviet Union would be willing to consider the matter if Egypt requested such assistance,[111] Egyptians received these assurances with considerable reserve. While the Cairo press reported financing offers from Japan and Switzerland, these reports were denied by responsible Egyptian officials. And despite rumors of a possible post-Suez American-Egyptian *rapprochement,* John Foster Dulles made it unmistakably clear that the United States had no intention to assist in the Sadd el-Aali project.[112]

With hopes for funds thus fading, a critical reassessment by

Egypt of the entire project was generally anticipated. Nasser still insisted that the High Dam was the keystone of his regime's program for improving his country's living conditions, and he outlined plans to initiate a five-year first stage which would require about 28 million pounds in foreign currencies.[113]

In technical discussions held in London between Egyptian representatives and members of the firm of Sir Alexander Gibb and Partners, major emphasis was placed on reviewing plans for the original cofferdams and diversion tunnels;[114] it was later indicated that construction of the entire dam would take eleven or twelve years, as opposed to Egypt's earlier optimistic expectations.[115] Moreover, there was some confusion as to the benefits that would accrue from the upstream cofferdam. In 1956, Colonel Helmy stated that it would have a 10-milliard capacity;[116] by November, 1957, he had increased this estimate to 13 milliards, although there had been no change in the plans.[117] He also failed to mention that the cofferdam would overlap almost the entire 5.5-milliard reservoir of the existing Aswan Dam.

There were other indications that original calculations of economic benefits to be derived from the High Dam needed to be revised. According to the board of international consultants, "Every year of delay in the completion of the diversion tunnels not only delays the completion of the Dam by at least one year, but it also increases the cost of the construction of the Dam on account of the restrictions which will be imposed on the regime in the existing Aswan Reservoir after the completion of the power station attached to the existing Aswan Dam. . . . Excavation of the diversion tunnels should be started without delay."[118] This was written in November, 1954. There was also evidence that Mr. R. R. Stokes, managing director for thirty years of the British firm which had supplied the control apparatus for all major works on the Nile inside Egypt since 1900, was at least partly correct when he claimed: "I have not discovered anyone in Egypt who has anything to do with agriculture who thinks this is a good project."[119] According to the *Economist,* senior officials at the Egyptian Ministry of Agriculture expected one rather than two additional million *feddans* to be irrigated as a

result of the High Dam.[120] A Sadd el-Aali pamphlet, published
in 1958, adjusted the government's official claims to 1 million
feddans to be reclaimed, another 700,000 converted from basin
irrigation, and 500,000 *feddans* of rice guaranteed annually—a
substantial drop from the 1955 figures.[121]

In the light of the above, it was not surprising when Dr.
Kaissuny, in May, 1958, announced that the High Dam "may
take second, not first priority."[122] He claimed that the two
major reasons for constructing Sadd el-Aali had been the need
for more arable land and the increasing demand for power. He
felt that, as a result of union with Syria, adequate land might
be available for agricultural expansion, and prospects for further
petroleum discoveries would reduce the cost of thermal power.
In his opinion, it seemed reasonable to invest first in the Suez
Canal, which would produce a better return; afterward, perhaps,
the High Dam project should be given serious consideration. For
obvious reasons, these comments were not recorded in the local
press, for the newspapers still were carrying enthusiastic articles
about the High Dam as the foundation stone for a new Egypt.

Government departments long since had learned not to include the High Dam in their various development plans. At the
Ministry of Industry, arrangements were being made to provide
thermal units required under the five-year plan for industry.
When asked about the added capital expenditures, in view of
the proposed High Dam hydro-electric scheme, one senior official
replied: "Oh, maybe these units will be amortized within ten
years; anyway, we need them."[123] According to a projection by
L'Electricité de France, Egypt will suffer a deficiency of electric
power during 1963-64 which will become increasingly acute;
this high demand could best be met if the first eight turbines of
the High Dam project commenced operations in 1964; otherwise,
serious overlapping in capital expenditure could occur.[124] In the
Ministry of Public Works, ranking officials viewed the High Dam
with great skepticism. According to one government official: "All
the drawings are ready for the Wadi el Rayan project and it
would take four years to execute. It would be better for Egypt
[than the High Dam]. And with 20 million pounds, another
500,000 *feddans* could be irrigated. This is enough for now."

The Chairman of the Egyptian Hydro-Electric Power Commission, speaking in Belgrade, stated that "the High Dam . . . guarantees a constant discharge annually. . . . [This] therefore accounts for irrigation engineers' adherence to the High Dam with remarkable tenacity, notwithstanding its defects, high costs, and constructional difficulties of which we are all aware and have been prepared to overlook on account of that important characteristic."[125]

The Sudan Takes Issue

As the economics of the High Dam underwent close scrutiny, prospects for an early water settlement with the Sudan remained slight. In 1957 and early 1958, several formal discussions were held, but the questions of indemnities for the inundation of the Wadi Halfa area and distribution of "surplus" water were not settled. By mid-1958, the Sudan was ready to test the irrigation canals in the first section of the newly reclaimed Managil scheme of the Gezira. Since this should only be done with Egypt's permission, a formal request was submitted on June 16.[126] When the Egyptians failed to reply, the Sudanese commenced to draw a nominal amount of timely water from the Blue Nile on July 2. Although this was a technical breach of the 1929 Nile Waters Agreement, the Sudanese insisted that Egypt's obstreperous attitude justified their independent action. The Nile of the summer of 1958 was exceedingly low;[127] and Egypt sought to blame her poor crops on the Sudanese action. In fact, however, the amount of water withdrawn for testing the Managil canals affected the flow of the river only negligibly. Egypt registered an official protest on July 9; subsequently, the Egyptian Foreign Ministry summoned all foreign ambassadors in Cairo to protest the Sudan's violation of an "international agreement."

The Sudan did not reply to the Egyptian protest until August 25. For the first time, the Sudanese government openly declared that it had never recognized the Nile Waters Agreement of 1929 as binding on the Sudan, claiming that the Sudan had not been an official party to it.[128] In private discussions, Sudanese officials suggested that existing "vested rights" would be recognized, but the refutation of the waters agreement was significant, for it reserved for the Sudan a wide latitude in future water negotiations. According to the Sudanese, they had tacitly refused, in January, 1956, to accept the 1929 agreement, an agreement which originally had been negotiated by the British. Egypt, cast in the strange role as a defender of Britain's colonial policy, claimed that "the British government concluded [the] agreement in the Sudan's name and in its [Britain's] capacity as the ruling authority in the Sudan at that time. The Sudan implemented the agreement under the condominium as an international entity. It does not stand to reason, therefore, that the Sudan should abandon and disown the agreement after attaining independence. Sudanese independence in itself cannot conceivably affect its commitments under international agreements."[129] Although this argument had some legal merit, the Egyptians were on weak ground. In 1951, Egypt had abrogated a 1936 treaty agreement with Great Britain on the grounds that Egypt, being occupied by British troops, had not acceded to the treaty of her own free will. When, in 1957, President Nasser was asked why the Sudan should not invoke similar logic to abrogate the 1929 agreement, he responded with a characteristic shrug.[130]

Egypt launched a strong campaign against the Sudan government. Fear was expressed that the Sudanese action would permit the British to exercise complete control over the sources of the White Nile. A direct appeal was made to the Sudanese people, over the head of their government, to prevent this encroachment upon the "indisputable rights of the Arab peoples of Egypt."[131] The intimation was made that the Sudan government, in league with the British, was seeking to injure Egypt. The Sudanese are proud people, however, and Egyptian threats served only to harden their resistance against their northern "brothers." When it became clear that the Sudanese would not be coerced, Egypt abruptly changed her tactics. Efforts were made to negotiate a waters agreement with Sudanese opposition political leaders, foremost among them Ismail el Azhari. But then a military coup in Khartoum deprived civilian political parties of their power.

Informed Egyptians and Sudanese believe that a water agreement may well be concluded in 1959. Egypt is under heavy pressure to provide sufficient water for her land reclamation schemes; and it seems apparent that the Sudan, as a last resort, is resolved to draw her water needs from the Nile with or without Egypt's approval. Now that the Sudan has embarked upon an ambitious 800,000-*feddan* extension of the Gezira Scheme, she will need substantially more water, especially during the timely period. Although she could drain off the Blue Nile's present natural flow, such an action would cause severe political repercussions. An agreement on the use of the High Dam waters should provide the Sudan with increased water supply at a nominal cost.*

The Sudanese have yet to accept Sadd el-Aali as the best solution to the Nile waters problem. They claim to prefer the equatorial lakes project, a series of small dams in the Sudan for irrigation and hydro-electric power, and a modified High Dam near Aswan.[132] Although it is impossible, at present, to assess the economic worth of this plan, the Sudan's desire to have extensive hydro-electric and irrigation facilities within her own borders is understandable. Likewise, Egypt finds it appealing to have the High Dam, with its reservoir, almost entirely under her sovereign control; fears of political manipulation of Nile waters never have been stilled.

The World Bank found little in the Sadd el-Aali project which would conflict with the principles of Century Storage.[133] But, in agreement with Dr. Hurst, it was observed that the High Dam was "complementary to the Equatorial Project," not an alternative.[134] Since the construction of the High Dam (perhaps in a modified form) could be completed long before the original Century Storage program could become effective, the Sudan has good reason to approve such a project. Further utilization of the Blue Nile, in conjunction with the Roseires Dam, would provide adequately for most of the Sudan's existing land-reclamation projects.

Current Prospects for the High Dam

No responsible hydrologist claims that the Sadd el-Aali alone will provide full utilization of Nile waters; extensive control is

---

* Egypt signed a Nile waters agreement with the Sudan on November 8, 1959.

required along the entire Nile. In the past, it has proved impossible to establish a development board with authority to deal with problems of the entire Nile Valley. A British plan along these lines was rejected in 1952, and both the Egyptians and the Sudanese have been unwilling to include outsiders in discussions on allocation of Nile water. President Nasser has stated privately that Egypt might accept a Nile Valley Development Board which included the Sudan and Ethiopia, but Uganda and the Belgian Congo would be excluded for they were under "foreign domination."[135] He believed that the necessary funds might be provided by the United States and the Soviet Union through an organ of the United Nations. It seems likely that, in the long run, a multinational organization will be created, for ultimate control of the Nile river will depend heavily upon agreement among the riparian states.

The history of the High Dam project entered a new phase on October 23, 1958. Nikita Khrushchev announced, during a Moscow visit by Field Marshal Abdel Hakim Amer, that the Soviet Union would provide Egypt with 400 million rubles (calculated by Egyptians as the equivalent of 37.5 million pounds)[136] in credits toward the construction of the High Dam. Subsequent technical discussions revealed how far President Nasser had veered from his original plans to finance the Sadd el-Aali. A major issue with the West had been the inability to obtain a firm commitment that foreign-currency requirements for the entire project would be underwritten; the tentative IBRD offer of a 200-million-dollar loan together with a proposed Anglo-American grant had, for many months, been considered inadequate. Two years later, Nasser accepted Soviet assistance which would cover only the construction of the "cofferdams stage." While the Soviets agreed to provide, at 2 per cent interest, credits to cover the foreign-exchange requirements of this stage (under the Anglo-American offer this was covered by outright grants), no public mention was made of assuring the foreign-exchange requirements for the entire High Dam project. Indeed, the Cairo press tended to discuss the cofferdams as if they were the High Dam.

While Egypt should be able to meet the local expenses of the "cofferdams stage," prospects of financing the internal costs of the High Dam scheme have not improved since 1956. While Sadd el-Aali still would seem beneficial to Egypt, its realization will hinge upon Egypt's ability to absorb the tremendous costs of construction. To some observers, Nasser's decision to seek Soviet assistance on the High Dam simply was another example of the economics of politics; in their opinion, Nasser acted under the compulsion of the High Dam's political importance. Perhaps this is true. Moreover, Nasser could not blink the fact that his military regime, after emphasizing Egypt's agricultural plight, had undertaken no major Nile development projects in over six years. It may well be that he also believes that Egypt's economy can support the enormous capital expenditures required by the High Dam project over more than a decade. At present, however, there is no assurance that the High Dam, as originally conceived, will ever be completed. The economic reservations voiced by the World Bank in 1955 and 1956 have not lost their validity.

VIII

Prelude to "Nasserism"

Egypt's International Position

During the period immediately following World War II, three major objectives guided Egypt's foreign policy: expulsion of the British from Egypt; the absorption of the Anglo-Egyptian Sudan into the Kingdom of Egypt; and prevention of a Jewish state in Palestine.

In all of these objectives, Egypt experienced initial frustration. In October, 1946, the British and Egyptian Foreign Ministers reached an agreement for the evacuation of all foreign troops from Egypt by September, 1949. A subsequent misunderstanding over the future status of the Sudan, however, voided the Sidky-Bevan Agreement.[1] While Great Britain did, of her own volition, withdraw all troops from Lower Egypt and station them in the Suez Canal Zone, this concession did not mute the rallying cry of "Egypt for the Egyptians." And the status of the Sudan remained unresolved during the early postwar years.

After a humiliating military defeat in the Arab-Israeli war of 1948, all the Arab combatants, excluding Iraq, signed armistice agreements with Israel. According to the terms of the Egyptian-Israeli agreement signed on February 24, 1949: "The establishment of an armistice between the armed forces of the two Parties is accepted as an indispensable step toward the liquidation of armed conflict and the restoration of peace in Palestine."[2] Egypt and other Arab countries, however, claimed that, pending a peace treaty, a "state of war" continued to exist with Israel.[3] Egypt invoked this explanation to justify her denial of Suez Canal passage to Israeli ships and cargo. Although the United Nations Security Council passed a resolution condemning this

206

interference with Suez shipping as "inconsistent with the objectives of a peaceful settlement between the parties of a permanent peace in Palestine set forth in the Armistice Agreement,"[4] no exit from this impasse was in sight. The United Kingdom had tens of thousands of troops patrolling the Canal Zone, but they were not ordered to ensure freedom of navigation through the Canal, as "guaranteed" in the Constantinople Convention of 1888.

In May, 1948, when the Arab armies entered Palestine, no Arab government accepted the partition plan recommended by the United Nations General Assembly on November 29, 1947. In accordance with the United Nations Charter, the Security Council alone had the authority to make decisions, while the General Assembly was limited to "discussions and recommendations." Thus, when a strongly partisan Assembly voted to divide Palestine into separate Arab and Jewish states,[5] the Arab delegates refused to accept this "recommendation." By the time this matter was presented to the Security Council for debate, however, the Assembly action had become a *fait accompli*. When Arab troops sought to block the implementation of the U.N. partition plan by force, they were soundly defeated by a small, ill-equipped Jewish defense force. It was only long after Israeli forces occupied territory substantially beyond the original borders proposed for a Jewish state in 1947 that the Arabs saw fit to support the General Assembly partition plan.

Opposition to Israel provided a unifying force within the Arab world, culminating in the Arab Collective Security Pact of 1950. Yet Egypt, the largest of the Arab states, was ill prepared to take military action against her enemy to the north. The Egyptian army, poorly commanded and badly beaten in the Palestine campaign, was in no condition to conduct another war; indeed, only a British threat that Great Britain was prepared, under the terms of the Anglo-Egyptian Treaty of 1936, to come to the aid of Egypt had forced Israel to withdraw her troops from Egyptian soil in 1949. Egypt expressed her hostility to the new state of Israel through diplomatic aloofness and a general economic boycott; active political agitation, however, was directed primarily against the British.

The subject of Britain's withdrawal from Egypt was again

raised during talks between Field Marshal Sir William Slim, Chief of the Imperial General Staff, and Wafdist Premier Mustapha Nahas in June, 1950. Sir William insisted that Egypt be linked with Great Britain in a defense pact. He categorically excluded American participation in such a pact, stating, "America is out of this; it has nothing to do with the Middle East."[6] When Nahas flatly refused to permit foreign troops to remain in Egypt, the negotiations collapsed. The Wafd government adopted a distinctly neutralist foreign policy, and, in protest against the British "occupation," Egypt refused to contribute forces to the U.N. contingent in Korea.[7]

By late 1951, Egypt's relations with Great Britain had deteriorated. When fluctuations in the cotton market buffeted Egypt's already fragile economy, Nahas sought to divert the country's attention away from domestic to foreign affairs. He pressed vigorously for a revision of the 1936 Anglo-Egyptian Treaty which regulated the status of British forces in the Canal Zone, and for the acceptance of Egyptian jurisdiction over the Sudan. When Great Britain refused to meet his demands, the Prime Minister tabled two decrees before Parliament on October 8, 1951. These decrees called for the abrogation of the 1936 treaty and for the unilateral installation of Farouk as King of the Sudan.[8] During the same period, Great Britain and the United States, in association with France and Turkey, sought to establish a Middle East Defense Organization (MEDO) which would encompass the Arab Middle East.

British military strategists deemed a base in the Suez Canal Zone vital to the success of this plan; therefore, on October 13, 1951, a proposal was submitted to the Egyptian government whereby Egypt would become a founding member of such a pact.[9] Since, however, an accompanying British note made evacuation of the Canal Zone contingent upon acceptance of this pact (which would permit foreign troops, including British, to be stationed in the Suez Canal Zone), the Egyptian Government flatly rejected the invitation to join the MEDO.

On October 16, Parliament approved the abrogation of the existing Anglo-Egyptian treaty and proclaimed Farouk King of the Sudan. Great Britain refused to recognize these unilateral actions, and the Suez Canal Zone immediately became the scene of sporadic violence. Egyptian laborers, numbering over thirty-five thousand, were forbidden to work for the British; an embargo was placed on all fresh fruit and other foodstuffs entering the Zone; and guerrillas harassed British installations and personnel. In one engagement, British troops killed forty-two Egyptian policemen, wounding another fifty-eight.[10] After the mob violence in Cairo on January 26, King Farouk dismissed the Nahas government and, during the next six months, until the military takeover, four successive prime ministers followed policies which were less antagonistic toward the British.

Egypt Ousts the British

The accession to power of the Free Officers brought some change in Egypt's diplomatic tactics, but for the first two years the major guidelines of Egyptian foreign policy remained essentially the same. The Suez, Sudan, and Palestine issues still commanded top priority; the problem of Palestine, however, was accorded the least attention of the three. "With Israel," Nasser explained, "a battle would indefinitely postpone internal reform, and the government has said that reform was the key foundation to its *raison d'être*."[11]

There is no firm evidence that Egypt was then seriously considering peace negotiations with Israel (although Egyptian officials often hinted at such possibility in private conversations with Western visitors). Yet, other Arab states bitterly scored what they considered Egypt's growing moderation vis-à-vis Palestine. Efforts to minimize tension along the Gaza truce line strengthened the suspicion of other Arab states that Egypt was seeking a separate peace. Indeed, when the government's censors passed an article in a weekly magazine, *Rose el Youssef*, which suggested the need for a *modus vivendi* with Israel,[12] the hope grew in Western circles that the military junta was charting a fresh, new approach to the entire problem of Palestine.

This optimism, however, was unwarranted. The problem of Palestine had become an emotional issue throughout the Arab Middle East, and no Arab leader (with the exception of King

Abdullah of Transjordan, who subsequently was assassinated)
had dared express publicly a desire for peace with Israel. Moreover, the clamors of the Moslem Brethren, who advocated all-out
war against Israel, precluded any conciliatory policy which might
have been contemplated by the military junta. Thus, while some
Israel-bound ships were allowed to traverse Egyptian territorial
waters on their way to Elath,[13] the list of Israeli "war matériel"
not permitted to pass through the Suez Canal was expanded to
include "food stuffs and all other commodities which are likely
to strengthen the war potential of the Zionists in Palestine in any
way whatever."[14]

The moderate, even conciliatory nature of official government
actions toward Israel also was in sharp contrast to public
statements issued by ranking members of the military junta. Lt.
Colonel Hussein Shafei of the Revolutionary Command Council
stated that "Israel cannot possibly bring anything but danger to
Egypt,"[15] and Major Salah Salem, then Minister of National
Guidance, dismissed Israel as "an artificial state which is bound
to disappear."[16] Gamal Abdel Nasser, speaking as Prime Minister, announced that "nobody can force the Arabs to accept
peace with Israel or to recognize her as an established state. We
believe that we can reverse the position in Palestine to its natural
state and return the land to its people and its owners. I believe
in the rights of Arabs in Palestine and I have faith in Arab
nationalism which shall triumph over borders and artificial
lines."[17]

The lull in the cold war with Israel obviously was a tactical
maneuver by the military junta. Egypt was willing, at least over
the short run, to shelve the Palestine question pending the
achievement of the more immediate objective of expelling the
British. The "truce" thus was to be only a temporary one. As
General Mohammed Naguib, then Prime Minister, expressed it:
"After we have liberated ourselves from the enemy who is
camped in our midst, we will work for the liberation of Palestine
and the realization of the aspirations of her sons."[18]

It was in the Sudan that the Free Officers scored their first
diplomatic victory. Egypt had long coveted the Sudan, but Great
Britain had consistently blocked Cairo's expansionist schemes

during the twentieth century. Although Farouk had been proclaimed King of Egypt and the Sudan and this title had been
recognized by the Arab and some Asian countries, this did not
change the reality of Britain's administrative hold over the Anglo-
Egyptian Sudan. Extension of Egypt's political control over her
southern neighbor became one of the primary objectives of the
new regime—an objective which was implicit in General Naguib's
references to a "greater Egypt."[19] But the Free Officers knew full
well that the British would not accede to Egypt's demands of
sovereignty over the Nile Valley. Thus, they decided upon a
flanking maneuver. In the fall of 1952, Naguib and Salah Salem
met with the leaders of various Sudanese political parties. They
agreed to champion the Sudan's right to self-government and,
within three years, self-determination. The British, thus confronted with a "legitimate" demand for self-determination, were
hard put to refuse. On February 12, 1953, an Anglo-Egyptian
agreement was signed which provided for the rapid "Sudaniza-
tion" of administrative posts and for self-determination after
three years.

The Egyptians clearly envisaged Sudanese independence as a
prelude to absorption of that country into Egypt. They banked
on Egypt's influence in Sudanese affairs and on the esteem with
which the Northern Sudanese regarded President Naguib, himself
part Sudanese. Cairo supported a merger of Sudanese political
parties into the National Unionist Party, headed by Ismail el
Azhari and heavily subsidized by the Egyptian government. In
November, 1953, elections the NUP won a majority of seats in
Parliament. By 1954, tentative plans were being considered for
the transfer of Egyptian farmers to uncultivated areas of the
Sudanese Gezira Scheme,[20] and Egypt's plans for the proposed
distribution of Nile waters to be stored by the High Dam were
based a priori on the conviction that Khartoum would readily
do Cairo's bidding. But, much to Egypt's chagrin and surprise,
the Sudanese did not seem willing to exchange control by the
British for control by the Egyptians. With the departure of the
British a certainty, many of the Sudanese who had been vocal
supporters of a union with Egypt found the appeals of independence more gratifying.

Already there was growing irritation in the Sudan at Egypt's heavy-handed interference in Sudanese affairs. It was an open scandal that Egyptian funds had "bought" seats in Parliament (the price for a seat in July, 1954, it was rumored, had been 2,000 pounds).[21] Nor did Naguib's political eclipse help relations between Cairo and Khartoum. After nearly a year as Prime Minister, Azhari did not feel beholden to his Egyptian "brothers"; in a private interview in July, 1954, he gave detailed reasons why the Sudan would not benefit from an economic or political union or federation with her northern neighbor.[22] Dawood Abdel Latif, Deputy Governor of Equatorial Province, commented tersely: "When Egypt offered to help rid the Sudan of the British, we said thank you very much. Now that the British are gone, we say to the Egyptians, thank you very much, and good-bye."[23]

For all their importance, the problems of Palestine and the Sudan were peripheral to the major issue of the British in the Suez Canal Zone. Britain long had been a dominant factor in Egypt's life; after the occupation of the 1880's, the British Residency in Cairo exercised firm control over local politics for well over a generation, and as late as 1942, the British Embassy could order King Farouk to replace his Prime Minister. Moreover, England normally was by far Egypt's largest trade customer and supplier, and the volume of Egyptian postwar imports was, in part, dependent upon access to the enormous amount of blocked sterling accumulated in London during the war years. Increased friction with Great Britain over the Canal Zone in 1951-52 had been reflected in a drop in Egypt's foreign trade. The military junta, therefore, was anxious for a peaceful settlement with Britain, if only to put Egypt's economy once more on a more solid footing. There was another factor, however, which impelled the Egyptian government on the road toward such a settlement—the prospect of American aid. The United States had become a major force in the Eastern Mediterranean, and the position taken by W. Averell Harriman in the Anglo-Iranian oil dispute suggested that America's influence throughout the Middle East would increase to the detriment of the British. It was, however, unmistakably clear that the United States, in deference to her European ally, was unwilling to grant massive assistance to Egypt until the Suez dispute had been resolved equitably.

While Great Britain had agreed in principle, as early as 1946, to evacuate the Canal Zone, first a dispute over the Sudan and then the issue of the proposed Middle East Defense Organization deadlocked negotiations. And although Naguib and Nasser, both of whom had been known for their pro-Western sympathies, recognized the benefits of a friendly settlement with Great Britain, the Free Officers were willing to accept no less than the unconditional evacuation of the British.[24] Moreover, the junta saw little reason for committing Egypt to a Western-oriented defense pact. Even in 1952, when Mohammed Naguib expressed Egypt's willingness to join an over-all alliance for the defense of the Middle East once her "national aspirations" had been satisfied,[25] other RCC members had suggested that such a treaty, to conform with the Arab Collective Security Pact, should include only Arab states.[26]

In an attempt to reach a compromise that would satisfy the British and at the same time prove politically acceptable to the Egyptian people, the military junta, in November, 1952, requested that Great Britain again enter into negotiations on the evacuation of the Canal Zone.[27] But the British, already smarting from the diplomatic turn of events in the Sudan, were unwilling to grant major concessions to the Egyptians.

The Suez Canal military installations, in which about eighty thousand U. K. troops were garrisoned, had long been considered the pivot of Britain's Middle East defense. The British were willing to evacuate their troops, but only at the price of re-entry rights and continued control over extensive military installations. The Egyptian military junta was reluctant to grant these concessions, fearing that they would provide grist for local political opposition groups, especially the Moslem Brethren.

When the negotiations stalled in late 1952, Gamal Abdel Nasser pledged that the British troops would be expelled from Egypt, by force if necessary. "It will not be a proper, official war," he threatened. "It will be a commando war, guerrilla war. British soldiers will be killed on the streets. Commando actions will be conducted on such a large scale as to make the British feel they are paying an inordinate price for the occupation of our country."[28]

The United States, anxious to anchor Egypt to the West, sought to intervene in the dispute.[29] Nasser, while he publicly rejected these overtures, privately welcomed the good offices of the American Ambassador, Jefferson Caffery. Nasser realized that a protracted guerrilla war against the British would prejudice Egypt's ambitious plans for internal development. This is why he dropped a broad hint to a London *Observer* correspondent: "We are soldiers and we are realists. We know that we cannot maintain such an immense base. We know that we will want technicians."[30]

Negotiations resumed on April 27, 1953, but faltered once again when Nasser categorically refused to discuss any defense pact which would explicitly link Egypt and other Arab states to NATO.[31] When the talks finally collapsed in early May, the Egyptian government decided upon a comprehensive policy of coercion. Armed Egyptians infiltrated the Canal Zone, and the Ministry of the Interior placed severe restrictions on all commercial transactions with British forces in the area.[32]

After John Foster Dulles visited Cairo in May, 1953, and held extensive talks with members of the RCC, President Eisenhower, in a letter of July 15, 1953, promised President Naguib that the United States would consider favorably Egyptian requests for armaments and economic aid immediately following the signing of a Suez settlement.[33] Shortly afterward, Anglo-Egyptian negotiators met in informal discussions, and by late September, members of Colonel Nasser's office jubilantly announced that an agreement was "as good as signed."[34] But when Great Britain insisted upon the right to reactivate the Suez base if Turkey were attacked (a provision which would have linked Egypt's defense with a NATO country), Salah Salem, spokesman for the Egyptian negotiating team, announced that agreement with the British was "impossible."[35]

Nasser, convinced that the United States had failed to use her influence with Britain in behalf of Egypt's "legitimate" claims, launched a scathing tirade against America. In a public speech he declared: "The so-called 'free world,' particularly the United States, proclaim they are helping to attain self-determination and are helping underdeveloped countries to advance. We consider such talk as opium administered by the 'free world' to enslaved peoples so that they may remain under its domination and not seek liberation."[36] He dismissed suggestions that Egypt might receive economic assistance from America by asserting that he did "not believe that the United States will help us. It is Britain's ally and both have a common, predetermined policy."[37] Earlier, President Naguib had suggested that America had "given Egypt the anesthesia, while Britain applied the scalpel."[38]

At this juncture, the Egyptian government decided to play a new card in the cold war with Great Britain: the threat of neutralism. In October, 1952, the Egyptian government had not rejected a suggestion from Pakistan's Prime Minister that a third world bloc, composed of Afro-Asian nations, be formed.[39] Indeed, at that time Abdel Mony Said Salama, a ranking official in the Ministry of Social Affairs' Labor Department, published a book in which he stressed the desirability of a neutralist bloc composed of India and other "peaceful" countries.[40] Although Naguib was on record as stating that neutrality, in the event of a major conflict between East and West, was impossible,[41] representatives of twelve Afro-Asian countries, convening in Cairo on December 23, 1952, at the invitation of the Egyptian government, held the first meeting of its kind outside the United Nations.[42] Rather than adopting a "neutralist" program, however, the delegates to this meeting simply voiced their support of the Arab position on Palestine, on West German reparations to Israel, and on the French policy in North Africa. It was only after Nehru's second visit to Cairo, in June, 1953, that the junta's threat of "neutralism" took on substance. On the eve of Nehru's departure for New Delhi, an Egyptian government spokesman "hinted strongly . . . that Egypt would align herself with the neutralist bloc of Asian nations in an effort to end Britain's 'imperialist' occupation of the Suez Canal Zone."[43]

In mid-1953, Naguib warned that Egypt might be compelled to obtain armaments from non-Western sources,[44] and reports circulated in Cairo of an offer by the Soviets to sell arms to

Egypt.[45] Few observers, however, took these reports seriously. But in December, 1953, the Egyptian ambassadors to London, Washington, and Moscow were summoned home. At the same time, there were reports that Nasser informed Dulles that Egypt was ready to opt for a policy of complete neutrality in the cold war.[46] Yet, there seemed to be no clear notion as to what this "neutrality" entailed. When American Ambassador Caffery informed Ahmed Hussein, Cairo's representative in Washington, that Egypt's new neutralist tendencies would endanger prospects for future American assistance, Dr. Hussein quickly denied that Egypt was even considering recognition of Communist China or an alliance with the Soviet Union within the United Nations.[47] And Major Salah Salem's description of Egypt's "new" policy was deliberately vague: "You can call it neutrality or anything else you like. Some may differ on the definition of the word neutrality, but what we really mean is that we take a hostile attitude and refuse to cooperate in any way with anyone who stands against our dignity and our freedom and that we cooperate [with] and support anyone who helps and supports us."[48]

To give substance to its threats, the military junta, in January, 1954, signed a commercial agreement for petroleum with the Soviet bloc. Two months later, the Soviet and Egyptian legations in Cairo and Moscow respectively were raised to embassies. During the same period, the Soviet Union for the first time used the veto in support of an Arab country when she rejected a Security Council resolution criticizing Egypt's exclusion of Israeli shipping from the Suez Canal. Yet, it was clear that Egypt's flirtation with the Communist bloc was a tactical maneuver aimed at the British. Nasser himself seemed to backtrack when he acknowledged: "It is not useful to speak of neutrality, because it has no meaning, especially in war time, unless the country is strong enough to maintain neutrality."[49]

The British, in any event, refused to be impressed by these vague threats, and Nasser decided upon a major concession: he would accept the British demand for the re-entry of her troops into the Canal Zone in the event Turkey was attacked. But he remained adamant in his refusal to link Egypt with MEDO. He told a Lebanese reporter: "Egypt's attitude toward military pacts has not changed. From the very first moment I explained to the British and Americans that the responsibility for the defense of the Middle East rests on the shoulders of Arab states alone, and that neither Egypt nor the Arab states will allow any outside state to interfere with the defense of the Middle East."[50] In private discussions with Western diplomats, however, Nasser did not exclude the possibility of an indirect link between Egypt and a NATO country.

On July 27, 1954, an Anglo-Egyptian settlement was initialled. All British troops were to be evacuated within twenty months after the agreement was signed; British civilian technicians were permitted into the Canal Zone, and Great Britain was granted the right of military access to her former bases if, within seven years, Turkey or any Arab state was attacked by an "outside power." "After the Suez settlement," Nasser later reflected, "there is nothing standing in the way of our good relations with the West. But this hammering . . . for pacts will only keep alive the old suspicions in the minds of the people . . . and the Communists know well how to exploit these suspicions. . . . It is a matter of group psychology with deep roots and, until the Arabs realize that there is no longer any hidden domination or control in pacts, any pressure to obtain them will be dangerously premature."[51]

Nasser had brought the Suez question to a successful conclusion, and he had every reason to believe that the British and Americans would soon honor his requests for military and economic aid. With Egypt's major foreign policy problem thus resolved, and with his internal political position consolidated, Nasser turned to the task of mending Egypt's political fences with her Arab neighbors.

Previously, other Arab states had criticized Egypt for her moderation vis-à-vis Israel and had turned a cold shoulder to Egypt's plea for an Arab boycott of the British pending an agreement on Suez.[52] Their reactions to a call by General Naguib for a united Arab front (under Egyptian leadership) had been equally frigid.[53] The emerging leaders in the Arab world, notably Syria's Colonel Adib Shishakly and Iraq's Nuri es Said, were wary of the revolutionary fervor and pan-Arab ambitions of

Egypt's ruling junta. Moreover, Colonel Nasser did not allay these suspicions with his outspoken criticism of Arab affairs. "We, the Arab nations," he charged in one such outburst, "are the cause of the loss of Palestine and our leaders the main reason why. . . . They [the Arab leaders] speak of 'insidious Israel' but they do nothing except talk. Arab unity is imaginary, not a real thing."[54] Such blunt language was anathema to conservative Arab leaders. Egypt's brief flirtation with neutralism also disturbed other Arab governments, a majority of whom were firmly committed to a pro-Western policy.

Push for Arab Unity

Until mid-1954, Egypt's attitude toward other Arab states was conditioned primarily by the struggle with Great Britain over the Suez Canal Zone. Nasser's interest in the Arab world had been limited to the objective of preventing any Moslem defense agreements with the West—at least until a Suez settlement was signed—lest such a move weaken Egypt's bargaining position.[55] Nasser's lack of concern for inter-Arab affairs was highlighted by his reported statement, during a conversation with the Syrian Ambassador in May, 1954, that "Egypt did not care whether Syria linked herself with Iraq or Jordan, as long as there was public support for the policy."[56]

After the Suez settlement, however, this attitude changed markedly. Nasser set the tone by again emphasizing that Egypt was anxious "to make the Arab Collective Security Pact the sole authorized instrument of defense of the Arab states,"[57] and Salah Salem visited King Saud to discuss the "possible unification of the Arab countries against pressure to participate in Western-sponsored military alliances."[58] Cairo papers spoke of sinister plots to isolate Egypt from the Arab world and singled out Iraq for vitriolic attacks.[59] In the wake of an announcement that Egypt and Saudi Arabia proposed a unified military command, Salah Salem visited Lebanon and Yemen in quick succession. Then, on the second anniversary of the Revolution, Premier Nasser made a major policy speech. He asserted that "the aim of the Revolutionary government is to make the Arabs a united nation with all its people cooperating for the common cause. . . . The Arabs' problems are also the problems of Egypt. . . . The Revolutionary government is looking with pleasure to close relations between the Arabs and the other states of the Afro-Asian bloc."[60] These statements, while in accord with the nebulous ideas which Nasser had expressed previously in his *Philosophy of the Revolution*, heralded a new phase in the policies of Egypt's military government: the drive for Arab hegemony.

Recognizing that Arab strength rested with unified action, Nasser was willing to work, at least over the short run, for the establishment of a powerful Arab bloc within the framework of the existing political *status quo*.[61] In order to revitalize the Arab Collective Security Pact, he even considered a *rapprochement* with Iraq. He was quoted as saying: "Nuri [es Said] is in power in Iraq. This is the time to reach an understanding with him."[62] It was with this mandate that Salah Salem was dispatched to Sarsank in August, 1954, to conduct discussions with top Iraqi leaders. The reports as to what transpired during these meetings have been contradictory. A leading Cairo weekly claimed that closer Arab military cooperation was agreed upon and that Iraq pledged to support a united Arab front against any Western military pact;[63] in return, Egypt promised not to stand in the way of Iraq-sponsored unity schemes (especially a projected Iraqi-Syrian federation).[64] Nuri es Said, however, gave a substantially different account of Egypt's commitments; he revealed that Major Salem, in addition to approving a common Arab defense organization, had agreed that an Arab state (presumably Iraq) should join the Turco-Pakistani Pact as a link between the Arab and Moslem defense community.[65]

Subsequent events suggested that Nuri's version was correct, and that Salah Salem had gone beyond the spirit, if not the letter, of his instructions. Upon his return from Sarsank, Major Salem was relieved of his official posts and granted a "leave of absence"; the next day he was reinstated as Minister of National Guidance and Minister of State for Sudanese Affairs. The rumor in Cairo was that Nasser, through the momentary demotion of Salem, was trying to "unbind" himself of any promises that the Major made to Nuri in behalf of the government.

Nuri, in any event, arrived in Cairo on September 15, to confer privately with Nasser. After two days of discussions, a press conference was held at the Iraqi Embassy; when Nuri stated that the Arabs must cooperate with the Western Powers, Nasser remained silent.[66] Iraq, under the shadow of the Soviet threat, felt obliged to link herself with a Western defense pact; Egypt felt no such compulsion. Thus, the proposed Egyptian-Iraqi reconciliation was stillborn.

Ironically, during this same period, Egypt's relations with Britain and the United States improved noticeably. Until August, 1954, while her traditional sources of Western supply were blocked, Egypt often was obliged to obtain armaments through clandestine channels. Moreover, scores of German ex-Wehrmacht officers, some of them originally commissioned by Farouk's government, supervised the training of the Egyptian army. The military mission under General Otto Farmbacher remained, even after the initialling of the Suez agreement, but Britain's traditional influence in Egypt's military affairs was expected to reassert itself after the October, 1951, embargo on the sale of British (and, indirectly, NATO) arms to Egypt was lifted. And the United States responded favorably to Egyptian requests for modern American military equipment. American officials probably were heartened by an RCC policy background paper which concluded that the only possible danger to the Middle East on a global scale was invasion from the Soviet Union.[67] On November 6, 1954, a 40-million-dollar American economic assistance agreement was signed in Cairo.

Nasser had intimated, before the Suez agreement, that Egypt might be willing to accept an indirect military tie with the Atlantic Alliance.[68] By late 1954, however, Nasser was definitely unwilling to commit his country to a military alliance directed specifically against the Soviet Union; instead, he seemed anxious to develop the Arab Collective Security Pact with Western arms.

The Arab League Council, convened at Cairo in December, 1954, discussed in detail the subject of military alliances. When, without further consultation with the Arab League, Iraq announced, on January 12, 1955, her intention of concluding a mutual defense pact with Turkey, Nasser reacted violently. While the regime's semiofficial daily newspaper, *Al Gomhouria*, castigated the Iraqi action, Nasser called an emergency meeting of Arab Prime Ministers for January 22. Nuri es Said, pleading ill health, did not attend, and delegations from Iraq, Yemen, and Libya arrived late for the policy conference. Nasser was blunt: Iraq had violated the Arab Collective Security Pact, and Egypt would withdraw from the Pact the moment Iraq signed her projected defense agreement with Turkey.[69] The other Arab leaders, however, refused to support Nasser's stand, and, after a mission was sent to Baghdad to confer with Nuri, the conference of Arab Prime Ministers ended on an indecisive note.

On February 24, 1955, the Turco-Iraqi Pact was signed in Baghdad; the following month, Great Britain acceded to the Pact. This, claimed Nasser, was proof that the Baghdad Pact was an instrument designed to cripple Egypt's position in the Arab world and to permit Great Britain to regain the political influence lost following the agreement to withdraw from the Suez Canal Zone. Nasser's professed fear of Western domination was not alleviated by Eden's rejoinder before the House of Commons, immediately after England had joined the Baghdad Pact: "I think that by so doing we have strengthened our influence and our voice throughout the Middle East."[70]

Nasser, in his attack upon the Baghdad Pact, claimed to be motivated only by "Arab national interests." But there were more deep-seated reasons. During this period, Egypt was beginning to gain international recognition; within a month Nasser had met with Tito once and Nehru twice, and some Arab leaders were beginning to turn toward Cairo for political guidance. While Egypt and Iraq historically had been contenders for leadership of the Arab world, Nasser assumed that the West would support a "progressive" Egypt's bid for the dominant role. According to Robert Doty, a *New York Times* correspondent who interviewed Nasser in April, 1955, implicit in his statements was the idea "that the United States and Great Britain had violated a 'gentleman's agreement' that Egypt should be permitted to take the lead in constructing a purely Arab defense alliance free from formal links with outside powers."[71] In the light of these circumstances, much of Nasser's original hostility to the Baghdad Pact (and Iraq as the only Arab member) may have stemmed from chagrin at having his ambitions thwarted by the West. Nasser was not one to accept a setback graciously. And so, in support of Major General Mohammed Salah Harb's policy statement of early February that "Egypt will remake the Arab world,"[72] Nasser launched a bitter campaign against Iraq and the British, whose covert support he had solicited a few months before.

The Baghdad Pact thus marked a major turning point in the evolution of Egypt's leadership: the revolutionary drive which had toppled the old regime and its supporting structure in Egypt now turned outward, and "Nasserism" became a driving force in the Arab world. A major incident along Israel's border helped spark this transformation. Through 1954, Egypt's relations with Israel had been relatively quiescent. Although an Israeli ship, the *Bat Galim*, was confiscated when it approached the Suez Canal, over sixty ships travelling to and from Israel had traversed the Canal safely between 1951 and 1954.[73] While Palestinian refugees frequently crossed into Israel, it was evident that the Egyptian government wanted to avoid open fighting along the border—if for no other reason than the fact that massive plans for internal development left few funds for the expansion of the Egyptian army.[74]

"Up to February 28, 1955," reported a Western writer, "Egypt had been rather less active against Israel than the other Arab countries."[75] On that day, however, a strong Israeli force attacked Egyptian military positions in the Gaza area, leaving behind thirty-eight Egyptian dead and thirty-one wounded.[76] Israel claimed that the attack had been provoked by numerous *fedayeen* ("death squad") raids mounted from Gaza—a claim which was not substantiated by Henry Byroade, the American Ambassador in Cairo, United Nations Mixed Armistice Commission reports, and *The New York Times* chronology for the preceding six months.[77] This reprisal raid, like that of October, 1953, may indeed have been designed in part to curb infiltration across Israel's borders; it was, however, more than coincidental that this "tough" policy was adopted six days after David Ben Gurion had been confirmed as Israeli Defense Minister.

The Gaza raid had an important impact on Nasser's relationship with his army. Previously he had been able to restrain the military's demands for modern equipment by pointing to the high cost of Egypt's internal development; after Gaza, however, this explanation no longer seemed valid. Indeed, it is unlikely that Nasser really wanted to restrain the army any longer. His ambition for Egyptian hegemony called for a strong military build-up. The Gaza attack provided him with a convenient excuse.

Western attempts to explain Nasser's sudden and full-scale venture into foreign affairs have leaned heavily upon an "activist" interpretation of Nasser's motives. According to this theory, Nasser, by the end of 1954, had recognized the futility of a short-term solution to Egypt's domestic problems. Given the country's existing physical and human resources, Nasser's program of economic and social reform had been commendable, but the immediate results were not encouraging. The contention is that some of Nasser's closest advisers, including Ali Sabry, persuaded the Premier during the winter of 1954-55 that he would be foolhardy to rest his political fortunes on domestic accomplishment—that his political survival would depend upon the success of Egypt in international affairs.[78] Walter Laqueur, a leading Western analyst of the Middle East, even went so far as to suggest that "if any ruler was ever driven by sheer force of circumstances to seek salvation in an 'activist' foreign policy, Colonel Nasser was."[79] This theory, while it may have some validity, ascribes too much of the "organic" to Nasser's policy. Nasser is a tactician rather than a strategist; he tends to react rather than to initiate. During the critical period under discussion, his policy was shaped by a variety of circumstances, among them his discussions with Nehru and Tito, the clash with Iraq over the Baghdad Pact, and the Israeli attack on Gaza. The disappointing pace of Egypt's internal development may have been a factor in Nasser's shift to an aggressive foreign policy, but it was not *the* factor. In fact, the government's allocations for internal development increased substantially after early 1955.

The year 1955 was a busy one for Gamal Abdel Nasser. Increasingly an adherent to the thesis that those countries which did not support Egypt's policies were her enemies, Nasser sought to make Cairo the capital of the Arab world. Al Azhar University, the theological center of the Islamic world, was mobilized for this purpose. Cairo's near-monopoly over Arab education enabled Egypt to place thousands of teachers in Arab countries, while many Arab and African students attended classes at the University of Cairo. Egypt had engaged in this type of "infiltration" long before Nasser came to power; but now the pace quickened noticeably. Exportation of technical experts, conferences in Cairo, and political agitation among the peoples of the Arab world—these became hallmarks of Egyptian policy. Voice of the Arabs, a half-hour program on the Egyptian home service in 1953, was beamed to Arab countries for nearly eight hours daily[80]—and the programs were pitched not to Arab governments but to the Arab masses.

On the diplomatic front, Nasser sought to organize a "southern tier" alliance to counter the Baghdad Pact. Major Salah Salem, the RCC member responsible for Arab affairs, was dispatched to Beirut and Damascus toward the end of February, and, on March 2, 1955, Egypt and Syria announced agreement on a unified military command. Salem and Syrian Foreign Minister Khaled el-Azm proceeded to Amman, then continued on to Saudi Arabia, where a three-nation statement was issued on March 6 in support of a joint defense. Three days later, after Yemen evinced interest in a new Arab pact, it appeared that Nasser had successfully constructed an Arab bulwark against Western military alliances. At the same time, a strong campaign was waged against Iraq and that "stooge of Western imperialism," Nuri es Said.

Nasser was becoming committed to a crusade in the name of Arab nationalism. Increasingly, those who opposed Cairo-dictated policies were castigated as "traitors to Arab nationalism." The conservative governments of the Arab world, be they monarchies or inbred political hierarchies, were highly vulnerable to such an assault. Nasser, by blaming Arab failures on Western "imperialism" and the political "old order," quickly became the hero for the restive urban Arab masses. Moreover, Nasser's propaganda campaign had an undeniable appeal, for it was designed to restore pride to the Egyptian and, incidentally, the Arab people. He sincerely believed that the Arabs could best cope with the conflicting currents of the cold war as a unified bloc—one led, of course, by Egypt. In 1954, Nasser had been content to speak for Egypt; a year later he assumed the role of spokesman for the "Arab people." On the third anniversary of the Egyptian Revolution, Nasser declared: "We are a peace-loving nation, but in order to preserve peace, we must be ready to fight to defend our country. *By our country I mean the whole Arab world.*" (Italics added.)[81]

"Positive Neutrality" Is Born

Nasser rapidly was becoming the most important single Arab personality: he also was extending his influence to the Asian world. At the conference of Afro-Asian countries held in Bandung during April, 1955, Nasser was feted as the leading representative of the Arab delegations. At the final informal reception of the Conference, he was seated at a small table reserved for Sukarno, Nehru, U Nu, and Chou En-lai.[82] His journey to Asia took him outside the Middle East for the first time; he could not help but be impressed by his warm reception in New Delhi and the respect accorded him by the leaders of Asia. Moreover, the discussions with these leaders at Bandung helped him to synthesize a doctrine tailored to his current objectives. As he later told an Indian journalist: "My visit to India proved a turning point in my political understanding. I learned and realized that the only wise policy for us would be [one] of positive neutrality and nonalignment. Coming back home, I found out from the response it had that it is the only possible policy which could get the broadest support from the Arab people."[83]

Nasser returned to Egypt with a noticeably enlarged sense of his importance. Successive visits to Cairo by the Prime Ministers of Thailand and India and by President Sukarno of

Indonesia enhanced his confidence. Nasser became an avid student of the tactics which Tito and Nehru used to good advantage. He recognized in them a perfect instrument for putting pressure on the West. But they did not blunt his aggressive bent. He held Britain and the United States responsible for the Baghdad Pact. He attacked the British for the Sudan's desire to become a fully sovereign republic. He accused Britain of restricting imports of Egyptian cotton, the United States of dumping surplus cotton stocks to the detriment of traditional Egyptian markets,[84] and the French of repressing Arab nationalism throughout North Africa.

Nasser's aggressive plunge into Arab politics required a more belligerent attitude toward Israel. Voice of the Arabs broadcast a speech by a member of Nasser's personal staff which called for the "extermination of Zionism in the second round of the Palestine war."[85] The Cairo press played down the effect of Israeli raids on Egyptian military positions, but Egypt could not afford to countenance successive defeats along the Palestine front. Thus, the *fedayeen*, trained in reconnaissance and guerrilla-war tactics, were organized by Lt. Colonel Mustafa Hafez of Egyptian army intelligence. The first recruits were enlisted in the Gaza Strip soon after the Israeli attack of February 28,[86] and, according to Abba Eban, then Israel's Ambassador to the United Nations, the *fedayeen* conducted their first raid into Israel in August, 1955.[87] United Nations reports indicate that "an organized series of raids" from the Gaza Strip followed Israel's occupation of a demilitarized zone along the truce line of August 22, 1955;[88] these raids, which resulted in twenty Israeli casualties, precipitated a massive retaliatory attack which razed the Egyptian military base at Khan Yunis.[89]

Yet, although the blockade against Israeli-bound ships transiting the Gulf of Aqaba was tightened, there was little evidence that Nasser was willing seriously to challenge Israel so long as he continued to lack the necessary military strength. In May, 1955, and again in September, 1955, he agreed to a limited withdrawal of Egyptian and Israeli troops from the armistice lines under U.N. supervision; on both occasions, the Israeli government refused.[90] It must have been embarrassing for the self-professed champion of Arab nationalism to be unable to defend his own borders against Israel.

Nasser sought to strengthen his power-political position by establishing closer relations with the Soviet Union. In an August interview with a correspondent for *Le Monde*, the Premier described his position on the cold war: "To those who ask me whether I prefer the United States or Russia, I say that I prefer Egypt. Our actions should be prompted solely by our country's interests."[91] The Russians, who had been sharply critical of Egypt's military junta until early 1955, were now ready to support Nasser's anti-Western "neutralism." The initiative in the *rapprochement* came as much from Cairo and Damascus as it did from Moscow.[92] Its main catalyst was the Communist arms shipment to Egypt.

IX

The West at Bay

Soviet Arms for Nasser

The junta made known its desire for modern armaments soon after its coup in July, 1952. Because Great Britain, during the Suez Canal Zone dispute, had applied an embargo on arms shipments to Egypt, the RCC approached the United States for military assistance. A mission headed by Ali Sabry (later Nasser's chief political adviser) arrived in Washington during the fall of 1952, but returned empty-handed after several months of negotiations.[1] While some American equipment, including ambulances and light weapons for the police, was received by Egypt, Nasser claimed that America made large shipments of weapons contingent upon a Suez settlement with the British;[2] this condition was made explicit in a letter President Eisenhower sent to President Naguib on July 15, 1953.[3] Moreover, Britain and the United States sought to isolate Egypt from other sources of supply. Some weapons were received from East Germany,[4] and Swedes helped establish machine gun and automatic rifle factories in Mahdi, a suburb of Cairo.[5] But the United States persuaded Spain to cancel armaments contracts totalling over 3 million dollars with the Egyptian government on the grounds that they were contrary to the provisions of the Spanish-American Military Aid Agreement.[6] Even after the lifting of the British arms embargo in August, 1954, the West was reluctant to meet Egypt's military requests. While Great Britain, after receiving cash payment in advance, often would extend delivery over several years,[7] the United States seemed determined to condition military aid on the acceptance of an American training staff in Cairo.[8] Nasser rejected this condition, claiming it to be an infringement upon Egypt's sovereignty.

By the spring of 1955, Nasser desperately needed new weapons for his army. The military, his major source of political strength, had demanded modern equipment for nearly three years; after the Israeli raid on Gaza and with the rise of Egypt's new ambitions in the Arab world, the officers' demands could no longer be denied. Although an Egyptian request for armored vehicles and artillery pieces was not filled by the United States in the winter of 1955,[9] Nasser appeared willing—even anxious— to receive his military requirements from the West. On June 9, 1955, Nasser informed American Ambassador Byroade that if the United States "won't give me equipment, I must get it from Russia." The same message was conveyed to the British.[10] While, in July, the British agreed to sell two destroyers to Egypt (two had been sold to Israel the previous month),[11] and while some 1953 and 1954 military contracts with the French were being filled,[12] the major Egyptian requests were made directly to the United States. On June 30, the United States government agreed "in principle" to supply Egypt with 27 million dollars of armaments, including a limited number of tanks, aircraft, and artillery.[13] Ostensibly, the negotiations then bogged down over a payment dispute; when quoted a cash price in dollars, the Egyptians wanted deferred payment, preferably in Egyptian pounds.[14] Officially, the matter still was under negotiation on September 27, 1955.[15] Apparently, President Eisenhower could have facilitated this sale to Egypt had American policymakers deemed such a move desirable.[16]

There are, however, indications that the question of payment was not the main reason for the failure of the negotiations. According to Jefferson Caffery, American Ambassador to Cairo until January, 1955, "He [Nasser] wanted military assistance without any conditions, and we had conditions."[17] In reply to Senator Hubert Humphrey's question, "Is it not true that the Egyptians offered to buy arms from the United States, and we offered to sell, but our price was too high?," Admiral Arthur Radford, former Chairman of the Joint Chiefs of Staff, stated: "I don't think that was the real reason. What they wanted to buy, as I recall them, were types of weapons we did not want them to buy. Maybe the price had something to do with it, but in my opinion it was not really the controlling factor."[18]

At least through 1954, Western military dealings with Egypt seemed to be based on the premise that under no circumstances would the RCC turn to the Soviet bloc for weapons. Some of the preconditions for Western arms shipments, as well as the embargos on weapons already purchased but not yet delivered, made it difficult for Nasser to equip his military force. He later told a British member of Parliament that, after the Gaza attack of February 28, "my soldiers were ineffective, the refugees in the Gaza Strip rioted against my inability to protect them, and the army officers in Cairo reminded me of their previous warning that I was spending too much on social services and too little on re-equipping the army. From that moment I had to take the Palestine problem seriously and be prepared to return blow for blow. . . . I pleaded with them [the West], but to no avail. So I turned to Russia and told the Soviet Ambassador frankly that I wanted to arm quickly and could afford no hard currency. I got the answer I wanted in four days."[19]

This is not to suggest that the West should have provided Egypt with weapons simply to prevent an Egyptian arms deal with the Soviets. There would have been no assurance that Egypt, once having obtained Western equipment, might not have turned to the Soviet bloc in any event. Moreover, America's global-strategic interests militated against providing Egypt with the equipment needed to completely modernize and mechanize her military forces. In all likelihood, therefore, the circumstances made it impossible for the West to match the attractive arms offer made by the Communist bloc. Whatever the reasons, the West did not prevent the Communists from scoring a major political coup when, on September 27, 1955, Gamal Abdel Nasser announced the conclusion of a massive armaments agreement with Czechoslovakia (later admitted by Nasser to be a front for the Soviet Union).

Presented with a *fait accompli*, there was little that the West could do. George Allen, an American Assistant Under-Secretary of State, hurried to Cairo to confer with Nasser, but his trip served further to enhance Nasser's prestige throughout the Arab world. Several days later, during a speech at the Egyptian Military Academy, Nasser disclosed the contents of two "secret documents," one British and the other French; they were presented as "conclusive proof" that, although Israel, rather than Egypt, was suspected of aggressive military intentions in 1955, the West permitted extensive shipments of arms to the state of Israel.[20]

Nasser's acceptance of arms from the Soviet bloc (then rumored to be in the amount of 80 million dollars, repayable in cotton)[21] represented a Western political defeat of the first magnitude: it made Nasser the hero of the Arab masses, and, at the same time, opened wide the Middle East doors to the Soviet Union. The West could draw little comfort from Nasser's statement: "With these arms we will be all right. . . . We will have enough."[22]

Subversion in the Arab World

His bold challenge of the West in the arms issue spurred Nasser's drive to organize the Arab world. Only the preceding month he had been forced to admit the failure of a policy vital to Egypt's plans for the Nile Valley and Africa south of the Sahara: with the dismissal of Major Salah Salem as Minister of National Guidance and Minister of State for Sudanese Affairs, Nasser claimed that the "book was wiped clean" and that Egypt was ready to recognize the Sudan as an independent republic.[23] The previous policy of subverting Ismail el Azhari's government ostensibly was abandoned, and Major Salem, the implementor of Nasser's policy directives on the Sudan, was held responsible for past frictions in Egyptian-Sudanese relations. It became clear that the Sudan would not easily succumb to the mystical appeals of a Cairo-oriented Arab nationalism. Elsewhere in the Arab world, however, the Nasser bandwagon gained momentum. The traditional political structure of the Arab world was crumbling; Nasser capitalized upon this fact by placing himself at the head of a "liberal" movement.

Nasser's drive to "remake" the Arab world was spearheaded by the activities of Egyptian military attachés. In Amman, Colonel Salah Mustapha was credited with keeping Jordan out of the Baghdad Pact,[24] and Lt. Colonel Kamal Mohamed Hinnawi, military attaché in Baghdad, was declared *persona non grata.*[25] The Iraqi Minister of Interior accused Mohamed Issa, a member of Hinnawi's staff, of possessing explosives and directives for a group plotting against the government.[26] Subsequently, after extensive contacts with disgruntled Palestinian refugees in Jordan, Colonel Mustapha was "mysteriously" assassinated by a bomb received through the mail; Colonel Hinnawi was rewarded for his efforts by becoming Nasser's personal press secretary. Attempts to undermine existing Arab governments opposed to Nasser became commonplace, and it was even reported that King Saud had foiled an assassination plot planned by Egypt.

Nasser, meanwhile, made bold advances on the diplomatic stage. The "southern tier" defense organization, left in limbo in March, 1955, reached a more concrete stage of development when formal military alliances were concluded with Syria, Saudi Arabia, and Yemen. Although Jordan expressed a willingness to "coordinate defense plans" with Egypt, a joint communiqué of May 6, 1956, made no provision for a unified command or full military cooperation.[27] As an aftermath to King Hussein's dismissal of the Arab Legion's commander, General Glubb Pasha, a meeting of the heads of state of Saudi Arabia, Syria, and Egypt was called in Cairo; its purpose was to provide assistance for their "sister country," Jordan, following the departure of the British.

Nasser was anxious to consolidate his position as leader of the Arab world. Juxtaposed with his vicious campaign throughout the Arab world, including North Africa, was Nasser's persistent plea that he did not wish to be established as "supreme over all the countries of the Arab world."[28] Fearful that such an impression might force Arab governments hostile to him into a common alliance, he reiterated: "Our interests are the interests of the Arabs. . . . Our policy is not to favor Egypt over the Arab area."[29] And in all fairness to Nasser, the charge that he sought to establish a personal Arab empire was perhaps premature. There is no denying that he called for the liberation of the Arab world from Morocco to Baghdad,[30] but this was not incompatible with the broad aims of Arab nationalism; it also was an acceptable tenet of Arab nationalism that independent Arab countries, like Egypt, should help liberate those areas still under foreign domination. Western and Arab officials, however, were apprehensive that "liberation" was equivalent to absorption into Egypt's sphere of influence.

Uneasy Truce with Israel

Nasser's attitude toward Israel was conditioned by immediate military considerations. Although he found it fruitful to announce his desire "to restore to the people of Palestine their right to freedom and life,"[31] he probably agreed with Admiral Radford's assessment that Israel's fighting force was superior to the Egyptian army.[32] Egypt was then receiving armaments from the Soviet bloc; other weapons were arriving in bulk from Great Britain, France, Belgium, and Italy.[33] While these weapons were being absorbed into Egypt's military establishment, Israel, in the event of a showdown, would have won a smashing victory. But, again to quote Admiral Radford, the Israelis would "have reason to be concerned when the Egyptians have learned to use their new equipment."[34]

Israel, meanwhile, continued to play to Nasser's weakness. In 1955, five major "retaliatory raids" were launched across the Egyptian truce lines, and on each occasion substantial losses were inflicted upon the Egyptian defenders.[35] Nasser, lacking the means for a retaliation in kind, relied upon the paramilitary *fedayeen*. While these armed infiltrators certainly disturbed Israel's sense of security, their exploits were publicized in the West far out of proportion to their actual deeds. The *fedayeen*, as distinguished from less organized Palestinian refugees who had been infiltrating Israel's borders continually since 1949, first were "unleashed" in August, 1955, following the Israeli occupation of an observation post near the demarcation line.[36] Israel's reaction was to destroy the *fedayeen* base at Khan Yunis. Then, in November, the day after Ben Gurion returned as Prime Minister, an Israeli attack against el Sabha resulted in fifty Egyptians killed and forty captured; the government in Cairo, in order to placate local public opinion, reported a nonexistent counterattack.[37] In April, 1956, after an Israeli attack on Kissufim left over 60 Arabs dead and another 120 wounded[38] (only

9 of the casualties reportedly were soldiers), Nasser retaliated by ordering intensified *fedayeen* action.[39] Only through the efforts of Dag Hammerskoljd was an unconditional cease fire implemented on April 18.

Internal pressures in Egypt as well as in Israel made lasting peace along these two countries' common border practically impossible. Moreover, Israel was surrounded by a hostile Arab world—one which was committed to a "state of war" against the successor to the Palestinian mandate. Israeli leaders watched with growing apprehension as Arab states, especially Egypt, increased their military potential. In some Israeli circles there was even talk of a "preventive war." Egypt, for her part, seemed content to play a waiting game, confident that time favored the Arab cause.

Nasser, in private conversations with Western visitors, made it clear that a settlement of the Palestine problem was not in the offing. He insisted upon restoration of the 1947 partition boundaries, resettlement, and compensation for the Arab refugees—demands which were at odds with the political realities of the situation. Major Salem, while still a member of the RCC, probably expressed the thinking of Egypt's leadership when he asserted: "We reject peace with Israel, even if she accepted the United Nations' decisions, because we are unable to ignore the danger of Israel and Israel's position. . . . If Egypt opens her doors to Israel, she is doomed. . . . Our economy would be wrecked and so would our morality and our military forces."[40] Whatever her motives, Egypt, while not prepared officially to recognize the existence of Israel, was anxious not to provoke a war with her antagonist. As one Egyptian expressed it, "We wish to maintain a nonbelligerent 'state of war'."

Nasser Against the West

While Nasser sought to keep the conflict with Israel within bounds, he scored successes in other areas. His political victories came at the expense of Western interests in the Arab world. The West, and especially Great Britain, had been staunch supporters of Middle East monarchies, and "Nasserism" increasingly undermined the position of these rulers. Moreover, Nasser more than once suggested publicly that the Arab countries could seriously cripple Western Europe's economy by withholding Middle East oil supplies.[41] Although the West had tentatively supported the plan to construct the High Dam, the anti-Western tenor of Nasser's policy throughout the Afro-Arab world raised serious doubts, especially in London and Paris, as to the wisdom of supporting Gamal Abdel Nasser actively. Eden sought to woo Egypt by proposing a Palestinian settlement favorable to the Arabs,[42] but Nasser, while he applauded Eden's Guild Hall speech, refused to cease his anti-British policy. France was able to "buy off" Egypt's violent crusade against the French in North Africa by resuming arms shipments to Egypt, but this respite was brief; the French felt compelled to reimpose an embargo on light weapons for the Middle East only three months later.[43]

By spring of 1956, the rift between Egypt and the Western Big Three had widened. French Foreign Minister Christian Pineau's trip to Cairo, in an effort to stop Nasser's support for the Algerian rebels, appeared fruitless. Nasser asserted that "for months no commando fighter had gone from Egypt to North Africa,"[44] but there was no guarantee that further Egyptian arms and Egyptian-trained soldiers would not be smuggled to Algeria. The Foreign Office in London was chagrined at Nasser's persistent and violent attacks against Great Britain's sphere of influence throughout the Arab countries and East Africa. Selwyn Lloyd, in a visit to Cairo, made it perfectly clear to Nasser that denial of Persian Gulf oil revenues to England would be considered a warlike act;[45] but this warning did not halt the Egyptian attack upon other vulnerable British positions throughout the area. Nasser, in an interview with a London *Observer* correspondent, claimed that Great Britain had wrecked an Anglo-Egyptian *rapprochement* by plunging into the Baghdad Pact.[46] A British Foreign Office spokesman, with Prime Minister Eden's personal approval, retorted: "In spite of the Sudan agreement, the treaty over the Canal Zone, the offer of British help for the Aswan [High] Dam, and consistent British efforts to establish better relations, Egypt has not ceased from actions and propaganda directed against Britain and governments in treaty relations with Britain."[47]

While Nasser's policies in the Arab world clashed headlong

with the interests of Great Britain and France, he did not abandon the hope of gaining the support of the United States. He calculated that America's prime policy objectives in the Middle East, aside from maintaining good relations with her NATO allies, were twofold: to check Communist infiltration and to protect Western oil interests. Sensing that he might be able to play on Dulles' fear of Soviet Communism, Nasser drafted a carefully couched appeal to America. He summed up the essence of his thesis in an interview with *The New York Times*' Cairo correspondent:

> I say that the Third World War is going on right now. We are in it. It is an invisible war. It is a war of nationalists all over the world to gain their independence. It is a psychological war and you cannot fight it with tanks. You Americans are concentrating on military bases. With atomic weapons and hydrogen bombs these bases are useless, and because of these new weapons I do not believe that anyone will start a "hot" war. You can have your military bases. But I say that around each one of them there will be a thousand nationalist bases, and the Communists are winning them over.
>
> Do you not look at a map of the world and wonder why the Soviets are winning this war? The only way to win this war is to support the nationalist struggle along the lines of the United Nations Charter, the Atlantic Charter, and your Bill of Rights. You will upset your allies, Britain and France, but you will have the whole world with you. . . . The United States is the greatest country in the world, but you can do great harm to the world if you continue to support colonialism against the philosophy of your revolution. . . . If I had continued to allow our cotton to pile up, simply because of a hypothetical fear of what might happen if we dealt with the Communists, I would have been a fool. Our Revolution would have failed and extremist elements would have arisen to overthrow us. . . . The Communists have already been in the Middle East for a long time. In Egypt we have already destroyed their organization and the Egyptian Communists are no longer a threat to us. The Communist threat from inside is greater in Lebanon and Syria and even in Iraq, where you have a defense pact against Communism.[48]

This thesis apparently was not accepted in Washington, for Egypt's relations with the Western Big Three continued to deteriorate. There were reports that further armament deals, bringing the total to about 250 million dollars, had been concluded with the Soviets;[49] and Egypt's diplomatic recognition of Communist China caused new consternation in Washington. Ranking French officials, disturbed by Egypt's direct participation in the Algerian war, publicly branded Nasser as "the Egyptian dictator"[50] and accused him of suffering from megalomania.[51] For ten weeks in the spring of 1956, the British Embassy frostily maintained none but administrative contacts with the Egyptian government.[52] Against this background, it should not have come as a great surprise when the United States and Great Britain withdrew their offers to assist in financing Egypt's proposed High Dam.

Nasser, accompanied by Nehru, was returning home from Brioni following a meeting of "neutralist" leaders when he received word of Dulles' action. Already the week had brought the Egyptian President two diplomatic setbacks: the Soviet Union had concluded a sizable petroleum deal with Israel, which dealt a severe blow to the Arab economic boycott, and Tito and Nehru did not subscribe fully to Nasser's views on Algeria and on the question of Palestine. Nasser's drive for international recognition was in danger of losing momentum. For those who were familiar with Nasser's character, there was little doubt that he would react violently to Dulles' rebuff; but American officials privately dismissed Nasser's threats to build the High Dam without Western assistance as "somewhat hysterical."[53] There was speculation in Cairo that the United States Information Service might be closed or that diplomatic relations with the United States might possibly be severed, but diplomats felt that the Soviet's apparent unwillingness to finance the Dam gave Nasser little tactical leeway.

Nationalization and Its Aftermath

Thus, it came as a shock when, on July 26, 1956, Gamal Abdel Nasser announced the nationalization of the Universal Maritime Suez Canal Company.[54] In some respects this was, as Dulles phrased it, an "angry act of retaliation."[55] But it was motivated by more than pique. Egypt had long coveted the Suez Canal Company and the profits which went to French and British shareholders. Even before the Revolution, some Egyptians[56]—particularly Mustapha el Hefnaoui, a lawyer who had written a doctoral dissertation in Paris on Egypt and the Suez Canal—had urged that the Egyptian government claim a greater share of the Canal revenues. Only four months after the Revolution, Dr. Hefnaoui was invited to lecture at the Officers' Club in Zamalek; at the conclusion of his speech, in which he advocated revocation of the Canal Company's concession, Mohammed Naguib told him that the lecture should be used as the government's "blueprint."[57] One of Naguib's colleagues, Colonel Gamal Abdel Nasser, however, insisted that the British must first be expelled from the Canal Zone.[58] Over the next several years some articles in the local press publicized the "injustices" committed by the French-controlled Canal Company,[59] and Hefnaoui continued to expound his pet thesis, but little more was done except to establish an advisory board to supervise the "Egyptianization" of Canal posts pursuant to the expiration of the Company's concession in 1968.[60] In 1955, Nasser held a five-hour conference with Dr. Hefnaoui in which the two men discussed in detail the possible methods by which Egypt could invalidate the existing Suez Canal concession; at the close of the meeting, Nasser suggested another meeting in 1960 "so that we can complete the job."[61] Later a team of army officers was delegated to investigate possible Company violations of the original Suez Canal concession.[62]

The nationalization of the Suez Canal Company had been considered by Egypt long before the withdrawal of an American offer for the High Dam. In August, 1956, President Nasser declared publicly that he had contemplated the possible nationalization of the Canal Company for over two and a half years,[63] and his close associate, Mohamed Hassanein Heikal, wrote that, following the evacuation of the Canal Zone by the British (June 18, 1956), this was the "year for the Canal."[64] Perhaps, as on other occasions, Heikal was guilty of ex post facto rationalization, for the members of the Egyptian board appointed to oversee the

Canal Company's operations were ill prepared to assume actual management.

The Western Big Three reacted violently to Nasser's nationalization. There was, however, no sound legal ground on which Nasser's move could be challenged, for Nasser, in his speech of July 26, had offered compensation to Company shareholders, and ample precedent supported Nasser's claim that the Suez Canal Company was, in fact, an Egyptian company subject to Egyptian laws.[65] Moreover, there was no evidence that Nasser, by his act of nationalization, had violated the Constantinople Convention of 1888, for the Suez Canal Company had never been entrusted explicitly with the maintenance of freedom of passage through the Canal. The initial reaction of Britain, France, and the United States was to apply economic pressure against Egypt by freezing Egyptian assets in their countries. Plans were also initiated to call a London Conference of twenty-four nations, ostensibly to establish an international control over the Suez Canal. The case for the Western Powers was tenuous for, as an American official observed: "There is no doubt that Egypt has the right, if she wishes, to nationalize the Suez Canal Company, assuming that adequate payments are made. If Nasser does not go further and does not disrupt the operation of the Canal, then everything will be all right."[66]

Britain and France, however, were in no mood for legalistic scruples; they recoiled at the thought of the Suez Canal coming under Egypt's "unfettered control."[67] Prime Minister Eden expressed the British (and French) view: "Some people say that Colonel Nasser promised not to interfere with shipping passing through the Canal. Why, therefore, don't we trust him? The answer is simple. Look at his record. Our quarrel is not with Egypt, still less with the Arab world. It is with Colonel Nasser."[68] President Nasser reacted with the aplomb usually expected of Whitehall. In his rejection of the invitation to the London Conference he gave a clear statement of Egypt's sound legal position: although he refused to surrender control of the new Suez Canal Authority, he did express a willingness to sponsor, with other 1888 Convention signatories, a conference for the purpose of reviewing the Constantinople Convention.[69] There followed two London Conferences, not attended by Egypt, the creation of a Suez Canal Users' Association (which, by Dulles' admission, was not prepared to "shoot its way through the Canal"),[70] and the establishment of "six principles" for the operation of the Canal, negotiated with the assistance of the United Nations Secretary-General. These, however, were empty moves in the face of the *fait accompli*: the Suez Canal was an integral part of Egyptian territory, and Nasser's government had assumed responsibility for the functions previously executed by the Universal Maritime Suez Canal Company.

Western military action over the Suez Canal issue would have been justified only if Egypt had interfered with shipping in the Canal. Yet, the Egyptians were scrupulously careful not to provide the West with legal provocation. Even though they did not abandon their claim of a "state of war" against Israel, two Haifa-bound freighters were permitted through the Canal.[71] When some shippers refused to pay tolls to the Egyptian Suez Canal Authority, Nasser, to avoid an incident, permitted them to make payment to the French office of the expropriated Company. Even after most of the qualified Canal pilots had left their jobs at the behest of the old Canal Company, Mahmoud Yunis, formerly an army colonel, and a skeleton crew managed to keep ships moving through the Canal without undue delay.

There were indications that Egypt might make political use of her control of the Canal. Before the nationalization, the Egyptian government had notified the United States Ambassador in Cairo that all American warships desiring passage through the Canal must give ten days' prior notice if Egypt was to be "responsible for the safety of the ships."[72] On another occasion (following the arms deal with the Soviets), an American ship carrying Turkish troops had been detained until the number of troops was ascertained.[73] But pending a recurrence of such actions after the expropriation of the Canal, the West had no legal ground for revoking the nationalization by force.

British and French leaders, however, from the outset of the crisis had reserved the right of military action as a "last resort." And Prime Minister Anthony Eden and Premier Guy Mollet did not accept the "six principles" negotiated at the U.N. On October 16, 1956, Eden and Selwyn Lloyd conferred with Mollet and Christian Pineau in Paris. It is generally believed that the final decision to invade Egypt was made at this meeting.

Suez and Sinai

In many respects, Israel had far more justification for an attack against Egypt than did France or Great Britain. The French were enraged by Nasser's support for the Algerian rebels. But Nasser was not the cause of the Algerian rebellion, and the French belief that a victory in Suez could atone for the failures of the Algerian campaign, let alone end the Algerian war, was a masterpiece of circuitous logic. Great Britain, on her part, focused on Nasser the resentments engendered by a frustrating series of setbacks in the British Empire. But if the British believed that by defeating Nasser they could arrest the tide of nationalism which battered their last remaining imperial footholds, they were guilty of a grievous misreading of history.

Israel, however, in her attempt to force a showdown with Egypt, did have the support of cold logic. Although Henry Byroade, former American Ambassador in Cairo, did not believe that Egypt was planning an attack on Israel,[74] Israeli leaders had reason to fear the Arabs' continued military build-up. According to Admiral Radford, by the end of 1956, "the total [military] hardware supplied by Russia to the Middle East countries at cheap prices" was estimated by the United States at 328 million dollars.[75] In the light of the Arabs' avowed ambition to "push Israel into the sea," the idea of a "preventive war" was a persuasive one. An equally important motive was Israel's desire to open the Gulf of Aqaba to Israeli shipping. On July 11, 1955, David Ben Gurion declared: "We shall ensure free passage through the Gulf [of Aqaba] to Elath, if necessary with the help of the Israeli navy, air force, and army."[76] Several months later, an American diplomat noted that Israel's avowed intention to remove the Egyptian blockade of the Gulf of Aqaba within the coming year could lead to a "preventive war."[77]

Israel's attitude toward the Aqaba issue was summed up by

Ben Gurion before the Knesset: "The future of the Negev depends on this free outlet. Its existence, safe and free, will turn Elath into a port of international importance, and it may transform Israel's geopolitical position. I believe that the crucial point of historical importance is the opening of the Straits of Elath to the unimpeded passage of Israeli and international navigation. Nothing can ensure the development of the Negev and our future economic independence more than that."[78] Given an Israeli decision to attack Egypt, it seemed reasonable to suppose that carrying out such an action in concert with France (and, perhaps, Great Britain) would make forceful opposition by the United States less likely. Indeed, there was irrefutable evidence of coordinated French-Israeli planning in the attack against Egypt;[79] Hanson Baldwin, military editor of *The New York Times*, also claims that Great Britain had some prior knowledge of Franco-Israeli intentions.[80]

In any event, on October 29, Israeli parachutists landed deep in Egyptian territory, while ground forces crossed the truce lines. The first Israeli communiqué named the Suez Canal as a target of the attack, but subsequent Israeli government communiqués claimed the elimination of *fedayeen* bases as the major military objective.[81] During the first day, Israel's full fighting force, especially her air force, was not committed to battle; instead, several brigade spearheads were ordered to conduct probing operations. In retrospect it would appear that Israel was prepared to withdraw from Sinai if circumstances proved unfavorable; moreover, Israeli leaders calculated that the Egyptians, if they initiated massive air attacks, would bear the onus of a full-scale war. As one observer remarked, Israel had initiated "more than a retaliatory raid and less than a war."

The United States, upon being apprised of the invasion, suggested a meeting of the signatories of the Tripartite Declaration (which guaranteed existing Arab-Israeli armistice lines), but the British and French were reluctant to take steps against Israel. Instead, after a hurried meeting in London, Eden and Mollet, on the afternoon of October 30, authorized a joint communiqué which was then handed to Egyptian and Israeli diplomatic representatives. The note requested both parties to

cease all warlike action and to withdraw their military forces
to a distance of ten miles from the Canal. So that the freedom
of transit through the Suez Canal could be assured, Egypt was
asked to permit the temporary occupation of Port Said, Ismailia,
and Suez by Anglo-French forces; failure of both combatants
to reply in the affirmative to this note within twelve hours would
"necessitate Anglo-French intervention in such strength as necessary to secure compliance."[82]

A State Department official subsequently described this note
as "the most brutal ultimatum in modern history."[83] At the
time Israel was "ordered" to "withdraw" to a distance of ten
miles from the Canal, its advance force, a single parachute
battalion, was over thirty miles from the Suez Canal.[84] Egyptians,
for their part, were asked to withdraw completely from Sinai
and the entire Suez Canal Zone, leaving Israel in full control of
the Gaza area and most of Sinai. In a speech before the House
of Commons later that day, Prime Minister Eden declared: "In
order to separate the belligerents and to guarantee freedom of
transit through the canal by the ships of all nations, *we have
asked the Egyptian government to agree that Anglo-French
forces should move temporarily into key positions at Port Said,
Ismailia, and Suez*. I repeat, temporarily . . . British and French
forces will intervene in whatever strength may be necessary to
secure compliance." (Italics added.)[85] In other words, the British
and French were determined to land troops in Egypt regardless
of Egypt's decision.

Eden invoked various justifications for his government's proposed action. On one occasion he explained the ultimatum as
the execution of the government's obligation to "take such steps
as are essential to protect the lives of their citizens and vital
rights such as are here at stake—I ought to add, vital international rights."[86] The claim also was made that Egypt, apparently overnight, had become a bastion of Soviet Communism in
the Middle East—despite the fact that Allan Noble, British
Minister of State for Foreign Affairs, had, on November 19,
1956, discounted the urgency of the "Soviet threat in Egypt."[87]
Anthony Head, British Minister of Defense, expressed his government's objectives more candidly on November 8: "The whole

point of this is that the Canal cannot and must not be solely the concern of the Egyptian government. That is what all this has been about."[88]

The overthrow of Nasser's government seemed to be a primary target of the Anglo-French action. A British-controlled Cyprus radio station broadcast in Arabic that the Anglo-French forces only wanted to rid Egypt of "that traitor" Nasser who had "almost delivered our country [Egypt] into Moscow's clutches."[89] A British-French communiqué from Cyprus acknowledged the following official leaflet which was scheduled for distribution throughout the Egyptian Delta: "Remember that we have the might to attain our objective, and we shall use all of it if necessary. Your choice is clear. Either accept the Allied proposals or accept the consequences of Nasser's policy, which will bring heavy retribution not only to the few who are guilty, but also to you, the many who are innocent."[90] As an editorial in *The New York Times* concluded, the "unannounced but major aim of the British and French military action was to bring about the overthrow of Nasser."[91]

According to a London *Times* correspondent, "the British Government's decision to intervene in Egypt was taken without the advice of nearly all senior diplomatic representatives in the area. . . . Reactions in nearly all of them [British embassies and legations] appear to have ranged from initial frank disbelief to talk of its being potentially a disaster."[92] These representatives had informed Whitehall that the present situation in the Arab world was far different from that of ten or twenty years before, and the efficacy of blatant British military intervention had been greatly reduced by the changed circumstances. The strong reaction against the Baghdad Pact was indicative of the new mood in the Arab world.

The Anglo-French military action was set in motion soon after Egypt's rejection of the October 30 ultimatum. On October 31, British and French planes bombed Egyptian air bases and systematically demolished other military targets. Simultaneously, the Israeli army swiftly moved across Sinai. As a result of the Suez crisis, Nasser had withdrawn about thirty thousand troops from Sinai (including the bulk of his armor) late in the summer, redeploying them near the Suez Canal.[93] This left the Eighth Infantry Division, composed primarily of Palestinians and Egyptian National Guardsmen, the Third Infantry Division, and four additional battalions to guard the Gaza area and all of Sinai.[94] Israel's fighting force of nine brigades, of which eight actually were committed to battle, seemed slightly superior in size to the Egyptian army in Sinai.[95] Israel's initial attack was launched against lightly defended positions which were overrun without serious opposition. Mobile Israel spearheads, often overextending their logistical support, then swept across Sinai in little over four days, with the fall of Sharm el-Sheikh on the Gulf of Aqaba delayed until November 5, only because the attacking Israeli brigade had to travel over hundreds of kilometers of difficult terrain before reaching its objective.

On occasion, when provided with strong defensive positions, the Egyptian army fought bravely, if ineptly. At the battle of Mitla Pass, an Israeli brigade was stopped momentarily,[96] and at Abu Agueila (or, more accurately, Un Sheham) an Egyptian brigade was able to hold out for more than two days. Then, inexplicably, the Egyptian commander ordered "every man for himself," and the position was abandoned at night with the guns left unspiked. Apparently, the decision was prompted by a serious shortage of water, but few of the soldiers survived the forced trek across the barren desert.[97] After an Egyptian garrison withdrew from its position at Ras Nasrani to the less well-fortified bunkers of Sharm el-Sheikh, these soldiers also mounted a brief, but stout resistance.[98] In the wake of bombing and strafing attacks by B-17 Flying Fortresses and by Mustangs, Israeli troops stormed the fortifications and fought for six hours before securing the position; 200 Egyptians were killed in the fighting.[99] In most other encounters with the Israeli enemy, Egyptian troops were quickly routed.

There can be no doubt that the Israeli fighting force defeated the Egyptians in Sinai in 1956. The Israelis, in flexibility of action and mobility of troops, proved far superior to the scattered Egyptian defenders. Some circumstances suggest, however, that, without assistance from the British and French, Israel's victory might not have been so overwhelming. Egypt had numerical air superiority over Israel at the start of the campaign, and the Egyptian air force commanded about fifty Ilyushin bombers.[100] Even with the recent addition of French Mystères IV to the Israeli air force, the danger of Egyptian bombing attacks against Israel would have required a large part of Israel's air force to fly air cover over Haifa, Tel Aviv, and Jerusalem. It appears, however, that much of this mission was undertaken by elements of the French air force, flown to Israel on October 29 specifically for this task.[101] There was also evidence that the French gave tactical air support to Israel's military operations in Sinai.[102] In any event, air superiority, a prerequisite for the bold tactics executed by Israel in Sinai, was ensured after October 31 by the Anglo-French destruction of Egyptian air fields.

The official Egyptian account of the Sinai campaign stresses the military significance of the Anglo-French intervention. Egyptian strategy called for the deployment of massive reinforcements across the Canal and into Sinai; this was begun shortly after the initial Israeli attack.[103] On the night of October 30 (after the Anglo-French ultimatum had been delivered), the Israeli air force discovered several large Egyptian convoys traveling east from the Canal Zone with their headlights on full;[104] scores of trucks, tanks, and troop carriers were destroyed with rockets and napalm. It was not until late Wednesday, October 31, that Cairo gave a withdrawal order to all troops in Sinai not already committed to battle.[105] Although this move was well conceived (the threatened Anglo-French invasion could trap Egyptian forces in Sinai), it had no apparent effect on the outcome of the battles of Abu Agueila, Rafah, Sharm el-Sheikh, and others. Indeed, there were indications that some major units of the Egyptian army were out of touch with headquarters from the start of hostilities.[106]

Israel's smashing victory in Sinai (between 1,000 and 3,000 Egyptians killed and about 5,600 captured, as contrasted with 171 Israeli dead and one prisoner)[107] attested to the tactical excellence of Israeli officers and the mobility of their units. Yet, as Israeli brigades reached el Arish and beyond, their lines of supply became dangerously overextended. If, at that point, the

Egyptian air force, poorly trained though its pilots were, had been capable of flying effective sorties against the enemy, and if Egyptian reinforcements which had crossed the Canal were available to mount a massive counterattack, the outcome of Israel's Sinai campaign might have been different.

The British-French campaign was badly conceived and woefully executed. It took Britain nearly three months to assemble the forces considered necessary for an invasion of Egypt—this despite the fact that, following the evacuation of the Suez Canal base, a British mobile ready reserve of twenty-five thousand troops in England supposedly was prepared to move anywhere in the world within seventy-two hours. On October 31, the bombing of Egyptian installations began in the face of only token opposition; Nasser apparently was unwilling to sacrifice his inexperienced pilots in such an uneven conflict. The bombings continued relentlessly for five days, yet there were no signs of an invasion.

If, as John Campbell claims, the British and French "expected a quick military success, whereby they would seize the Canal and oust Abdel Nasser before anybody else could do very much about it,"[108] they went about this task in an unprofessional manner. The French were willing to stage a direct paratroop assault upon the bulk of the Canal Zone[109] on the assumption that Anglo-French air cover could prevent effective counter-attacks by Egyptian armor. The British, however, were exceedingly cautious, for they wished to keep Allied casualties to a minimum.

By the time British landing craft dispatched from Malta had lumbered into view off Port Said and the first paratroopers were dropped on November 5, world opinion had already been roused against the invasion. The Soviets threatened the "aggressors" with missile warfare, while the dispatch of Russian "volunteers" to Egypt seemed possible. The following morning, British and French troops landed on the quays and beaches of Port Said; after a temporary cease fire and sharp resistance from the civilian population, elements of the combined force advanced along the road to Ismailia. Much against French wishes, however, a cease fire was proclaimed over the entire battle area at midnight,

November 6. At a minimum, the French were anxious to seize
the entire Canal. They deemed this a relatively simple task;
however, Anthony Head, Britain's Minister of Defense, believed
that such an operation would take another seven days.[110] Foreign
Minister Pineau explained to the French National Assembly:
"France was under the moral and material necessity of accepting
the British decision."[111]

The Anglo-French invasion ended in dismal failure. Its
avowed objective, to maintain freedom of passage through the
Canal, was defeated when Nasser, soon after the bombing
attacks, blocked the Canal by sinking ships along its entire
length. And before troops had landed in Port Said, the fighting
in Sinai had ceased. The British and French did not seize the
Suez Canal, and Gamal Abdel Nasser was still firmly entrenched
as leader of Egypt. He had been handed a smashing military
defeat: an Egyptian destroyer, the "Ibrahim el Awal," had been
captured intact by the Israelis (a humiliating experience without
precedent in twentieth-century naval history); perhaps half of
Egypt's air force had been destroyed;[112] many thousands of
soldiers had been killed or captured; and much of the new Soviet
military equipment had been destroyed.

But the intervention of Britain and France shrouded Nasser
in the robes of a martyr, and he played this role to the hilt. His
army's poor performance in Sinai was blamed upon the Anglo-
French attack, and this explanation contained enough truth to
make it plausible to a great majority of Egyptians. Moreover,
the resistance of the citizens of Port Said provided Nasser with a
potent rallying-cry: "Port Said . . . has proved to the world
that Egypt will never surrender!"[113] In short, a resounding military defeat turned into a political victory for Gamal Abdel
Nasser.

X

The Tactics of "Positive Neutrality"

Nasser Recoups

One aftermath of Suez was the possibility of a U.S.-Egyptian *rapprochement*. Cairo officials noted America's apparent lack of foreknowledge of the military attacks on Egypt and applauded her forceful action to bring about a cease fire.[1] Indeed, Nasser's close advisers believed that the United States was preparing to "come to terms with Arab nationalism."[2]

There were, however, few indications that Nasser had fundamentally changed his anti-Western policies; according to Ambassador Jefferson Caffery, who had once been extremely close to Gamal Abdel Nasser, "Nasser does want to make Egypt the dominant power in the Middle East. . . . He does want to be the strongest man in the Middle East, and sometimes he doesn't care where the chips fall."[3] It was questionable, therefore, whether the United States would abandon her support of traditional allies and conservative governments in the Arab world in favor of a man who had enhanced his personal ambitions to the detriment of Western interests in the Middle East.

Egypt's hopes of a reconciliation were quickly dashed when a request for 435,000 tons of American wheat and flour was turned down. Before the Suez crisis, considerable wheat had been shipped to Egypt under Public Law 480 which permitted payment in local currency (part of which could then be turned back to the local government for development projects). This time the request was flatly refused, the official reason being that authorizations under P.L. 480 had been nearly exhausted.[4] Authorization for the 1956-57 CARE program for 55 million dollars worth of food was buried under red tape.[5] Egypt, severely pressed for hard currencies and suffering from a food shortage, took this as a deliberate rebuff; Nasser then turned to the Soviet Union for food supplies, which were purchased in soft currency at slightly above world-market prices.[6]

Nevertheless, Nasser was anxious to gain American support. Implicit in his overtures to Washington was the fear that he could become too beholden to the Communist bloc. Since Nasser, however, was unwilling to abandon his aggressive policies in the Afro-Arab world, America pursued a policy of isolating Egypt and, to a lesser extent, Syria, politically and economically. Egyptian government funds, which had been blocked in July, 1956, remained frozen through 1957, and permits to export lubricating oil and mechanical spare parts to Egypt were difficult to obtain. The British and the French gladly cooperated in this campaign.

On the political level, vigorous efforts were made to drive a wedge between Nasser's Egypt and the rest of the Arab world. Following the proclamation of the Eisenhower Doctrine, King Saud visited the United States and announced his support of the Doctrine; at the time, this was considered a notable victory for Western policy. Subsequently, Richard Nixon journeyed across the African continent, visiting several of the peripheral Arab nations; James Richards, appointed as Eisenhower's special representative to promote the Doctrine, toured a number of countries in the Middle East. Egypt at one time seriously considered receiving Richards in Cairo. Wing Commander Ali Sabry announced that he would welcome a visit by Ambassador Richards and the Foreign Ministry made diplomatic preparations.[7] Richards, however, saw fit to by-pass Cairo on his homeward journey.

America's policy of open hostility toward Egypt, which included formal American participation in the Baghdad Pact military committee, seemed to stem the tide of "Nasserism" momentarily. Yet, the central shortcoming of American policy was its support of the political "old order" to the apparent exclusion of the liberal elements in Arab society. By the spring of 1957, the Arab Middle East was split into two camps—pro- and anti-West. A climax in this struggle came in Jordan, where pro-Western King Hussein, in opposition to the Cabinet headed by Sulimon Nabulsi, sought to keep his distance from Nasser. After two weeks of uncertainty, during which Hussein was accused by Cairo of a "palace coup" while he claimed to have suppressed an Egyptian-sponsored coup against the monarchy, Nasser's drive to subvert other Arab states suffered a severe, if momentary, setback.[8] The strong backing given Hussein by King Feisal of Iraq and by King Saud destroyed what semblance of Arab harmony had remained after the February meeting in Cairo of King Saud, King Hussein, President Kuwatly of Syria, and Nasser. More significant, the defeat of the pro-Nasser forces in Jordan indicated that Nasser could be stopped; this encouraged the Hashemites of Jordan and Iraq to suspend their long-standing feud with the Saudi royal family, and the three countries aligned against Egypt.

Yet, Nasser did not allow defeat in Jordan to deter him. The activities of Egypt's military attachés in other Arab countries continued unabashed. Already an attaché had been expelled from Libya, another declared *persona non grata* in Iraq, still another had left Saudi Arabia, and strong complaints had been registered concerning the activities of Egyptian attachés in Lebanon, the Sudan, and Tunisia.[9] Moreover, Nasser was assured of thousands of potential agents as 2,472 teachers were approved by the Egyptian government in 1957 for work in the Arab world.[10] Then, Egypt was linked directly to a plot to assassinate King Saud.[11]

In answer to charges that he was attempting to undermine existing Arab governments and political institutions, Nasser struck a pose of outraged innocence. The reports on Egyptian military attachés, according to him, were "black propaganda," except for Libya, where a colonel "went crazy."[12] This explanation, however, contradicts a speech he reputedly made to Egyptian military commanders in March, 1957. In this speech, which was published in an Iraq daily[13] and later proclaimed a "fake document" by the Egyptian government,[14] Nasser reportedly declared: "Those who delude themselves into believing that [Arab] unity can be achieved with honeyed words alone must open their eyes wide and see the Egyptian army of today. . . .

Military attachés are . . . a gamble we took. . . . There is this irregular war which costs us little, but which costs our enemies much."[15]

Nasser's vigorous campaign to organize the Arab world continued throughout 1957. At times, for tactical reasons, the attacks against King Hussein or Nuri es Said abated; on occasion, Cairo's propaganda machine turned its venom against the Western-oriented government of Lebanon. Arms and troop shipments were part of this campaign: jet fighter planes were given to Saudi Arabia,[16] small arms were presented to Tunisia[17] (during a critical period in Habib Bourguiba's relations with the West), and "basic elements" of the Egyptian armed forces were stationed in Syria during a widely publicized "threat" of an invasion by Turkish troops.[18] The end result was that Nasser retained his great popularity among the Arab peoples, but, with the exception of Syria, failed to gain the favor of any Arab government. Symptomatic of this failure was the absence of Arab-country contingents in the annual military parade held in Cairo on July 23, 1957.

Nasser spent much of 1957 resisting Western attempts to isolate him diplomatically; and he did this, as was his wont, with aggressive countertactics. This was evident in the manner in which he treated various organs of the United Nations. Egypt's Foreign Minister, Mahmoud Fawzi, was technically correct when he claimed before the United Nations that "the United Nations Emergency Force can be stationed in Egypt or operate there only with our consent. These forces are in Egypt only in relation with the present attack on Egypt. The force is not in Egypt as an occupation force, nor as a replacement for the invaders, nor to clear the Canal, nor to settle any problem in relation to the Suez Canal or Palestine, or any other matter."[19] Yet, Nasser's treatment of early UNEF contingents and Egypt's abrupt return to Gaza belied the good faith in which the force has been created. His refusal to permit the complete clearance of the Suez Canal under U.N. auspices until such time as Israeli forces had completely withdrawn from Sinai and Gaza[20] also was popular with Egyptians. This was another affront to the United Nations.

Problems of "Positive Neutrality"

Nasser, while he exercised little restraint in his campaign against Arab opponents and the West, was careful not to provoke further hostilities with Israel. Egypt had not recovered from her military defeat in 1956. While legalisms could be argued boldly before the United Nations, Nasser was unwilling to challenge Israel frontally. An unresolved issue was freedom of passage through the Gulf of Aqaba. Nasser realized that interference with shipping going to the Israeli port of Elath would be regarded by Israel as a *casus belli*.[21] Because Israel's right of passage through Aqaba was internationally recognized, and in the face of America's firm pledge to support Israel's right, Nasser meekly accepted the stationing of a UNEF garrison at the head of the Gulf indefinitely. With the United Nations also "protecting" Egypt in Gaza, Nasser was obliged to look elsewhere for major political victories.

Nasser found few such opportunities in Asia. Close relations were maintained with Asian countries and with "neutralist" leaders such as Nehru and Sukarno (who reciprocated Nasser's warmth by stating that Indonesia desired a "guided democracy" such as that practiced in Egypt), but it was obvious that Egypt would find political leadership of the Asian bloc a difficult objective. Even in 1957, Nehru had expressed serious misgivings over the tactics employed by his erstwhile neutralist protégé, President Nasser. This did not prevent Premier Nehru, Premier Mohamed Daoud of Afghanistan, and others from visiting Cairo, but they came as political equals, not as disciples of Nasser's "positive neutrality."

The possibilities for victories in Asia thus limited, Nasser turned to the African continent. In 1953, Colonel Nasser had written: "I would say, without exaggeration, that we cannot, even if we wish to, in any way stand aside from the sanguinary and dreadful struggle now raging in the heart of Africa between five million whites and two hundred million Africans. . . . The people of Africa will continue to look up to us, who guard the northern gate of the continent and who are its connecting link with the outside world."[22] Although Cairo subsequently had paid little attention to the African movement (indeed, there were very few Egyptians knowledgeable in African affairs south of the Sahara), an Islamic Congress was established, a major purpose being to provide scholarships for African students and dispatch Islamic missions throughout the African continent.[23] There were sporadic efforts, also, to arouse indigenous groups in Ethiopia and elsewhere against their existing governments, but Egypt's propaganda machine was not heavily committed to this campaign.

During 1957, Egypt's involvement in Africa became more pronounced. Plans to erect an Islamic center in Somaliland were accelerated, and efforts were made to encourage more young African leaders to establish themselves in exile in Cairo; those friendly to the Egyptian government often received monthly stipends from Egyptian intelligence. In coordination with efforts to buy the support of African nationalist leaders, direct agitation among African peoples became governmental policy. Thus, in the summer of 1957, the Voice of Free Africa,[24] patterned after the Voice of the Arabs, entered the airwaves. Multilanguage broadcasts harangued African listeners to drive the "white dogs of the oppressor countries of the West" from their lands.[25]

Back in November, 1954, Mr. Chandra of the Indian Communist Party's Central Committee had proposed an Afro-Asian solidarity conference.[26] The suggestion was not received enthusiastically at the time, and it was not until 1957 that this idea was implemented. According to Anwar Sadat, in early 1957 a delegation from the Asian Solidarity Committee (generally regarded as a pro-Communist organization)[27] met with Nasser and requested that an Asian conference be held in Cairo.[28] Reputedly on Sadat's initiative, the conference was extended to include Africa. By March, Nasser agreed to a conference in Cairo as a means to show that "Dulles could not isolate Egypt."[29]

The Afro-Asian People's Solidarity Conference opened on December 26, 1957. Its orientation was strongly anti-Western. Even Anwar Sadat, presiding officer of the Conference, showed annoyance at the blatant pro-Communist views expressed by many delegations.[30] It was decided to establish a permanent organization in Cairo under the direction of an Egyptian secretary-general. This conformed with Egypt's desire for a front organization through which she could influence African affairs, but it was an open question whether the organization would be controlled by Egypt or by the Communists. Representatives of both the Soviet Union, which had been invited to the Cairo meeting as an Asian nation, and the People's Republic of China were installed as deputy secretary-generals of the permanent body, and the Communists had, in the past, earned a well-deserved reputation for subverting "popular" organizations. Some observers even speculated that Nasser was providing the Communists with entry into Africa in return for Soviet economic assistance and political support.

Egypt's past record in the Sudan gave the lie to Egyptian claims of sincere African nationalist sentiments. And his ambitions on the African continent confronted Nasser with a dilemma. He seemed sincere in his desire for friendlier relations with the West; reconciliation would mean improved trade relations. At the same time, however, he was unwilling to brake his anti-Western drive throughout the Middle East and Africa. Nasser expressed surprise to Western visitors that these activities should prevent the West from embracing him as a friend. Earlier, he had tried to explain away anti-Western attacks in government newspapers as being designed "only for local consumption." Whatever his rationalizations, American and British diplomats saw little reason to support a government actively committed to an anti-Western policy.

Great Britain and France reluctantly had permitted their ships to pay tolls to the Egyptian Suez Canal Authority after the Canal was reopened. There seemed no other recourse. But both countries were unwilling to make further major concessions to Egypt. Egypt, on the other hand, desired friendly relations with Britain, for the scarcity of sterling seriously hampered trade negotiations with all but the Communist bloc. Nasser even went so far, in a July, 1957, television broadcast to the British people, to deem it the "duty" of Britain and Egypt to resume diplomatic relations.[31] An Arab diplomat made this revealing observation: "The British he [Nasser] merely distrusts, the French he loathes."[32]

There was strong sentiment among Cairo shopkeepers and even among Egyptian technicians and civil servants for the restoration of friendly relations with Great Britain. The British, however, were not anxious to reach a settlement at the price of releasing blocked sterling assets which might bolster Nasser's political position. Instead, they firmly supported America in her policy of the political and economic isolation of Egypt. American enmity was not to Nasser's liking, for it prejudiced his game of economic and political neutralism. So even when he publicly criticized the United States for a "policy of invasion from within," he was careful to temper this charge with acknowledgment of American support during the Anglo-French-Israeli military action.[33]

In an effort to restore to Egypt's foreign affairs the balance which he had found so profitable in 1955, Nasser gave orders that all branches of the government and the press present Egypt as a strictly neutral country.[34] Nasser also seemed ready to jettison the term "positive neutrality," with its unfavorable connotations in the West, with the more euphemistic "nonalignment."[35] These gestures, however, had little effect. While West Germany, Italy, Greece, Spain, and other West European countries maintained normal relations with Egypt, the Western Big Three remained aloof. Indeed, their position seemed to harden when Nasser, in December, 1957, disclosed a plot against his government reputedly masterminded by the British.[36]

Under the circumstances, Egypt was forced to rely more heavily than ever upon the Communist bloc for her economic needs. But Nasser's greater dependence on the Soviets for armaments, food, and for cotton markets did not reduce Egypt to the status of a satellite. Nasser wished to maintain his freedom of action with regard to both East and West, and, on occasion, he dealt bluntly with his Communist friends. On his authorization, for example, a widely publicized Soviet film festival was abruptly closed and a Hollywood "Western" substituted. The Soviet films were banned for their detailed scenes on how to subvert a police force and how best to sabotage a factory.[37] It was later reported that Nasser's differences with the Soviets over their failure to fulfill commercial contracts prompted the Russian Ambassador's abrupt departure for the Soviet Union in June, 1957.[38]

The Soviets, on occasion, sold Egypt goods at prices above those prevailing on the world market and, at times, cotton sold to Eastern Europe was discounted on Western markets.[39] Yet, Russia, in her effort to "neutralize" the Arab world, generally was careful not to antagonize the Egyptian government. Instead of forcing conditions upon Egypt, the Soviets were content to extend their power gradually. Three years before, Nasser had been violently opposed to foreign military missions in Egypt; he even objected to the German military mission which had come to Egypt upon the official invitation of the Egyptian government.[40] In 1957, referring to the Soviets, he stated, "I don't mind missions if I ask for them, but I don't like them imposed on me as a condition of aid."[41] His conduct of foreign affairs also did not reflect strict adherence to his professed "neutralism"; on the United Nations vote on Hungary, for example, Nasser explained that "Egypt abstained out of gratitude for the Soviet Union's position on Suez."[42]

Ali Sabry, Nasser's chief political adviser, explained that he could not afford to look too closely to see if the Soviets were consuming their cotton purchases, and, even if Czechoslovakia were violating her trade agreement with Egypt, a stoppage of cotton sales to the Czechs would be a "political blow."[43] To rectify this situation, he proposed a political formula which he wished to apply to foreign trade. Political independence could be maintained, he asserted, if one-third of Egypt's exports went to the West, another third to the Communists, and the remainder to the "others."[44] If nothing else, this would have assured the marketing of at least two-thirds of Egypt's annual cotton crop. This stratagem reputedly had been recommended to President Nasser by Marshal Tito in 1956.[45]

While ostensibly seeking a "balanced" policy, however, Nasser leaned more heavily on Communist support. In November, 1957, the Russians agreed in principle to provide Egypt with industrial credits totalling 62 million pounds. This, to Western observers, amounted to a virtual Soviet lien on the Egyptian

economy. But Nasser professed not to see any broad implications
in this agreement. "I must say," he declared, "that up to this
moment I have noticed absolutely nothing which could confirm
the suspicion that the Soviet Union might want to intervene in
our internal affairs or influence our politics in a certain direction.
. . . It was *we* who asked the Soviet Union for help, and, to tell
the truth, each time this help was immediately given to us and
without political conditions."[46] Discounting the actions of local
Communists (which generally were ineffectual) and assuming
that Nasser accepted at face value Communist support of Arab
nationalism, this statement seemed generally correct at the end
of 1957.

Nasser's Drive for Arab Hegemony

The next year began auspiciously for Nasser. In 1956, just
before the nationalization of the Suez Canal Company, planning
for a close Egypto-Syrian political alliance had reached an
advanced stage; although a series of crises intervened, by November, 1957, a joint session of the Egyptian and Syrian Parliaments
had unanimously approved a federal union between the two
countries.[47] Two months later these plans approached fruition.

But in January, 1958, the federation idea was dropped in
favor of a more comprehensive merger. According to President
Nasser, Syrian political leaders "came to me saying everything was
a mess. I met with all except the Communists. They told me,
'Only you can save us. Liquidate our parties and join us to
Egypt.' "[48] Other reports suggested that the sudden decision for
a full union was prompted by the alarming growth of Communist influence in Syria.[49] These reports seemed to be borne out
when, on February 1, Nasser established himself as absolute ruler
over the United Arab Republic (Egypt and Syria) and provision
was made for a single political party—the National Union. Soon
afterward, Khaled Bakdash, leader of the Syrian Communist
Party, hurriedly left with his family for Moscow.[50] To counter the
Egyptian-Syrian merger, King Feisal and King Hussein hastily
proclaimed an Arab Federation of Iraq and Jordan, agreeing to

closer political and economic unity than provided for in the draft charter of the United Arab Republic. King Hussein claimed this federation to be truly representative of Arab nationalism.

At first Nasser treated the Hashemite federation with measured politeness. He even sent King Feisal congratulations for the "blessed step" which one day might lead to a "greater union."[51] Within several weeks, however, his mood changed, and the "artificial federation" became the target of vitriolic attacks. In Damascus he declared: "They [imperialists and Zionists] want to set up an artificial union which does not represent the will of the people but follows the plans drawn up by imperialists to divide the Arab peoples."[52] He soon extended his campaign of vilification to other Arab countries: "Every one of the sons of the Arab nation feels today that there must be an end to traitors and agents, so that we can establish real freedom, as well as the unity which will be the realization of all our hopes, in the whole of the Arab homeland. . . . The only obstacle which stands in the way of Arab solidarity today . . . are the traitors and the agents of imperialism."[53]

On February 5, Nasser made a speech before the National Assembly which foreshadowed a new aggressive burst against other Arab states. "In the lives of nations," he stated, "there are generations ordained and solely chosen by destiny to witness decisive turning points in the history of mankind. . . . This generation of the Egyptian nation is one of those generations ordained to live great moments of transition, moments that are like pageants of sunrise."[54] In short order, he mounted a hostile campaign against the governments of Iraq, Jordan, Lebanon, Saudi Arabia, and the Sudan. (Perhaps he had some justification in the case of Saudi Arabia, for there was strong evidence that agents for King Saud had paid 1.9 million pounds for the assassination of President Nasser.)[55]

Nasser's campaign against the Sudan was grossly miscalculated. In 1902, some Egyptian territory was placed under the Anglo-Egyptian Sudan to facilitate problems of administration; for over fifty years, the Egyptian government had made no formal move to claim this land. Then, on February 1, 1958, a note delivered to the Sudanese Permanent Under-Secretary in the Ministry of Foreign Affairs demanded that all territory above 22° latitude be handed over to Egypt.[56] This was followed by two further notes in which Egypt expressed the intention to conduct a plebiscite for the United Arab Republic in the disputed areas on February 22. On February 17, Sudanese Foreign Minister Mohamed Mahgoub announced that Egyptian troops were being moved to areas belonging to the Sudan.[57] Amid strong popular support, the Sudanese government rejected Egypt's virtual ultimatum.

In retrospect, it appears that President Nasser was "misinformed and had to contend with a firmer government . . . than he had expected."[58] The Sudan, herself holding a national election on February 27, brought the entire matter before the United Nations Security Council, whereupon Egypt abruptly agreed to postpone her frontier claims. But the Sudanese did not rest content merely to obtain a retraction of Egypt's earlier ultimatum; instead, they held their own election in the disputed territories. By the end of February, the Sudanese government had scored a clear-cut victory over Nasser.

Despite his experience in the Sudan, Nasser had good reason to believe that many of the Arab states were under severe pressure to reach an accord with the United Arab Republic; and the fact that Nasser had, indeed, gained support of political liberals in an area still supporting some elements of the political "old order" prompted the absolute monarch of Yemen to federate with the U.A.R. At this juncture, the United States apparently reconsidered its policy of actively opposing a man so widely revered by the masses throughout the Arab Middle East. Moreover, earlier fears that Nasser would be an easy victim for Communist subversion proved unfounded; Egypt's economic dependence upon the Communist bloc had, by necessity, increased substantially, but Nasser had, at least for the moment, retained a large degree of political independence. And Nasser's desire to establish a politically more balanced pattern of trade was reflected by his heavy discounts on cotton purchased in hard currencies—discounts introduced as an inducement to Western buyers.

A *Fleeting* Rapprochement

The West revised its policy cautiously. A few million pounds sterling were unfrozen in London. Then funds were released for the continuation of an Egyptian-American land reclamation scheme in Lower Egypt. West Germany encouraged Egyptian overtures for economic credits. And the United States let it be known that Egyptian government funds frozen in America would be released immediately upon the announcement of a financial settlement with the Universal Maritime Suez Canal Company. In return, Cairo's propaganda machine softened its attacks on the United States until, in early April, Nasser ordered a halt to all direct attacks against America and John Foster Dulles.[59] To observers in Cairo it appeared that Nasser wished to mend his political fences with the West before departing on his much-heralded journey to the Soviet Union. While Nasser was visiting Moscow, an agreement on the Suez Canal Company was reached, Egyptian assets in America were released, and West Germany provided Nasser's government with massive industrial credits.

Nasser, obviously concerned lest his visit to the Soviet Union have unfavorable repercussions in the West, proceeded on his trip with extraordinary caution. Originally, his plane had been scheduled to stop at Budapest, where he was to meet Communist chief Janos Kadar and review a military guard of honor. He firmly refused to do either. While in the Soviet Union, strong attacks were being hurled at Marshal Tito by Khrushchev and other Communist chieftains; Nasser deliberately sent his "neutralist" friend a warm note on the occasion of a Yugoslav national holiday. A new, conciliatory Nasser returned to Cairo. "I know and feel," he declared, "that the people of the United States aim and work for peace. I know and you, fellow brethren, know, that when Eden, Guy Mollet, and Ben Gurion committed aggression against our country, free peoples rose against this aggression and free people in Britain and France shouted against this aggression. . . . The world wants peace. . . . Before I left for the Soviet Union, I was informed by the United States that it would pursue a new policy towards the U.A.R., that it would recognize our right to pursue a policy of positive neutralism. . . . I feel that this policy, for the maintenance of which we have struggled, this independent policy of positive neutralism and nonalignment, has finally triumphed, having been recognized by the two strongest powers in the whole world, the Soviet Union and the United States."[60] An Egypto-Western *rapprochement* had been achieved, but it was almost immediately cut short by the outbreak of violence in Lebanon.

The West, or at least the United States, seemed willing to condone Nasser's broad claims of Arab unity; there was even no violent reaction when an influential Cairo weekly published a map of the United Arab Republic as envisaged in 1998: Lebanon and Israel had disappeared as political entities, and the Arab world and portions of "black" Africa were included within the shaded area of the U.A.R.[61] The United States, however, looked askance at Nasser's overt subversion of existing Arab governments, especially when those governments favored the West. Although Lebanon's President Camille Chamoun was partly responsible for the crisis which erupted in Lebanon in May, 1958, the American government later made public unsifted intelligence reports which unquestionably confirmed that the United Arab Republic (Syria in particular) did indeed engage in "massive interference."[62] Reports by a special United Nations investigating team notwithstanding, rebel soldiers were recruited and trained in Syria, and extensive arms shipments, including heavy machine guns and mortars, were smuggled to rebel bands.

There is evidence to suggest that both Nasser and the United States wished to reach a quick settlement of the Lebanese affair; Nasser, however, felt firmly committed to the rebelling "nationalists," and America could hardly abandon the staunchly pro-Western Chamoun without suffering a political defeat of the first magnitude. Thus, the two countries again drifted toward open hostility. By mid-June, Mohamed Hassanein Heikal was authorized to write: "The truth revealed by the current events in the Lebanon is that America has not changed her policy, but has merely changed her approach. . . . This policy is [still] aimed at dealing a devastating blow to Arab nationalism, thus foiling all its aspirations."[63] But Nasser was careful not to let his relations with the United States deteriorate completely (a multimillion dollar contract for dredging the Suez Canal was given to three American firms in June), for he was acutely aware of the need to protect his position vis-à-vis the Soviets.[64] At the same time, the Communists sought to commit Nasser categorically to the side of the Lebanese rebels.

Perhaps, if Lebanon had been an isolated case, friendly relations between Nasser's government and the United States could still have been possible. But the July 14 *coup d'état* in Iraq signalled an open split. The United States government immediately held Nasser responsible for the coup and warned against new moves in Lebanon and Jordan. It is not clear to what extent Nasser was implicated in the Iraqi coup. The categorical charge, however, that he was *directly* responsible for the events in Baghdad seemed to credit him with inordinate powers of organization. Certainly, Nasser had sought to whiplash the forces of Arab nationalism; and in so doing, he had contributed to the overthrow of pro-Western governments. But it is doubtful that he had a detailed master plan of conquest. As he explained with apparent candor during the turbulent events of 1958: "It is our policy to have flexibility. We don't have any detailed program."[65] Yet, the immediate American reaction, even before details of the revolt in Baghdad had become known, was to blame Nasser; United States troops quickly were moved into Lebanon, and the British returned to Jordan in an effort to shore up the existing government.

Nasser, then visiting Tito, made a hasty trip to Moscow for consultations with Khrushchev, then stopped in Damascus for meetings with Iraq's Deputy Premier before his return to Cairo. He obviously was pleased with the events in Iraq, for not only had Nuri es Said been eliminated, but it was generally believed in Cairo that the "strong man" of the ruling military junta was Colonel Abdel Salem Mohamed Aref, well known for his pro-Nasser sympathies. As the crisis deepened, the possibility of further Western military intervention existed, and Khrushchev reportedly offered Nasser the use of Russian "volunteers."[66] By

September, however, the crisis had abated. To the supporters of
"Nasserism" it appeared time to gather the spoils of their latest
victories.

"Nasserism" on the Wane

On the surface, events of mid-1958 indicated a new ground-
swell of "Nasserism." Yet, no new victims fell to the drive conducted from Cairo in the name of the "Arab nation." Indeed, it
seemed that the tide of "Nasserism," having reached its crest,
was gradually receding.

Jordan was the first to stem the tide. In 1957, when Jordan
was considering a sharp break with Great Britain, Egypt, Syria,
and Saudi Arabia agreed to underwrite the annual subsidy paid
to the Jordanian government by the British. This amount—12.5
million pounds—represented a sizable portion of Jordan's annual
revenue. Following the political upheaval during the spring of
1957, only Saudi Arabia adhered to her commitment. Nasser
later explained: "Our aid to Jordan was based on the unification
of the Syrian, Egyptian, and Jordanian armies in the defense of
supreme Arab interests. But the King of Jordan suddenly reversed this trend and turned his policy upside down. To have
extended aid to him under those circumstances would have meant
encouraging him to adopt a policy that runs counter to the
supreme interests of the Arabs."[67] It was interesting that these
words were uttered by a man who previously had excoriated the
West for offering assistance "with strings attached."

King Hussein, long at odds with the Nasser government,
expelled various members of the U.A.R. Embassy during the first
half of 1958; then, when the U.A.R., after the coup in Baghdad,
recognized Iraq as separate from the Arab Federation, Hussein
severed diplomatic relations with the U.A.R. There was considerable speculation that Hussein's government was in momentary
danger of being overthrown. Nasser's designs on Jordan, however, had to reckon with the Israeli threat to occupy West
Jordan in the event of Jordan's absorption into the U.A.R. He
realized, also, that integration of Jordan into the U.A.R. would
be a heavy financial burden upon an already overstrained Egyp-

tian treasury. Moreover, King Hussein, in his refusal to give way before "nationalist" intimidations, had rallied powerful support and seemed capable of withstanding Cairo's campaign of subversion.

Tunisia also stood firm in the face of Nasser's enticements and attempts at subversion. Habib Bourguiba never had been friendly to Nasser, and with the disclosure in March, 1958, of a plot to assassinate Bourguiba, purportedly planned by a Tunisian exile in Cairo and initiated by men carrying Egyptian travel documents, Tunisian-Egyptian relations deteriorated to the breaking point.[68] It therefore seemed surprising when, in September, 1958, Tunisia applied for membership in the Egyptian-dominated Arab League. The reason for this move was quickly revealed, however, when the Tunisian delegate, in his first League meeting, complained: "The League follows only one direction, works for one side, obeys the orders of one member. We must avoid the possibility of one member of the League falling into the habit of disregarding the opinions of others."[69] Four days later, the Tunisian government broke off diplomatic relations with the United Arab Republic. The following month, Bourguiba announced the discovery of still another Egyptian-supported conspiracy against his government, and again Nasser denounced Bourguiba's accusations as "pure fabrications."[70] There was, however, strong Arab sympathy for Bourguiba's position. He seemed to express the feelings of other Arab leaders when he asserted sarcastically: "To intervene permanently in the internal affairs of others is not, so far as I know, a method of being neutral."[71]

Nasser, sensing growing opposition in the Arab world, effected a fortuitous *rapprochement* with Saudi Arabia. Perhaps in the opinion that this conciliation would strengthen the mystique of Arab unity, he dispatched Field Marshal Amer to meet with King Saud and Premier Feisal. At the same time, however, Cairo initiated concerted attempts to overthrow the existing government in the Sudan.

Aly Khashaba, previously accused of subversion in Iraq, Lebanon, and Saudi Arabia, arrived in Khartoum as Counselor of the U.A.R. Embassy in mid-July.[72] Within a week, it was reported that an attempted pro-Nasser coup had been foiled and that Khashaba had been expelled for suspicious activities.[73] Subversion having failed, efforts were made to win over Sudanese opposition leaders—a campaign which seemed destined for success when Ismail el Azhari, leader of the National Unionist Party, and others visited Cairo and reputedly were ready to conclude a "deal" in early November. But on the day originally scheduled for the reopening of the Sudanese Parliament (at which time the pro-Western government of Abdullah Khalil was expected to receive a vote of no confidence), a military *coup d'état*, engineered by General Ibrahim Abboud (formerly a close military colleague of Khalil), resulted in the dissolution of all political parties. Nasser's ambitions in the Sudan were blocked, at least temporarily.

These failures seemed strange in the light of Nasser's acknowledged potential for controlling the Arab world. He was, after all, the most popular personality in the Arab Middle East. Cairo was the center of Arab education, and many front organizations, including the Arab League and the International Confederation of Arab Trade Unions, had their headquarters in Cairo and received their "guidance" from Egyptians. It became evident, however, that Egypt did not use these "front organizations" to best advantage. The Arab League, for example, was generally considered to be in the shadow of Egypt's Foreign Ministry, and many of the officials, including the Secretary-General, were Egyptians; the League was thus discredited as a representative Arab organization.

The International Confederation of Arab Trade Unions was another case in point. Originally, when this organization was formed in Damascus in March, 1956 (with headquarters in Cairo), its avowed aims included the establishment of "unity of the Arab Nation" and "ensuring a better life for workers in the Arab fatherland."[74] A token annual subsidy was received from the Labor Department of the Egyptian Ministry of Social Affairs and Labor ostensibly for the achievement of these goals.[75]

According to Helmy Ibrahim (relieved of his post at the International Labour Organization in Geneva for what his colleagues call "leftist" activities, and at that time attached to the

Egyptian Labor Department while also directing the International Affairs Section of the Arab Confederation), the Confederation started as a trade-union movement. When interviewed in August, 1958, however, he was unable to offer any evidence that the Confederation had advanced the cause of labor.[76] Instead, he placed heavy emphasis on the political role which was "inflicted" upon the Confederation by the Suez crisis and the military attacks.[77] Since then, according to his explanation, all of the Confederation's efforts were devoted to coping with crises in Syria, Lebanon, Jordan, and elsewhere.[78] When asked to list the Confederation's major achievements, he promptly referred to the blowing up of an oil-pumping station in Syria in November, 1956. (According to a reliable source, Major Toiema provided 100,000 pounds to Anwar Salama, then on the Confederation's Executive Council, to prevent the flow of Iraqi oil across Syria.) A second "achievement" during this same period, according to Ibrahim, was the refusal by Sudanese airline workers to refuel "enemy" (British and French) planes.[79]

The Confederation, while Pan-Arab by definition, was firmly controlled by Egyptians; authority was concentrated in the hands of two men—Fathy Kamal, long a member of the Egyptian trade-union movement, and Helmy Ibrahim, a shrewd politician with a distinct aversion to any physical exertion. They both were accused of being Communists, but one of their closest colleagues softened this charge by categorizing them merely as "opportunists." The organization was run in flagrant disregard for its constitution. Although the Executive Council was obliged to meet at least once yearly to review the Secretary-General's actions and pass on matters of policy, only one such meeting had been held by late 1958, and this was in May, 1957; since then, no further meetings had been called, for they are "pretty expensive" and "Fathy Kamal did not consider it worthwhile."[80] When Fathy Kamal was presented with a catalogue of his violations of the constitution, he ascribed them to the fact that the delegates were "hot-headed" when the constitution was drafted.[81]

The Confederation once was described as a "travel agency and telegraph office," for much of its energy was expended in dispatching Arab labor delegations to Communist countries for

official visits and receiving reciprocal delegations from East
Europe and Communist China. Under Kamal's and Ibrahim's
leadership, the Confederation increasingly turned from Arab
labor problems and devoted major efforts to establishing close
ties with Communist organizations. An example of this policy was
a Confederation-sponsored meeting, in September, 1958, to discuss the problem of Algeria—a meeting arranged in conjunction
with the World Federation of Trade Unions (a Communist-
controlled organization). Ibrahim, without informing the government Labor Department or the Ministry of Foreign Affairs,
dispatched invitations only to those labor organizations which
were friendly to the WFTU; Yugoslav unions, three of India's
four leading trade-union bodies, and other "neutral" or pro-
Western groups were excluded. After forceful government intervention, the "conference" was transformed into a "committee,"
thus losing some of its propaganda value.

Now that the Confederation has departed so obviously from
its announced objectives, it seems to have lost much of its potential appeal in the Arab world. Instead, the Confederation, as
reflected by its top leadership, had assumed a strongly pro-
Communist orientation which often has proved embarrassing to
the government.*

The Egyptian government experienced equal failure with
another mass-appeal front organization, the Afro-Asian Solidarity
Committee. The Committee's task was clear to its employees: it
was to provide the spearhead for Nasser's movement to capture
the leadership of "black" Africa. Toward this end, young exiled
African leaders were put on the payroll. But the Committee was
singularly ineffective. After a year in operation, its greatest
accomplishment seemed to consist in the fact that it had assembled the most attractive secretaries in Cairo. Moursy Saad el-Din,
the man actually responsible for administering the Committee,
stated frankly in an interview that his main source of background
information on Africa came from John Gunther's *Inside Africa*.
When the Committee was first organized, there were fears among
Western observers (and even some Egyptian government officials) that the Committee would be dominated by the Commu-

---

* Significantly, in 1959, Fathy Kamal was voted out of office.

nists. Although the Soviet and Communist Chinese Deputy Secretary-Generals were extremely active, Moursy (also associated with the Ministry of the Interior's Censorship Department), at Nasser's instructions, limited their effectiveness.[82]

The greatest challenge to Egypt's African ambitions, as they were expressed through the Afro-Asian Solidarity Committee, came from President Kwane Nkrumah of Ghana. Nkrumah, like Nasser, wished to be recognized as the leader of African nationalism. With this in mind, he organized the Accra Conference of independent African states in April, 1958. In stark contrast with the Afro-Asian meeting in Cairo, a resolution was adopted at Accra which favored "nonentanglement" with either of the Great Power blocs. Alleged subversion by Western, Communist, and African countries (the Sudan complained about Egyptian activities) was a topic of discussion in closed meetings.[83] The Secretary-General of the Afro-Asian Solidarity Committee, Yussef Sebai, hastily called a press conference to explain that the Accra meeting was merely an extension of the Bandung and Cairo Conferences.[84] But this face-saving gesture could not hide the fact that Nasser had suffered a defeat at Accra.

Although Egypt played host to many African students (over three hundred were given scholarships by the Islamic Congress alone),[85] and several African national groups were subsidized by the Egyptian government,[86] most Africans living in Cairo, even some of those paid by Egyptian intelligence, were openly suspicious of Nasser's intentions toward Africa. To them, Nkrumah rather than Nasser seemed the natural leader of Africa south of the Sahara.

When Nkrumah visited Cairo in June, 1958, Nasser gave him a lavish reception; in an unprecedented display of "unity and friendship," posters bearing pictures of Nasser and Nkrumah were distributed throughout Cairo. This, however, did not prevent Nkrumah from hinting publicly of the political gulf separating the two leaders. Nkrumah voiced his disappointment that Nasser had chosen not to attend the Accra Conference.[87] Then, in a final joint communiqué, while the two men reaffirmed the principles adopted at the Bandung and Accra Conferences, no mention was made of the Afro-Asian People's Solidarity Conference.[88] By December, as Nkrumah prepared to sponsor an African "people's" conference of his own, his rift with Nasser became more open; like many others, he criticized Nasser for introducing Communist influences into African affairs.[89] Nasser's African fortunes were on the decline as increasing numbers of African territories and independent states began to regard Nasser as a foreigner and a non-African.

By the end of 1958, Nasser had made no significant headway in his drive for leadership of "black" Africa. Indeed, there were many signs that, in the face of Nkrumah's strong challenge and the listless response of several important African groups, he had decided to slow down his campaign, at least temporarily. This was reflected in the activities of the Afro-Asian Solidarity Committee, which turned its attention almost entirely to Arab and Asian matters. Nasser's political setback in Africa was matched by a similar rebuff in Asia, where his peculiar brand of neutralism was proving unpalatable to many of the Asian "neutralists." Nehru, for example, refused to give his personal support to the Afro-Asian Solidarity Committee because of its strongly pro-Communist orientation, and an Indonesian delegate, with the knowledge and approval of his government, protested the seating of the Soviet Union at an Afro-Asian Economic Conference in Cairo, claiming that Russia was neither African nor Asian.[90] This limited Nasser's opportunities for political victories to the Arab world; but here, too, his position had been weakened.

Early in the year, after the creation of the United Arab Republic and the formation of the United Arab States, many observers took it for granted that "Nasserism" soon would engulf the Arab Middle East. By the year's end, however, Egyptian Pan-Arabism had claimed no new adherents; and this failure, unlike that of the post-Suez era, could not easily be blamed on "Western imperialism" or Arab "stooges of imperialism." Instead, it suggested that "Nasserism" was rapidly becoming outmoded. Nasser's concept of Arab nationalism had fed primarily upon negative themes: anti-Westernism, anti-imperialism, and anti-monarchism. The fact that Nasser had initiated no significant Pan-Arab economic measures seemed to trouble neither the masses nor the elites—the middle-class civil servants, teachers, and army officers—in the Arab world. Nasser's promise of Arab unity seemed to them a panacea.

The Syrians had been the first to surrender their nationality. It was not long, however, before Baathists like Akram Hourani and Michel Aflek were appalled by the appearance of Egyptian proconsuls in Damascus. The warm speeches in February turned to bitter recriminations in April, as Syrians struggled against total absorption into a Greater Egypt. President Shukry Kuwatly was retired with the rank of "first Arab citizen"; then Major General Afif Bizri, chief of the Syrian army, was removed from his post and appointed to a nonexistent U.A.R. planning commission. Sabry el-Assaly, formerly Syrian Prime Minister, was unceremoniously dropped as U.A.R. Vice-President, while Akram Hourani was demoted and "strong man" Abdel Hamid Serraj was placed directly under Egypt's police chief, Zacharia Mohieddine. Certainly there was cause for Egyptians to refer to Syria as their "northern province."

At least over the short run, Egypt's pilot project of "Arab unity" in Syria had ended in failure, and the unsuccessful experiment pointed up a fact which had long since become obvious to more sophisticated Cairenes: the Egyptian Revolution was dead, and "Nasserism," as a symbol of revolutionary nationalism in the Afro-Arab world, was becoming a bit jaded. In essence, " 'Nasserism' is not an ideology, but an attitude of mind."[91] Only when the Syrian Baath Party entered into an alliance with Nasser in February, 1958, could he embrace, in the Baathist creed, a cohesive Arab ideology. By July, however, the Baathists had broken with the Egyptian leader. Thus, when the July revolution overthrew the monarchy in Iraq, Nasser found his influence rapidly waning. "Nasserism," as an emotional force among the Iraqi masses, spent itself with the defeat of the "old order." Nor could Nasser offer the new military regime in Baghdad anything in the way of an effective operational program.

In short, "Nasserism" exerted an effective appeal in the Arab world so long as men like Nuri es Said served as the whipping boys of Arab nationalists. In their place, however, emerged leaders with whom Nasser was ill prepared to cope. Men like Habib Bourguiba, General Kassem, and General Ibrahim Abboud of the Sudan seemed to have strong popular support, and Egypt could hardly criticize their governments for espousing principles which Nasser's own junta had embraced but a few years before. Although Nasser still appeared to many Arabs as the modern-day Saladin of the Arab world, he could no longer pose as *the* Arab leader. Arab leaders drew another lesson from the Syrian example. "An alliance between a big and a small power," Nasser had declared in 1955, "is an alliance between the wolf and the sheep, and it is bound to end with the wolf devouring the sheep."[92]

By fall of 1958, Nasser seemed resigned, at least for the moment, to do little except to consolidate his gains in the Arab Middle East. Anwar Sadat, the man responsible for receiving visiting Arab dignitaries from the Arabian Peninsula and the Persian Gulf, declared: "Now we need solidarity, but we don't need political federation. Once we achieve solidarity, then the events will tell."[93] Although he acknowledged that Arab nationalism was not based upon equality, he admitted readily that there could be no political federation between sheikhdoms and the U.A.R.[94] This statement seemed in line with the general recognition in Cairo that Egypt had neither the resources nor the personnel to absorb new "provinces" into the U.A.R.; indeed, Egypt seemed incapable of caring even for Syria. Instead, greater emphasis was placed on regional Arab projects. Plans for convening an Arab oil conference in Cairo approached implementation, and, on the U.A.R.'s initiative, it was agreed to establish an Arab development fund, with member-nations providing capital estimated at 20 million pounds.[95] Moreover, the Egyptian Chambers of Commerce sponsored a meeting of representatives from Arab states to discuss the possibilities of creating an Arab common market.[96]

Nasser and the Communists

Nasser, by late 1958, clearly had lost much of his former initiative in foreign affairs. The West still was reluctant to sanction his Pan-Arab ambitions; Jordan, Lebanon, Iraq, the Sudan, and Tunisia remained cool to his overtures; and the Communists were becoming openly hostile. Local Communist opposition posed a delicate problem, for the Soviets had just promised to extend credits for the first stage of the High Dam, and much of Egypt's foreign-trade transactions were with the Communist bloc. Nasser communicated his fears to the American Embassy in Cairo; he warned that the Communists were taking over the government in Iraq.[97] The Americans responded cautiously: they encouraged a West German bid to participate in the first stage of the High Dam (it was refused), and an agreement was signed to provide 24.9 million dollars of surplus wheat to the U.A.R., payable in Egyptian currency.[98] After these and other efforts to "hedge" his international position, Nasser felt ready to mount a frontal attack against Arab Communists.

Khaled Bakdash, leader of the Syrian Communist Party, publicly had been denouncing Syria's union with Egypt, and in a major speech at Port Said, Nasser chose to challenge the Communists on this issue. He announced to a nationwide radio audience: "The Communist Party in Syria declared its refusal to participate in national unity and to join a National Union. They refuse that this nation should be united to fight against the enemies of Arab nationalism and Arab unity. They even object to Arab nationalism and Arab unity. Some members announced last week that they advocated separation and that there should be no unity or Arab nationalism."[99] This attack was followed by the arrest of scores of Syrian and Egyptian Communists.

As Iraq became increasingly hostile to the United Arab Republic, Cairo prepared an offensive against Iraqi Communists. Although care was taken not to criticize the Soviet Union directly, Egyptian censors passed an article which charged that the Communists considered a country's "positive neutrality" as merely an interim stage leading to that country's alignment with the Communist world.[100] While local papers were condemning Iraqi Communists for attacks on the Koran and mosques,[101] Mohamed Hassanein Heikal was careful to distinguish between "world Communism" and the "application of Communist principles" in individual countries.[102]

Nasser's anti-Communist campaign appeared, for a time, to be an excellent tactical gambit: he was able to crush the major opposition within the U.A.R.; he gave the Western powers pause to reconsider their aloofness toward his government; and he gained a convenient platform against Iraq, rapidly re-emerging as his strongest rival for leadership in the Arab Middle East. Yet, if Nasser's attacks on Communism were only a "tactic," Nikita Khrushchev failed to appreciate this. The Soviet Premier, in his speech before the Twenty-first Soviet Communist Party Congress, declared that fighting against Communists and other progressive parties "is a reactionary business." He objected strenuously to the campaign in "some countries" against "progressive forces" under the "false slogan of anti-Communism."[103] Mohamed Hassanein Heikal took Khrushchev to task for interfering with internal U.A.R. affairs; in his rebuttal of Khrushchev's charges, he specifically denied that the Cairo charges were leveled against international Communism, claiming the activities of the Syrian Communist Party as their only target.[104]

During the following month, an uneasy truce was maintained between the Egyptian and Soviet leaders. Khrushchev tried to pour oil on troubled waters by acknowledging in a personal letter to Nasser that Cairo's attitude toward Communism was "a matter of internal policy which concerned the United Arab Republic alone."[105] But events in Iraq made it obvious that Nasser no longer merited the full support of the Soviet Union. As Western analysts long had predicted, Khrushchev was rapidly finding the objectives of international Communism incompatible with Gamal Abdel Nasser's professed policy of constructing a united Arab bloc.

Egyptian-Soviet relations reached a nadir following Colonel Shawaf's abortive uprising in March, 1959, against General Kassem's Iraqi government. In retort to Nasser's denial of any link with the revolt and the accusation that "Communist agents of a foreign power" were trying to split the United Arab Republic of Egypt and Syria, Premier Khrushchev accused Nasser of seeking to annex Iraq and chided the Egyptian President for being "a rather young man and rather hot-headed . . . [who] took upon himself more than his stature permitted."[106] Then Khrushchev continued with a veiled threat: "That is harmful; he shouldn't do it. He might strain himself."[107]

Nasser, soundly defeated in Iraq and sharply dressed down by Khrushchev, reacted with customary violence. He declared heatedly: "We do not accept Premier Khrushchev's protection of Arab Communists. . . . We reject subordination . . . because we fought hard . . . for our independence. . . . We shall defend it to the last drop of our blood."[108] As this bitter exchange continued, an Egyptian minister for the first time acknowledged publicly that the Communist world was opposed to Arab nationalism.[109] The government-supported Middle East News Agency claimed that Russia had dropped her support of "Nasserism" and was engaged in "a plan directed toward dominating the Arab nation."[110]

The climax of Nasser's attack came on March 30, 1959, when he uttered his strongest criticism of international Communism:

We tried not to make the local activities of Arab Communists in Iraq or Syria a reason for any clash with Russia as long as Russia did not interfere in our affairs. We were trying to convince ourselves that the Communist Parties in our countries were independent of international Communism. We found that they were not, and that was why I called them Communist stooges. They carried out orders and instructions to liquidate patriotic and national elements in order to place our country inside the zones of Communist influence. We were suddenly faced by flagrant interference in our internal affairs by Russia. There was concrete evidence of an alliance between the Russian leaders and Communists working against us inside our country.[111]

Some Western observers evinced surprise when, after this mutual recrimination, a Soviet-U.A.R. reconciliation was quickly effected following a personal letter from Nikita Khrushchev to President Nasser. For those familiar with Egypt's past diplomatic maneuvers, however, this move was not unexpected, for Nasser could ill afford to break completely with the Communist bloc. Egypt's army had been re-equipped with nearly 400-million-dollars worth of Soviet weapons, and Egypt's ambitious five-year plan for industrial development was dependent upon Soviet financing. Moreover, in the light of a Soviet agreement to construct the first stage of the High Dam with Soviet technicians and 100 million dollars in credits, and the fact that the Communist bloc provided markets for about 60 per cent of Egypt's annual cotton exports, Nasser was loath to jeopardize this assistance without a prior Western commitment.

During Nasser's brief but violent anti-Communist crusade, his relations with the West had improved noticeably. East German efforts to establish diplomatic relations with the U.A.R. were rebuffed, a financial agreement was reached with Great Britain, and Italy's Prime Minister concluded a successful visit to Cairo. The American government hesitantly considered granting the massive assistance which Nasser claimed as prerequisite to Egypt's adoption of a sincerely "neutralist" policy. Western policy makers also were encouraged by Nasser's efforts to remove some of the obstacles in the U.A.R.'s relations with Jordan and Lebanon.[112]

But these various moves did not necessarily signify a long-range trend. On previous occasions, Nasser had made tactical moves designed to gain Western support, only to lash out violently against the West and its supporters several months later. There also was no assurance that Nasser, motivated by little except his ambitions for himself and Egypt, might not again seek the assistance of the Communist bloc in his desire to dominate the Arab Middle East.

Nasser had beaten a tactical retreat from his *de facto* alliance with the Soviets, and for this the West was grateful. But any assumption that Nasser's policies had undergone a fundamental change was premature. Instead, it was appropriate to recall a compliment Nasser once tendered his "neutralist" friend, the President of Yugoslavia: "Tito is a great man. He showed me how to get help from both sides—without joining either."[113]

XI

Nasser's New Egypt in Perspective

Modern Egypt always has been a difficult country to govern. Physical control has been a relatively simple task, for the Egyptians are by nature a submissive people. But positive plans for development continually have been defeated by Egyptian inertia and lack of public responsibility. True, in the past, "strong men" —such as Mohamed Ali, dictator of Egypt for over forty years, and Khedive Ismail—have imposed their will on Egypt. When they passed from the stage, however, their accomplishments were dissipated by the ineptness of their successors and by the apathy of Egypt's ruling classes.

The nationalist revival during the period of British occupation revealed a public awareness among a segment of Cairo's population, but this seldom was transacted into positive achievements. Instead, the Egypt of 1952 was a stagnant country. Beset by political strife, successive national governments did little to foster the country's development. An archaic structure of land ownership, abysmal living conditions among the great majority of the population, an economy geared to benefit a privileged few, and political instability—this was the legacy after thirty years of independence.

The existing political parties abdicated their right to govern. In their struggle with the King and their quest for power and office, they treaded ruthlessly on the welfare of their country. Egypt's political structure blocked progress, rooted as it was in the *status quo*. No parliament controlled by wealthy landowners and Cairo's privileged social elite would support sweeping reform programs to the detriment of the vested interests.

Few groups were untainted by the corruption which permeated Cairo. Many ranking civil servants owed their positions to partisan politics; landowners gained protection from the Wafd; businessmen were dependent upon the government for favors; and high ranking military officers often owed their posts to the King's personal support. Only the middle-class military—the captains, majors, and colonels, and, perhaps, a few generals—had the moral credentials for a *bona fide* movement of reform. And, after the sordid manipulation of the Alexandria cotton market and the collapse of national government in 1952, only the military was prepared to take action in the name of the people.

Humiliated in the 1948 Palestine War, the Egyptian army generally had done little to distinguish itself. In its ranks, however, was a cadre of sincere and talented, though inexperienced, officers, and it was they who toppled the government in 1952. Initially, a junta sought to establish a nonpartisan civilian government, but this body proved unwilling to initiate the reforms desired by the young officers. Thus, the job of governing fell to the Free Officers by default. Governing had not been their initial purpose, and they were ill prepared for the task; but they alone were in a position to raze the "old order." And the destruction of the "old order" was a prerequisite for the implementation of profound reforms.

Rapid development in Egypt required an authoritarian government, and it became increasingly obvious that the Revolutionary Command Council could not measure up to the task. Instead, a single leader, a man with dictatorial powers, was needed. Gamal Abdel Nasser became dictator of Egypt in April, 1954. His was a difficult task. The country had not rallied to the military movement. Moreover, there was no panacea for Egypt's problems, and his every move drew the sniping attacks of those without the responsibilities for government. To his credit, he approached his mission boldly. Easy as it was to be irresolute, he determined what was best for Egypt, then forcefully sought to impose his will on the country and his reluctant military colleagues. He alone assumed final responsibility for the success or failure of his policies.

Unfortunately, his drive for internal development soon was tempered by external considerations. Nasser claimed the role of unifier of the entire Arab world. Moreover, he was embarrassed by Egypt's military inferiority vis-à-vis Israel. While economic and social development still progressed at a commendable pace, Nasser placed increasingly heavy emphasis on Egypt's foreign relations. Undoubtedly, Nasser realized that this would have a detrimental effect on Egypt's future internal development, for a massive military establishment would severely strain Egypt's limited resources.

There is no single explanation for Nasser's aggressive plunge into foreign affairs. Following his personal consolidation of power, the prospect of dealing primarily with domestic policies certainly held little attraction for a man of Nasser's tactical abilities. And, in Nasser's mind, the restive Egyptian people, destined for a long period of austerity until the development programs bore fruit, probably required the "bread and circuses" of an anti-imperialist witch hunt.

In 1955, Egypt was passing through a transitional period. The government had provided handsome incentives to attract foreign investments; 40 million dollars of American technical assistance was forthcoming; the West was prepared to finance the foreign-exchange requirements of the mammoth High Dam scheme; internal development projects were gaining momentum. Egypt's internal programs required Nasser's personal and constant supervision—especially since few of Nasser's colleagues had the ability or authority to initiate the programs necessary for Egypt's sound development.

Instead, Nasser sought an international reputation: he became deeply involved in Arab world politics, and he embarked on an aggressive policy which alienated his Western friends. This campaign was not without some provocation or justification—for, at times, Great Britain, the United States, as well as several Arab governments had not behaved with consummate wisdom or tact. But this was no reason for Gamal Abdel Nasser to abandon the statesmanship which he had employed to Egypt's great advantage during the Revolution's first thirty months.

The Nasser of 1955 was essentially the same man who had engineered a coup three years before. He was exceedingly ambitious for himself and for Egypt; he worked far harder than did his colleagues; and he was content to live an austere life free of the extravagant luxury often associated with military dictators. His greatest attribute was his extraordinary skill as a tactician. Perhaps it was too much to expect such a man to content himself with the difficult and often monotonous task of internal development: this taxed his administrative abilities while providing little scope for those skills which he had used to such advantage in besting Mustapha Nahas, Mohammed Naguib, the Moslem Brethren, and the British in Suez.

The same energy which had been devoted to internal reform subsequently was directed outward onto the international scene. Nasser's successes were undeniable. He became the symbol of Arab nationalism to the Arab masses. His program of "positive neutrality" gained a degree of respectability through his association with Nehru and Tito. Confident of Soviet support, he mounted a vigorous attack against British and French interests throughout the Arab world. But these successes benefited Egypt little. Nasser, as the self-styled champion of Arab nationalism, heightened the pitch of his anti-Western attacks, derided his opponents in the Arab world as "stooges of imperialism," and scored notable victories. But, as he had discovered earlier in Egypt, destroying was easier than building.

Nasser deemed the High Dam the cornerstone of Egypt's economic development. Thus, it was a severe blow to Egypt when the West withdrew its offer to finance the Dam. John Foster Dulles made this move in retaliation for Nasser's aggressive tactics. The Egyptian President, even if he could justify his actions in terms of "sovereignty" and "dignity," could not blink the fact that his foreign adventures have postponed the construction of the High Dam, essential to Egypt's future well-being, by at least two years.

Egypt benefited from the Anglo-French attack on Suez. She obtained unquestioned control over the Canal, from which she should net an amount in excess of 10 per cent of her annual national budget. Moreover, as an aftermath to the attack on Port Said and Egypt's military defeat in Sinai, foreign control over Egyptian banks and insurance companies has almost been eliminated. As "compensation" for the Anglo–French–American blockade of Egyptian assets, Nasser was awarded a Soviet industrial credit for 62 million pounds. This was small compensation, however, for the economic losses implicit in his estrangement from the West.

The year 1957 was a critical one for Egypt. She weathered the West's diplomatic isolation, initiated an industrial development program, and convened a National Assembly. Ironically, however, Gamal Abdel Nasser, the hero of the Arab masses, was becoming less popular at home. The internal-development program, sharply curtailed during the Suez crisis of 1956, certainly gave Egyptians little cause for rejoicing. The National Assembly, symbolic of the "new Egypt," proved uncomfortably embarrassing to the regime. President Nasser, anxious to end the period of political transition (originally proclaimed in 1953), had opened the carefully screened Parliament amid great fanfare. But when some members displayed startling independence, the government felt obliged to end the entire parliamentary experiment abruptly. Without question, the Revolution of 1952 was on the decline, and the military was reluctant to relinquish its authority. Instead, the "transitional period" was extended indefinitely.

In 1958, Nasser again sought victories abroad. He triumphantly incorporated Syria into the United Arab Republic, but the regime, already hard-pressed to manage Egypt's domestic affairs, was ill equipped to shoulder the economic burdens of Syria. In the wake of the Syrian merger came the Iraqi revolution, which some called Nasser's greatest victory to date. With the demise of Nuri es Said, however, "Nasserism" seemed to lose its momentum. Because many of the Arab countries already had overthrown the "treacherous old order," there remained few scapegoats on which Egypt could vent her ire. Moreover, Nasser and his tired corevolutionaries lacked an operational program for economic and social development which they could pass on to other nationalist leaders.

Nasser did not play his cards well. In 1954, when Egypt represented a liberal force in the Arab world, Nasser could well have afforded to be charitable to his Arab neighbors. His control over the religious and secular center of learning for the Arab Middle East gave him a tremendous advantage which he could have used wisely. Instead, he embarked upon a destructive policy, ostensibly to make the dream of a single Arab nation a reality. In this, however, he has failed. Egypt's difficulties in Syria —her "northern province"—have brought the sudden realization to many Arab leaders that Nasser had little to offer to the "newly liberated" Arab nations.

These failures seem to have had a sobering effect on Nasser. At least for the present, he appears to realize that the once-irresistible force of "Nasserism" has lost its momentum. He is making a serious attempt to develop a more constructive policy toward the Arab world. Nasser still has strong appeal among the Arab masses, but he is discredited with most Arab governments. It will be a difficult task for him to gain the confidence of the very men whom he sought to undermine not so long ago. But if he is sincerely concerned with the welfare of the Arab world, he must do just that. He still is the most competent leader in the Arab world, the man who best can provide cohesion to the Arab drive for political and economic maturity. His ultimate success will depend on the extent to which he will subordinate his personal ambition for the well-being of his Arab "brothers."

"Positive neutrality" has been the guideline of Nasser's foreign policy since 1955. His desire to maintain Egypt's independence of action is undeniable—and, in this context, his adherence to neutrality is far more sincere than most Western observers are wont to believe. But his aggressive anti-Western posture for much of the past four years has compelled even such a convinced Asian neutralist as Nehru to dissociate himself from Nasser's "neutralist philosophy." "Neutralism" for Nasser is not a philosophy but a blanket of morality in which he has sought to shroud his aggressive tactics. Nor has he executed "neutralist" tactics with outstanding skill. By alienating the West, he has estranged the Soviet bloc's rival bidder for Egypt's favor and thus had undercut his country's value on the auction block of "neutrality."

There has been evidence of late that Nasser is trying to redress this mistake. After his clash with Nikita Khrushchev over Iraq, he seems anxious to restore the balance to Egypt's policy which proved so profitable in 1955. President Nasser is no Communist, nor is he anxious to further Communist aims in the Arab and African worlds. But in his desire to extend Egypt's hegemony over the Afro-Arab world, he has, in the past, accepted massive Communist-bloc support. He may do so again.

Moreover, although Egypt's flirtations with the Communist bloc have brought the cold war into the Arab heartland, Nasser has not become a tool of the Soviets. Indeed, Communist economic penetration in Egypt could be curbed if the West were willing to underwrite the bulk of Egypt's cotton exports.

Nasser is skilled in the game of political survival; he has also been extremely lucky. He has played the cards of "positive neutrality" for high stakes and, to date, bluff and courage have kept him in the game. But Egypt has benefited little from Nasser's international adventures. Much has been undertaken in the name of lofty principles, yet Egypt has paid a high price for Nasser's tactical successes.

Originally, internal reform and development was the Revolution's *raison d'être*. Ultimately, it is by the achievements in these fields that Nasser will be judged. Egypt is a poor country—poor in physical as well as human resources. At the time of the Revolution, the new regime faced a substantial balance of payments deficits, a much-reduced General Reserve Fund, and a crisis in cotton marketing. Industry provided a nominal proportion of the national income and only six million *feddans* under cultivation were available to produce sustenance for twenty-one million people.

Today, seven years later, Egypt has made substantial progress. Gross examples of waste are in evidence—the results of bad planning, inefficient implementation, and inexperienced management. By Western standards, the results are not outstanding. But one must gauge the military's achievements against the accomplishments of previous civilian governments. For example, the Aswan hydro-electric plant, under consideration for many years, is under construction; an iron and steel company, expensive by Western yardsticks, has been constructed; and roads have been built, railway equipment replaced, the High Dam project undertaken and numerous educational and social programs initiated.

Progress has not met original expectations. But this failure is not peculiar to Egypt: planning in underdeveloped countries invariably is overly ambitious. The shortcomings of specific programs have been obvious. And, perhaps, Egypt's long-range planning is ill-conceived. Moreover, Egypt still has not attained an adequate level of economic and social development. This, however, does not detract from the significant progress made by the military regime.

Nasser can claim less success in internal politics. His elimination of domestic opposition was a masterpiece of political legerdemain. One by one, the opposition first was isolated, then destroyed. His hesitant efforts to build a new political structure suggest, however, that the military period of "transition" may continue indefinitely.

Nasser has shown concern over his regime's lack of permanence. His government, as distinct from Nasser as an individual, has no "mandate from the people." His sudden death would result in chaos, for no obvious successor has been groomed to take his place. On several occasions, Nasser cautiously has attempted to build a bridge between the military and the civilian population. But his fear of relinquishing personal authority, together with his lack of a political philosophy, have rendered these efforts ineffective.

Nasser's government is authoritarian. But it is clear that a less forceful government could not have imposed the discipline necessary to achieve even the nominal development Egypt recently has experienced. Nasser now must provide for the future, for the popular support commanded by him will not automatically be transferred to his ultimate successor. Instead, a national political structure, commensurate with Egypt's new responsibilities, must be constructed. This will entail risks on Nasser's part, for it will mean granting a platform to elected representatives of the people; it will mean less censorship of the press; it will mean subjecting the military and civilians to a single standard. Indeed, such moves will encourage a political opposition which, in turn, may render governing more difficult. But only through a gradual diffusion of power—power which now is so jealously guarded by Nasser—can the Revolution be consummated.

The Egyptian people owe a great deal to President Nasser. He assumed leadership over a country in a time of despair.

Through courageous determination and reckless opportunism he has since managed to make his subjects proud to be Egyptians. Certainly, many of them are deluded by his government's "pie-in-the-sky" promises. But today, Egypt has a far better chance to maintain, or even increase, her per capita standard of living than it had seven years ago. Nasser has made many mistakes. His foreign adventures have cost Egypt dearly. But, in the final balance, Nasser has done Egypt a great service. He has broken the vicious circle of poverty and lethargy and has started Egypt on the positive path of development.

At the time of the 1952 coup, Gamal Abdel Nasser was only thirty-four years old. Since then, he has matured rapidly. No longer must he worry about being "accepted," for he has established himself as an exceptionally qualified leader. Moreover, he has the experience of seven turbulent years in power. In the past, Nasser's impulsive desire to be in the limelight has prompted him to overplay his hand. Recent events suggest that he is gaining moderation with the passage of time. His failures in Syria and Iraq have been sobering; and his frontal attack on Communism, in March and April of 1959, suggests that he will hesitate in the future before again committing himself heavily to Communist support. The ultimate decision is Nasser's. If he so chooses, he can become one of the great personalities of the twentieth century, at least within the Afro-Asian world. But, paradoxically, he can achieve this distinction only if he tempers his personal desire to dominate the Arab world and concentrates instead on meeting the manifold needs of his nation.

NOTES

Chapter I

Prelude to Takeover

1. Jean and Simonne Lacouture, *Egypt in Transition* (London: Methuen & Co., 1958), p. 128.
2. *The New York Times,* February 26, 1954.
3. *Ibid.*
4. Anwar el Sadat, *Revolt on the Nile* (London: Allan Wingate, 1957), p. 14.
5. *Ibid.*, p. 43.
6. Sadat, in a personal interview on September 2, 1958.
7. Lacouture, *op. cit.*, p. 132.
8. Sadat interview.
9. *Ibid.*
10. *Ibid.*
11. Khaled Mohieddine, in a personal interview on September 13, 1958.
12. Rashed el Barawy, *The Military Coup* (Cairo: Renaissance Bookshop, 1952), p. 191.
13. Lacouture, *op. cit.*, p. 134.
14. Mohieddine interview.
15. Sadat, *op. cit.*, p. 84.
16. Mohieddine interview.
17. *Jewish Observer and Middle East Review* (London), July 25, 1952.
18. Lacouture, *op. cit.*, p. 140.
19. Sadat, *op. cit.*, p. 97.
20. Lacouture, *op. cit.*, p. 141.
21. *Ibid.*, p. 143; Sadat interview.
22. Barawy, *op. cit.*, p. 196.
23. Mohammed Naguib, *Egypt's Destiny* (New York: Doubleday & Co., 1955), p. 95.
24. *Ibid.*, p. 90.
25. Mohieddine interview.

26. Lacouture, *op. cit.*, p. 143; Mohieddine interview.
27. Barawy, *op. cit.*, p. 201.
28. Lacouture, *op. cit.*, p. 145.
29. Mohieddine interview.
30. *Jewish Observer and Middle East Review*, July 25, 1952.
31. *Al Misri*, October 28, 1952.
32. Lacouture, *op. cit.*, p. 146.
33. Sadat interview.
34. Naguib, *op. cit.*, p. 109; Sadat interview; Sadat, *op. cit.*, p. 131.
35. Sadat interview; Naguib, *op. cit.*, p. 110.
36. Mohieddine interview.
37. Lacouture, *op. cit.*, p. 148.
38. *Ibid.*, pp. 150-51.
39. Gamal Abdel Nasser, *The Philosophy of the Revolution* (Cairo: Dar el Maaref, 1954), p. 19.
40. *Ibid.*
41. *Jewish Observer and Middle East Review*, August 1, 1952.
42. Sadat interview; Lacouture, *op. cit.*, pp. 156-57.

Chapter II

Coup and Consolidation

1. *Jewish Observer and Middle East Review* (London), August 1, 1952.
2. Gamal Abdel Nasser, *The Philosophy of the Revolution* (Cairo: Dar el Maaref, 1954), p. 20.
3. Khaled Mohieddine, in a personal interview on September 13, 1958.
4. Jean and Simonne Lacouture, *Egypt in Transition* (London: Methuen & Co., 1958), pp. 163-64.
5. *The New York Times*, July 31, 1952.
6. According to a once-prominent official of the outlawed Moslem Brethren who wishes to remain anonymous; *see also*, Ishak Musa Husaini, *The Moslem Brethren* (Beirut: Khayat, 1956), p. 127.
7. Anwar el Sadat, in a personal interview on September 2, 1958.
8. *Misr Egyptian News Agency Weekly Review*, January 16, 1954. Subsequently referred to as *MENA*.
9. Lacouture, *op. cit.*, p. 162.
10. *The New York Times*, August 9, 1952.
11. *Ibid.*

12. *Ibid.*, August 11, 1952.
13. *Ibid.*, August 14, 1952.
14. *MENA*, August 16, 1952.
15. Mohammed Naguib, *Egypt's Destiny* (New York: Doubleday & Co., 1955), p. 154.
16. Ahmed AbdullahToiema, in a personal interview on April 8, 1958.
17. Abdel Mony Said Salama, an important official in the Labor Department of Egypt's Ministry of Social Affairs and Labor, in a personal interview on July 10, 1958; Hussein Shafei, in a personal interview on August 26, 1958.
18. *Jewish Observer and Middle East Review*, August 22, 1952.
19. Walter Z. Laqueur, *Communism and Nationalism in the Middle East* (2nd ed.; New York: Frederick A. Praeger, 1957), p. 48.
20. *The New York Times*, August 16, 1952.
21. Sadat interview.
22. *Jewish Observer and Middle East Review*, September 26, 1952.
23. *The New York Times*, September 28, 1952.
24. *Ibid.*, September 30, 1952.
25. *Ibid.*, September 26, 1952.
26. *Ibid.*, October 1, 1952.
27. *MENA*, October 11, 1952.
28. *Ibid.*, October 18, 1952.
29. *Ibid.*
30. *Ibid.*
31. *The New York Times*, November 17, 1952.
32. *MENA*, December 6, 1952.
33. Rashed el Barawy, *The Military Coup* (Cairo: Renaissance Bookshop, 1952), pp. 201, 204.
34. *MENA*, June 20, 1953.
35. Toiema, in a personal interview on April 26, 1958.
36. Naguib, in a personal interview on August 28, 1953.
37. Lacouture, *op. cit.*, p. 176.
38. Tom Little, *Egypt* (New York: Frederick A. Praeger, 1958), p. 223.
39. *The New York Times*, October 2, 1953.
40. *Jewish Observer and Middle East Review*, November 6, 1953.
41. *MENA*, July 11, 1953.
42. *Jewish Observer and Middle East Review*, December 4, 1953.
43. *Ibid.*, December 11, 1953.
44. *MENA*, November 28, 1953.

45. *Ibid.*, January 16, 1954.
46. Lacouture, *op. cit.*, p. 179.
47. *Ibid.*, p. 181.
48. Sadat interview.
49. Little, *op. cit.*, p. 228.
50. Sadat interview.
51. *Ibid.*
52. *The New York Times*, March 1, 1954.
53. Lacouture, *op. cit.*, p. 184.
54. Sadat interview.
55. *Ibid.*
56. Lacouture, *op. cit.*, p. 184.
57. *The New York Times*, March 1, 1959.
58. Lacouture, *op. cit.*, p. 185.
59. *The New York Times*, March 1, 1954.
60. *Ibid.*, February 2, 1954.
61. *Ibid.*, February 28, 1954.
62. *Ibid.*, March 28, 1954.
63. *Ibid.*, March 2, 1954.
64. *Ibid.*, March 3, 1954.
65. *Ibid.*, March 10, 1954.
66. *Jewish Observer and Middle East Review*, March 12, 1954.
67. *The New York Times*, March 22, 1954.
68. *Ibid.*, March 26, 1954.
69. *Ibid.*, March 21, 1954.
70. *Ibid.*
71. *Ibid.*, March 27, 1954.
72. *Ibid.*
73. *Ibid.*, March 28, 1954.
74. *Ibid.*
75. Lacouture, *op. cit.*, p. 190.
76. *MENA*, April 3, 1954.
77. *The New York Times*, April 1, 1954.
78. Little, *op. cit.*, p. 213.
79. *The New York Times*, March 30, 1954.

Chapter III

The Entrenchment of the Military Regime

1. Gamal Abdel Nasser, in a speech on July 22, 1954, commemorating the second anniversary of Egypt's Revolution.

2. *Misr Egyptian News Agency Weekly Review,* October 23, 1954. Subsequently referred to as *MENA.*
3. *Ibid.,* June 12, 1954.
4. *Ibid.,* July 10, 1954.
5. Nasser, in a personal interview on August 19, 1954.
6. Nasser speech.
7. *MENA,* July 24, 1954.
8. *Ibid.,* June 5, 1954.
9. *Ibid.,* August 28, 1954.
10. Tom Little, *Egypt* (New York: Frederick A. Praeger, 1958), p. 254.
11. *Jewish Observer and Middle East Review* (London), August 6, 1954.
12. *MENA,* August 28, 1954.
13. Nasser interview.
14. *The New York Times,* September 26, 1954.
15. *Ibid.,* October 8, 1954.
16. *Ibid.,* September 14, 1954.
17. Anwar el Sadat, in a personal interview on September 9, 1958.
18. *Ibid.*
19. *Ibid.*
20. *MENA,* October 30, 1954.
21. *Ibid.*
22. *The New York Times,* October 31, 1954.
23. *Ibid.*
24. Ishak Musa Husaini, *The Moslem Brethren* (Beirut: Khayat, 1956), p. 137.
25. *The New York Times,* November 12, 1954.
26. Jean and Simonne Lacouture, *Egypt in Transition* (London: Methuen & Co., 1958), p. 193; *MENA,* November 27, 1954.
27. *The New York Times,* November 28, 1954.
28. Nasser, in a speech on June 1, 1956, before the General Cooperative Congress.
29. *The New York Times,* October 13, 1954.
30. *MENA,* December 24, 1955.
31. Lacouture, *op. cit.,* p. 271.
32. *MENA,* January 15, 1955.
33. Sadat interview.
34. Lacouture, *op. cit.,* p. 268.
35. *Jewish Observer and Middle East Review,* March 25, 1955.
36. *MENA,* June 2, 1956.
37. *The New York Times,* Section VI, August 19, 1956.

38. *MENA*, April 2, 1955.
39. *Ibid.*, July 10, 1954.
40. *The New York Times*, May 20, 1955.
41. *MENA*, May 21, 1955.
42. *Ibid.*, May 28, 1955.
43. *Ibid.*, January 28, 1956.
44. Nasser speech, June 1, 1956.
45. *Ibid.*
46. *MENA*, June 23, 1956.
47. *Jewish Observer and Middle East Review*, August 16, 1957.
48. *The New York Times*, December 1, 1956.
49. *Al Shaab*, November 12, 1956.
50. *Cairo Press Review*, November 22, 1956.
51. *Al Gomhouria*, November 30, 1956.
52. *The New York Times*, December 1, 1956.
53. *New York Herald Tribune*, April 26, 1957.
54. As quoted by Barrett McGurn, *New York Herald Tribune*, April 26, 1957.
55. *New York Herald Tribune*, April 29, 1957.
56. *Cairo Press Review*, May 11, 1957.
57. *Al Gomhouria*, June 17, 1957.
58. *Al Shaab*, June 19, 1957.
59. *The New York Times*, July 3, 1957.
60. Anwar Salama, in a personal interview on August 29, 1957.
61. *Cairo Press Review*, July 23, 1957.
62. *Ibid.*, August 13, 1957.
63. *Ibid.*
64. *The New York Times*, August 13, 1957.
65. *Ibid.*
66. *Jewish Observer and Middle East Review*, August 23, 1957.
67. *Cairo Press Review*, August 26, 1957.
68. *Ibid.*, August 23, 1957.
69. *Ibid.*, September 3, 1957.
70. Ali Sabry, in a personal interview on September 12, 1957.
71. *Cairo Press Review*, August 15, 1957; *Jewish Observer and Middle East Review*, November 29, 1957.
72. *Jewish Observer and Middle East Review*, November 29, 1957.
73. *Ibid.*
74. *Ibid.*, November 1, 1957.
75. *The New York Times*, November 13, 1957.
76. *Egyptian Economic and Political Review* (Cairo), February, 1956, p. 41.

77. *Al Ahram,* December 16, 1957; *Cairo Press Review,* December 16, 1957.
78. *Jewish Observer and Middle East Review,* January 17, 1958; *Cairo Press Review,* January 8, 1958.
79. Mohamed Hassanein Heikal, in a personal interview on September 12, 1957.
80. Nasser, in a speech on December 5, 1957, before the General Cooperative Congress.
81. *Ibid.*
82. *Ibid.*
83. *Ibid.*
84. *Ibid.*
85. *Al Akhbar,* August 25, 1958.
86. *Akhbar el Yom,* January 4, 1958; *Al Ahram,* January 5, 1958; Sadat interview.
87. Sadat interview.
88. Ahmed Abdullah Toiema, in a personal interview on April 26, 1958.
89. *Ibid.*
90. An Egyptian citizen who does not wish to be identified.
91. Sadat interview.
92. Mohamed Abou Nour, in a personal interview on September 21, 1958.
93. *Ibid.*
94. *Ibid.*
95. *The New York Times,* January 2, 1959.
96. Mahmoud Riad, an Under-Secretary at the Ministry of the Interior, in a personal interview on August 31, 1958.
97. *Ibid.*
98. *Al Gomhouria,* June 17, 1957.

Chapter IV

Agriculture and Agrarian Reform

1. Mohamed el Abd, *Egyptian Agrarian Reform System of Land Requisition* (Cairo: Higher Committee for Agrarian Reform, 1955), p. 9.
2. Abdel Razzak Sidky, *Progress of Egyptian Agriculture in Five Years* (Cairo: Ministry of Agriculture, 1957), p. 6.
3. George L. Harris (ed.), *Egypt* (New Haven, Conn.: Human Relations Area Files, 1957), p. 193.

4. National Production Council, *Permanent Council for the Development of National Production* (Cairo: n.p., 1955), p. 28.

5. Sayed Marei, *Agrarian Reform in Egypt* (Cairo: Société Orientale de Publicité, 1957), p. 193.

6. *Observations on the Urbanization and Distribution of Agricultural Population in Egypt* (Cairo: Higher Committee for Agrarian Reform, n.d.), p. 9.

7. Doreen Warriner, *Land Reform and Development in the Middle East* (London: Royal Institute of International Affairs, 1957), p. 11.

8. Charles Issawi, *Egypt at Mid-Century* (New York: Oxford University Press [for the Royal Institute of International Affairs], 1954), p. 135.

9. *Middle East Economist and Financial Service* (Forest Hills), February, 1952.

10. Marei, *op. cit.*, p. 23.

11. *Jewish Observer and Middle East Review* (London), August 22, 1952.

12. Marei, *op. cit.*, p. 44.

13. *Ibid.*

14. *Ibid.*, pp. 27, 247.

15. Marei, *Outline of Land Reform in Egypt* (Cairo: Higher Committee for Agrarian Reform, n.d.), p. 9.

16. *Land Reform in Figures* (Cairo: Higher Committee for Agrarian Reform, 1954), p. 1.

17. William Thweatt, "The Egyptian Agrarian Reform," quoting a letter from Nikolai Koestner, *Middle East Economic Papers, 1956* (Beirut), p. 149.

18. National Bank of Egypt, *Economic Bulletin*, Vol. VI, No. 3, 1953, p. 215.

19. Marei, *Outline of Land Reform in Egypt*, p. 16.

20. Thweatt, *op. cit.*

21. Marei, *Agrarian Reform in Egypt*, p. 366.

22. Mohamed Abdel-Wahab Ezzat, text of a speech delivered at the Center on Land Problems in the Middle East (Cairo: Higher Committee for Agrarian Reform, 1955), p. 4.

23. National Bank of Egypt, *Economic Bulletin*, Vol. VI, No. 3, 1953, p. 215; Marei, *Agrarian Reform in Egypt*, p. 57.

24. *Land Reform in Figures*, p. 1.

25. Marei, in a personal interview on October 5, 1958.

26. *Areas Distributed Up to September, 1954* (Cairo: Higher Committee for Agrarian Reform, 1954), p. 1.

27. Marei, *Outline of Land Reform* (2nd ed.; Cairo: Higher Committee for Agrarian Reform, 1956), p. 27.

28. Marei, in a personal interview on July 6, 1957.

29. *Agrarian Reform Program of Land Distribution, July 23, 1957* (Cairo: Agrarian Reform General Organization, 1957), p. 2.

30. *Cairo Press Review*, July 12, 1958.

31. *Al Ahram*, July 29, 1958.

32. Marei, *Agrarian Reform in Egypt*, p. 69.

33. Warriner, *op. cit.*, p. 44.

34. *Statutes of Zaafaran Cooperative Society* (Cairo: Higher Committee for Agrarian Reform, 1955), p. 27.

35. Marei, *Agrarian Reform in Egypt*, p. 69.

36. Mahmoud Fawzi, in a personal interview on September 20, 1958.

37. Marei, *Agrarian Reform in Egypt*, p. 171.

38. Marei, in a letter of June 3, 1959 to the writer.

39. Marei, *Agrarian Reform in Egypt*, p. 99.

40. *Ibid.*, pp. 378-79.

41. *Ibid.*, p. 92.

42. Warriner, *op. cit.*, p. 37.

43. Marei, in a personal interview on July 13, 1956.

44. Warriner, *op. cit.*, p. 32; Thweatt, *op. cit.*, p. 156.

45. Ahmed el- Alfi, Director of the Agrarian Reform's Economic Department, in a personal interview on September 28, 1958.

46. Marei interview, October 5, 1958.

47. *Ibid.*

48. Marei, *Agrarian Reform in Egypt*, p. 160.

49. Marei interview, October 5, 1958.

50. *Ibid.*

51. UNRWA Bulletin No. 5, November, 1952, p. 2.

52. Marei, *Agrarian Reform in Egypt*, p. 393.

53. Eva Garzouzi, *Old Ills and New Remedies in Egypt* (Cairo: Dar al Maaref, 1958), p. 90.

54. Warriner, *op. cit.*, p. 39.

55. *Al Shaab*, July 14, 1956.

56. *Cairo Press Review*, October 18, 1957.

57. *Al Shaab*, April 28, 1958.

58. Warriner, *op. cit.*, p. 32.

59. Marei, at a press conference on July 29, 1954.

60. Warriner, *op. cit.*, p. 31.
61. Marei letter, June 3, 1959.
62. *Mudiriat Al-Tahreer*, Liberation Province Pamphlet No. 1 (Cairo: Chiati, 1954), p. 12.
63. Warriner, *op. cit.*, p. 52.
64. Garzouzi, *op. cit.*, p. 108.
65. Marei interview, July 6, 1957.
66. Omar Sabry, Ali Sabry's younger brother and an authority on agricultural affairs, in a personal interview on September 10, 1958.
67. Marei interview, October 5, 1958.
68. *Revolution After Five Years* (Cairo: Egyptian Department of Information, 1957), p. 31.
69. Personal interview with a staff member at Liberation Province, April 19, 1958.
70. *Cairo Press Review*, May 27, 1958.
71. Sabry interview.
72. Garzouzi, *op. cit.*, p. 111.
73. Mohamed Hassanein Heikal, in a personal interview on September 12, 1957.
74. Rifki Anwar, Director of what originally was the EARIS Project, in a personal interview on September 30, 1958.
75. Anwar interview.
76. National Production Council, *op. cit.*, pp. 67-68.
77. *Goals of the Revolution* (Cairo: n.p., n.d.), p. 6.
78. Warriner, *op. cit.*, pp. 21-22.
79. Marei interview, October 5, 1958.
80. *Agriculture in Egypt* (Cairo: n.p., 1958), p. 3.
81. Mansour el Sayed, in a personal interview on September 15, 1958.
82. Sidky, in a personal interview on July 29, 1953.
83. Issawi, *op. cit.*, p. 116.
84. Sabry, in a personal interview on September 15, 1958.
85. Marei interview, July 13, 1956.
86. Marei, *Agrarian Reform in Egypt*, p. 184.
87. *Ibid.*, p. 122.
88. *Al Shaab*, February 8, 1958.
89. Hussein Shafei, in a personal interview on August 26, 1958.
90. Mahmoud Fawzi, *Nawag: a Pilot Experiment for Solving the Problem of Fragmentation in Egypt* (Cairo: Agrarian Reform General Organization, 1958).

91. "Agricultural Statistics," *Monthly Bulletin of Agricultural Economics, Statistics, and Legislation* (Cairo), January, 1957, p. 2.
92. Ministry of Finance and Economy, *Statistical Pocket Year-Book, 1955* (Cairo: Egyptian Government Press, 1956), p. 36; Statistical Department of the Presidency of the Republic, *Statistical Pocket Year-Book, 1957* (Cairo: General Organization for Government Printing Offices, 1958), p. 42.
93. National Bank of Egypt, *Economic Bulletin*, Vol. XI, No. 2, 1958, pp. 210-11.
94. Sidky, *op. cit.*, p. 17.
95. National Production Council, *op. cit.*, p. 34.
96. Marei interview, October 5, 1958.

Chapter V

Education and Social Development

1. George L. Harris, ed., *Egypt* (New Haven: Human Relations Area Files, 1957), p. 5.
2. Mirrit Boutros Ghali, *The Policy of Tomorrow* (Washington, D.C.: American Council of Learned Societies, 1953), p. 7.
3. Charles Issawi, *Egypt at Mid-Century* (New York: Oxford University Press [for the Royal Institute of International Affairs], 1954), p. 73.
4. Issawi, *op. cit.*, p. 67.
5. *The Atlas of Services* (Cairo: The Permanent Council for Public Welfare Services, 1955), p. 58.
6. Data obtained from the General Buildings Foundation (formerly School Buildings Foundation), October, 1958.
7. Eva Garzouzi, *Old Ills and New Remedies in Egypt* (Cairo: Dar al Maaref, 1958), p. 26.
8. Data obtained from the General Buildings Foundation, October, 1958.
9. Mahmoud Abou Sennar, in a personal interview on September 21, 1958.
10. Ibrahim Afifi, Assistant Director-General of the Teacher Training Program at the Ministry of Education, in a personal interview on September 11, 1958.
11. Ministry of Finance and Economy, *Statistical Pocket Year-Book, 1955* (Cairo: Egyptian Government Press, 1956), p. 21.

12. Statistical Department of the Presidency of the Republic, *Statistical Pocket Year-Book, 1957* (Cairo: General Organization for Government Printing Offices, 1958), p. 26.

13. *Ibid.*, p. 6.

14. Sadek H. Samaan, *Value Reconstruction and Egyptian Education* (New York: Bureau of Publications, Teachers College, Columbia University, 1955), p. xiii.

15. Ministry of Finance and Economy, *Statistical Pocket Year-Book, 1954* (Cairo: Egyptian Government Press, 1955), p. 23.

16. *Statistical Pocket Year-Book, 1957*, p. 28.

17. *Misr Egyptian News Agency Weekly Review*, December 24, 1955. Subsequently referred to as *MENA*.

18. Ahmed Neguib Hashim, then Permanent Under-Secretary at the Ministry of Education, in a personal interview on April 3, 1958.

19. *Al Gomhouria*, September 5, 1958; *Al Shaab*, September 5, 1958.

20. *Ministry of Municipal and Rural Affairs: Its Achievements Prior to the Revolution and During Five Years of the Revolution Government* (Cairo: n.p., 1957), p. 5. Subsequently referred to as *Ministry of Municipal and Rural Affairs, Achievements;* Aziz Yassin, an Under-Secretary at the Ministry of Municipal and Rural Affairs, in a personal interview on August 4, 1958.

21. *Statistical Pocket Year-Book, 1954*, p. 22; *Statistical Pocket Year-Book, 1957*, p. 26.

22. Garzouzi, *op. cit.*, p. 22.

23. Gamal Abdel Nasser, in a speech on July 13, 1955, at the opening of the Bernesht Combined Service Unit.

24. *The Permanent Council for Public Welfare Services* (Cairo: Société Orientale de Publicité, 1955), p. 7.

25. *Ibid.*, p. 13.

26. *The Permanent Council for Public Services* (Cairo: Egyptian Department of Information, n.d.), p. 46.

27. Abdou Sallam, a ranking official at the Permanent Council for Public Welfare Services, at a press conference on August 22, 1956.

28. *Ibid.*

29. Salah Ismail, in a personal interview on July 24, 1956.

30. Personal observation, August, 1956.

31. Abdou el Fattah el Ziat of the Combined Service Units Administration, in a personal interview on August 19, 1957.

32. Garzouzi, *op. cit.*, p. 145.
33. Mohamed Shalaby, in a personal interview on May 16, 1958.
34. Hussein Shafei, in a personal interview on August 26, 1958.
35. Shalaby interview.
36. Shalaby, *Rural Reconstruction in Egypt* (Cairo: Egyptian Association for Social Studies, 1950), p. 36.
37. *Cairo Press Review*, August 21, 1958.
38. Yassin interview.
39. *The Combined Centers of Egypt: A New Development in Rural Welfare Programs* (Cairo: n.p., April, 1957), p. 1.
40. Shalaby interview.
41. Ziat interview.
42. *Policy of Generalizing Potable Water for Drinking and Domestic Purposes* (Cairo: Ministry of Municipal and Rural Affairs, 1958), p. 23.
43. Mohamed Abu Nosseir, in a personal interview on September 25, 1958.
44. *Ibid.*
45. *Ibid.*
46. *Progress Since the Revolution* (Cairo: Ministry of Social Affairs, n.d.), p. 31.
47. Mustapha Kamal Fuad of the Housing Cooperatives Department at the Ministry of Social Affairs and Labor, in a personal interview on August 2, 1958; Ahmed Rifaat, Assistant Under-Secretary in charge of housing matters at the Ministry of Municipal and Rural Affairs, in a personal interview on October 1, 1958.
48. Information supplied by Fuad Abou Zaghla, Director of the Public Relations Department at the Ministry of Municipal and Rural Affairs, August, 1958, and Ahmed Rifaat, September, 1958.
49. Data obtained from the Popular Housing and Development Company, October, 1958.
50. Fuad interview; Mr. Hismet of the Civil Servants Insurance and Pension Fund, in a personal interview on October 4, 1958.
51. Fuad interview.
52. Rifaat interview.
53. Ibrahim Khalil of the Popular Housing and Development Company, in a personal interview on October 1, 1958.
54. Data obtained from the Popular Housing and Development Company, October, 1958.

55. *Ministry of Municipal and Rural Affairs, Achievements*, p. 13.
56. *Housing Problems in Egypt* (Cairo: Ministry of Municipal and Rural Affairs, 1954), p. 7; data obtained from the Popular Housing and Development Company, October, 1958.
57. Fuad interview; information supplied by Fuad Abou Zaghla, August, 1958, and Ahmed Rifaat, September, 1958.
58. Fuad interview.
59. Rifaat interview.
60. Data obtained from the Housing and City Planning Department, Ministry of Municipal and Rural Affairs, October, 1958.
61. Nasser, in a speech on July 27, 1958, delivered at the official opening of the iron and steel factory at Helwan.
62. Ahmed Abdullah Toiema, in a personal interview on April 8, 1958.
63. Anwar Salama, in a personal interview on August 22, 1957.
64. Mohamed Wasfy, in a personal interview on September 1, 1957.
65. Toiema, in a personal interview on April 26, 1958.
66. *Ibid.*
67. Ahmed Ismail, Director-General of the Labor Department at the Ministry of Social Affairs and Labor, in a personal interview on May 18, 1958.
68. *The Egyptian Social Security Scheme* (Cairo: Egyptian Government Press, 1950), p. 52.
69. Institute de l'Assurance et de l'Epargne des Travailleurs, *Rapport sur les Activités de l'Institution en cours de l'Anné 1956 et Bilan Arrêté en 31 Decembre, 1956* (Cairo: n.p., 1957), p. 2.
70. Wasfy interview.
71. Salama interview.
72. *Al Gomhouria*, December 23, 1957.
73. Hismet interview.
74. Data obtained from the Civil Servants Insurance and Pension Fund, October, 1958.
75. National Bank of Egypt, *Economic Bulletin*, Vol. XI, No. 3, 1958, p. 266.
76. Abbas Ammar, former Minister of Social Affairs, in a press conference on July 24, 1953.
77. Issawi, *op. cit.*, p. 245.
78. Ministry of Finance and Economy, *Statistical Pocket Year-Book, 1953* (Cairo: Egyptian Government Press, 1954), p. 19; *Statistical Pocket Year-Book, 1957*, p. 24.

79. *Ministry of Municipal and Rural Affairs, Achievements,* pp. 8-11.
80. Khalid Mohamed Khalid, *From Here We Start* (Washington, D.C.: American Council of Learned Societies, 1953), p. 125.
81. *Egyptian Economic and Political Review* (Cairo), December, 1957, p. 82.
82. Toiema interview, April 26, 1958.
83. Memorandum from Zaki Imam, Director-General of the Agricultural Cooperatives Department at the Ministry of Social Affairs and Labor, September, 1958.
84. Shafei interview.
85. Mohamed Korani el Badawi, in a personal interview on September 25, 1958.
86. Nasser, in a speech on June 1, 1956, before the General Cooperatives Congress.
87. Toiema interview, April 8, 1958.
88. Nasser, in a personal interview on June 28, 1958; Shafei interview.
89. Shafei interview.
90. *Ibid.*
91. Nasser, in a speech on July 22, 1957, commemorating the fifth anniversary of Egypt's Revolution.

Chapter VI

Economics and Industrialization

1. A. A. I. el Gritly, "The Structure of Modern Industry in Egypt," *L'Egypte Contemporaine* (Cairo), Nos. 241-42, November-December, 1947, pp. 434-35.
2. *Ibid.,* p. 458.
3. *Ibid.,* pp. 377-78.
4. *Ibid.,* p. 385.
5. Said el Naggar, *Industrialization and Income with Special Reference to Egypt* (Cairo: Fouad I University Press, 1952), p. 137.
6. Charles Issawi, *Egypt at Mid-Century* (New York: Oxford University Press [for the Royal Institute of International Affairs], 1954), p. 169.
7. *Jewish Observer and Middle East Review* (London), March 28, 1952.

8. *The New York Times*, May 11, 1952.
9. *Proceedings of the Eleventh Plenary Meeting of the International Cotton Advisory Committee* (Washington, D.C.: International Cotton Advisory Committee, 1952), pp. 217-18.
10. *The New York Times*, May 18, 1952.
11. National Bank of Egypt, *Economic Bulletin*, Vol. VI, No. 3, 1953, p. 189.
12. Data obtained from the office of Hassan Abbas Zaki, Minister of the Treasury, September, 1958.
13. National Bank of Egypt, *Economic Bulletin*, Vol. VI, No. 3, 1953, p. 210.
14. *Ibid.*, Vol. V, No. 4, 1952, p. 289.
15. Gamal Abdel Nasser, in a speech on July 22, 1954 commemorating the second anniversary of Egypt's Revolution.
16. *Jewish Observer and Middle East Review*, June 29, 1953.
17. National Bank of Egypt, *Economic Bulletin*, Vol. VI, No. 3, 1953, p. 185.
18. *Ibid.*, p. 189.
19. Nasser speech.
20. Nasser, at a press conference on July 24, 1954.
21. National Bank of Egypt, *Economic Bulletin*, Vol. IX, No. 1, 1956, p. 19.
22. *Ibid.*, p. 22.
23. Ministry of Finance and Economy, *The Budget Report for the Year 1956-57* (Cairo: Egyptian Government Press, 1956), p. 18.
24. Mohamed Hassanein Heikal, in a personal interview on September 12, 1957.
25. Ministry of Finance and Economy, *The Budget Report for the Year 1955-56* (Cairo: Egyptian Government Press, 1955), p. 27.
26. *Egyptian Economic and Political Review* (Cairo), June, 1955, p. 25.
27. Ministry of Finance and Economy, *The Budget Report for the Year 1955-56*, p. 21.
28. *The New York Times*, July 5, 1956.
29. Data obtained from the office of Hassan Abbas Zaki, Ministry of the Treasury, September, 1958.
30. *Al Ahram*, September 17, 1956.
31. *The New York Times*, January 17, 1957.
32. *Al Gomhouria*, January 24, 1957.
33. Abdel Moneim el Banna, Director of Research at the Ministry

of Economy and Commerce, in a personal interview on July 9, 1958.

34. Ministry of Finance and Economy, *The Budget Report for the Year 1957-58* (Cairo: Egyptian Government Press, 1957), p. 12.
35. *Al Ahram*, October 30, 1956.
36. *Cairo Press Review*, February 11, 1957.
37. National Bank of Egypt, *Economic Bulletin*, Vol. X, No. 1, 1957, p. 40.
38. *Egyptian Revolution in Three Years* (Cairo: Egyptian Department of Information, 1955), p. 71.
39. Mahmound Ibrahim, *A Memorandum on Objectives and Techniques of Planning in Egypt* (Cairo: National Production Council, 1956), p. 6.
40. Ministry of Industry, *Industry After the Revolution and the Five-Year Plan* (Cairo: Egyptian Government Press, 1957), p. 89. Subsequently referred to as Ministry of Industry, *Five-Year Plan*.
41. *Ibid.*, p. 97.
42. *Ibid.*, p. 101.
43. *Ibid.*
44. *Ibid.*, p. 125.
45. *Ibid.*, p. 175.
46. *Ibid.*, p. 198.
47. *Ibid.*, p. 107.
48. *Ibid.*, p. 106.
49. *Akhbar el Yom*, August 10, 1957.
50. National Bank of Egypt, *Economic Bulletin*, Vol. X, No. 3, 1957, pp. 230-31.
51. *Ibid.*, p. 230.
52. Banna interview.
53. Aziz Sidky, "Industrialization of Egypt and a Case Study of the Iron and Steel Industry" (Doctoral dissertation, Harvard University, 1951), p. 57.
54. Arthur D. Little Company, *Opportunities for Industrial Development in Egypt* (Cairo: Egyptian Government Press, 1955), p. 41.
55. National Production Council, *Permanent Council for the Development of National Production* (Cairo: n.p., 1955), p. 18.
56. *Ibid.*, p. 17.
57. Frederick Harbison and Ibrahim Abdel Kader Ibrahim, *Hu-*

man Resources for Egyptian Enterprise (New York: McGraw-Hill, 1958), pp. 24-25.

58. Sidky, in a personal interview on March 19, 1958.
59. Nasser, in a personal interview on September 11, 1957.
60. *Misr Egyptian News Agency Weekly Review,* August 28, 1954.
61. Ministry of Industry, *Five-Year Plan,* p. 102.
62. Yehia Molla, Director-General of the Industrial Organization Department at the Ministry of Industry, in a personal interview on March 31, 1958; *The New York Times,* November 22, 1957.
63. Molla, in a personal interview on May 28, 1958.
64. Molla interview, March 31, 1958.
65. Ministry of Industry, *Soviet-Egyptian Technical Agreement of January 29, 1958* (Cairo: Egyptian Government Press, 1958), pp. 6-8.
66. Data obtained from the National Planning Commission, September, 1958.
67. *Jewish Observer and Middle East Review,* December 6, 1957.
68. Nasser, in a speech on November 27, 1958.
69. National Production Council, *op. cit.,* p. 14.
70. Eva Garzouzi, *Old Ills and New Remedies in Egypt* (Cairo: Dar el Maaref, 1958), p. 56, quoting from the Industrial Bank's *Economic Bulletin,* Vol. I, No. 1, 1957.
71. *Ibid.,* p. 58.
72. National Bank of Egypt, *Economic Bulletin,* Vol. X, No. 2, 1957, p. 157.
73. *Ibid.*
74. *Ibid.,* Vol. XI, No. 2, 1958, p. 148.
75. *Ibid.,* p. 103.
76. *Ibid.,* p. 94.
77. Molla, in a personal interview on April 10, 1958.
78. Nasser speech, July 22, 1954.
79. Hussein Shafei, in a personal interview on October 6, 1958.
80. Nasser, in a speech on July 27, 1958, delivered at the official opening of the iron and steel factory at Helwan.
81. Nasser, in a speech on June 1, 1956, before the General Co-operative Congress.
82. *Journal de Commerce et Maritime* (Alexandria), February 13, 1958.
83. Nasser speech, November 27, 1958.

84. Arthur D. Little Company, *op. cit.*, p. 101.
85. *Cairo Press Review*, August 17, 1956.
86. *Egyptian Economic and Political Review*, October, 1954, p. 32.
87. Abdel Moneim el Badawi, a former brigadier in the Egyptian army now employed in the administration of the iron and steel company, in a personal interview on March 30, 1958.
88. Molla interview, March 31, 1958.
89. National Production Council, *op. cit.*, p. 245.
90. Ahmed el Sharabassy, "Irrigation in Egypt and the Renaissance," *Egypt Today, 1953-54* (Cairo: Dar el Maaref, 1954), p. 76.
91. Ministry of Industry, *Five-Year Plan*, p. 12.
92. Hydro-Electric Power Department, *Description of Aswan Dam Hydro-Electric Scheme* (corrected to July, 1958 [Cairo: Ministry of Public Works, 1958]), p. 6.
93. Mohamed Hassanein Heikal, in a personal interview on September 12, 1957.
94. Mohamed Ahmed Selim, a member of the National Production Council, at a press conference on August 19, 1956.
95. National Production Council, *op. cit.*, p. 190.
96. Nasser speech, November 27, 1958.
97. *Cairo Press Review*, December 5, 1958.
98. *Al Shaab*, May 4, 1957.
99. *Cairo Press Review*, December 25, 1957; National Bank of Egypt, *Economic Bulletin*, Vol. XI, No. 2, 1958, pp. 178-79.
100. Data obtained from the Economic Organization, October, 1958.
101. *Al Ahram*, January 22, 1958.
102. National Bank of Egypt, *Economic Bulletin*, Vol. IX, No. 3, 1956, pp. 226-27; *Al Ahram*, January 22, 1958.
103. Data obtained from the Egyptian Central Exchange Control, July, 1958.
104. *Middle East Economist and Financial Service* (Forest Hills), July-August, 1958, p. 7.
105. Mahmoud Yunis, Managing Director of the Suez Canal Authority, at a press conference on May 7, 1958.
106. *Mideast Mirror* (Beirut), August 17, 1958.
107. Nasser speech, November 27, 1958.
108. *Middle East Economist and Financial Service*, November, 1958.

109. *Ibid.*, October, 1958.
110. *Proceedings of the Sixteenth Plenary Meeting of the International Cotton Advisory Committee* (Washington, D.C.: International Cotton Advisory Committee, 1957), p. 134.
111. Mustapha Khalifa, an Under-Secretary at the Ministry of Commerce, in a personal interview on August 19, 1957.
112. National Bank of Egypt, *Report of the Fifty-Eighth Ordinary General Meeting* (Cairo: n.p., 1958), p. 15.
113. Ministry of Finance and Economy, *The Budget Report for the Year 1956-57*, p. 18.
114. National Bank of Egypt, *Economic Bulletin*, Vol. XI, No. 2, 1958, p. 105.
115. *Ibid.*
116. *Ibid.*, p. 108.
117. *Roads Under the New Regime* (Cairo: National Production Council, 1955), pp. 14-15; Mohamed Ibrahim Sobhi, an ex-army officer employed at the Ministry of Communications, in a personal interview on September 10, 1958.
118. Sidky, at a press conference on April 8, 1958.
119. Salah Nassim, in a personal interview on October 5, 1958.
120. Nasser, in a speech on July 26, 1956.
121. *Egyptian Economic and Political Review*, October, 1955, p. 29; Statistical and Census Department of the Ministry of Finance and Economy, *National Income for 1953: Official Estimate* (Cairo: Egyptian Government Press, 1955), p. 10.

Chapter VII

The High Dam

1. H. E. Hurst, *The Nile* (London: Constable & Co., 1952), pp. 155-58.
2. John Marlowe, *A History of Modern Egypt and Anglo-Egyptian Relations, 1800-1953* (New York: Frederick A. Praeger, 1954), pp. 268-69.
3. Ministry of Public Works, *Irrigation and Drainage in Egypt— 1950* (Cairo: Egyptian Government Press, 1950), p. 15.
4. Hurst, *op. cit.*, p. 310.
5. Personal interview with the resident engineer at the Jebel Aulia Dam, July 12, 1954.
6. Sadd el-Aali Department, *Report on Sadd el-Aali Project*

(Cairo: Misr Press, February, 1955), p. 2. Subsequently referred to as *Sadd el-Aali Report, February, 1955.*

7. Hurst, *op. cit.,* p. 243.
8. H. E. Hurst, R. P. Black, Y. M. Simaika, *The Future Conservation of the Nile* (Cairo: Société Orientale de Publicité, 1946), pp. 19-21.
9. *Ibid.,* p. 9.
10. Hurst, *op. cit.,* p. 317.
11. Hurst, Black, Simaika, *op. cit.,* p. 86.
12. *Ibid.,* pp. 82-83.
13. Press conference at the Ministry of Public Works, July 29, 1954.
14. Hurst, Black, Simaika, *op. cit.,* pp. 76-77.
15. Hurst, *op. cit.,* p. 302.
16. Hurst, Black, Simaika, *op. cit.,* p. 30.
17. *Ibid.,* p. 5.
18. Ministry of Public Works, *op. cit.,* p. 23.
19. *Ibid.,* p. 19; Hurst, *op. cit.,* p. 287.
20. Hurst, *op. cit.,* p. 294.
21. Mohammed Naguib, in a personal interview on August 28, 1953.
22. Abdel Moneim Kaissuny, then Deputy Minister of Finance, at a press conference on July 29, 1954.
23. Gamal Abdel Nasser, in a speech on July 26, 1954.
24. *Egyptian Gazette,* May 17, 1958.
25. Hurst, *The Nile* (Typed revised draft of Mss., Chapter XVII), p. 23.
26. National Production Council, *Permanent Council for the Development of National Production* (Cairo: n.p., 1955), p. 137.
27. *Ibid.*
28. *Ibid.,* p. 147.
29. *Report by the Board of Consultants on Sadd el-Aali Project, November, 1954* (Cairo: Misr Press, 1955), p. 19. Subsequently referred to as *Sadd el-Aali Report, November, 1954.*
30. *Ibid.,* p. 2.
31. *Ibid.,* p. 14.
32. National Production Council, *op. cit.,* p. 148.
33. *Ibid.,* p. 133.
34. *Sadd el-Aali Report, February, 1955,* p. 10.
35. *Misr Egyptian News Agency Weekly Review, March 26, 1955.* Subsequently referred to as *MENA.*

36. National Production Council, *op. cit.*, p. 1.
37. *Sadd el-Aali Project* (Antwerp: n.p., 1958), p. 12.
38. *Sadd el-Aali Report, February, 1955,* pp. 20-21.
39. *MENA,* March 26, 1955.
40. *Sadd el-Aali Report, February, 1955,* p. 22.
41. *Report of the United Kingdom Trade Mission, February, 1955* (London: Her Majesty's Stationery Office, 1955), p. 20.
42. *Sadd el-Aali Report, February, 1955,* p. 2.
43. *The Nile Waters Question* (Khartoum: Sudanese Ministry of Irrigation and Hydro-Electric Power, 1955), p. 2.
44. Sir Harold McMichael, "Egyptian-Sudanese Relations," *Middle Eastern Affairs* (New York), March, 1959, p. 104.
45. Samir Helmy, *Towards the Full Utilization of the Waters of the Nile* (Cairo: Misr Press, 1955), p. 4.
46. Helmy, *op. cit.*, p. 4.
47. *The Nile Waters Question,* p. 13.
48. Helmy, *op. cit.*, pp. 16-17.
49. Hurst and Black, *Report on a Hydrological Investigation on How the Maximum Volume of the Nile Water May Be Made Available in Egypt and the Sudan* (Cairo: Misr Press, 1955), p. 5.
50. *The Nile Waters Question,* pp. 31-33.
51. *Ibid.,* p. 43.
52. Helmy, *op. cit.*, p. 20.
53. *MENA,* October 8, 1955.
54. *Ibid.,* April 9, 1955.
55. *Ibid.*
56. *The New York Times,* June 2, 1955.
57. *Ibid.,* September 7, 1953.
58. *Jewish Observer and Middle East Review* (London), December 18, 1953.
59. National Bank of Egypt, *Economic Bulletin,* Vol. VII, No. 2, 1954, p. 68.
60. Naguib interview.
61. *The New York Times,* October 14, 1955.
62. *MENA,* October 15, 1955.
63. *The New York Times,* October 18, 1955.
64. *Ibid.,* November 21, 1955.
65. *Ibid.,* December 17, 1955.
66. *Ibid.,* December 8, 1955.
67. *Ibid.,* December 18, 1955.

68. *Ibid.*, December 19, 1955.
69. Morris Llewellyn Cooke, *Nasser's High Dam: Panacea or Politics?* (Washington: Public Affairs Institute, n.d.), p. 13.
70. *Ibid.*, p. 13.
71. *Ibid.*, p. 22.
72. *Ibid.*, p. 7.
73. *Ibid.*
74. *MENA*, February 11, 1956.
75. *The New York Times*, February 9, 1956.
76. Cooke, *op. cit.*, pp. 8-9.
77. Nasser speech.
78. *Ibid.*
79. *MENA*, February 4, 1956.
80. Nasser speech.
81. House of Commons, *Parliamentary Debates*, Hansard, Vol. 552, No. 157, Friday, May 18, 1956, col. 2419.
82. *The New York Times*, March 17, 1956.
83. *Ibid.*, April 28, 1956.
84. *Ibid.*, June 21, 1956.
85. *Ibid.*, April 2, 1956.
86. *Ibid.*, July 23, 1956; Wilton Wynn, *Nasser of Egypt* (Cambridge: Arlington Books, 1959), p. 159.
87. *The New York Times*, July 17, 1956.
88. *MENA*, July 18, 1956.
89. *Times Weekly Review* (London), August 2, 1956.
90. Nasser speech.
91. *Jewish Observer and Middle East Review*, July 20, 1956.
92. *The New York Times*, July 20, 1956.
93. *Ibid.*, July 21, 1956.
94. *Parliamentary Debates*, May 18, 1956, col. 2391.
95. John Robinson Beal, *John Foster Dulles: A Biography* (New York: Harper & Brothers, 1957), p. 260.
96. *Ibid.*, p. 258.
97. *Hearings Before the Committee on Foreign Relations and the Committee on Armed Services*, U. S. Senate, 85th Congress, 1st Session, on S. J. Res. 19 and H. J. Res. 117, Part. I, January-February, 1957 (Washington, D.C.: Government Printing Office, 1957), p. 465. Subsequently referred to as U. S. Senate, *Hearings*, Part I and Part II.
98. *The New York Times*, April 20, 1957.
99. *Ibid.*, July 15, 1956.

100. *Ibid.*, July 22, 1956.
101. *Al Ahram*, July 23, 1956.
102. *The New York Times*, July 25, 1956.
103. *Ibid.*, October 18, 1956.
104. Mohamed Hassanein Heikal, in a personal interview on September 12, 1957.
105. *Al Shaab*, July 23, 1956.
106. *The New York Times*, July 24, 1956.
107. *Congressional Record*, U. S. Senate, August 14, 1957, p. 13395.
108. *The New York Times*, August 22, 1957.
109. Samir Helmy, at a press conference on August 19, 1956.
110. Samir Helmy, in a personal interview on July 31, 1957.
111. *The New York Times*, October 20, 1956.
112. U. S. Senate, *Hearings*, Part I, p. 319.
113. Nasser, in a speech on July 22, 1957, at the opening of the National Assembly.
114. *Times* (London), April 12, 1958.
115. *Ibid.*, April 14, 1958.
116. Helmy press conference.
117. *Cairo Press Review*, November 23, 1957.
118. *Sadd el-Aali Report, November, 1954*, p. 2.
119. *Parliamentary Debates*, May 18, 1956, col. 2396.
120. *Economist*, November 1, 1958.
121. Sadd el-Aali Department, *The Pressing Need for Speeding Up the Realization of the Sadd el-Aali Project* (Cairo: Les Editions Universitaires d'Egyptes, 1958), p. 13.
122. Abdel Moneim Kaissuny, at a press conference on May 15, 1958.
123. Yehia Molla, in a personal interview on May 19, 1958.
124. *General Electrification Scheme for Egypt*, Vol. I (Paris: L'electricité de France, 1955), p. 13.
125. *Middle East Economist and Financial Service* (Forest Hills), September, 1957.
126. *The New York Times*, July 3, 1958.
127. Ahmed Ali Kamal, Director, Minister's Cabinet, Ministry of Public Works, in a letter of March 31, 1959.
128. *Al Gomhouria*, August 27, 1958.
129. *Cairo Press Review*, August 27, 1958.
130. Nasser, in a personal interview on September 11, 1957.
131. *Al Shaab*, August 27, 1958.
132. *Times* (London), September 23, 1958.

133. Cooke, *op. cit.*, pp. 20-21.
134. Hurst, *The Nile* (Typed revised draft of Mss., Chapter XVII), p. 25.
135. Nasser interview, September 11, 1957.
136. *Mideast Mirror* (Beirut), November 2, 1958.

Chapter VIII

Prelude to "Nasserism"

1. J. C. Hurewitz, *Diplomacy in the Near and Middle East* (Princeton, N. J.: D. Van Nostrand Co., 1956), Vol. II, pp. 271-73.
2. *Ibid.*, p. 300.
3. Security Council /549/ July 26, 1951, p. 8.
4. *Ibid.*, /558/ September 1, 1951, p. 2.
5. Alfred M. Lilienthal, *What Price Israel* (Chicago: Henry Regnery Co., 1953), pp. 48-73.
6. *Jewish Observer and Middle East Review* (London), February 8, 1952.
7. Tom Little, *Egypt* (New York: Frederick A. Praeger, 1958), p. 182.
8. *Ibid.*, p. 183.
9. Hurewitz, *op. cit.*, pp. 329-30.
10. *The New York Times*, January 26, 1952.
11. Gamal Abdel Nasser, in a personal interview on August 19, 1954.
12. *Jewish Observer and Middle East Review*, November 20, 1953.
13. *Ibid.*, July 31, 1953.
14. *Al Misri*, November 28, 1953.
15. *Jewish Observer and Middle East Review*, May 8, 1953.
16. *Ibid.*, May 14, 1954.
17. *Ibid.*, June 11, 1954.
18. *Ibid.*, January 30, 1953.
19. *Misr Egyptian News Agency Weekly Review*, November 1, 1952. Subsequently referred to as *MENA*.
20. Hussein Zulficar Sabry, Ali Sabry's brother, at that time one of the two or three Egyptians most responsible for Sudanese Affairs, in a personal interview in Khartoum on June 27, 1954.
21. Daniel Jumetongu, then chief bookkeeper in Juba of Equatorial Province, in a personal interview on July 8, 1954.

22. Ismail el Azhari, then Prime Minister of the Anglo-Egyptian Sudan, in a personal interview on June 27, 1954.
23. Dawood Abdel Latif, in a personal interview on July 2, 1954.
24. Little, *op. cit.*, p. 237.
25. *The New York Times*, December 11, 1952.
26. *Jewish Observer and Middle East Review*, May 1, 1953.
27. *Ibid.*, May 15, 1953.
28. *Ibid.*, January 2, 1953.
29. *Al Ahram*, March 3, 1953.
30. *MENA*, April 18, 1953.
31. *The New York Times*, April 13, 1953.
32. *Ibid.*, May 15, 1953.
33. Mohammed Naguib, in a personal interview on August 28, 1953.
34. *The New York Times*, September 29, 1953.
35. *Jewish Observer and Middle East Review*, October 16, 1953.
36. *Ibid.*, November 27, 1953.
37. *Ibid.*
38. Naguib interview.
39. *MENA*, October 11, 1952.
40. *Ibid.*, November 8, 1952.
41. *Ibid.*
42. *Jewish Observer and Middle East Review*, January 2, 1953.
43. *The New York Times*, June 25, 1953.
44. *MENA*, March 28, 1953.
45. *The New York Times*, August 18, 1953.
46. *MENA*, December 12, 1953.
47. *The New York Times*, January 7, 1954.
48. *MENA*, February 13, 1954.
49. *The New York Times*, April 20, 1954.
50. *Jewish Observer and Middle East Review*, June 11, 1954.
51. *The New York Times*, August 20, 1954.
52. *Jewish Observer and Middle East Review*, April 10, 1953.
53. *Ibid.*, April 17, 1953.
54. *Ibid.*, December 25, 1953.
55. *MENA*, March 16, 1954.
56. Little, *op. cit.*, p. 258; *MENA*, May 29, 1954.
57. *Jewish Observer and Middle East Review*, June 11, 1954.
58. *Ibid.*, June 4, 1954.
59. *MENA*, June 19, 1954; *Jewish Observer and Middle East Review*, June 25, 1954.

60. Nasser, in a speech on July 22, 1954, commemorating the second anniversary of Egypt's Revolution.
61. Walid Khalidi, "Nasser and the Arab World," *Middle East Forum* (Beirut), April, 1959, p. 30.
62. Little, *op. cit.*, p. 257.
63. *MENA*, August 28, 1954, quoting from *Akhbar el Yom*.
64. *Ibid.*, August 21, 1954.
65. *Jewish Observer and Middle East Review*, September 3, 1954; *ibid.*, February 18, 1955.
66. Little, *op. cit.*, p. 259.
67. *The New York Times*, September 3, 1954.
68. *Jewish Observer and Middle East Review*, August 20, 1954.
69. *Ibid.*, February 11, 1955.
70. House of Commons, *Parliamentary Debates*, Weekly Hansard, No. 320, April 14, 1955, col. 897.
71. *The New York Times*, April 4, 1955.
72. *Jewish Observer and Middle East Review*, February 11, 1955.
73. *Ibid.*, October 22, 1954.
74. Little, *op. cit.*, p. 268; *Jewish Observer and Middle East Review*, July 15, 1955.
75. Guy Wint and Peter Calvocoressi, *Middle East Crisis* (Middlesex: Penguin Books, 1957), p. 58.
76. *Hearings Before the Committee on Foreign Affairs*, House of Representatives, 85th Congress, 1st Session, on H. J. Res. 117, January, 1957 (Washington, D.C.: Government Printing Office, 1957), p. 396. Subsequently referred to as House of Representatives, *Hearings*.
77. *Hearings Before the Committee on Foreign Relations and the Committee on Armed Services*, U. S. Senate, 85th Congress, 1st Session, on S. J. Res. 19, H. J. Res. 117, January-February, 1957 (Washington, D.C.: Government Printing Office, 1957), pp. 746-47. House of Representatives, *Hearings*, p. 395.
78. *Jewish Observer and Middle East Review*, July 26, 1957.
79. Walter Z. Laqueur, *The Soviet Union and the Middle East* (New York: Frederick A. Praeger, 1959), p. 215.
80. Yehia Abou Bakr of the Voice of the Arabs staff, in a personal interview on July 7, 1958.
81. *The New York Times*, July 23, 1955.
82. Little, *op. cit.*, p. 267.
83. R. K. Karanjia, *Arab Dawn* (Bombay: Blitz, 1958), p. 187.
84. *The New York Times*, July 8, 1955.

85. *Jewish Observer and Middle East Review,* June 17, 1955.
86. *The Baltimore Sun,* April 12, 1956.
87. Abba Eban, in a speech before the United Nations General Assembly on November 1, 1956.
88. House of Representatives, *Hearings,* p. 397.
89. Background Note No. 23, Embassy of Israel, Washington, D.C., September 8, 1955.
90. Nasser, in an interview with representatives of the Associated Press and the Columbia Broadcasting System on September 27, 1957; Little, *op. cit.,* p. 270; *Jewish Observer and Middle East Review,* May 13, 1955.
91. *MENA,* August 6, 1955.
92. Laqueur, *op. cit.,* p. 190.

Chapter IX

The West at Bay

1. *Misr Egyptian News Agency Weekly Review,* October 1, 1953. Subsequently referred to as *MENA.*
2. Abdel Hakim Amer, in a personal interview on August 23, 1953; *U. S. News and World Report,* November 4, 1955.
3. *The New York Times,* July 31, 1954.
4. Gamal Abdel Nasser, in a personal interview on August 19, 1954.
5. *The New York Times,* March 11, 1956.
6. *Ibid.,* July 19, 1954; *ibid,* July 20, 1954.
7. *Ibid.,* September 27, 1955.
8. *Ibid.,* September 18, 1954.
9. *Ibid.,* September 26, 1954; *MENA,* April 2, 1955.
10. *MENA,* October 1, 1955; *ibid.,* November 14, 1955.
11. *The New York Times,* July 26, 1955.
12. *Ibid.,* November 12, 1955.
13. *Ibid.,* October 26, 1955.
14. *Ibid.,* February 26, 1955; *U. S. News and World Report,* November 4, 1955.
15. *Hearings before the Committee on Foreign Relations and the Committee on Armed Services,* U. S. Senate, 85th Congress, 1st Session, on S. J. Res. 19, H. J. Res. 117, January-February, 1957 (Washington, D.C.: Government Printing Office, 1957),

p. 715. Subsequently referred to as U. S. Senate, *Hearings*, Part I and Part II.

16. *Ibid.*, Part II, p. 730.
17. *Ibid.*, p. 783.
18. *Ibid.*, Part I, p. 438.
19. *Jewish Observer and Middle East Review* (London), January 27, 1956.
20. *MENA*, October 8, 1955; *Jewish Observer and Middle East Review*, October 7, 1955.
21. *The New York Times*, October 26, 1955.
22. *U. S. News and World Report*, November 4, 1955.
23. Nasser, in a personal interview on September 11, 1957.
24. *Jewish Observer and Middle East Review*, July 26, 1957.
25. *The New York Times*, January 12, 1956.
26. *Ibid.*, January 26, 1956.
27. *Middle East Journal* (Washington), Vol. 10, No. 3, Summer, 1956, p. 283.
28. *The New York Times*, June 27, 1956.
29. *MENA*, June 2, 1956, a translation of an interview with Nasser published in *Al Gomhouria*.
30. *Ibid.*, June 23, 1956.
31. *Ibid.*
32. U. S. Senate, *Hearings*, Part I, p. 438.
33. *The New York Times*, December 29, 1955; *Jewish Observer and Middle East Review*, June 1, 1956.
34. *Jewish Observer and Middle East Review*, June 22, 1956.
35. *Ibid.*, December 23, 1955.
36. *Hearings before the Committee on Foreign Affairs*, House of Representatives, 85th Congress, 1st Session, on H. J. Res. 117, January, 1957 (Washington, D.C.: Government Printing Office, 1957), p. 397.
37. Wilton Wynn, *Nasser of Egypt* (Cambridge: Arlington Books, 1959), p. 126.
38. Alfred M. Lilienthal, *There Goes the Middle East* (New York: The Devin-Adair Co., 1957), p. 169.
39. *Look*, June 25, 1957.
40. *Jewish Observer and Middle East Review*, January 7, 1955.
41. *MENA*, May 19, 1956; *Jewish Observer and Middle East Review*, December 25, 1953.
42. *MENA*, November 19, 1955.

43. *The New York Times,* November 26, 1955; *Jewish Observer and Middle East Review,* February 24, 1956.
44. *Jewish Observer and Middle East Review,* March 23, 1956.
45. Anwar Sadat, in a personal interview on September 2, 1958.
46. *MENA,* March 31, 1956, quoting from the London *Observer.*
47. *Jewish Observer and Middle East Review,* March 30, 1956.
48. *The New York Times,* April 2, 1956.
49. *Ibid.,* May 21, 1956.
50. *Ibid.,* May 28, 1956.
51. *Ibid.,* July 1, 1956.
52. Tom Little, *Egypt* (New York: Frederick A. Praeger, 1958), p. 281.
53. *The New York Times,* July 25, 1956.
54. U. S. Senate, *Hearings,* Part I, p. 453.
55. John Robinson Beal, *John Foster Dulles: A Biography* (New York: Harper & Brothers, 1957), p. 111.
56. Moustapha el Hefnaoui, *Les Problèmes Contemporains Posés par le Canal de Suez* (Paris: Guillemot et de Lamothe, 1951) ; Mahmoud Kamal, *Tomorrow's Egypt* (Cairo: Eastern Press, 1953).
57. Hefnaoui, in a personal interview on September 28, 1956.
58. *Ibid.*
59. *MENA,* July 18, 1953, a summary of an article from *Al Tahrir,* the Egyptian armed forces weekly.
60. *MENA,* July 11, 1953; Hefnaoui interview.
61. Hefnaoui interview.
62. E. V. Lawrence, *Egypt and the West* (New York: American Institute of International Information, 1956), p. 7, as translated from the Beirut newspaper *L'Orient,* July 13, 1956.
63. Nasser, at a press conference on August 12, 1956.
64. *Jewish Observer and Middle East Review,* August 17, 1956.
65. Nasser press conference; J. C. Hurewitz, *Diplomacy in the Near and Middle East* (Princeton, N. J.: D. Van Nostrand Co., 1956), Vol. II, p. 384.
66. Lilienthal, *op. cit.,* p. 182.
67. *Jewish Observer and Middle East Review,* August 3, 1956.
68. John Connell, *The Most Important Country* (London: Cassell & Co., 1957), p. 117.
69. Nasser press conference.
70. *The New York Times,* September 18, 1956.
71. Beal, *op. cit.,* p. 113.

72. U. S. Senate, *Hearings*, Part II, p. 745.
73. *Ibid.*, p. 746.
74. *Ibid.*, p. 714.
75. *Ibid.*, Part I, p. 416.
76. *Egyptian Economic and Political Review* (Cairo), August, 1955.
77. *The New York Times*, October 4, 1955.
78. *Jewish Observer and Middle East Review*, March 1, 1957.
79. Michael Foot and Mervyn Jones, *Guilty Men 1957* (New York: Rinehart & Co., 1957), p. 197; *The Observer* (London), November 25, 1956; Merry and Serge Bromberger, *Secrets of Suez* (London: Pan Books, 1957), p. 43.
80. *The New York Times*, Section VII, March 31, 1957.
81. *Ibid.*, October 31, 1956.
82. Connell, *op. cit.*, p. 190.
83. *Ibid.*
84. S. L. A. Marshall, *Sinai Victory* (New York: William Morrow & Co., 1958), p. 258.
85. *The New York Times*, October 31, 1956.
86. Foot and Jones, *op. cit.*, p. 16.
87. *Ibid.*, pp. 183-84.
88. *Ibid.*, p. 180.
89. *The New York Times*, November 3, 1956.
90. *Ibid.*, November 5, 1956.
91. *Ibid.*, November 9, 1956.
92. *Ibid.*, Foot and Jones, *op. cit.*, p. 191, quoting a dispatch from the London *Times*.
93. *The New York Times*, November 2, 1956.
94. Marshall, *op. cit.*, p. 267.
95. *Ibid.*, p. 268; *The New York Times*, Section VII, March 31, 1957.
96. Marshall, *op. cit.*, p. 89.
97. Robert Henriques, *100 Hours to Suez* (New York: The Viking Press, 1957), p. 125; Marshall, *op. cit.*, pp. 269-70.
98. Henriques, *op. cit.*, p. 99.
99. *Ibid.*, pp. 100-01; Marshall, *op. cit.*, p. 224.
100. Foot and Jones, *op. cit.*, p. 184.
101. *Ibid.*, p. 205; Bromberger, *op. cit.*, p. 84.
102. *Jewish Observer and Middle East Review*, November 23, 1956; Bromberger, *op. cit.*, pp. 11, 25-26; Foot and Jones, *op. cit.*, pp. 206-07.

103. Little, *op. cit.*, p. 301; Nasser, in a speech delivered at Al Azhar Mosque on November 9, 1956.
104. Marshall, *op. cit.*, p. 260.
105. *The New York Times*, November 2, 1956; Nasser speech.
106. S. L. A. Marshall in the *Detroit News*, January 10, 1957.
107. *The New York Times*, Section VII, March 31, 1957.
108. John C. Campbell, *Defense of the Middle East* (New York: Harper & Brothers [for the Council on Foreign Relations], 1958), p. 109.
109. The account in the Brombergers' book, while studded with factual errors, seems, in essence, to be a correct account of the Anglo-French military action.
110. *Jewish Observer and Middle East Review*, December 7, 1956.
111. Foot and Jones, *op. cit.*, p. 221.
112. *Newsweek*, December 3, 1956.
113. Nasser speech.

Chapter X

The Tactics of "Positive Neutrality"

1. Michael Foot and Mervyn Jones, *Guilty Men, 1957* (New York: Rinehart & Co., 1957), p. 217; *U. S. News and World Report*, December 7, 1956; *U. S. Hearings before the Committee on Foreign Relations and the Committee on Armed Services*, U. S. Senate, 85th Congress, 1st Session, on S. J. Res. 19, H. J. Res. 117, January-February, 1957, Government Printing Office, 1957, p. 446. Subsequently referred to as U. S. Senate, *Hearings*, Part I and Part II.
2. *The New York Times*, December 11, 1956.
3. U. S. Senate, *Hearings*, Part II, p. 777.
4. *Ibid.*, Part I, p. 168.
5. *Ibid.*
6. Mustapha Khalifa, then an Under-Secretary at the Ministry of Commerce, in a personal interview on August 19, 1957.
7. *New York Herald Tribune*, April 25, 1957.
8. *Orbis*, Summer, 1957, Vol. I, No. 2, pp. 136-37.
9. *The New York Times*, June 12, 1957; *Jewish Observer and Middle East Review* (London), July 26, 1957; *ibid.*, March 14, 1958.
10. *Jewish Observer and Middle East Review*, August 30, 1957.

11. *The New York Times*, May 4, 1957.
12. Gamal Abdel Nasser, in a personal interview on September 11, 1957.
13. *Jewish Observer and Middle East Review*, September 11, 1957.
14. *Akhbar el Yom*, August 24, 1957.
15. *Jewish Observer and Middle East Review*, July 26, 1957.
16. *Middle East Journal* (Washington, D.C.), Vol. XI, No. 4, Autumn, 1957, p. 417.
17. *The New York Times*, December 13, 1957.
18. *Middle East Journal*, Vol. XII, No. 1, Winter 1958, p. 65.
19. *Jewish Observer and Middle East Review*, November 30, 1956.
20. *The New York Times*, March 26, 1957.
21. *New York Herald Tribune*, April 20, 1957.
22. Nasser, *The Philosophy of the Revolution* (Cairo: Dar el Maaref, 1954), p. 69.
23. Nasser, in a personal interview on August 19, 1954.
24. *Times* (London), January 25, 1958.
25. *The New York Times*, January 21, 1958.
26. Walter Z. Laqueur, *The Soviet Union and the Middle East* (New York: Frederick A. Praeger, 1959), p. 307.
27. Irene W. Meister, "The Bandung Conference: An Appraisal," in Robert Strausz-Hupé and Harry W. Hazard (eds.), *The Idea of Colonialism* (New York: Frederick A. Praeger, 1958), p. 262.
28. Anwar Sadat, in a personal interview on September 9, 1958.
29. *Ibid.*
30. *The New York Times*, January 7, 1958.
31. *Economist* (London), January 18, 1958.
32. *The New York Times*, March 2, 1957.
33. Nasser, in a speech on July 26, 1957.
34. *The New York Times*, October 10, 1957.
35. Nasser interview, September 11, 1957.
36. Nasser, in a speech on December 23, 1957, delivered at Port Said.
37. *The New York Times*, January 23, 1957.
38. *Ibid.*, June 5, 1957.
39. Khalifa interview.
40. Nasser interview, August 19, 1954.
41. *Look*, June 25, 1957.
42. *Ibid.*
43. Ali Sabry, in a personal interview on September 12, 1957.

44. *Ibid.*
45. Laqueur, *op. cit.*, p. 277.
46. *Cairo Press Review*, November 25, 1957.
47. *Mideast Mirror* (Beirut), November 24, 1957.
48. *The New York Times*, April 2, 1958.
49. *Times* (London), January 17, 1958; *The New York Times*, February 7, 1958.
50. *The New York Times*, February 7, 1958.
51. *Ibid.*, February 15, 1958.
52. *Cairo Press Review*, March 3, 1958.
53. *Ibid.*, March 12, 1958.
54. Nasser, in a speech on February 5, 1958, before the National Assembly.
55. Nasser, in a speech on March 6, 1958.
56. *News Bulletin* (Khartoum: Information Center of the Republic of the Sudan), Year 2, No. 67, March 6, 1958.
57. *Times* (London), February 18, 1958.
58. *Mideast Mirror*, June 1, 1958.
59. *The New York Times*, April 13, 1958.
60. Nasser, in a speech on May 16, 1958, upon his return from Moscow to Cairo.
61. *Akher Saa*, March 12, 1958.
62. *The New York Times*, July 17, 1958.
63. *Al Ahram*, June 15, 1958.
64. *The New York Times*, June 17, 1958.
65. *Ibid.*, April 2, 1958.
66. *Ibid.*, July 21, 1958.
67. *Cairo Press Review*, April 7, 1958.
68. *The New York Times*, March 6, 1958.
69. *Mideast Mirror*, October 19, 1958.
70. *Cairo Press Review*, December 3, 1958; *The New York Times*, December 4, 1958.
71. *Mideast Mirror*, December 7, 1958.
72. *Time*, August 4, 1958.
73. *The New York Times*, July 24, 1958.
74. International Confederation of Arab Trade Unions, *Constitution* (Cairo: n.p., 1957), pp. 3-4.
75. Ahmed Ismail, Director-General of the Labor Department at the Ministry of Social Affairs and Labor, in a personal interview on May 18, 1958.

76. Helmy Ibrahim, in a personal interview on September 24, 1958.
77. *Ibid.*
78. *Ibid.*
79. *Ibid.*
80. *Ibid.*
81. Fathy Kamal, in a personal interview on September 25, 1958.
82. Moursy Saad el-Din, in a personal interview on August 8, 1958.
83. *The New York Times*, April 22, 1958.
84. Yussef el Sebai, at an Afro-Asian Solidarity Committee press conference on April 30, 1958.
85. Mohamed Mohamed Heiba, Director, Cultural Department of the Islamic Congress, in a personal interview on April 13, 1958.
86. *Times* (London), March 19, 1958; *ibid.*, April 2, 1958.
87. *Cairo Press Review*, June 16, 1958.
88. *Egyptian Gazette*, June 22, 1958.
89. *The New York Times*, December 9, 1958.
90. *Ibid.*
91. Laqueur, *op. cit.*, p. 316.
92. *Misr Egyptian News Agency Weekly Review*, July 9, 1955.
93. Sadat, in a personal interview on September 2, 1958.
94. *Ibid.*
95. *Cairo Press Review*, September 30, 1958.
96. *The New York Times*, December 7, 1958.
97. *Jewish Observer and Middle East Review*, November 28, 1958.
98. *The New York Times*, December 25, 1958.
99. Nasser, in a speech on December 23, 1958.
100. *Cairo Press Review*, December 29, 1958 (quoting an article which appeared in *Rose el Youssef*).
101. *Akhbar el Yom*, January 10, 1959.
102. *Al Ahram*, January 10, 1959.
103. *The New York Times*, January 28, 1959.
104. *Al Ahram*, January 28, 1959.
105. *The New York Times*, March 14, 1959.
106. *Mideast Mirror*, March 22, 1959; *The New York Times*, March 20, 1959.
107. *The New York Times*, March 20, 1959.
108. *Ibid.*, March 22, 1959.

109. *Mideast Mirror,* March 22, 1959.
110. *Ibid.*
111. *Ibid.,* April 5, 1959.
112. *The New York Times,* January 20, 1959; *ibid.,* March 26, 1959.
113. *Ibid.,* March 3, 1958.

Index

Abboud, Ahmed, 56, 138, 145, 169
Accra Conference, 269-70
Africa, 253-55, 268-70
Afro-Asian bloc, 215, 219, 225
Afro-Asian People's Solidarity Conference, 254-55
Afro-Asian Solidarity Committee, 254-55, 269-70
Agrarian Reform, 16-17, 75-94, 144, 158; see also Agricultural cooperatives
Agrarian Reform Bonds, 86-87, 89
Agricultural cooperatives, 82-85, 90, 92, 94, 103-06
Agricultural credit, 82-83, 88-89; see also Agricultural cooperatives
Agricultural production, 74-75, 106-07
Algeria, 235, 241, 268
Amer, Abdel Hakim, 6-7, 9-10, 25, 31, 35, 44, 47, 52, 55, 62, 156, 204, 265
Amin, Abdel Moneim, 14-15, 38
Anglo-Egyptian Sudan; see Sudan
Anglo-French military action, 58-59, 149, 242-44, 247-49, 256, 280
Aouda, Abdel Kader, 30, 33, 46
Aqaba Gulf, 210, 241-42, 245, 253
Arab Collective Security Pact, 207, 213, 218-22, 232
Arab League, 220-21, 265-66
Armaments, 51, 147, 166, 188, 194, 215, 217, 220, 223, 227-31, 233, 241, 246
Azhari, Ismail el, 183, 186, 202, 211-12, 266

Baghdad Pact, 221-23, 226, 250
Bandung Conference, 225, 269

Black, Eugene, 189-91, 197; see also International Bank for Reconstruction and Development
Boghdadi, Abdel Latif, 5-7, 23, 25-26, 31, 41, 52, 62, 67-68, 118, 122, 135, 150-51, 162-64, 168
British blocked sterling, 147-48, 165-66, 256, 261; see also Foreign exchange

Capital formation, 144-45, 157-58
Century Storage, 175-79
Collective farming, 85, 96-97, 104
Combined Service Units, 113, 118-20
Communist China, 148, 192, 195, 216, 255
Communists, 6, 15-16, 20, 27, 32, 34, 40, 42-43, 48-51, 54, 63, 72-73, 236, 258, 267, 273-75
Conspiracies; see Trials
Constitution, 13, 20, 22, 27, 53, 55, 66, 68
Cooperative movement, 69-70, 123-24, 133-34; see also Agricultural cooperatives
Cotton, 56, 107, 139-41, 143, 145-46, 166-67, 181, 208, 236, 256-57, 260, 276, 283

Deficit financing, 145-47, 158, 167-68
Development budgets, 143-44, 146-48, 172; see also Five-year plan for industry
Dulles, John Foster, 57, 187, 192-96, 198, 214

Economic Development Organization, 61, 72, 150, 160, 163, 168
Eden, Anthony, 221, 235, 239-41, 243

Education, 49, 61, 112-17, 224, 251, 254, 269
Egyptian-American Rural Improvement Service, 99-100, 261
Egyptianization, 60-62, 149-50
Egyptian-Sudanese Nile waters discussions, 183-86, 201-03; *see also* Sudan; Nile Waters Agreement of 1929

Farouk, King, 8-11
Fath, Ahmed Abdul, 9, 20, 39
Fedayeen, 222, 226, 234, 242
Five-year plan for industry, 152-55, 159-62
Foreign community, 55, 58-61; *see also* Religion
Foreign exchange, 142-43, 147-48, 155-56, 164-67; *see also* British blocked sterling
France, 148, 165, 187, 226, 231, 233, 235, 237, 239-44, 246-48, 250, 255
Free Officers, 4-11

Gaza raid, 51, 145, 222-23, 230
General Reserve Fund, 140-41, 143, 148
Gezira Scheme, 174, 183, 201, 203, 211
Great Britain, 179, 183, 187-89, 191, 194, 202, 206-17, 220, 226, 228, 231, 233-36, 239-45, 247-48, 250, 255-56, 276; *see also* Suez Canal military bases

Hassanein, Magdy, 67-68, 94-97, 169; *see also* Liberation Province
Health facilities, 132-33
Heikal, Mohamed Hassanein, 69, 145, 162, 192, 197, 238, 262, 273-74
Helmy, Samir, 64, 180, 184, 186, 188, 198-99; *see also* High Dam
High Dam, 57, 99, 144, 158, 179-205, 211, 235, 237, 275-76, 280
Hodeiby, Hassan el, 13, 17, 27-28, 33, 43-44, 46-47; *see also* Moslem Brethren
Housing, 122-27
Hurst, H. E., 175-76, 178-79, 184, 203

Hussein, Ahmed, 187, 193, 216
Hussein, Kamal el din, 6-7, 13, 29, 44, 68, 115-16, 135

Ibrahim, Hassan, 5-8, 26, 31, 35, 47, 163, 187
Imperialism, 55-56, 62, 215, 221, 224-25, 236, 259, 270, 280
India; *see* Nehru, Jawaharlal
Industry, 137-39, 142, 158-59, 168-69; *see also* Five-year plan for industry
  Ministry of, 151-52, 154-55, 159-60, 163, 200; *see also* Five-year plan for industry; Sidky, Aziz
International Bank for Reconstruction and Development, 164, 187-91, 197, 203, 205
International Confederation of Arab Trade Unions, 266-68
Iraq, 217-22, 223-24, 231-32, 251-52, 258-59, 263-64, 266, 271-75, 281; *see also* Baghdad Pact
Iron and steel factory, 144, 160-62
Israel, 12, 45, 206-07, 209-10, 216-18, 222-23, 226-27, 229, 231, 233-34, 240-48, 252-53, 262, 264, 279

Jews, 48-49, 60-61; *see also* Religion
Jordan, 231-32, 250-51, 258-59, 264-65, 272, 276

Kafr el Dawar, 14-15, 23, 127-28

Labor, 14-15, 23, 33-35, 40, 63-64, 71, 127-29
Land distribution, 79-82, 84-87, 93-94; *see also* Agrarian Reform
Land reclamation, 95-102, 107-08
Land requisition, 79-82, 86, 89
Lebanon, 218, 251-52, 259, 262-63, 265, 272, 276
Liberation Province, 67-68, 94-99, 182
Liberation Rally, 20-21, 23, 27-28, 33-34, 39-42, 54, 70-71
Libya, 251

Maher, Ali, 11, 14, 16-17, 19-20, 24, 32, 76-77
Mansour, Yussef Saddik, 14, 16, 38

Marei, Sayed, 77-78, 81, 83-87, 91-93, 97-98, 101, 103-04, 108; see also Agrarian Reform
Middle East Defense Organizations, 208, 213-14, 216-20; see also Baghdad Pact
Military attachés, 231-32, 251-52
Military tribunals; see Trials
Mohanna, Rashad, 8, 13-14, 19-20, 24
Mohieddine, Khaled, 5-8, 12-13, 16, 29-30, 35, 38-39, 50, 72
Mohieddine, Zacharia, 4, 6, 8, 13, 26, 31, 52, 60-62, 67, 160
Moslem Brethren, 3, 5-6, 12-13, 17-19, 23, 27-28, 30-35, 40, 42-47, 133, 210

Naguib, Mohammed, 7-12, 14-20, 23-25, 29-35, 39, 41-43, 45-46, 66-67, 179, 187, 210, 212-13, 215, 217, 228, 238
Nahas, Mustapha, 5, 13, 16-18, 26; see also Wafd
Nasser, Gamal Abdel, 3-5, 7-9, 11-13, 20, 23-26, 28-36, 38, 40-47, 50-55, 57, 62, 64, 68-70, 72-73, 134-36, 142-44, 157, 159-62, 185, 190-93, 196-99, 202, 204-05, 209-10, 213-28, 230-39, 244, 247-64, 269-76, 278-85
National Assembly, 53-54, 57, 62-72, 97, 116, 163, 259, 281; see also Parliament
National Bank of Egypt, 144, 146, 149-50, 153, 160, 163, 167-68
National budget, 140-44, 146-48
National debt, 143, 147, 157; see also Treasury Bills
National income, 139, 171, 182
National Planning Commission, 151, 160, 163
National Production Council, 101, 142-44, 151, 180-81
National Union, 53-54, 62-63, 70-72, 273
Nehru, Jawaharlal, 195-96, 215, 221, 223, 225, 237, 253, 270, 280, 282
Neutralism, 50, 192, 195, 215-16, 225-27; see also Nehru, Jawaharlal; Tito, Josip Broz

New Society, 59, 95, 134-36
Nile Waters Agreement of 1929, 174, 183, 185, 201-02

Palestine arms scandal, 12-13, 24
Palestine War of 1948, 6-7, 58, 206, 218, 278
Parliament, 13, 16, 19, 27, 30-34, 40, 52-53; see also National Assembly
Permanent Council for Public Welfare Services, 118-21, 144, 151
Persian Gulf, 235, 272
Petroleum, 139, 142, 148, 170-71, 200, 235-37, 267, 272
Port Said, 58-59, 122, 247-48
Press, 22, 32, 35, 39, 53-54

Radford, Arthur W., 229, 233, 241
Raouf, Abdel Moneim, 5-7, 46
Religion, 44, 48-50, 61-62, 132-33, 224, 254; see also Jews; Moslem Brethren
Revolutionary Command Council, 21, 23-25, 29, 32-35, 55
Rural development, 110-11, 121-22

Sabry, Ali, 52, 66, 160, 198, 223, 228, 250, 257
Sadat Anwar, 4-7, 10-11, 13, 24, 26, 31, 33-35, 38, 46, 50-51, 53, 55, 68, 70-72, 254, 272
Salama, Anwar, 63, 71, 128, 130
Salem, Gamal, 7, 26, 29, 31, 46, 55, 75, 78, 93, 187-88
Salem, Salah, 7, 25-26, 31, 34, 39, 55, 210-11, 214, 216, 218-20, 224, 231, 234
Saudi Arabia, 218, 224, 232, 250-52, 259, 264-65
Scientific farming, 102-03
Sequestration, 60-61
Shafei, Hussein, 9, 13, 25, 35, 39, 46, 72, 104-05, 120, 134-35, 160, 210
Shawki, Ahmed, 9, 25, 29, 39
Sidky, Aziz, 67, 151-55, 160, 163, 171; see also Industry, Ministry of
Sinai campaign, 57, 59, 242-48, 252-53
Social security, 129-32
Society of Free Officers; see Free Officers

Soviet Union and her satellites, 146, 148-49, 155-56, 159, 163, 166-67, 187-89, 192, 195-98, 204-05, 215-16, 220, 227, 228, 230-31, 233, 236-37, 241, 243, 247, 250, 254-58, 260-63, 268-70, 273-76, 280, 282-83, 285

Sudan, 174-75, 178, 181, 183-86, 189, 190, 193, 201-03, 206, 208-12, 226, 231, 235, 251, 255, 259-60, 265-66, 269, 271-72

Suez Canal, 43-45, 57, 148, 155, 164-67, 198, 200, 222, 237-40, 242-43, 248, 252, 255, 258, 261, 263

Suez Canal Company; *see* Suez Canal

Suez Canal military bases, 43-45, 145, 208-09, 212-15, 217-18, 235

Syria, 200, 217-18, 224, 250-52, 258, 262, 264, 271-74, 282-83

Tito, Josip Broz, 195, 221, 223, 226, 237, 257, 261, 263, 276, 280

Toiema, Ahmed Abdullah, 15, 23, 34-35, 70-72, 127-29

Treasury Bills, 141, 143, 145-47, 149, 158, 167-68

Trials, 20, 24, 33, 39-40, 46-48, 59, 62-66

Tunisia, 252, 265, 271-72

United Nations, 206-08, 216, 222, 226, 234, 240, 252-53, 257, 260

United States, 65, 99-100, 145, 148, 164, 180, 187-89, 191-98, 204, 212-16, 220-22, 226, 228-30, 236-43, 249-50, 253, 255-56, 261-63, 273, 276

Voice of the Arabs, 224, 226, 254

Wafd, 13-14, 16-19, 24, 30, 32, 48, 64

West Germany, 166, 179-80, 187, 220

Yemen, 218, 224, 260

Zaki, Hassan Abbas, 153, 168

Due